THE CAMBRIDGE COMPANION TO
THE *SUMMA THEOLOGIAE*

Arguably the most influential work of theology in the history of Christianity, Thomas Aquinas' *Summa Theologiae* has shaped all subsequent theology since it was written in the late thirteenth century. This *Companion* features essays from both specialists in Aquinas' thought and from constructive contemporary theologians to demonstrate how to read the text effectively and how to relate it to past and current theological questions. The authors thoroughly examine individual topics addressed in the *Summa*, such as God, the Trinity, eternity, providence, virtue, grace, and the sacraments, making the text accessible to students of all levels. They further discuss the contextual, methodological, and structural issues surrounding the *Summa*, as well as its interaction with a variety of religious traditions. This volume will not only allow readers to develop a comprehensive multi-perspectival understanding of Aquinas' main mature theological work but also promote dialogue about the vital role of the *Summa* in theology today.

PHILIP MCCOSKER is Director of the Von Hügel Institute and Fellow of St Edmund's College, University of Cambridge, and Departmental Lecturer in Modern Theology, University of Oxford. He is the editor of *What Is It that the Scripture Says?* (2006) and author of *Christ the Paradox: Expanding Ressourcement Theology* (2017). He is also the editor of the journal *Reviews in Religion and Theology*.

DENYS TURNER is Horace Tracy Pitkin Professor Emeritus of Historical Theology at Yale University. His most recent publications include *Julian of Norwich, Theologian* (2011) and *Thomas Aquinas: A Portrait* (2013).

CAMBRIDGE COMPANIONS TO RELIGION

This is a series of companions to major topics and key figures in theology and religious studies. Each volume contains specially commissioned chapters by international scholars, which provide an accessible and stimulating introduction to the subject for new readers and nonspecialists.

Other Titles in the Series

(continued after Index)

THE CAMBRIDGE COMPANION TO

THE *SUMMA THEOLOGIAE*

Edited by

Philip McCosker
University of Cambridge
University of Oxford

Denys Turner
Yale University

CAMBRIDGE
UNIVERSITY PRESS

BX
1749
.T6
C26
2016

CAMBRIDGE
UNIVERSITY PRESS

32 Avenue of the Americas, New York NY 10013-2473, USA

Cambridge University Press is part of the University of Cambridge.

It furthers the University's mission by disseminating knowledge in the pursuit of education, learning, and research at the highest international levels of excellence.

www.cambridge.org
Information on this title: www.cambridge.org/9780521705448

© Cambridge University Press 2016

First published 2016

Printed in the United States of America by Sheridan Books, Inc

A catalog record for this publication is available from the British Library.

Library of Congress Cataloging in Publication Data
Names: McCosker, Philip, editor. | Turner, Denys, 1942– editor.
Title: The Cambridge companion to the *Summa theologiae* / edited by Philip McCosker, Denys Turner.
Description: New York : Cambridge University Press, 2016. |
Series: Cambridge companions to religion |
Includes bibliographical references and index.
Identifiers: LCCN 2015042946| ISBN 9780521879637 (hardback) |
ISBN 9780521705448 (paperback)
Subjects: LCSH: Thomas, Aquinas, Saint, 1225?–1274.
Summa theologica. | BISAC: RELIGION / Theology.
Classification: LCC BX1749.T6 C26 2016 | DDC 230/.2–dc23
LC record available at http://lccn.loc.gov/2015042946

ISBN 978-0-521-87963-7 Hardback
ISBN 978-0-521-70544-8 Paperback

For our students at Cambridge, Oxford, and Yale.

Contents

Contributors

Frederick Christian Bauerschmidt is Professor of Theology at Loyola University, Maryland.

David Burrell CSC is Theodore M. Hesburgh Professor Emeritus in Philosophy and Theology at the University of Notre Dame.

Francis X. Clooney SJ is Parkman Professor of Divinity, Professor of Comparative Theology, and Director of the Center for the Study of World Religions at Harvard Divinity School.

Sarah Coakley is Norris-Hulse Professor of Divinity at the University of Cambridge.

Brian Davies OP is Distinguished Professor of Philosophy at Fordham University.

Gilles Emery OP is Professor of Dogmatic Theology at the University of Fribourg.

Paul Gondreau is Professor of Theology at Providence College.

Paul J. Griffiths is Warren Professor of Catholic Theology at Duke University.

Nicholas M. Healy is Professor of Theology and Religious Studies at St John's University, New York.

Mark D. Jordan is Andrew W. Mellon Professor of Christian Thought at Harvard Divinity School.

James F. Keenan SJ is Canisius Professor of Theology and Director of the Jesuit Institute at Boston College.

Karen Kilby is Bede Professor of Catholic Theology at Durham University.

Andrew Louth is Professor Emeritus of Patristic and Byzantine Studies at Durham University.

John Marenbon is a Senior Research Fellow at Trinity College, Cambridge.

Herbert McCabe OP† was an editor of *New Blackfriars*, and taught in several Dominican houses.

Philip McCosker is Director of the Von Hügel Institute at the University of Cambridge and Departmental Lecturer in Modern Theology at the University of Oxford.

Jean Porter is John A. O'Brien Professor of Theology at the University of Notre Dame.

Timothy Radcliffe OP was Master of the Order of Preachers, and is a member of the community at Blackfriars, Oxford.

Eugene F. Rogers Jr. is Professor of Religious Studies at the University of North Carolina, Greensboro.

Christoph Schwöbel is Professor of Systematic Theology at Tübingen University.

Kathryn Tanner is Frederick Marquand Professor of Systematic Theology at Yale Divinity School.

Denys Turner is Horace Tracy Pitkin Professor Emeritus of Historical Theology at Yale Divinity School.

Pim Valkenberg is Professor of Religion and Culture at The Catholic University of America.

Olivier-Thomas Venard OP is Professor of New Testament Studies and Deputy Director of the École biblique et archéologique française, Jerusalem.

Acknowledgements

Above all, we would like to thank the scholars who have written this book for their expertise, collaboration, and extreme patience. The original idea for this *Companion* – when we were both located in Cambridge – came from Kate Brett at Cambridge University Press: we thank her for her inspiration and encouragement. The project was taken on in due course by Laura Morris and Alexandra Poreda, and finally brought firmly to eventual publication by Beatrice Rehl and Isabella Vitti, all through the disruptions of our own several criss-crossing transatlantic moves as well as the illnesses of a number of contributors. In the course of the preparation of the volume, one of its contracted contributors, Servais Pinckaers OP, died before his essay was complete: we would like to record our appreciation here for his scholarship on Thomas and ethics more broadly. Brian Davies OP, one of our contributors, is also the literary executor for Herbert McCabe OP, another of our contributors. He undertook the careful editing of Herbert's text for this publication: for this, as well as the permission to publish the piece here, we are extremely grateful. We also wish to thank Pauline Matarasso for translation work *en route* and John Trappes-Lomax for vital assistance at the end. Any infelicity remains ours alone.

Abbreviations

ad	*ad* ('to the nth argument', indicating a specific reply to a specific argument in an article)
arg	*argumentum* ('argument', referring to a specific argument within an article)
Blackfriars	St Thomas Aquinas, *Summa Theologiae: Latin text and English translation, Introductions, Notes, Appendices and Glossaries*, ed. Thomas Gilby *et al.* (60 volumes; London: Eyre & Spottiswoode, 1963–74; Cambridge: Cambridge University Press, 2006)
corp	*corpus* ('body' of an article)
DV	*De Veritate*
obj	*objectio* ('objection', referring to a particular objection in an article)
PG	J.-P. Migne (ed.), *Patrologiae cursus completus ... Series Graeca* (Paris: 1857–66)
PL	J.-P. Migne (ed.), *Patrologiae cursus completus ... Series Latina* (Paris: 1844–64)
prol	*prologus* ('prologue' or introduction to a part, question, or article)
SCG	*Summa contra Gentiles*
ST	*Summa Theologiae*
Torrell I	Jean-Pierre Torrell OP, *Saint Thomas Aquinas. Volume 1: The Person and His Work* (Rev. ed.; Washington, DC: Catholic University of America Press, 2005)
Torrell II	Jean-Pierre Torrell OP, *Saint Thomas Aquinas. Volume 2: Spiritual Master* (Washington, DC: Catholic University of America Press, 2003)

WA   Martin Luther, *D. Martin Luthers Werke: Kritische*
            Gesamtausgabe (Weimar: Böhlau, 1883–1993)
WATR   Martin Luther, *D. Martin Luthers Werke: Kritische*
            Gesamtausgabe, Tischreden (Weimar: Hermann Böhlaus
            Nachfolger, 1912–21)

A Note on Citations of the *ST* and other Texts by Thomas Aquinas

Citations of the *ST* in this volume follow this basic tripartite format: III.3.5. The initial capital roman letters indicate the part (in this case the third part), the second element in arabic numerals indicates the question within that part (in this case the third question), and the third element in arabic numerals indicates the article within that question (in this case the fifth article). The second part of the *ST* is divided in two sub-parts: I-II and II-II. More elaborate references will indicate the precise location within an article using further indicators found in the list of abbreviations. These are clearly explained in Frederick Christian Bauerschmidt's chapter in this volume. Other texts by Thomas are cited in standard format. These are published in many editions and online: bibliographical references to the best editions can be easily found, for example, in Bauerschmidt's *Thomas Aquinas: Faith, Reason, and Following Christ* (Oxford University Press, 2013), 317–22.

Introduction

PHILIP MCCOSKER and DENYS TURNER

What need is there for yet another collection of essays on Thomas Aquinas? The obvious, and non-defensive, answer to that question is that we need any and as many as are worthwhile, as many as contribute to his reception within the theological and philosophical communities – those communities being as many and various as they are, they need as many and various Thomases. And Thomas being the kind of generative thinker that he is, his writings invite and reward endlessly, even occasionally cacophonously, plural engagements.

This volume, moreover, is less than a comprehensive account of the theology of Thomas Aquinas, being confined as it is to the Thomas whose theological mind can be discerned in a particular text, his *Summa Theologiae*. Though our collection no doubt will contribute to the dominance of that text within the contemporary reception of Thomas' thought, it is worthwhile noting now that it would be possible to give an account of Thomas' theology, in its different way as comprehensive, and in its different way as limited, as that to be found in the *Summa*, but based entirely on his biblical commentaries, especially those on the gospels of Matthew and John.

There is therefore something distinctive about a collection of papers on the text of the *Summa Theologiae* alone. Our focus on Thomas' mature 'systematic' work of theology, so central to the theological canon, yields different dividends. In addition to exploring Thomas' own views on many theological topics and methodological questions, our contributors show how one can still do theology with this seminal text. Our volume has quite a bit to say (and show) on how that might be done. It thus necessarily differs in focus from its stable-mate edited by Norman Kretzmann and Eleanore Stump, *The Cambridge Companion to Aquinas* (Cambridge: Cambridge University Press, 1993), for this latter volume attends principally to the thought of the philosopher whom, Thomas believes, he has to be if he is to have any sort of credibility as a theologian. These two Thomases should ideally be read side by side. Both are needed and they fit together, indeed frequently they are identical. At any rate this volume is intended to complement that earlier volume. In its multi-perspectival dimension it is also doing something significantly different from the recent single-author guides to the *Summa Theologiae* by Bauerschmidt, Davies, Loughlin, McGinn, and Torrell.[1] It is closest to Andreas Speer's edited collection but differs from it in its theological focus.[2] Some of the dividends by which we have been struck in our collection include: the thoroughgoing importance of *convenientia*, or fittingness, in the *Summa*; the ubiquity of the Holy Spirit in Thomas' teaching; the aporetic nature of Thomas' christology and anthropology; the forgotten centrality of the life of Christ in his thought; the way in which Thomas complicates facile East/West theological cleavages; and the overall importance of the practical, especially in the form of moral theology, for the whole: it is all geared to action.

One recent development in the reception of Thomas' *Summa* is a plurality and diversity of interpretations, whether of its overall structure and purpose, or of the relative significance of the two main sources known to him of classical Greek philosophies in Aristotle and Plato, or of the influence on his theology of Muslim thought, especially that of Avicenna (as Ibn Sina was known in the Latin West), or the Jewish theologian Maimonides, or indeed of the relative roles of scripture and philosophy. In this collection of papers we have tried to represent no one school of interpretation alone, but rather as many as possible. The heterogeneity of readings, of styles of presentation, of views about the nature, purpose and context of the text means that no reader should expect an easily identified consistency in the matter of the interpretation of the *Summa*. One should, rather, expect to find represented a broad, though by no means entirely comprehensive, representation of the main approaches to the reading of Thomas' *Summa* in contemporary scholarship. This should encourage readers to come up with their own interpretations of Thomas' text in dialogue with others.

[1] See Frederick Christian Bauerschmidt, *Holy Teaching: Introducing the Summa Theologiae of St Thomas Aquinas* (Grand Rapids: Brazos, 2005); Brian Davies, *Thomas Aquinas's Summa Theologiae: A Guide and Commentary* (Oxford: Oxford University Press, 2014); Stephen J. Loughlin, *Aquinas's Summa Theologiae: A Reader's Guide* (London: T&T Clark, 2010); Bernard McGinn, *Thomas Aquinas's Summa Theologiae: A Biography* (Princeton: Princeton University Press, 2014); Jean-Pierre Torrell OP, *Aquinas's Summa: Background, Structure, and Reception* (Washington, DC: Catholic University of America Press, 2005).

[2] Andreas Speer (ed.), *Thomas von Aquin: Die Summa Theologiae. Werkinterpretationen* (Berlin: de Gruyter, 2005).

Because, unusually, this Cambridge Companion is focussed upon a text rather than a complete oeuvre or single theme, we have introduced a whole initial section devoted to the question of what kind of text it is, and how it should be read. We thought it important to attend to the preliminary questions of what Thomas' purpose was in writing it; of how, for Thomas, the description of the author at work in composing the *Summa* is incomplete without reference to the sources of his theology in a life of prayer; of how the structure of the text reveals its primary purpose to be the construction of a coherent moral theology appropriate for the training of Dominican preachers. We thought it important to give an account of the relative places and roles of scripture and philosophy in Thomas' text and likewise to give some account of the distinctively medieval conception of theological (and philosophical) teaching method and argument structure.

Thereafter, in the central Part II of our collection, the essays address broad themes in the *Summa*. This is not to say that in all cases they address 'sections' of the text, for, though others, including some of our contributors, disagree, in general it is not our view as editors that the structure of the *Summa* is determined by discrete sections or, as some call them, 'treatises,' on discrete and detachable subject matters. Were one to suppose this to be so, it would come as a shock to most readers to discover that Thomas' set-piece discussion of grace is confined to but seven 'questions' of the *Prima Secundae*. In fact it would be more to the point to stress that the doctrine of grace is so pervasively present throughout the whole *Summa* that, like the air we breathe, you would notice how present it is in the work only when, exceptionally, it seems to be missing. Though, understandably, the *Summa* is rarely read from cover to cover, it is important at least to acknowledge that the ordering of its agenda is determined, as Thomas emphatically insists in the work's general prologue, by pedagogical considerations bearing on the training of his fellow Dominican preachers and confessors. The structure of the *Summa* betrays Thomas' sense of a learning curve for theological neophytes. You will not get your christology right in the Tertia Pars, he implies, unless you have got in place first your doctrine of God, one and three, in the Prima Pars; and the over-arching pastoral purpose of the *Summa* – considerably more than half of the work's total volume is devoted to what we today would call moral and pastoral theology – demands that it be enclosed within that framework, of God one and three at the outset, and of the incarnation of that triune God in Christ in the final part. The *Summa*, in short, is an intricately connected whole. It cannot be read without distortion as a series of separable 'treatises'.

Inevitably, however, we editors had to allocate topics to our fellow contributors on some principle of division of labour, and though we vary much in how exactly we approach our task, on the whole we have seen our purpose to be that of inviting the reader in to particular aspects of Thomas' theological temperament: and there, once again, one discovers not a singleness, but a multiplicity of voices and perspectives fully reflective of the multi-valency of the text of the *Summa* itself. It is, for example, necessary to give due place to the importance that Thomas attached to a sort of pre-theological rational argument for the existence of God; equally, it is important to stress the ultimacy in Thomas' theology of the apophatic – for Thomas at the beginning, in the middle and threading through to the end of theology there is mystery: we do not, and cannot, know what God is. But take both approaches together, and the reader will find that they converge on the same Thomas Aquinas: there is but one God and that one God is, as Thomas himself says, both the 'formal object' of '*Sacra Doctrina*' and ultimately unknowable whether by reason or by faith (I.12.13*ad*3) – and yet it is precisely with this God that by means of that grace of the Spirit which is charity we are made 'one' through Christ and the Church.

We have also attempted, in Part III, to give weight to the work's historical and contemporary relevance within a broader range of Christian theological traditions, from its most natural environment in the Roman Catholic traditions, to those Christian traditions other than the Roman Catholic, whether variously Eastern Orthodox or Reformed and for whom, in Thomas' own times or in recent decades, the *Summa* has become a common source; and then finally it seemed worth adding some reflections on the work's reception, whether actual or possible, within some of the non-Abrahamic religious traditions. Thomas Aquinas – or rather a distinctly odd version of him as a, or even *the*, 'Christian philosopher' – used to be the private and closely guarded 'official' possession (and weapon) of a Roman Catholic church in search of a distinctive theological identity, one moreover marked by its hostility to much in the philosophies of the modern age. More ecumenical and inter-religious times, together with their considerably improved grasp of history and hermeneutics and their theologically more generous scholarship, have reconnected Thomas' theology with the common traditions of the mainstream Christian churches which results in an immeasurably enhanced theological payback to all. The Thomas whom we as editors have come to know in the course of assembling this collection of essays would certainly have approved of this revision of his place within the history of

Christian theology as a '*doctor communis*', a common resource for all traditions.

Perhaps the over-riding impression of Thomas' theology as represented by the *Summa Theologiae* that we hope the reader of this volume will be left with is that in that vast work there converge an implacable commitment to rational coherence, obedience to the laws of logic, and pedagogical purpose, with a sense that the whole enterprise of theology is shot through with unresolvable mystery. For Thomas, logic and philosophy, indispensable to the theologian, have nonetheless missed the mark if that ultimacy of the mystery of God is not what they lead to, just as the task of the 'doctor' of the sacred, the task of the theologian, is betrayed if it leads the student to anything other than the even deeper mystery of faith.

Part I

Reading the *Summa Theologiae*

FREDERICK CHRISTIAN BAUERSCHMIDT

Those who have been reading the *ST* for a while might forget the difficulties that it poses to the novice reader. Perhaps harder to forget are the difficulties posed by the vast secondary literature and the various schools of approach that seem endlessly locked in fierce, if at times arcane, battles over how the *Summa*, and Aquinas' work in general, is best understood. Yet over the years I have found the *Summa* to be one of the most rewarding texts to teach precisely because many of its initial difficulties *can* be overcome as students master its idiom and begin to acquire a basic knowledge of some of the critical questions which it has engendered.

READING THE SUMMA THEOLOGIAE

While the secondary literature on Aquinas is helpful, in the end it is more important to read the *ST* than to read about it. Yet simply opening the text often leads readers to quickly close it, as they see arguments and counter-arguments, divisions and subdivisions, as well as a variety of unfamiliar technical terms and constant reference to debates between authorities ancient and medieval. We might wonder what we need to know, or perhaps who we ought to be, before we start reading the text. We certainly ought to have some basic familiarity with the vocabulary of Aristotle, the sort of familiarity that might be gained from reading Aquinas' own Aristotelian *Vade Mecum*, *De Principiis Naturae*, so as not to be baffled or misled by this terminology, which pervades the *Summa*. Likewise, the reader ought to have a basic familiarity with the contents of the Bible, both the principal figures and the overall arc of the biblical narrative, as well as some knowledge of the history of Christian doctrine, particularly the contributions of Augustine. While good English language translations of the *Summa* are available, a reader who is not afraid to use a Latin dictionary will often benefit by checking a translation against Aquinas' fairly simple Latin.[1]

The articles

The smallest unit of the *Summa* is the 'article' – *articulus* in Latin meaning a small joint, member, or part (see II-II.1.6*corp*). Small though they are, the articles shall command the largest share of our attention here. The articles follow the pattern of the medieval 'disputation,' a classroom exercise in which philosophical and theological questions were debated. They begin with a statement of the point that is at issue; these are given by Thomas at the beginning of the collection of articles known as a 'question' (see later in this chapter), but are typically repeated by editors at the beginning of the corresponding article. These are followed by opening arguments known as 'objections,' typically two to four in number, that offer reasons for one way of answering the question posed in the title. Then follows what is almost always a single argument for the other way of answering the question posed, which is introduced by the words *sed contra* ('on the other hand'). After this comes what is known as the 'body' or *corpus* of the article, in which Thomas offers his answer to the question. The article concludes with responses to the opening objections and, on a few occasions, to the *sed contra*. This dialectical path to truth, also known as the *quaestio*, is discussed in detail by John Marenbon in his contribution to this volume, so I will simply offer some practical suggestions for how one might go about reading an article in the *Summa*.

The objections offer initial arguments and authoritative statements that will prove, in the course of the article, to be in some way inadequate to the task of answering the question. These should not, however, be viewed as straw men set up by Aquinas so that we can admire his skill in knocking them down. In the prologue to the *Summa* Thomas complains about the 'swarm of pointless ... arguments' found in many disputations, and we can presume that he is setting out to do something different. So the arguments found in the objections are never pointless; indeed, Aquinas generally thinks that they are rather good arguments and deserving of our attention. The more truth found in the objection, the better it serves Aquinas' purposes.

The objections are sometimes simple arguments from authority – that is, they cite a statement from scripture or the church fathers or a

---

[1] The sixty-volume 'Blackfriars' edition of the *Summa*, originally published in the 1960s and recently republished in paperback by Cambridge University Press, helpfully presents the Latin text and English translation on facing pages. Unless otherwise noted, all translations of Aquinas in this volume are from this edition.

non-Christian philosopher such as Aristotle that would seem to incline one to answer the question in a particular way. Thus in I.2.1, which addresses the question of whether God's existence is self-evident, the first objection offers the statement by John of Damascus that 'the aware-ness of God is implanted by nature in everybody,' which would incline one to say that the existence of God is self-evident to us. At other times, the objections offer a very compressed argument that does not rest on an authority. In the same article of the *Summa* we find in the second objection a version of Anselm's argument for God's existence from the *Proslogion*, which seems to imply that God's existence is self-evident to anyone who knows that the word 'God' means 'that than which nothing greater can be thought,' yet we find no invocation of Anselm's author-ity. Finally, these arguments sometimes invoke an authority as part of a larger argument, as in the third objection of I.2.1, in which the saying of Christ from Scripture – 'I am the way, the truth and the life' – forms the basis for the claim that God is truth, which serves as a premise in the argument for the self-evidence of God's existence based on the self-evidence of truth. An attentive reader of an article of the *Summa* ought to note the sort of arguments being made in the objections.

The objections sometimes argue from more or less the same per-spective; in the case of I.2.1 they are all arguing for the self-evidence of God's existence in terms of an implicit knowledge that only needs to be made explicit. At other times, however, the objections represent dif-ferent perspectives. For example, in the very first article of the *Summa*, addressing the question of whether there is 'another teaching required apart from philosophical studies,' the two objections both answer 'no,' but for quite different reasons. The first adopts a 'fideist' position and appeals to the authority of scripture – 'be not curious about things far above thee' (Ecclesiasticus 3:22) – to argue that what is beyond human reason cannot be investigated by human beings at all but must be, pre-sumably, accepted on faith. The second adopts a 'rationalist' position and points to Aristotle's designation of one part of philosophy as 'theol-ogy' or 'divine science' to argue that there is nothing that goes beyond the range of human reason, not even the being of God. Again, an atten-tive reader ought to note whether the objections represent different fac-ets of one position, or two opposed positions, since Thomas often locates his own view somewhere between opposed positions.

If the objections are never flat-footedly wrong, the *sed contra* is rarely flat-footedly right. Though typically representing something closer to Thomas' position, it is often inadequate taken on its own. Sometimes it is a simple quotation of an authority, while at other times it offers the sketch of an argument, but rarely more than a sketch. In a few cases, it offers an argument that is no closer to Aquinas' final view than the objections. A notable instance of this is III.65.1, on the question of the number of the sacraments, in which the five objections argue for their being fewer than seven and the three arguments *sed contra* argue for their being more. A careful reader of the *Summa* will keep in mind that even though a quick glance at the *sed contra* can often give a very general idea of how Thomas will proceed in response to the question posed, it will not do so infallibly. Thomas' own position often takes the form of a careful balancing of the truths found in both the objections and the *sed contra*.

How does Aquinas go about this balancing of truths? In the body or *corpus* of the article, as well as in his specific replies to the objections, he adopts a number of intellectual strategies for addressing the question at issue. Any attempt to list these strategies must always be partial, but readers will soon come to recognize certain characteristic moves that Thomas makes within an article, and it is worth mentioning a few of them.

Aquinas frequently settles a question, or begins to settle a question, by making a distinction. Thus, in addressing the question of whether it was necessary for the Word to become incarnate in order to save humanity, Aquinas notes that there are two ways in which a means can be said to be necessary to a particular end, and proceeds to distinguish between the necessity of a means that is an absolute requirement to reaching a goal – in the way that one must necessarily eat in order to live – and the necessity of a means that allows one to reach a goal in the best possible way – in the way that a horse might be necessary for a long journey (III.1.2). Readers should see that while these distinctions are very important in Thomas' resolution of questions, and need to be attended to and grasped in order to understand his resolution of the question, they are deployed with a good deal of flexibility according to the requirements of the particular issue under discussion. The distinctions are never drawn simply for their own sake and the reader must always ask, 'why is *this* distinction important for *this* question?'

In addition to making distinctions, Thomas makes arguments; indeed, he is careful at the outset of the *Summa* (I.1.8) to clarify the way in which theology is 'argumentative' (in Latin, *argumentativa* – i.e., probative). These arguments are not, however, all of the same sort. Some of the arguments might properly be termed 'demonstrations' or proofs. As a good Aristotelian, Thomas distinguishes between proving *why* something is the case (what he calls a *demonstratio propter quid*) and proving *that* something is the case (a *demonstratio quia*), and notes that only the former is a demonstration 'in an unqualified sense.'[2] The 'why-demonstration' would be something like a proof in geometry, in which one sees not simply the truth of the conclusion, but how it flows from the premises. It does not seem to me that such arguments play a very prominent role in the *Summa Theologiae*, not least because the source of the truth of conclusions in theology – the middle term of the premises, if you will – is God, whose essence remains irreducibly mysterious to us.[3] However, 'that-demonstrations' do find a place in the *Summa*, in what Thomas calls the 'preambles' of faith, which are those things concerning God that are, at least in principle, within the power of unaided human reason to demonstrate. The most notable of these preambles is, of course, God's existence, for which Thomas offers sketches of five different demonstrations (I.2.3). In these cases, the middle term is not God's ungraspable essence, but God's effects in the world. Here, we have a demonstrative argument, though not a demonstration in an unqualified sense. Even such qualified 'that-demonstrations' from premises derived from natural reason do not feature prominently in the *Summa*, which is not surprising, since Thomas thought that such knowledge of God was apparent 'only to few, and even so after a long time and mixed with many mistakes' (I.1.1). More often one finds arguments that 'borrow' premises from God's own self-knowledge, which God has shared with us in historical revelation.

Often a revealed truth accepted on faith serves as the major premise in an argument and a truth known through natural human reason serves as the minor premise, resulting in what later scholastics called a 'theological conclusion.' Of course, in Thomas this form of argumentation is not as wooden as my description makes it sound; rarely does one find a neatly laid out syllogism. But we can see something of how this form of reasoning works in Thomas in the example of his discussion of whether Jesus had any acquired human knowledge.[4] In the *Summa* Thomas argues that in addition to divine, beatific and prophetic knowledge, Jesus also had knowledge gained in the way ordinary for humans: by abstraction from sense data (III.9.4). Aquinas' argument, diffused over the body of his response, is that we hold on faith that Christ is perfect in his divinity and perfect in his humanity, but we know that human perfection entails

---

[2]   *Commentary on Aristotle's Posterior Analytics*, 1.23a, Richard Berquist trans. (Notre Dame, IN: Dumb Ox Books, 2007), 106.

[3]   See I.12.13.

[4]   This example is suggested in Victor White OP, *God the Unknown* (New York: Harper, 1956), 13.

the acquisition of knowledge by abstracting from sense data, therefore Christ must have acquired knowledge in this way. Such an argument is in one sense 'reasonable,' since it follows a normative pattern of human reasoning, yet in another sense transcends reason, because it draws its major premise – Christ's perfect divinity and humanity – from a truth that can only be known by faith.

Aquinas often employs an even looser form of argumentation that later tradition has called the 'argument from fittingness' (*argumentum ex convenientia*). In this sort of argument, Thomas is not seeking to establish a necessary conclusion, but to engage the reader in an act of persuasion that might be described as 'aesthetic': he is attempting to display the decorous convergence of a variety of truths, so as to manifest the contours of a particular truth of faith. To choose one example among many, Thomas argues for the fittingness of the incarnation based on the convergence of other things that Christians believe about God: that God is the highest and most perfectly self-communicating good, that our faith is strengthened by direct communication from God, that a visible guide better leads us into right action, that human presumption is best cured by the display of divine humility, and so forth (III.1.1–2). Such arguments are not absolutely probative, but depend on one's willingness to intellectually step back, so as to be able to gain a wider view of the beauty of what God has shown us, its sheer fittingness. This beauty will probably not convince an unbeliever (though one ought not to underestimate the persuasive power of beauty), but it will surely move the Christian to greater love of God by virtue of the intellect's deeper grasp of the interlocking patterns of divine revelation.

Thomas' sense of fittingness manifests itself in non-argumentative ways as well. One can often detect typical ordering patterns that recur frequently in Thomas' discussion of different issues. For instance, questions are often addressed by viewing them from the perspective of the fourfold Aristotelian scheme of causality or, particularly on questions concerning salvation, from the perspective of the twofold working of grace: withdrawing us from evil and advancing us in goodness. Theological issues are often discussed according to a threefold pattern derived from the theological virtues of faith, hope and love. Thus, in exploring the ways in which it is fitting that Christ be really present in the Eucharist, Thomas discusses how the Eucharist fulfills the *hope* expressed in the sacrifices of the Old Law, how Christ's bodily presence is an expression of his *love* toward his friends, and how the hidden sacramental presence of Christ's body makes his humanity an object of *faith* (III.75.1). An awareness of these patterns, which are often left implicit by Thomas, can help readers understand why his discussions take the particular shape they do.[5]

It is worth mentioning, in addition to what one often finds in Thomas' arguments, what one does *not* find: concrete examples or images or illustrations. Or at least one rarely finds useful ones. For all that I have said about the 'aesthetic' aspect of Thomas' way of arguing, this is a highly abstract aesthetic; his is not the sort of mind that readily produces examples. The examples he does employ are often simply ones recycled from Aristotle or other sources, and these tend to be based either on outdated science (e.g. the influence of heavenly bodies on the sublunar world) or are so abstract as to leave the more sensually-minded completely in the dark. Thomas requires readers who are willing to operate at a certain level of abstraction, or are willing to find their own images and examples.[6]

In all of this, it is most important to take the article as a whole, and not simply focus on the arguments found in the body of the article. It is worth recalling that an *articulus*, while internally differentiated, is in fact a basic unit and ought to be read as such. It is frequently difficult to understand Thomas' own position without having first grappled with, and seen the point of, the objections. And often the most interesting point that Thomas makes in an article will be contained not in the body, but in a reply to an objection. Some readers might wish to read the article straight through; others might find it helpful to read the objections in a cursory manner, only to return to them once they have read the body of the article and read each one in conjunction with Thomas' reply to it. The best strategy for reading an article of the *Summa* is reader-specific and may in fact vary from article to article.

Questions, treatises, and parts

Much of the labour of reading the *ST* takes place in the workshop of the article. It is here that one grapples with Thomas' actual arguments. At the same time, one ought to attend to the larger structures in which the articles are embedded.

Articles are grouped by Thomas into 'questions.' What Thomas does in the questions of the *Summa* is to break an issue down into its

---

[5] These patterns perhaps served as mnemonic devices intended to help the Dominican friars, whom Thomas taught, to recall specific arguments while preaching or disputing.

[6] For those who cannot come up with their own examples, the writings of the late Herbert McCabe are a rich source of examples and images to illustrate Thomas' arguments. See, for example *On Aquinas* (London: Burns and Oates, 2008).

micro-issues – the articles – while ordering those articles in a coherent way, such that not only is the larger issue comprehensively addressed, but also one article flows into the next, to form a cumulative argument. A failure to discern this can often leave readers wondering why, within a question, articles can seem to repeat themselves. When confronted by an article that seems to repeat what was said in the immediately preceding article, we ought to look more deeply for the subtle ways in which the article is advancing the argument of the question as a whole.

To take one of the shorter questions as an example: in III.5 Thomas addresses in four articles the issue of the aspects of human nature that Christ takes to himself in becoming incarnate. Thomas begins with two presumptions in place: human beings are a unity of body and soul, and in speaking of the incarnation we are speaking of Christ becoming a true human being. So Thomas asks in the first article whether in the incarnation Christ took on a true body, to which he answers yes, since one cannot be human without being embodied. In the next article he seems to repeat substantially the question from the first article, asking whether Christ had a 'carnal' or 'fleshly' body. In asking this, he is further refining his investigation, for while we know that Christ took on a body, we still do not know what *sort* of body Christ took on: a body subject to suffering and change, such as earthly beings have, or an incorruptible body, such as (Thomas thought) the heavenly bodies are. Thomas says that it must have been the former, since the Gospel stories would seem to be deceptions if Christ could not suffer. In the third article he turns to the other half of the equation: does Christ have a human soul? He answers yes, basing his answer both on the scriptural narratives that show Jesus engaged in activities such as being angry, sad and hungry, which are passions of the soul, as well as on the Aristotelian view that the soul is the form of the body, and thus to have a truly human body Jesus must have a truly human soul. In the fourth article, asking whether Christ took on a human mind, he again seems to repeat his inquiry, even noting in his reply that the negative view can be refuted by the arguments from the preceding article. Yet this article adds a nuance lacking from the article that preceded it. Christ did not simply take on a soul that animated his body, but he took on a soul that made him live in the way that is particular to human beings: the life of a rational animal. This is important because Christ becomes incarnate to save us from sin, which is an affliction unique to beings possessed of reason. Thus Thomas spells out over four articles why it is fitting that Christ possess both a body that can suffer and a soul that can reason. In stepping back from the particulars of the arguments in the individual articles and taking in the scope of the question as a whole, the reader gains further insight into what it means for Christ to possess human nature in its integrity.

Commentators on Aquinas will often speak of the questions of the *Summa* as being gathered into larger structures known as 'treatises,' largely based on Thomas' practice of pausing periodically between questions to give a prospective view of what is to come in the next group of questions and how he will organize his discussion. These remarks can be valuable for a reader seeking to see how questions are interrelated, though one ought not to think of the treatise as necessarily being a complete discussion of a particular topic. Often important points on a particular topic can be found scattered throughout the *Summa*.

The division of the *Summa* into its three parts – with the first part dealing with God and creation, the second with human action, and the third with Christ and the sacraments – has generally been seen as highly significant and has been much discussed. More details on these discussions concerning the rationale for the structure can be found in Mark Jordan's essay in this volume. Here it shall suffice to say that, while there are many theories about the structure of the *Summa*, I am not convinced that these theories make very much difference in the act of reading the *Summa*. It certainly is a fruitful exercise to step back and try to absorb the grand sweep of what Thomas is setting about in the *Summa*, but it often does not make very much difference to the actual work of following its particular arguments. Certainly there are important points to notice about the structure: the presence in the first part, which might otherwise be mistaken for a 'natural theology,' of Aquinas' Trinitarian theology; the attention, unique in the medieval *Summa*-genre, given to human moral action in the second part; the grouping together of sacraments and christology in the third part. But one does not need a theory about the structure of the *Summa* before one begins to read it, and indeed one ought not to develop or adopt a theory about its structure *before* one has spent sufficient time with the text.

The *Summa* in its context

In reading the *Summa Theologiae* we ought to have some idea of its intellectual context: both the context of Thomas' writings as a whole and the context of medieval theology. The *Summa* is, without question, Thomas' masterpiece, and one often finds there Thomas' views in their most mature and clearly articulated form. Yet one can gain much from reading, for example, Thomas' discussions in the *Summa* about whether Theology is *scientia* or whether God's existence can be demonstrated, in light of his commentaries on Aristotle's *Posterior Analytics* or Boethius's *De Trinitate*. Likewise, one attains new insights into Aquinas' discussions of natural knowledge of God and of the workings of operative grace by reading his commentary on Paul's letter to the Romans.

One can also gain much from reading Thomas in light of other medieval theologians. One has a better grasp of what Thomas is criticizing in I.2.1*ad*2 if one has read Anselm's *Proslogion*. One understands better Aquinas' views on the demonstrability of the world's creation in time if one contrasts them with his contemporary Bonaventure's views on the same subject. One even gains insight into Thomas from reading later medieval theologians, such as Duns Scotus and Ockham, who reject certain aspects of his thought. Readers must bear in mind that the *Summa* is part of a vast, ongoing conversation, and it is important to become familiar with the other voices in that conversation.

It is also important to bear in mind the ends for which Thomas wrote the *Summa*, which seem to have been related to the intellectual formation of Dominican friars.[7] It is often helpful to ask oneself what the pedagogical purpose would be of a particular argument or distinction that Thomas makes and how it would aid those preparing for the Dominican tasks of preaching and the care of souls through the sacrament of penance.

READING ABOUT THE *SUMMA THEOLOGIAE*

The conversation in which the *Summa* is a part has also developed into a conversation *about* the *Summa*. While it is more important to read the *Summa* than to read about it, it would be mere hubris to think that one can get by without making use of the treasury of reflection that subsequent centuries have bequeathed to us regarding this text. I will briefly mention some of the most significant genres of writing about the *Summa* as well as a few specific works that might be particularly useful to those undertaking to read the *Summa*.

---

[7] See Leonard E. Boyle OP, *The Setting of the Summa Theologiae of St Thomas* (Toronto: Pontifical Institute of Medieval Studies, 1982). For a rich development of Boyle's work, see M. Michèle Mulchahey, *'First the Bow is Bent in Study...' Dominican Education before 1350* (Toronto: Pontifical Institute of Medieval Studies, 1998). My own recent effort to read Thomas in his Dominican context is much indebted to the scholarship of Boyle and Mulchahey. See Frederick Christian Bauerschmidt, *Thomas Aquinas: Faith, Reason and Following Christ* (Oxford: Oxford University Press, 2013).

Commentators

Commentaries on the *Summa Theologiae* began to be produced in the 15th century and soon became a significant theological genre. Perhaps the most important single commentary is that of the 16th century Dominican Thomas de Vio, more commonly known as Cajetan, which the editors of the Leonine edition of Thomas' works chose to include with the *Summa*. Other important commentaries, among the many that were written, include those by Francisco de Vitoria (*c.* 1483–1546), John Poinsot, known as John of Saint Thomas (1584–1644), and Charles René Billuart (1685–1757), as well as the cooperative commentary produced by the Carmelites of Salamanca during the 17th century. Unfortunately for those who are relative novices in reading Latin, very little of this commentarial literature has been translated. One may gain a sense of this literature, however, from English translations of the commentaries on various parts of the *Summa* written by the 20th century French Dominican Reginald Garrigou-Lagrange. His work not only embodies the spirit of the commentators, in the close analysis of the text and the making of ever-finer distinctions, but also conveys much of the substance of their discussions. Though Garrigou-Lagrange's work has become somewhat unfashionable since the Second Vatican Council, it remains an invaluable point of entry into an important body of secondary writings on the *Summa Theologiae*.[8]

Historians

In the late 19th century, after Leo XIII's encyclical *Aeterni Patris* (1879) commended the study of scholasticism in general and Thomas Aquinas in particular, historical investigation of Thomas and his times began in earnest and has much enriched the study of Thomas. Though he was once described by a 20th-century Thomist as 'a channel connecting us directly with intelligible truth,'[9] Thomas was a man of his times, and some knowledge of those times is valuable for reading Thomas. Information about the political, ecclesiastical and academic climates in which Thomas worked will help us appreciate the forces that contributed

---

[8]   The commentaries of Garrigou-Lagrange on the *Summa* that have been translated into English include: *The One God* (St Louis: Herder, 1943), *The Trinity and God the Creator* (St Louis: Herder, 1952), *Christ the Savior* (St Louis: Herder, 1950), *Grace* (St Louis: Herder, 1952), *Beatitude* (St Louis: Herder, 1956), *The Theological Virtues – Vol. 1: Faith* (St Louis: Herder, 1965).

[9]   A. G. Sertillanges, *St Thomas and His Work* (London: Burns, Oates & Washbourne, 1932), 111.

to the shaping of Thomas' theology.[10] Knowledge of Thomas' historical context can also help us to distinguish what is particular in his work and what is commonplace, when he is simply repeating common medieval attitudes and perspectives, and when he is making a distinctive contribution.[11] Furthermore, knowledge of the historical context of the *Summa* can help us have a better grasp of the possible ends for which he wrote and why he addressed the questions he did in the way he did.

It is also helpful to have some sense of the 'history of effects' of Thomas' work – that is, the way in which he has influenced subsequent discussions in theology, philosophy, politics and so forth. The work of Thomas in general, and the *Summa Theologiae* in particular, has had considerable influence both within Roman Catholicism and outside of the Catholic Church, though the nature of that influence has varied in different times and places.[12] In addition, some sense of the various 'schools' among Thomas' followers can give readers an appreciation of the variety of approaches that can be taken to Thomas and of interpretations that can be given to his work.[13]

Philosophers and theologians

In addition to the venerable commentarial tradition and to more recent historical studies, there is also a wealth of articles and monographs on the *Summa*, as well as helpful general introductions. These works reflect the variety of approaches to Thomas mentioned above. Among the secondary works on Thomas, one broad distinction stands out: that between those who read Thomas primarily from a philosophical perspective, and those who read him from a theological perspective.

While no one would deny that the *Summa Theologiae* is a work of theology, some would claim that it is possible and profitable to isolate for study the philosophical moves that Thomas makes. Even among those who agree with Thomas' theological positions, some see his major

---

[10] The state of the art biography is Torrell I.

[11] Marie-Dominique Chenu, *Toward Understanding St Thomas* (Chicago: Regnery, 1964) remains invaluable. More recently, see Torrell II, and Bernard McGinn, *Thomas Aquinas's Summa Theologiae: A Biography* (Princeton: Princeton University Press, 2014).

[12] See Romanus Cessario OP, *A Short History of Thomism* (Washington, DC: Catholic University of America Press, 2005), as well as the fascinating study by Marcus Plested, *Orthodox Readings of Aquinas* (Oxford: Oxford University Press, 2012).

[13] For the early 20th century, see Helen James John, SND, *The Thomist Spectrum* (New York: Fordham University Press, 1966). For the later 20th century, see Fergus Kerr (ed.), *Contemplating Aquinas: On the Varieties of Interpretation* (London: SCM, 2003).

achievements as philosophical.[14] Particularly since the Second Vatican Council, in the wake of which many theologians, freed from the necessity of being some sort of 'Thomist,' turned away from Thomas, much of the creative interest in Aquinas has been in the realm of philosophy. But the reading of Thomas as a thinker primarily of philosophical importance is at least as old as Leo XIII's *Aeterni Patris*, which prescribed the study of Thomas' *philosophy* as the cure for the ills of modernity. The explicit or implicit bracketing of Thomas' theological concerns can be carried out in various ways. In some cases, the author, while seeing Thomas' philosophy as distinct from his theology, and without treating his theology *per se*, still sees his philosophy and theology as part of a unified project.[15] In other cases, the author explicitly rejects Thomas' theology, but still finds philosophical value in his writings.[16] In still other cases, the author makes no particular reference to Thomas' Christian theology at all, but simply focuses on a particular philosophical question.[17] Monographs and articles in this genre are quite useful, though one must bear in mind that, by bracketing the theological, they give only a partial picture of what Thomas was setting out to do in the *Summa Theologiae*.

There has been in recent years a revival of interest in Thomas as a theologian, an end to what Karl Rahner called the 'uncanny silence' surrounding Aquinas in the immediate post-conciliar period. Rather than seeing his theology as a grace note in what is essentially a philosophical undertaking, a number of significant recent works, without ignoring Thomas' philosophical gestures, have taken as primary what Thomas has to say about the Trinity, Christ, and salvation.[18] Perhaps an

---

[14] See, for example, the remarks of Fernand Van Steenberghen, *The Philosophical Movement in the Thirteenth Century* (Edinburgh: Nelson, 1955), 96–98.

[15] For a classic example, see Etienne Gilson, *The Christian Philosophy of St Thomas Aquinas* (New York: Random, 1956).

[16] For example, Anthony Kenny, *Aquinas on Mind* (London: Routledge, 1993).

[17] For example, Ralph McInerny, *Aquinas and Analogy* (Washington, DC: Catholic University of America Press, 1996). McInerny, of course, does not completely ignore what Aquinas says about God, but treats this as a matter of natural theology and not Christian theology.

[18] To mention just a few works of many: for general introductions from a theological perspective, see Otto Hermann Pesch, *Thomas von Aquin: Grenze und Größe mittelalterlicher Theologie. Eine Einführung* (Mainz: Matthias-Grünewald-Verlag, 1988) and Nicholas M. Healy, *Thomas Aquinas: Theologian of the Christian Life* (Aldershot: Ashgate, 2003); for a collection of essays giving an introduction to Thomas on various theological topics, see Thomas Weinandy, Daniel Keating and John Yocum (eds), *Aquinas on Doctrine: A Critical Introduction* (London: T&T Clark, 2004). For examples of constructive engagements with Thomas for contemporary theological

indication of the return of interest in Thomas' theology can also be seen in the attention that philosophers are paying to Aquinas' discussion of Christian doctrines. For example, Eleonore Stump, in a book on Aquinas in a series entitled 'Arguments of the Philosophers' pays meticulous attention to the arguments Aquinas makes concerning incarnation and atonement.[19]

Thomas identifies himself in the prologue to the *Summa Theologiae* as a 'teacher of catholic truth' (*catholicae veritatis doctor*) and to understand the true 'catholicity' of his teaching, one must see it as a whole in which philosophical moments are integrated into the pursuit of the truth of the God revealed in Jesus Christ. The holistic reading that a work like the *Summa Theologiae* demands of us is part of the challenge, and the delight, that it offers to its readers.

purposes see Matthew Levering, *Scripture and Metaphysics* (Oxford: Blackwell, 2004) and, from a Protestant perspective, R. Michael Allen, *The Christ's Faith: A Dogmatic Account* (London: T&T Clark, 2009).

[19]   Eleonore Stump, *Aquinas* (New York: Routledge, 2003).

Dominican spirituality

TIMOTHY RADCLIFFE OP

Spirituality is not a word often associated with St Thomas' *Summa*. It is defined by *The Oxford Dictionary of the Christian Church* as 'people's subjective practice and experience of their religion, or the spiritual exercises and beliefs which individuals or groups have with regard to their personal relationship with God.'[1] This seems remote from the rigorous, logical argumentation of the *Summa*. Thomas did not have a spirituality in this modern sense. He lived before the break-up, at the beginning of the fourteenth century, of the unity of theology, philosophy, ethics, and spirituality. He could not have imagined the study of theology as a merely intellectual exercise. Studying, praying, and living virtuously were interpenetrating dimensions of a life open to God's grace.

His spirituality was intellectual and moral. The *Summa* is 'in its structure and method, prayer ... both an exhortation to contemplation and an act of contemplation.'[2] It is also a preaching of the gospel. Thomas is often contrasted with St Dominic, a wandering preacher who left hardly any writing, but they truly are brethren. 'The perfection of Christian life consists in charity – primarily in the love of God, and secondarily in love of neighbour' (II–II.184.3*corp*). And the most perfect act of charity is to share the gospel with others, which is why the most perfect state of life, he argued, is that of preachers and teachers. The writing of the *Summa* is an act of charity, an expression of God's friendship for humanity, and thus a work of the Holy Spirit and part of the spiritual life of a friar of the Order of Preachers.

The Prologue of the *Prima Pars* tells us that the *Summa* was written for 'beginners.' These were probably the young friars whom Thomas taught from 1265 to 1268 at Santa Sabina, on the Aventine in Rome,

---

[1] F. L. Cross, *The Oxford Dictionary of the Christian Church*, ed. E. A Livingstone (3rd ed.; Oxford: Oxford University Press, 1997), 1532.
[2] A. N. Williams, 'Mystical Theology Redux: The Pattern of Aquinas' *Summa Theologiae*', *Modern Theology* 12/1 (1997), 56.

the priory given to Dominic by Pope Honorius III in 1219. Fergus Kerr OP believes that 'these would have been run-of-the-mill students who were being trained to preach in the vicinity of the priories in which they had joined the Order. Unlike Thomas himself, they would not have been destined to proceed to the great international universities to study theology.'[3]

According to Thomas, these students were hindered from learning because of 'the swarm of pointless questions, articles, and arguments' in other works. He wished to offer a presentation which follows the *ordo disciplinae*. This is more than just putting the questions in a logical order; the very idea of 'order' is suggestive of his underlying spirituality.

St Dominic's principal legacy to his brethren was a form of government which directed the Order towards its end, 'preaching and the salvation of souls', according to the Primitive Constitutions. Thomas wrote an orderly account for friars whose lives were directed to a specific end, unlike monks who had no other purpose than to praise God. But embedded in the structure of the *Summa* is the longer journey of every human being towards God, in whom alone we may find our happiness and fulfilment. So the *ordo disciplinae* pointed these itinerant friars towards their final goal, the vision of God. Dominic's spirituality was incarnate in the government of the Order for the preaching of the gospel; Thomas' government of the material expresses a purposeful spirituality, ordered to the goal of the Christian life. The prologues offer the clearest signposts on the journey, and so we shall look to them for clues to the *Summa*'s spirituality.

Thomas never finished the *Summa*. In 1273 he had an experience, significantly at Mass, which prevented him from writing anything more. He said, 'Everything that I have written seems like straw in comparison with what I have seen, and what has been revealed to me.' It is not that this mystical experience suggested that all his writing was a waste of time. It was the fruition of the pilgrimage, intellectual and spiritual, that the *Summa* is, a glimpse of the goal.

This is a journey towards the one who is pure existence, *ipsum esse*. Existence is not something that God has; it is the utter act of the one who spoke to Moses from the burning bush saying 'I am who am.' Thomas' God is not the static entity of classical theism, but pure dynamism; 'He takes seriously the thought that the word "God" might actually be better regarded as a verb.'[4] David Burrell translates Thomas as

[3] Fergus Kerr, *After Aquinas: Versions of Thomism* (Oxford: Blackwell, 2002), 165.
[4] Kerr, *After Aquinas*, 187.

asserting, 'To be God is to be to-be.'⁵ God's happiness is identical with this act of being, in which God enjoys himself utterly.

Everything is created to come to its own perfection, to be as fully as possible. Thomas sees things not statically but in terms of their potential flourishing. So the study of Christian theology is not the dry exploration of ideas about God. It is our response to God, in whom we shall find the happiness for which we are made. So these 'beginners' who followed the *ordo* of the *Summa* were not just learning what to preach in their itinerant ministry; they were beginning their journey home to God. We are created *ad imaginem Dei*, in the image of God. But for Thomas this '*ad*', which means 'towards', implies a dynamic process, of coming to be, flourishing as God intended. As Kerr writes, 'a small bit of grammar carries a good deal of theology.'⁶

Dominic's form of government was also designed to preserve the unity of the Order. The brethren were quickly scattered all over the known world. The Order might easily have fragmented; but the preachers of the Kingdom, into which is gathered the whole of humanity, must remain one. We preach God's will for the unification of humanity in his Son. The *Summa* is marked by the same concern for unity. The questions are not just ordered to an end, but express a more or less unified theological vision. One of the ways in which we come to flourish is in becoming one, from Thomas' controversial insistence on the unity of the human person, body and soul, to the unity of humanity in Christ, and the unutterable unity of God. Theological questioning heals divisions and tensions at every level of our being, personal and communal, ecclesial and political, drawing us into the oneness of God.

This seems to put an extraordinary weight upon study. How can it have this spiritual import? The prologue opens with reference to the role of the 'teacher of Catholic truth'. *Veritas* is the motto of Thomas' religious order. The impulse for the Order's foundation came from Dominic's encounter with the Albigensian heresy in the south of France. It is fundamental to human dignity, and part of how we are made *ad imaginem Dei*, that we are capable of knowing the truth. Knowledge is not just about things. To know the truth is, in some sense, to become what is known. Thomas frequently quotes Aristotle's words, 'the soul, in a way, is everything.' To know is not to look dispassionately at something with a scientific eye. It is to open oneself to its being, which is its truth.

---

⁵ David B. Burrell, *Aquinas, God and Action* (Notre Dame, IN: University of Notre Dame Press, 1979), 54.
⁶ Kerr, *After Aquinas*, 124.

It is a passivity by which one's being is enlarged. 'Knowing is a new way of being on the knower's part.'[7] For us living after Descartes, this may seem bizarre. For us knowledge implies disengagement, distance, detachment. For Aquinas it is part of how we come alive, realise our potential as rational beings who are attuned to the meaning and being of things.

Charles Taylor distinguishes between the 'porous self' of pre-modernity, and the 'buffered self' which came into existence in the eighteenth century.[8] Thomas lived in the world of 'the porous self'; one's sense of self was founded on relationships with other beings, human and spiritual. One is a 'we' before one is an 'I'. The 'buffered self' is essentially private, pre-existing its involvement with others. McCabe contrasts the modern view, 'that society is made of individuals', with the older view, 'that the individual is made of societies.'[9]

We can either dismiss Thomas' spirituality, and its underlying epistemology, as merely of antiquarian interest, founded on an outdated understanding of what it means to be a human being. Or, we may read it as a critique of fundamental assumptions of our culture. It is, of course, impossible for us to become thirteenth-century men and women and inhabit Thomas' world, but we may find in Thomas a fruitful challenge to our contemporary self-understanding. Thomas' account of knowledge rings true in some ways. When we come to know and love someone, then we do become open to them, vulnerable to their way of being alive; our humanity is enlarged. Novels and films extend our sympathies, and invite us to be in the world differently. Without having to pretend that the Enlightenment never happened or to surrender our hard won sense of individuality, the idea that 'the soul, in a way, is everything' invites us to be free of a suffocating sense that our identities are founded on detachment and separation.

If knowing is not, then, a private affair of the solitary ego, but is embedded in my belonging to others, then obviously thinking together is part of our communal life. Argument is not the duelling of eighteenth-century gentlemen but one of the ways in which we build and sustain the community of truth. Dominic debated with Albigensians so as to draw them back into the community of the Church, and not to condemn them. These young friars, for whom Thomas was writing, were

---

[7]   Kerr, *After Aquinas*, 30.
[8]   Charles Taylor, *A Secular Age* (Cambridge, MA: Harvard University Press, 2007), 35–43.
[9]   Herbert McCabe, *God Matters* (London: Geoffrey Chapman, 1987), 231.

from their earliest days in the Order trained to argue with each other.[10] Thomas asserted that 'if anyone wants to write back against what I have said, I shall be delighted, because there is no better way of disclosing truth and confuting error than by arguing with people who disagree with you.'[11] The whole of the *Summa* is founded on considering the arguments of opponents, taking them seriously, modifying and refining one's opinions in the light of their objections, and seeking the larger truth in which we can be one. During his composition of the *Summa*, he was engaged in disputations with people on just the subjects about which he was writing.[12] The solitary labour of writing drew life from constant immersion in public debate.

Disputation also belongs to our journey towards our end. Disobedience to reason is a kind of disobedience to God[13]. So we obey God's call to share his life by reasoning with each other. And because argument is part of our spiritual journey towards the one who is love, then necessarily it must be charitable. Of course academic disputes in Thomas' time were often as bitter as they are today, but Thomas, at least, almost never dismissed the arguments of his opponents as rubbish. Uncharitable reasoning would be a sort of contradiction in terms, a subversion of one of the ways in which we engage with each other. Thomas was even known to refuse to reply to a vicious attack on his views by a new Master of Arts, because 'he did not wish to spoil the new Master's day.'[14]

If the topic about which we think and argue is 'catholic truth', and ultimately the truth of God, then our knowing is necessarily enmeshed with our loving. Thomas' exploration of thinking and willing, knowing and loving, come together in his treatment of the gift of wisdom (I-II.45). Here we see, argues Thomas Heath OP, how 'knowledge of the goodness of an object causes us to love it; love then brings about a different and better kind of knowledge; this new appreciation deepens the love which, in turn, intensifies the appreciation and so on.'[15] So thinking about catholic truth is inherently bound up with love. It is a truth that cannot be known dispassionately. And this great intellectual even concedes that the 'little old lady' (*vetula*) who is

---

[10] Simon Tugwell (ed.), *Albert and Thomas: Selected Writings* (New York: Paulist Press, 1988), 210.

[11] *De Perfectione*, §30, quoted by Tugwell, *Albert and Thomas*, 337.

[12] Tugwell, *Albert and Thomas*, 253.

[13] *DV*, 11.1, 17.5.

[14] Tugwell, *Albert and Thomas*, 230.

[15] *Blackfriars* 35, 200.

burning with the love of God will know more than 'a scholar full of his own superiority'.[16]

So, for these early Dominicans, debate was more than a matter of the cold acquisition of knowledge. It was a foretaste of the joy of the beatific vision. Albert the Great, Thomas' master, talked of the pleasure of seeking the truth together: '*in dulcedine societatis quaerere veritatem*'.[17] Thomas was frequently called the *felix doctor*, the happy teacher. Those who pursue wisdom are, he writes, 'the happiest that anyone can be in this life.'[18] They share in wisdom's play in the presence of God (Proverb 8:30).[19] By study one's mind and heart are open to God who is pure joy, a small glimpse of our final end.

But here we reach the most profound challenge of Thomas' spirituality, which is that in this life we are joined to God as to the unknown: 'We cannot know what God is, but only what he is not; we must therefore consider the ways in which God does not exist, rather than the ways in which he does' (I.3*prol*). Even the proofs of the existence of God are less opposed to atheism than to those who think God's existence is obvious. In Thomas' world, in which virtually everyone believed in God, he had to establish that it was a matter of faith. In itself God's existence is evident, but not for us (I.2.1) The proofs are, paradoxically, the first step in letting go our pictures of God, painfully liberating ourselves from the grip of what seemed to his contemporaries an obvious, sacramental way of looking at the world, filled with divine splendour. Kerr argues that 'far from being an exercise in rationalistic apologetics, the purpose of arguing for God's existence is to protect God's transcendence.'[20]

The proofs are, in a way, the first step in that negative path, the *via remotionis*, by which we let go all false images of God. We draw near to God by stripping our mind of all concepts that seek to contain God. This is the most profoundly ascetical exercise, far more radical than fasting. This is the spirituality of the theologian who, writes Torrell, 'must abandon idols and turn toward the living God (Acts 14:14). He must renounce the constructions of his own mind, personal idols that have no less a hold.... Negative theology is the intellectual form of our respect and adoration in confrontation with God's mystery.'[21] Herbert

---

[16] Torrell II, 98.
[17] Albert the Great, *Commentarii in octo libros politicorum*, book 7, quoted in Tugwell, *Albert*, 30.
[18] *Sententia libri Ethicorum*, 10.11.
[19] Janice L. Schultz and Edward Syman (eds), *An Exposition of the 'On the Hebdomads' of Boethius* (Washington, DC: Catholic University of America, 2001), 5.
[20] Kerr, *After Aquinas*, 58.
[21] Torrell I, 34, 35f.

McCabe OP calls this Thomas' 'sanctity of the mind'. Legend has it that as a child he insistently asked: 'What is God?'. All of his life was devoted to attempting to answer questions, but this was the question that defeated him. McCabe writes: 'As Jesus saw that to refuse the defeat of the cross would be to betray his whole mission, all that he was sent to do, so Thomas knew that to refuse to accept defeat about this one question would be to betray all that he had to do, his mission.'[22] It is only in the beatific vision, when we are so united with God that God becomes 'the form of the intellect', that we shall see God as he is, sharing in God's self-knowledge and utter happiness. The intellectual asceticism of this life is an opening of our minds and hearts to receive this gift. Dominic insisted that the brethren be beggars for their bread. For Thomas, the intellectual life is the opening of our minds to receive this ultimate gift, a sharing of God's own being, deification.

This may all seem aridly intellectual, the pilgrimage of a mind, but the *Secunda Pars*, devoted to our moral life, sets it firmly in our lives as rational but bodily beings, passionate, desiring animals. Morality is not fundamentally about obeying rules. It is, again, dynamic, becoming the sort of people, as Kerr writes, 'who would be fulfilled only in the promised bliss of face-to-face vision of God.' 'Ethics for Thomas is … motivated by anticipated happiness.'[23] Given the centrality of this moral vision in the *Summa*, placed between the doctrines of Creation and the Incarnation, Tugwell can go so far as to say that 'the whole of the *Summa* can be seen as an exercise in moral theology',[24] just as it is all an exercise in spirituality.

The Prologue to the *Prima Secundae* gives us the foundation of Thomas' ethical spirituality, the goodness of creation and human freedom. Thomas' understanding of us as moral agents, made in the image of God, is based on his doctrine of creation, 'that God is the exemplar cause of things and that they issue from his power through his will.' The Dominican Order was initially founded to confront Albigensianism in the south of France. This was one of those outbreaks of dualism which periodically infect Western Europe. Thomas' doctrine of creation rejected its claim that the world is evil. His understanding of what it means to be human was rooted in this anti-dualism. It is not surprising that the only two miracles attributed to Thomas concern food! His most contentious claim was the fundamental unity of the human being. The soul is

---

[22] McCabe, *God Matters*, 236.
[23] Kerr, *After Aquinas*, 130.
[24] Tugwell, *Albert and Thomas*, 336.

the form of the body. The journey towards God described here is made by rational animals, passionate beings. One of his favourite quotations was 'nothing in the mind if not first in the senses.' He scandalised his contemporaries with assertions such as that 'the soul is not the whole person. My soul is not me.'[25] It was this insistence that provoked the first attacks on Thomas, especially by the Franciscans, and even by some of his Dominican brethren.

There cannot be a vast gulf between nature and grace, because nature too is a gift from God. Thomas asserts that so long as something exists, 'God must be present to it, and present in a way in keeping with the way in which the thing possesses its existence' (I.8.1). The cultivation of the virtues, then, is not the imposition of an alien life on an utterly corrupt humanity. As Thomas famously says in many and various ways, grace perfects nature and does not destroy it. Despite the wounding of sin, we retain a desire for God. 'God has thus left, at the deepest level of every being, a desire to return to him.'[26] Our passions need to be healed rather than suppressed, liberated for our deepest desire, which is for God. They are ruled by reason but, recalling Aristotle, 'not by the despotic rule of a master towards his slave, but by the civil and royal rule which governs free men who are not entirely subject to dictate' (I–II.17.7*corp*). This is evocative, surely, of Thomas' experience of Dominican government, the ruling of free friars who would not accept being pushed around!

Thomas inherited from Aristotle the belief that 'friendship is what is most necessary to live'. In his own words, 'Among all the things that a human being needs, other humans are the most necessary to him.'[27] But Aristotle's conception of the friendship of the free citizens of the Greek city is transformed, in the light of John 15:15, 'I call you no longer servants but friends.' Our natural need for friendship, whether in marriage or the city, is gathered up into our sharing in the friendship which is the life of the Trinity. Through the presence of the Holy Spirit in our lives, we become friends of God, and the Father and the Son come to make their home in us. This deep sensitivity to friendship was surely rooted in his experience of the fraternal life of the Order. We know little of Thomas' own friendships – clearly Reginald, his socius on his travels for many years, was a close friend – but friendship was characteristic of the early brethren, for example, St Dominic's love of

---

[25] Quoted by Torrell II, 257 (see *In I ad Corinthios*, 14.19, lect. 2, n. 924).
[26] Torrell I, 343.
[27] *SCG* III.128.1, translation modified from Torrell, II, 281.

the brethren. There were also many examples of the friars' easy friendship with women. Jordan of Saxony, Dominic's successor, who died shortly before Thomas became a Dominican, was famous for his deep friendship with the Dominican nun, Blessed Diana d'Andalò.[28] In the next century, there was the friendship of St Catherine of Siena and Blessed Raymond of Capua. The spiritual life is a graced flourishing of what is most natural to us.

The second fundamental intuition of Thomas' ethics is the conviction that the moral life is an expression and embrace of our freedom. In the Prologue to the *Prima Secundae*, he says that we are made in the image of God, because the human being 'is intelligent and free to judge and be master of himself.' He will examine how the human being is 'the source of actions which are his own and which fall under his responsibility and control.' The radical transcendence of God, to whom we are joined as to the unknown, means that there is no competition for power between God and humanity. God's grace makes us free. Kerr writes, 'Thomas sees no conflict between God's working in everything and everything doing its own thing, so to speak. Or rather: he is well aware of the temptations, common in his day and ours, to see rivalry between God's sovereign freedom and human autonomy, either making God an item in the world or reducing creatures to puppets. "It seems difficult for some people," he remarks, "to understand how natural effects are attributed to both God and to a natural agent" (*SCG* III.70.1).'[29] So God gives us our part in the realization of God's will. Our prudent moral action is a sharing in God's providential government of the world. One of the ways, surprisingly, in which we may do this is through prayer. Prayer for Thomas was above all asking for things. Our prayers do not change God's mind, but rather it is God's will that things happen in accordance with our prayers. So we have in prayer what Thomas calls 'the dignity of causality'.

This sense of human freedom again reflects the spirituality of Dominic's Order. Dominic handed over the government of the Order to the brethren, confident in their responsibility. He was famous for his trust of the brothers. When he sent out his youngest friars to preach, the Cistercians warned him that he would lose them. Dominic replied, 'I know for certain that my young men will go out and come back, will be

---

[28] See further Gerald Vann OP, *To Heaven with Diana! A Study of Jordan of Saxony and Diana d'Andalò with a translation of the Letters of Jordan* (Reprinted; New York: iUniverse, 2006).

[29] Kerr, *After Aquinas*, 43f.

sent out and will return; but your young men will be kept locked up and will still go out.'[30]

In the *Tertia Pars* the spirituality of the *Summa* finds its synthesis. God responds to our thirst for happiness by drawing near to us as we are, flesh and blood, in the Incarnation of the Son and the sacramental life of the Church. Once again the prologue signposts the way on which we are embarked; Jesus Christ 'showed in his own person that path of truth which, in rising again, we can follow to the blessedness of eternal life. This means that after our study of the final goal of human life and of the virtues and vices we must bring the entire theological discourse to completion by considering (*consideratio*) the Saviour himself and his benefits to the human race.'

The pilgrimage into which Thomas is initiating those young friars here reaches towards its consummation, 'the blessedness of eternal life.' But we are flesh and blood; 'Nothing in the mind unless first in the senses.' So Thomas stresses that Christ *shows* us the path of truth; we shall *consider* Christ himself, for in him the end of the journey is made visible and tangible. It belongs to God's friendship with humanity to show himself in Jesus, 'so that knowing God under visible form, we might be enraptured into love of the invisible.'[31] Torrell points out that this formulation, from the *SCG*, is probably taken by St Thomas from the Christmas Preface. His theology is rooted in the celebration of the liturgy, in which our faith is visibly expressed.

In Christ we see the one in whom humanity and divinity are united, and so can hope to attain unity with God ourselves. In Christ, God takes us by the hand to lead us into friendship. This contemplation of the life and death of Jesus offers more than just a moral example. Knowledge, again, is transforming. By seeing God in Jesus, we begin the process of becoming like God. Thomas is writing for a culture in which faith needed to be made manifest, incarnate. It was often said that Dominic preached as much by example as by word. One of Thomas' favourite quotations was 1 John 3:2: 'Beloved, we are God's children now; it does not yet appear what we shall be, but we know that when he appears we shall be like him, for we shall see him as he is.' The saints are 'deiform', transformed by the vision of God (I.12.6), and this begins in our *consideratio* of Christ. Thomas offers us thirty-three questions on the mysteries of Christ's life, one for each year of his life. It is a thoroughly trinitarian

---

[30] Simon Tugwell OP (ed.), *Early Dominicans: Selected Writings* (Mahwah, NJ: Paulist, 1982), 91.
[31] *SCG* IV.54, n. 3927.

spirituality; we are configured to the Son by the mediation of the Holy Spirit, for the Spirit is the giver of all gifts. The Word offers us the teaching, and the Spirit makes us able to receive it.

This visibility finds its climax in the Eucharist. Lay people, who rarely went to communion, longed to see the host lifted up after consecration. Eamon Duffy asserts that 'seeing the host became the high point of lay experience of the Mass.'[32] In the host was made tangible the one in whom humanity and divinity are joined, the promise of beatitude. But for Thomas, the visibility is not just as of an object. The sacraments 'belong to the general category of signs' (III.60.1). David Bourke wrote that 'the very act of producing meaning and the act of causing are one and the same.'[33] They effect what they mean. They are signs that speak to us. The Eucharist nourishes us as meaning made flesh.

We are caught up in the very happening of redemption in the mysteries of Christ's life. Thomas, we have seen, has a dynamic spirituality; we flourish by sharing the life of God who is pure act. Through the sacraments, one becomes 'a participator not merely in the fruits of the Passion but in the death, Resurrection, and "newness of life" of Christ himself.'[34] One shares in the present happening of grace. Thomas refers to Christ not just as risen but rising now, *homo resurgens*. 'The historical Christ, today glorified, touches us by each of the acts of his earthly life, which is the bearer of a divinizing life and energy.'[35]

So Thomas' exploration of the Eucharist, which is almost the last subject touched upon in the *Summa*, is the climax of his spirituality. It responds to the hunger of our minds for meaning, of our wills for delight, our bodies for nourishment, and that deepest need of all, for friendship with each other in God. All that is given here. It is fitting that it was in the Eucharist that Thomas had that mystical experience that was the glimpse of the end of the journey, towards which his *Summa* pointed. It is reported that shortly before he died, when the Eucharist was brought to him, Thomas said: 'I receive you, price of my soul's redemption, I receive you, viaticum for my pilgrimage, for whose love I have studied, kept watch and laboured and preached and taught.'[36]

---

[32] Eamon Duffy, *The Stripping of the Altars: Traditional Religion in England 1400–1580* (New Haven: Yale University Press, 1992), 94.
[33] *Blackfriars* 56, xxi.
[34] Ibid., xxiii.
[35] Torrell I, 139.
[36] Tugwell, *Albert and Thomas*, 265.

Structure

MARK D. JORDAN

Thomas' *ST* is rarely read whole, yet an overarching structure is its distinguishing theological achievement. The structure clarifies inherited doctrines while integrating them into a cumulative pedagogy for which God's incarnation is the singularly appropriate response to the moral needs of an embodied human learner. Many readers, medieval and modern, have lost sight of the structure – often because they were interested in excerpting particular passages or in extracting principles for application elsewhere. They have treated the *Summa* as a loose dictionary with separate entries rather than as a single curriculum. Despite those readings, the sequence of the *Summa* remains the principal structure through which it intends to shows its lessons about divine revelation and to produce its pedagogical effects.

Two famous and relatively recent interpretations of the *Summa*'s structure can suggest how much theology there is in it and how stubbornly it resists summary. From the late 1930s on, Marie-Dominique Chenu argued that the *Summa* followed the great arc of the *exitus* and *reditus*, the transit of all creatures from a divine origin back to a divine end.[1] As Chenu understood perfectly well, this arc would hardly be unique to the *Summa*. Thomas himself explicitly invokes *exitus/reditus* to explain the division into four books of Peter Lombard's *Sentences*,

[1] Marie-Dominique Chenu, 'Le plan de la *Somme théologique* de Saint Thomas,' *Revue Thomiste* 47 (1939), 93–107, reprised in his *Introduction à l'étude de saint Thomas d'Aquin* (Montreal: Institut d'études médiévales, 1954), 255–276. For reactions to Chenu through 1998, see Brian Johnstone, 'The Debate on the Structure of the *Summa Theologiae*,' in Paul van Geest, Harm Goris, and Carlo Leget (eds), *Aquinas as Authority* (Leuven: Peters, 2002), 187–200. For a more recent critique of Chenu, see Rudi te Velde, *Aquinas on God: The 'Divine Science' of the Summa Theologiae* (Aldershot: Ashgate, 2006), 11–18. For critical elaborations of Chenu, see Thomas O'Meara, *Thomas Aquinas Theologian* (Notre Dame: University of Notre Dame Press, 1997), 56–64; Jean-Pierre Torrell, *Aquinas's Summa: Background, Structure, and Reception* (Washington, DC: Catholic University of America Press, 2005), 17–62; and Bernard McGinn, *Thomas Aquinas's Summa Theologiae* (Princeton: Princeton University Press, 2014), 66–69.

by his time a required work for university curricula in theology.[2] Before Thomas ever explained it, the pattern was a commonplace of theological composition. Adopting it, Thomas affirmed the traditional notion that a work of theology ought to narrate a redemptive history, not least as an ideal curriculum for its readers.

More recently, and much more specifically, Leonard Boyle argued from circumstantial evidence that Thomas conceived the *Summa* as a response to educational problems in his own religious community.[3] At the time the formation of most Dominican friars led them through selections of scripture, canon law, and moral cases so that they could preach and hear confessions. In the *Summa*, Thomas showed how to arrange such scattered material within a more fundamental pattern of Christian doctrine. He understood the local pedagogical problem in terms of the universal condition of human learning on the way to blessedness in God.

Both accounts are plausible, but they are hardly the same. Juxtaposing Boyle with Chenu only sharpens questions about the theology written into the *Summa*'s structure. How is the grand historical cycle of *exitus/reditus* actually helpful to a community of preachers and confessors? If the most profound Christian doctrines ought to bear fruit in the care of souls, how in fact do they? It is possible to start on these questions with the clues about Thomas' intentions as he began the *Summa*, but then the clues have to be tested against the achieved structure of his text. That structure traces the historical cycle, but it looks especially to history's center, the incarnation of God.

THE INTENTIONS OF THE *SUMMA*

Thomas did not write elaborate prefaces, but his prefatory remarks do provide clues, not least because they are precise in their brevity. Thomas opens the *Summa* with the briefest of prologues on the obligations of the Christian teacher.[4] The teacher is obliged to provide not only for

---

[2] Thomas, *Super Sent.* I.2 divisio textus (ed. Mandonnet – Moos 1:57).

[3] Leonard E. Boyle, *The Setting of the Summa Theologiae of Saint Thomas* (Toronto: PIMS, 1982), reprinted in James P. Reilly (ed.), *The Etienne Gilson Lectures on Thomas Aquinas* (Toronto: PIMS, 2008).

[4] As might be expected, the duties of teaching figure in a number of Thomas' explanations of his compositional purposes, beginning with his inaugural declaration as a doctor or licensed teacher of theology (the *principium*, *Rigans montes*). For a more exact appreciation of the very short prologue to the *Summa*, it is helpful to compare it with the *proemium* to the *Scriptum super Sententiis*, the first nine chapters of *Summa contra Gentiles* I, and the *prologus* to the 'Lectura Romana' on *Sententiae* I (which I count as an authentic work).

the accomplished, but also for those just beginning. So the intention of the *Summa* is to 'deliver what belongs to the Christian religion (*Christiana religio*) in the way that befits the teaching of beginners (*incipientes*).' Modern readers are liable to suppose that 'religion' means doctrine and that the 'beginners' have only just undertaken its academic study. Boyle rightly observed that the words have another sense for Thomas. Later in the *Summa*, 'religion' names both a virtue of devotion to God and the vowed ways of life that school one in it (II-II.81–91, II-II.186–189). 'Beginners' might then refer to those in early stages of religious formation – to 'novices,' as Thomas will call his intended readers a few lines later in the prologue. Such beginners need teaching that offers effective truth about their divine destination. So Thomas' prologue continues with criticism of theological texts that fail to offer it. They multiply 'useless questions, articles, and arguments.' They do not proceed according to an appropriate order of study. They produce both 'distaste and confusion' through pointless repetition. The *Summa*, by contrast, promises to teach 'briefly and clearly' only what is useful, according to an appropriate order, and without alienating duplication.

Thomas' stated intentions might seem clichés, but their deliberateness can be verified in the circumstances of the work's composition. In 1265, Thomas was assigned to open a house of studies for the Dominicans in Rome.[5] The assignment was not unexpected, since he had been teaching for the last six years outside universities in Dominican houses throughout central Italy. Now he was asked to open his own school as a sort of bridge between ordinary pastoral training and advanced academic study. During his first year at Rome, Thomas tried redoing his commentary on the *Sentences* of Peter Lombard. He proceeded with a simpler structure than he had used ten years earlier at the university in Paris, and he excluded many of his own technical elaborations. Still, after revisiting parts of the Lombard's first book, Thomas set the project aside and turned instead to what became the *Summa*. His decision is surprising. Peter Lombard's order of topics was recognizably a variation on the structure of the Nicene creed, that venerable form for Christian catechesis. Why not prepare beginners by taking them through the creedal pattern as reflected in a canonical academic work?

In the *Summa*'s prologue, Thomas faults theologians who follow the sequence required by the exposition of an authoritative text without

5   For the reconstruction of the circumstances, see Boyle, *Setting*, 9–12; Torrell I, 142–5; M. Michele Mulchahey, *'First the Bow is Bent in Study...': Dominican Education before 1350* (Toronto: PIMS, 1998), 278–306.

consulting the needs of beginners. The complaint only makes sense if the sequence of the underlying text is in fact unsuitable for beginners. It is not hard to fill in the implied judgment about Peter Lombard's creedal pattern. The Nicene creed contains no moral and little sacramental teaching. While those omissions are perfectly understandable given the creed's intended uses, they become significant defects when its pattern is adopted for the education of preachers. Peter Lombard's solution, if it is one, divides moral teaching into two segments: will, grace, and sin are treated in connection with the fall of Adam and Eve (II.25–44), while the theological virtues and the commandments appear as an enormous excursus tethered somehow to a consideration of Christ's virtues (III.23–40). The Lombard's lengthy discussion of the sacraments follows immediately, but in a separate book devoted to 'the doctrine of signs' as opposed to the 'doctrine of things' (IV.1–42). In sum, Peter Lombard fits pastoral topics within the creedal pattern by splitting the moral discussion incoherently and detaching the incarnation from the sacraments of Christian life.

Thomas abandoned variations on this pattern to invent the *Summa*. He divided his new work into three parts. The first treats God's essence and the distinction of persons in the Trinity, God as creative exemplar, and the creatures that proceed from God. The second part considers 'the motion of the rational creature towards God.' It is further divided into two sections. The first of them presents moral matter generally or 'universally': the end of human life, the elements of properly human action, and both the intrinsic and extrinsic principles of human acts. The second section surveys moral questions compendiously under the headings of the main virtues before integrating them into states or ways of life. *Summa* III presents Christ as the way by which the rational creature can reach God. The finished portion of this last part teaches the appropriateness of divine incarnation, the lessons of Christ's earthly life, and the efficacy of his sacraments as extensions of his saving work. Thomas broke off writing the *Summa* at III.90.4, in the middle of the discussion of the sacrament of penance. He had promised to proceed from it to the sacraments of orders and matrimony before ending with immortal life.

Even in such bald summary, the structure of *Summa* evidently improves on Lombard's *Sentences*. First, it unifies the treatment of moral matter, while distinguishing more cogently between elements or principles and composite actions. Second, it brings together incarnation and sacraments in a single motion of divine communication. Third, the *Summa* shows the usefulness of the whole of theology to the soul's motion towards God. Pastoral theology mirrors and depends on the fundamental order of creation. *Exitus/reditus* or any other narrative of divine providence is not presented as a cold fact, but as an exhortation to seek God. The intended reader of the *Summa* is not a remote spectator so much as an invited participant. Indeed, Thomas adapts the classical rhetorical form of the *synkrisis* or persuasive comparison of goals for the opening and the conclusion of the *Summa*'s moral part (I-II.1–6, II-II.179–189). This persuasion is completed by the *epideixis* or laudatory demonstration of incarnation as the most generous and effective pedagogy for embodied minds that have lost their way.

The *Summa* re-orients the received topics of theology towards the predicament of human souls. There are more questions about creatures in the first part than about God, and more about human beings than about the Trinity. The entire second part is a moral consideration of human life. The doctrine of Christ in the third begins with arguments for the appropriateness of an incarnate God as savior for humankind. The *Summa* devotes more questions to a moralized retelling of gospel events than to the metaphysics of the incarnation, and it gives more questions still to the sacraments as extensions of Christ's saving work (incomplete as that treatment remains). The beginners who are Thomas' intended readers most need from theology what it can teach them about their return to God. Indeed, for Thomas that is the justification for the existence of the 'science' or body of knowledge that is theology. Human beings had to be instructed by divine revelation about how to reach their end 'more appropriately and certainly' (I.1.1).[6] The *Summa* leads beginners through the many theological discourses that elaborate revelation without ever losing sight of their end.

TEXTUAL UNITS AND DIALECTICAL PROGRESS

By the standards of thirteenth-century academic composition, Thomas' *Summa* has a very simple textual articulation. It is divided into three large 'parts' consisting of 'questions' and 'articles.' There are no intermediate units, except perhaps for the division of the second part into two sections. By contrast, the *Summa of Brother Alexander*, one of Thomas' models, contains books, parts, inquisitions, treatises, questions, titles, distinctions, members, chapters, and articles. Thomas reduced the layers of textual division in part because he wanted to write 'briefly and clearly' for beginners.

---

[6] The uniqueness of theology as a teaching that offers both truth and blessedness is also the main point of the prologue with which Thomas began his review of Lombard's *Sentences* at the school in Rome.

Each 'article' in the *Summa* abbreviates a standard pattern of medieval teaching, the dispute. Whether written or performed, the dispute (or disputed question) is a device for arranging and judging contrary precedents on a controverted issue. Thomas presided over several series of public disputes and then edited them for publication. They explore knotted controversies, with inherited arguments for and against each point often running into the dozens. For the *Summa*, Thomas reduces controversy to its schematic minimum – most often three or four 'arguments' against the view he will sustain, one argument for it, a very short determination of the issue, and then succinct replies to the arguments. An article can be so brief because it is not meant to stand on its own. Thomas explains the meaning of the word 'article' with reference to clauses of the creed: it 'signifies a mutual adaptation (*coaptatio*) of certain distinct parts' (II-II.1.6). The articles of the *Summa* are also such parts, carefully arranged in relation to one another to make up a question. The fundamental unit of dispute in the *Summa* is the question rather than the article.

To better address beginners, why didn't Thomas abandon the question form altogether, as he had done successfully in the *SCG* and as he would do again in the *Compendium of Theology*? Perhaps he wanted to accustom his readers to the argumentative procedures prevailing in academic theology. He may also have judged that even a simplified imitation of living dispute is the safest form for theological reflection on inherited texts. It highlights the always contestable processes of theological interpretation and so resists the temptation to imagine a timeless orthodoxy beyond human learning. The dialectical play of the articles within a question also mirrors the 'motion' of learning that Thomas constructs at much larger scale throughout the *Summa*. Later readers began to separate groups of questions into 'treatises,' and they studied separately the 'treatise on law' or the 'treatise on the sacraments.' Not only does this add a layer of textual organization that Thomas refused, it can disrupt his dialectic by interposing topical boundaries. The *Summa* reduces textual units to propel the reader through the dialectic of the whole.

Thomas provides a running table of contents in the prologues to those questions at which his dialectic takes a significant step. One way to appreciate the order of the *Summa* is to string those divisions together into a single outline. Unfortunately, the interspersed prologues are announcements rather than explanations, and they often mark divisions of unequal size or importance. Thomas seems sometimes to change his mind on the way from a division of topics to their elaboration. A few questions appear in transposed order, while others are inserted without announcement.[7] More importantly, Thomas stretches groups of questions without prior comment when the complexity of the material requires. For example, opposed vices are enumerated when announcing the questions under faith, hope, and prudence, but not under charity, justice, fortitude, or temperance. It is no coincidence that the last four are the most complex sequences of questions in the moral part of the *Summa*. In short, Thomas is perfectly willing to expand the dialectic as he proceeds into particular topics. His tables of contents are progressive, and the actual sequence of questions in a segment may modify preliminary descriptions of them.

Dialectical sequences appear at every level of the structure. Within an article, there is clearly a progression from the arguments or 'objections' (as we tend to say in English), through the reasoning 'On the contrary,' to 'I answer that it should be said that ...'. Some readers forget that the comments on the objections are an indispensable further step. In them Thomas qualifies or applies principles announced too abstractly in the body. Within a question, there is an equally important progression through the articles. Simple distinctions or models proposed in early articles are amended in later ones. The same is true from question to question. Later questions in a sequence can qualify or correct initial views. The description of the New Law, for example, stretches and in some ways undoes the overly neat definition of law proposed fifteen questions earlier (compare I-II.106–108 with I-II.90). Learning theology well requires a dialectical adjustment even of announced topics.

THE EMBODIED HUMAN LEARNER

The order of topics in the *Summa* must locate practices of caring for souls within the fundamental professions of Christian faith. Thomas does this by attaching the pastoral matter of the second part to two fundamental doctrines. He secures it on one side to the creation of human beings as embodied minds. He carries it forward on the other side to divine incarnation, the life of Christ, and Christ's legacy of bodily sacraments. The moral part of the *Summa* arises from a preliminary account of the human creature and issues in a retelling of the deeds of incarnation undertaken for that creature's rescue.

---

[7]   For examples of transpositions, compare the prologue to I-II.22 with the actual order of I-II.24–25 or the prologue of II-II.39 with II-II.40–42. For examples of insertions, see I.26 on divine happiness and I.105 as a second effect of divine governance.

By medieval standards, no single part of the *Summa* is a self-contained treatise of human nature. Indeed, the *Summa* omits a number of topics that medieval readers would have expected in that kind of treatise, including basic human physiology and a model of the senses, outer and inner. As Thomas explains, the theologian studies the details of the human body only so far as it has bearing on the soul, and within the soul attends only to intellect and appetite, for which all other powers are 'preambles' (prologues to I.75, I.78, and I.84).[8] Thomas then divides the theological topics between the first and second parts in order to treat them quite differently. He presents the intellect quickly in *Summa* I. Then, after a cursory introduction to sensory appetite, will, and free choice, Thomas postpones any discussion of their acts into the moral consideration of *Summa* I-II (I.84*prol*). The postponement may seem awkward, but it is meant to focus the reader's attention on a single point in the first part: the human being is distinguished from other creatures as an intellect that learns through the body. A woman or a man is not an intuitive, angelic intellect trapped somehow in alien flesh from which it must hope to escape intact. Human beings have abstractive intellects that must learn their relation to the creator through sensory experience. Thomas' teaching about human beings starts from the cognitive consequences of their embodiment.

If *Summa* I emphasizes humanity's location on the boundary of intellect and body, *Summa* II represents the hybrid being's motion towards its highest end through both intellect and will. That single sentence can hide the sprawl of moral topics Thomas is expected to treat. The second part of the *Summa* is by far the longest in the text we receive. It contains almost three times as many questions as the first part. Even if it had been finished, the third part is hardly likely to have reached the 189 questions of *Summa* II-II, much less the 303 questions of the whole second part. Those hundreds of questions elicit Thomas' boldest structural innovations. Thomas had to contend in them not only with the deficiencies in Peter Lombard's version of the creedal pattern, but with

---

[8] It follows that no part of the *Summa* was intended to be a separable *philosophy* of human nature – despite the efforts of many generations to extract one. For a recent example in English, which is candid about its methodological disagreements with Thomas, see Robert Pasnau, *Thomas Aquinas on Human Nature: A Philosophical Study of Summa Theologiae Ia 75–89* (Cambridge: Cambridge University Press, 2002), especially 10–16. My own view is that Thomas never intends to write just as a philosopher, since he held that Christians were called to a knowledge beyond philosophy. On this point, I endorse the views of Victor Preller in 'Water into Wine', in Jeffrey Stout and Robert MacSwain (eds), *Grammar and Grace: Reformulations of Aquinas and Wittgenstein* (London: SCM, 2004), 253–267, especially 262.

a confused inheritance of pastoral material, unconvincingly arranged under competing and often bewildering schemes. Moral prohibitions were often classed according to the lists of 'capital' or chief sins, but they could also be grouped according to the Ten Commandments – or by *ad hoc* patterns such as sins against God, against neighbour, and against self. For moral prescriptions, Thomas' predecessors resorted to lists of the virtues, but also to the beatitudes in the Sermon on the Mount or the 'gifts' of the Holy Spirit in Isaiah 11. Many earlier treatments are encrusted with moral tales and interrupted by homiletic flights. Others adopt a legal tone, imitating codifications of civil or ecclesiastical laws. The texts that Thomas inherited also borrowed indiscriminately and tacitly from philosophical accounts of the human soul, with its faculties and passions, its capacities and vulnerabilities.

In the *Summa* II, Thomas begins by dividing this mass of material. He combines teaching on the end, elements, and principles of human morality (*Summa* I-II). Only then does he analyze exemplary judgments on the main kinds of human actions (*Summa* II-II). The distinction between these two sections is something like that between a study of musical instruments and a review of a performance played on them. Thomas describes the components of human action before he follows them into moral actions, into a history. Thomas intends that the two sections should be read in order, then, remembering their different interests and conventions for representing human powers and acts.[9]

The emphasis on embodiment in the first part's questions on human intellect carries forward into *Summa* I-II. One obvious example is the space given over to the passions: the group of 27 questions is one of the largest. Such sustained attention might seem to contradict the principle of theological selectivity, to digress from theology into natural philosophy. In fact, Thomas spends attention on the passions because he wants to represent them as an occasion and an example of theological pedagogy. He begins by explaining that the passions are not mere bodily reactions, but that they are morally good or morally bad so far as they 'lie under the command of reason and the will' (I-II.24.1). In the questions that follow, images of command, obedience, and rule or measure

---

9   Thomas clearly intends that the *Summa* be read from beginning to end. He makes that clear in small details (such as internal cross-references) and in large arguments. The sequence is particularly important in understanding the relation of *Summa* I-II to II-II. Still it is worth asking whether contemporary readers might actually grasp Thomas' moral pedagogy more easily by starting with his conclusion in *Summa* III and then retracing the textual path to it. See Mark D. Jordan, *Teaching Bodies: Moral Formation in the Summa of Thomas Aquinas* (New York: Fordham University Press, 2016).

(*imperium, obedientia, regula*) appear on every side. Political and regal governance is exercised in a city by means of education, habituation, and rational persuasion; so too within the soul, in its relations to the bodily affects and impulses that power the passions. The space given to them reminds the reader that the project of moral education begins in intimate relation to the body.

The importance of embodiment appears in another way in the delayed entry of grace and its pairing with law. In Peter Lombard, grace appears immediately after the discussion of free choice (*Sententiae* II.26, in general, and II.28–29, before the fall). Thomas justifies delaying its treatment within *Summa* I-II when he describes it as one of two *exterior* principles of human acts leading towards the good and given by God. God 'instructs by law' and 'helps by grace' (I-II.90*prol*). The reader is brought to law and grace from inside the human soul, from the prior study of the internal starting-points of human action. Thomas' approach does not denigrate God's assistance. It helps readers by starting with what is nearer to hand in their embodied experience. *Summa* I-II begins with the highest human end because only the end renders actions intelligible. The sequence of questions then follows the human approach to the end, beginning with the primary possibility of choice and ending with the uniquely efficacious gift of grace (I-II.6*prol*).

Thomas makes his boldest rearrangement of traditional topics in *Summa* II-II, which is at once his most lucid and most detailed representation of the situation of human embodiment. He begins by acknowledging that the great temptation for any more detailed moral teaching is to run on endlessly, through every variety of virtue, gift, vice, precept, and counsel, illustrating each with abundant cases. Thomas proposes instead two simplifying principles. First, he unites in a single cluster of questions a virtue, the corresponding gifts, the opposed vices, and the attached affirmative or negative precepts. Second, he sets intellectual virtues aside and traces all of the moral virtues back to the three theological and four cardinal. He insists that the consideration of the vices should not distend this list of seven. Vices must be subordinated to virtues. They must also be distinguished by real differences rather than by accidental ones: 'vices and sins are distinguished by species according to their matter and object, not according to other differences of the sins, such as 'of the heart,' 'of the mouth,' and 'of the deed,' or according to weakness, ignorance, and malice, and other such differences' (II-II*prol*).[10]

---

[10] The division according to 'heart, mouth, and deed' comes to Thomas through Peter Lombard *Sententiae* II.42.4. The division according to 'weakness, ignorance, and

The bold reorganization in *Summa* II-II depends on rejecting all secondary classifications, however vivid, in favor of the essential.

Thomas' insistence on essential classifications of virtues and vices reinforces underlying theological lessons. It recapitulates the teleological structure of *Summa* I-II, since it refuses to let moral pedagogy be determined by deviations from the highest human end. It reminds the reader that sin exists only as privation, that it can be understood only as defect or derailment. More fundamentally, and perhaps too obviously, the entire effort to teach the virtues and vices presupposes that sin is something of which human beings can repent, from which they can be redeemed. This possibility of moral instruction after sin follows from the conditions of embodied human experience. For angelic minds, Thomas has taught, there is no possibility of repentance (I.64.2). The character of the angels' minds and appetites means that any deliberate choice fixes them immutably. For human souls, the cognitive and volitional circumstances of moral learning leave open the possibility of repentance until death – that is, until (temporary) disembodiment. The possibility of repentance is the precondition of moral re-education. In this way, the project of *Summa* II-II presumes and displays human embodiment, not least by calling for a teaching that can address fallen souls convincingly.

THE INCARNATE TEACHER, HIS LIFE, AND HIS SACRAMENTS

The most famous objection against the structure of Thomas' *Summa* is that it delays the appearance of Christ until the third part. How can any properly Christian theology so postpone the arrival of Christ and the scriptural narrations of his life? A quick reply to the objection is that Christ, his deeds, and his teachings appear throughout the *Summa*. He is mentioned in the prologue to the work and then regularly from its first question on. A more extended reply might begin in this way: So far as the *Summa* is preoccupied with the learning of embodied, discursive reason and will, it has been preparing for Christ's appearance from the doctrine of divine creation onward – and most specifically from the questions on human understanding in *Summa* I. But Thomas must wait until this the end of the moral part to justify the incarnation persuasively. It makes

malice' descends through *Sententiae* II.22.4. Thomas deploys both distinctions in other passages, even within the *Summa*, though he is always careful to point out that they are not classifications by genus or essential species.

no sense for him to assert that God becomes incarnate for the sake of human salvation until it is somewhat clear why human beings require to be saved, from what moral condition and by which moral means.

Many readers have come to the third part expecting either a reaffirmation of orthodox patristic positions or an anticipation of the Tridentine condemnations of Protestant views. They assume that *Summa* III is principally concerned with the metaphysics of the hypostatic union or with forensic models of justification and atonement. Thomas knows many of the patristic debates, of course, and he treats them generously. Yet he wisely resists entering into medieval anticipations of some later polemics. (With both justification and grace, readers after the Reformation must pay particular attention to what Thomas does *not* ask or argue.) Still Thomas' main concern in *Summa* III is rather to show the *convenientia* of the incarnation down to its scriptural details – to display for admiration the appropriateness or fittingness of how God took flesh for human education. Arguments about whether God proceeded appropriately or in due form are the most prominent and the most common arguments in the teaching about incarnation. Thomas rehearses them in relation to the fact and the manner of God's assuming a human nature, to Christ's deeds and attributes, and to his institution of sacraments. Read whole, *Summa* III is a long praise of the pedagogical appropriateness of God's becoming human in order to teach.

Arguments about *convenientia* are often denigrated by contrast with strict demonstration. In the *Summa 'against the Gentiles'*, Thomas himself insists that such arguments lack demonstrative force and ought not to be pressed on unbelievers as if they were strict demonstrations (see especially I.9 [2]). If reasoning about *convenientia* is not demonstration, it is still pedagogically valuable. For certain topics, it might be pedagogically indispensable. An act of giving or teaching can be judged appropriate only in relation to the situation of a particular recipient. The reiteration of *convenientia* arguments around the incarnation means to show that the incarnation opens 'the way for us to move towards God' (IIIprol). Thomas' arguments in *Summa* III justify incarnation as the wisest response to the needs of fallen human learners. They do this first abstractly, then by a sustained reading of the narrative of Christ's life (III.27–59). It is pedagogically appropriate not just that God become incarnate, but that God become incarnate in the kind of life that the gospels narrate for Jesus of Nazareth. The structure of the *Summa's* third part asserts the important connection of the incarnation, the life of Christ, and the Christian sacraments. They are linked by a single pedagogical principle – which is a single theological insight.

Embodied intellects learn best from bodily signs. For the *Summa*, sacraments are bodily signs that cause the grace that they signify. They are able to do this through Christ's incarnation – indeed, though the Passion. The three unrepeatable sacraments of baptism, confirmation, and ordination confer a sacramental character that becomes a source for the actions of Christian life, especially 'worship of God according to Christian ritual' (III.63.1*ad*1; cf. III.62.5*corp*). 'Believers are configured to [Christ's] priesthood through sacramental characters' (III.63.3*corp*). Sacramental worship is both a declaration of faith and an education in Christian action. Any priest's duty is to offer sacrifices, but 'sacrifice' includes any external means for bringing participants closer to God (III.22.2). Priestly performance is moral pedagogy. Believers see this most vividly in the eucharist, which is for Thomas the principal act of divine worship. Sharing the eucharistic meal both requires and confirms membership in the body of Christ. This 'body' is more than a metaphor. Sacramental incorporation extends divine incarnation. Sacraments are signs and causes, initiations and celebrations of a new mode of embodiment through which human learning can be brought to its end.

In *Summa* III, Thomas supplies arguments of *convenientia* for each of the sacraments. Earlier in the *Summa*, he relies on Moses Maimonides when he wants to offer detailed readings of Israelite ceremonial law as a stage of a divine teaching (I-II.101–103). In those questions, Thomas argues that apparently irrational ceremony can be understood as part of a rational moral teaching for a specific segment of human history. In the detailed treatment of the Christian sacraments within *Summa* III, there are similar arguments – indeed, stronger ones, because, to Christian eyes, the burden of argument is lighter. Thomas wants to show that the sacraments, down to their details, are an appropriate and intelligible divine response to the condition of sinful embodied intelligences in bodies. His guide here is not, of course, Maimonides. He cites instead a range of Latin and Greek sources, relying especially on Ps-Dionysius, but also on John Chrysostom (or his imitator in the *Opus imperfectum*) and on John of Damascus.

A structure of theological teaching that flows from the appropriateness of incarnation, through a narrative of Christ's life (and of his mother's), to the sacraments can be found in several of Thomas' sources, but notably in John of Damascus, *De fide orthodoxa* (chapters 55–86). John presents the holy mysteries of God as a pendant to a narration of Christ's life. The sacraments are extensions not just of the fact of the incarnation, but of its unfolding in time – of its narration.[11] Another influence on the *Summa* of Thomas' new Greek learning can be seen in *how* he tells Christ's life. As might be expected of someone who supervised the compilation of a continuous gloss on the Gospels drawn largely from the Greek Fathers, the arguments for the *convenientia* of each event in Christ's life are richly supported by patristic sources – and, indeed, from the very sources excerpted for that *Catena aurea*. What bridges from the treatment of divine-human union to the sacraments is a meditated narrative of Christ's life as exemplary moral pedagogy. It gives the key to understanding why there are sacraments at all.

Thomas did not finish writing on the sacraments or begin to describe immortal life. The *Summa*'s abrupt interruption is not the conclusion that Thomas promised. Still his decision to break off writing – if a vision can be said to issue in a decision – may remind the reader that even a finished text could not have supplied the desired end of its own teaching. The *Summa* was written in aid of the learning of embodied intellects. Its pedagogy does not wish to be complete except in their beatitude.

---

[11] John of Damascus, *De fide orthodoxa: Versions of Burgundio and Cerbanus*, ed. Eligius M. Buytaert (St Bonaventure: Franciscan Institute, 1955), cap. 86 n. 3: 308.

Scripture

PIM VALKENBERG

Not many contemporary college students will be immediately confronted with Thomas Aquinas and his *ST* when they enter upon their first introduction to theology. Nor will they perceive Aquinas' style as particularly lucid or the contents of his argumentations as remarkably simple. Yet this was the idea that Aquinas had in mind when he wrote the prologue to his *Summa*: to 'convey the things which belong to the Christian religion in a style serviceable for the training of beginners'.[1] Although we do not exactly know the identity of the group of beginners for whom Aquinas began to write his *Summa Theologiae* when teaching at the Dominican house of studies in Rome around 1265,[2] we do know that he began by writing an introduction to this *Summa* that now appears to us as strikingly modern, since it poses such questions as: what type of scholarly investigation are we starting? How is this inquiry related to other scholarly endeavours? What are the sources that we use and how are they to be used? At the same time, Aquinas uses some notions that appear to be strikingly old-fashioned, such as *Sacra Doctrina*, the very subject-matter of the first question in the *Summa*. If you are an English speaking student, you would of course be inclined to associate this notion with 'doctrine', but that would not really help you to understand what Aquinas refers to here. The situation gets worse if we notice that Aquinas apparently identifies *Sacra Doctrina* with *Sacra Scriptura*, holy Scripture. Again, the average reader may think that they know what Scripture means, and again that would not help them to understand what Aquinas tries to say.

---

[1] Apart from the translation by Thomas Gilby in *Blackfriars* 1, I will occasionally use the recent partial translation by Frederick Christian Bauerschmidt, *Holy Teaching: Introducing the Summa Theologiae of St. Thomas Aquinas* (Grand Rapids: Brazos, 2005).

[2] See Torrell I, 142–59, and Mark Jordan, 'The *Summa*'s Reform of Moral Teaching – and Its Failures', in F. Kerr (ed.), *Contemplating Aquinas: On the Varieties of Interpretation* (London: SCM Press, 2003), 41–54.

Apparently, 'doctrine' and 'Scripture' are very closely connected in Aquinas' understanding of theology. This chapter will therefore begin by looking at the connections between these concepts in the very first question of the *ST* in order to tease out Aquinas' theoretical approach to Scripture as a major source of his theology. The second section will investigate whether Aquinas' practice is in line with his theory: does Scripture function as a major source in the *Summa*?[3] Finally, we will reflect on the implications of Aquinas' model of using Scripture in his theology for contemporary theological education both within the Christian tradition and in conversation with other traditions.

SACRED SCRIPTURE AND SACRED TEACHING

In the prologue to the *ST*, Aquinas talks about his function as *catholicae veritatis doctor*, a teacher of Catholic truth. It is his task to instruct those who are beginning to learn about this truth, and those who are advanced in this truth. This particular book, the *Summa Theologiae*, aims to help those who are new to this teaching (*Huius Doctrinae Novitii*). So the truth of the catholic faith is made manifest in a certain teaching, and it is the identity of this teaching (*Sacra Doctrina*) that is the subject matter of the very first question in the *Summa*: what is it and what does it cover?

It is remarkable that Aquinas starts his deliberations by talking about the necessity of this teaching. He hypothetically presupposes a situation that might well apply to many modern universities, even if they include a department of religious studies: many students might think that philosophy covers all there is to know about the basic questions of human life, so that a separate department of theology is superfluous if not perhaps contrary to 'real' science and scholarship. Similar lines of reasoning are brought forward in the first two arguments of I.1.1. These arguments function to make us aware of particular problems associated with what might seem a matter of course: the existence of a holy teaching as part of a human body of knowledge. In the replies to these arguments, Aquinas will show that he is aware of these problems and that he is willing to discuss them at the appropriate level of specificity. Yet the basis of his considerations is given, as so often in the *Summa*, in the form of a short quotation from Scripture in the argument *sed contra*.

---

[3] For a similar interpretation of Aquinas' theory and practice concerning Scripture, see Christopher T. Baglow, 'Sacred Scripture and Sacred Doctrine in Saint Thomas Aquinas', in Thomas Weinandy, Daniel Keating, and John Yocum (eds.), *Aquinas on Doctrine: A Critical Introduction* (London: T & T Clark, 2004), 1–25.

'All scripture is inspired by God and is useful for teaching, for refutation, for correction, and for training in righteousness' (2 Timothy 3:16).[4] Two claims are made in this Scriptural self-reference: Scripture is divinely inspired (or revealed, as Aquinas adds later on), and it is useful in certain forms of human reasoning. We will see how these few words from Scripture in fact contain the most important topics that Aquinas discusses in the first *quaestio* of his *Summa Theologiae*.

In his response Aquinas refers to an objective that is not usually connected with human reasoning or teaching, but that is nevertheless essential for a holy teaching: human salvation. While other forms of human knowledge rely on the power of human reason alone, and in so doing may even reach to a form of 'theology or divine science' – as the second argument says – as part of philosophy, human salvation requires a form of teaching according to divine revelation. Aquinas gives two reasons for this necessity, leading us to the core of his theological anthropology. In the first place, human beings are destined by God to reach an end that surpasses the grasp of their reason. Aquinas refers to a famous text from the prophet Isaiah – in a form quoted by St Paul in his first letter to the Corinthians – in order to show the origin of this theological principle: 'Eye has not seen, God, without you, the things that you have prepared for those that love you.'[5] If the goal that God has set for human beings is to be reached by them, they need such knowledge of these matters as surpasses human reason, and therefore they need to know about these matters by divine revelation. In the second place, we need instruction by divine revelation also about matters concerning God that we are able to investigate by our human reason. The reason why we need revelation here – or why revelation is useful here – is that finding the truth about God without revelation is difficult and a matter for a few elect. Aquinas, echoing an argument from Moses Maimonides, argues that revelation helps more human beings find an easier way to the truth about God.

Summarizing our analysis of this very first article of the *ST*, we may conclude that *Sacra Doctrina* is a teaching or a body of knowledge that

---

[4]   All quotations from Scripture are taken from *The Catholic Study Bible: The New American Bible* (Oxford: Oxford University Press, 2006).

[5]   In fact Aquinas does not give a literal quotation, but conflates Isaiah 64:3 with 1 Corinthians 2:9, according to the Vulgate. See Bauerschmidt, *Holy Teaching*, 32. It is significant that Aquinas gives the same quotation in the same form when discussing the possibility of witnessing the resurrection of Christ in III.55.1. See Wilhelmus G. B. M. Valkenberg, *Words of the Living God: Place and Function of Holy Scripture in the Theology of St Thomas Aquinas* (Leuven: Peeters, 2000), 103.

is holy because it is immediately connected with Scripture as a divinely inspired source of human reasoning. Because human beings need to know about God and the goal of their lives – when we know Aquinas a bit better, we may say: God is the goal of their lives – they need a form of teaching that surpasses their natural reason, and this teaching has to be given to them by God through revelation.

This first article of the *Summa Theologiae* reveals some of the most important theological principles that Aquinas employs in this work, but it by no means ends the methodological considerations in the first *quaestio*. Since we solely focus on the relation between *Scriptura* and *doctrina*, we have to gloss over most of the problems connected with the epistemological status of holy teaching as a *scientia*: a form of deductive knowledge that operates according to the rules that became normative since the third 'entrance' of Aristotle into the western medieval academic world.[6] But at the end of his reply to the Aristotelian position that no scientific knowledge is possible regarding individuals, Aquinas again appeals to revelation. He states that holy teaching indeed discusses individuals, but it does so because it refers to them as examples for our moral life, or it proclaims 'the authority of the men through whom divine revelation has come down to us, which revelation is the basis of sacred Scripture or doctrine'[7] At this place, Aquinas clearly identifies holy Scripture and holy teaching (*Sacra Scriptura Seu Doctrina*) because they are both derived from divine revelation. However, the reference to divine revelation serves mainly to support the authority of holy men – to whom Aquinas sometimes adds women[8] – as witnesses and transmitters of revelation. This indicates how the authority of textual sources (*auctoritates*) in holy teaching (*Sacra Doctrina*) proceeds from the authority of teachers (*doctores*) who have received a special ability to explain God's revelation to us. These teachers are the Prophets and the Apostles from the Bible, but also the Bishops, the Saints and the Doctors of the Church. For Aquinas, they are all included in Holy Scripture, since they all refer to the One who is the ultimate source of revelation and salvation: Jesus

---

[6] See Thomas Gilby, 'Appendix 6: Theology as Science' in *Blackfriars* 1, 67–87. Also, Per Erik Persson, *Sacra Doctrina: Reason and Revelation in Aquinas* (Philadephia: Fortress, 1970), and Herwi Rikhof, 'Thomas at Utrecht', in Kerr, *Contemplating* Aquinas, 105–136, here 112–115.

[7] I.1.2ad2.

[8] See, for instance, the role of Mary Magdalene as witness to Christ's resurrection in his commentary on John. See Matthew Levering, 'Reading John with St. Thomas Aquinas', in Thomas Weinandy, Daniel Keating, and John Yocum (eds.), *Aquinas on Scripture: An Introduction to his Biblical Commentaries* (London: T & T Clark, 2005), 99–126, 121–125 and III.55.1, with Valkenberg, *Words*, 102.

Christ. Aquinas refers to this divine source of holy teaching once more in his response to the question as to whether it is a *scientia* when he distinguishes between two types of sciences. Some sciences proceed from premises that are known by the natural light of intelligence – he mentions arithmetic as an example – while others proceed from premises that they accept from the light of a higher science – he mentions music that derives its principles from arithmetic. Now holy teaching, according to Aquinas, proceeds from principles that it accepts from the higher science that God and the blessed have of God. By distinguishing the full knowledge that God and the blessed in heaven have of God from the derived knowledge that the students of holy teaching have, Aquinas not only refers to the reality of the *visio beatifica*: (the vision of 'those who behold God face to face in heaven')[9] but he echoes one of St. Paul's most famous texts about our longing to overcome the limits of our perception of God as well: 'At present we see indistinctly, as in a mirror, but then face to face. At present I know partially; then I shall know fully, as I am fully known' (1 Corinthians 13:12).

The weakness and the power of holy teaching because of its derived status from the knowledge of God and the blessed, are the subject of discussion once again in the last three articles of the first *quaestio* of the *Summa*.[10] Article 8 discusses whether this holy teaching uses argumentative reasoning. Again, the epistemological status of holy teaching as a body of knowledge is at stake here, but this time the focus is on its mode of proceeding: does it proceed by reasoning and proving, or does it proceed by using authoritative quotations? If it proceeds by using *auctoritates*, its scientific status seems to be in jeopardy, but if it proceeds by argumentative reasoning, its status as a body of knowledge derived from revelation seems be problematic. Again, a rather surprising quotation from Scripture forms the basis of Aquinas' response here; it is another quotation from the Pauline letters in the New Testament, referring to the tasks of a bishop who should embrace 'the true message as taught so that he will be able both to exhort with sound doctrine and to refute opponents' (Titus 1:9). It seems strange that Aquinas refers to the tasks of a bishop when engaged in discussing the epistemological status of theology as a body of knowledge, yet this shows both the

---

9 Bauerschmidt, *Holy Teaching*, 35 note 17, and Gilby, *Blackfriars* 1, 11, in their commentaries on I.1.2corp.

10 I follow Bauerschmidt (*Holy Teaching*, 31–44) in his selection of articles 1–2 and 8–10 as the most important parts of I.1, and do not enter into a discussion of some places in the articles in between where Aquinas seems to identify *Sacra Scriptura* and *Sacra Doctrina*, such as I.1.3corp; I.1.4arg2; I.1.7arg2.

guiding role of Scripture for Aquinas where it mentions *sana doctrina*, and the ecclesial roots of holy teaching. Moreover, the quotation indicates the two basic tasks of holy teaching that Aquinas emphasizes time and again: to instruct the faithful, and to refute opponents.[11] In his response, Aquinas states that no science argues in proof of its premises; yet it argues from these premises in order to prove something else. In the case of holy teaching, these premises are the articles of faith (*articuli fidei*). Aquinas adduces a well-known example of this mode of proceeding, and again it is taken from Scripture, viz., the way in which St Paul adduces the resurrection of Christ in order to prove the general resurrection (I Corinthians 15:12). As concerns the refutation of opponents, this is done in holy teaching – Aquinas refers to *Sacra Scriptura* in his text – by distinguishing the type of revelation that the opponents accept as authoritative: if heretics accept the authoritative texts of holy teaching (*auctoritates sacrae doctrinae*), we use these texts in debate with them, and if they deny one article of faith, we use another article against them – which Aquinas saw as the mode of proceeding of Paul concerning the resurrection of Christ. If, however, the adversaries deny the entirety of divine revelation, it is not possible to prove the articles of faith by reason; it is only possible to solve the problems that they might bring up against faith.

Having explained the two basic functions of holy teaching and the limits of proving the articles of faith in his response, Aquinas comes back to the problematic status of reasoning by adducing authoritative texts in his reply to the second argument that stated that 'authority is the weakest ground of proof'.[12] In his reply, he explains how holy teaching uses reason and revelation as its two main sources. Since this teaching obtains its premises through revelation, it has to trust the authority of those to whom revelation was made, and therefore reasoning by adducing authoritative texts is the most appropriate way to proceed here. While an argument from authority may be weakest according to human reckoning, it is strongest when based on divine revelation. This implies that holy teaching employs different types of authoritative texts: it properly uses the authorities of canonical Scripture as cogent arguments – this phrase shows both the distinction between holy Scripture and holy teaching (holy teaching uses Scripture), and their close-knit relationship

---

[11] See, among others, *SCG* I.9; *Quaestio IV de quolibet* 9.3, and Aquinas' prologue to his commentary to the Gospel according to John.

[12] '*Locus ab auctoritate est infirmissimus*', I.1.8arg2, transl. Gilby, *Blackfriars* 1, 29. The quotation is attributed to Boethius.

(as proper and cogent arguments). Furthermore, the authoritative texts of the teachers of the Church (*doctores Ecclesiae*) are used as proper but probable arguments. This ecclesial aspect of Scripture explains why Aquinas can so easily make it an equivalent of holy teaching: Scripture for him is Scripture-as-interpreted-in-the-Church, and in that specific sense the creed (summarizing the basic premises from Scripture) and the teachers of the Church (explaining and applying Scripture in different contexts) may be said to be part of Scripture.[13] Authoritative texts from the philosophers may be used as well in holy teaching, but these are extraneous and probable arguments that can only be used with reference to questions that can be known by natural reason.

This distinction between three kinds of authorities in holy teaching corresponds to Aquinas' practice in holy teaching: wherever possible, he will base his teaching on the canonical Scriptures, 'for our faith rests on the revelation made to the Prophets and Apostles'[14] as the sole decisive argument in theological reasoning.[15] Although they do not have the same cogent nature, the writings of the teachers of the Church may be adduced as proper theological arguments as well, primarily insofar as they enfold or explain the truth of the canonical Scriptures. The writings of the philosophers, on the other hand, are assessed as extraneous arguments that belong to the level of natural reason which has a valid but limited use in holy teaching. Aquinas explains this with a phrase that recalls one of the basic expressions of his theology: 'Since therefore grace does not destroy nature but perfects it, natural reason should minister to faith as the natural inclination of the will ministers to charity.'[16] This means that we may use secular sources and natural reasoning in holy teaching as well, but we should be aware that it cannot prove faith but only make manifest some implications of this teaching related to questions that are accessible to natural reason. For the practice of holy teaching, this implies that there may be a difference between questions relating to articles of faith that are not accessible to natural reason, such as the Trinity and the Incarnation, where extraneous sources do not

---

[13] *Sacra Scriptura* thus should be interpreted as 'Scripture as read and interpreted in the Church', see Jean-Pierre Torrell, *Le Christ en ses mystères: la vie et l'oeuvre de Jésus selon saint Thomas d'Aquin* (Paris: Desclée, 1999), 28–29, and Michael Dauphinais and Matthew Levering, *Knowing the Love of Christ: An Introduction to the Theology of St Thomas Aquinas* (Notre Dame: University of Notre Dame Press, 2002), 3.

[14] I.1.8ad2, transl. Gilby, *Blackfriars* 1, 31.

[15] See Valkenberg, *Words*, 13–18 with references to other works by Aquinas.

[16] I.1.8ad2, transl. Bauerschmidt, *Holy Teaching*, 38.

have much to contribute, and questions relating to articles of faith that are accessible to natural reason, such as God's oneness and the goal of human life, where extraneous sources have a much greater contribution to make.[17]

After these quite technical considerations, it might come as another surprise that Aquinas indicates the manner of speaking of Scripture (*Scriptura*, not *Doctrina*) as the subject-matter of the final two articles of the first *quaestio*. Article nine discusses the phenomenon of metaphorical or symbolical language in Scripture that seems to be incompatible with the argumentative procedures discussed in the previous article. But again, Aquinas introduces a quotation from Scripture in the argument *sed contra* in order to point to the fittingness of Scripture here: 'I granted many visions and spoke to the prophets, through whom I set forth examples' (Hosea 12:10). Again, the quotation serves two purposes. On the one hand, it points to the prophets as receivers and transmitters of God's revelation; on the other, it shows that God uses likenesses and metaphors in speaking to these prophets. Therefore, Aquinas concludes, holy teaching (here he uses *Sacra Doctrina*) may use metaphors. In his response, Aquinas gives two reasons. In the first place, human knowledge starts with sense perception and therefore Scripture uses bodily metaphors in order to teach us spiritual truths. In the second place, Scripture is intended for all, and most people learn better by illustrations than by abstract ideas. Again, one can see how Aquinas has the wide perspective of human salvation before his eyes when he talks about holy teaching.[18] Article ten, finally, discusses another possible source of confusion: the patristic hermeneutical rule according to which one text of Scripture may have not only a literal sense, but spiritual senses as well, seems to introduce a form of indeterminacy that may hinder the use of Scripture in argumentative reasoning. In his response to this problem, Aquinas once again connects holy teaching immediately with Scripture and God's revelation: while other forms of teaching can only use words in order to convey meaning, God can use things as well to give meaning. If words signify things, that is their historical or literal meaning; but if words signify things that themselves signify other things, we talk about the spiritual sense of these words. Aquinas refers to an example that is frequently used in the Pauline letters of the

---

[17] In *SCG* IV.I, Aquinas indicates this as the difference between the mode of argumentation in book 4: mainly by the authority of holy Scripture, and the mode of argumentation in books 1–3: mainly by human reasoning.

[18] See I.1.1, and Jean-Pierre Torrell, *Recherches thomasiennes* (Paris: Vrin, 2000), 132.

New Testament: the Old Law is a *figura* (foreshadowing) of the New Law (see for instance Hebrews 10:1). Although these spiritual senses are important in the history of interpretation of Scripture, and in the spiritual life of the Church, they have their limits in holy teaching as a *scientia*, and therefore Aquinas remarks that the spiritual sense is based on the literal sense, which is according to the intention of the divine Author of Scripture, and therefore this is the only sense of Scripture from which arguments may be drawn. This should not be interpreted as a tendency in Aquinas to go from a 'spiritual' to a more 'rational' way of using Scripture in theology, but rather as an indication that he is aware of the different ways in which Scripture may be employed in different fields of scholarship. When Aquinas, who was a Master of holy Scripture (*Magister in sacra pagina*) in his academic life, used Scripture in his academic disputations, he would normally rely on argumentative reasoning and only use Scripture according to the literal sense; but when he explained Scripture and preached on Scripture as part of his academic religious tasks, he would have more occasion to enjoy the multiplicity of meanings and interpretations of Scripture.[19]

THE ROLE OF SACRED SCRIPTURE IN THE *SUMMA THEOLOGIAE*

The analysis thus far has explained why Aquinas joins the notions of Scripture and holy teaching so closely together in the introductory *quaestio* of his *Summa Theologiae* such that he can discuss them as equivalent. Now it remains to be seen whether Scripture indeed plays the part that Aquinas' introductory discussion seems to assign to it. A student who opens the *Summa* and begins to read in a random article of the first part of this book, may not find any reference to Scripture, and wonder if it plays any part at all.

Before we can explain how Scripture functions both in articles where its presence is obvious and in articles where it is quoted seldom or not at all, it is necessary to look at the structure of the *Summa* once again.[20] The discussion about this structure has for a long time been dominated by Marie-Dominique Chenu's proposal to read the *Summa* in terms of

[19] Reading and explaining Scripture; preaching on Scripture, and discussing themes from Scripture with the students were the basic tasks of the *Magister in sacra Pagina*. So Aquinas' most important daily task (his 'graduate course') was not explaining theological texts, but explaining Scripture. See Torrell, *Initiation à saint Thomas d'Aquin*, 79–108.

[20] See the preceding chapter by Mark Jordan in this volume.

the neo-Platonic movement of exit and return (*exitus* and *reditus*) of all things from and to God.[21] One of the hotly debated problems with this proposal is that it seems to forge a strong metaphysical bond between the first and the second part of the *Summa*, only to relegate its third part (on Christ and the sacraments) to the plane of contingency, almost as an afterthought. Recently, Rudi te Velde has proposed to read the structure of the *Summa* differently, and, following Aquinas' prologue to I.2, to distinguish between God, human beings, and Christ as acting subjects in the three parts of the *Summa*.[22] Following Torrell, te Velde connects this analysis of the structure of the *Summa* with the central notion of salvation in the very first article of the introductory *quaestio*. Human beings are created by God for a destination that they cannot reach by natural reason alone; therefore, they need holy teaching that originates in the witnesses of the revelation given by God. The central notion of salvation returns in Aquinas' prologue to the third part of the *Summa*, in which he talks about Jesus Christ as the Saviour. 'Although the introductory question of the *Summa* remains silent about Christ, one might argue that the word *salus*, which is frequently used in the first article in connection with the necessity of sacred doctrine, implicitly refers to Christ as the one by which man's salvation is brought about'.[23] Te Velde's argument can be strengthened by the consideration that Christ is the main *doctor* of holy teaching, while the prophets and the apostles assist in this teaching of faith insofar as they refer to Christ.[24]

One of the consequences of Chenu's thesis is that he singled out some parts of the *Summa* as 'biblical theology': these would be the parts in which Thomas Aquinas would discuss biblical themes such as creation (I.90–102), Old and New Law, and grace (I-II.90–108), Christian life (II-II.171–189) and the mysteries of the life of Christ (III.27–59).[25] Although Chenu is certainly right in observing that Aquinas introduces a wealth of biblical materials in these parts of his *Summa Theologiae*,

---

[21] Marie-Dominique Chenu, *Introduction à l'étude de Saint Thomas d'Aquin* (Paris: Vrin, 1950), 255–276. For a contemporary survey of these discussions, see Brian Johnstone, 'The Debate on the Structure of the *Summa Theologiae* of St Thomas Aquinas: from Chenu (1939) to Metz (1998)', in Paul van Geest, Harm Goris, and Carlo Leget (eds), *Aquinas as Authority* (Leuven: Peters, 2002), 187–200.

[22] See Rudi te Velde, *Aquinas on God: the 'Divine Science' of the Summa Theologiae* (Aldershot: Ashgate, 2006), 9–35.

[23] Ibid., 22.

[24] Nicholas M. Healy, 'Introduction' in Weinandy *et al.* (eds), *Aquinas on Scripture*, 1–20, here 13–14.

[25] Chenu, *Introduction*, 222 and 271. See also Michel Corbin, *Le chemin de la théologie chez Thomas d'Aquin* (Paris: Beauchesne, 1974), 800.

his thesis seems to imply that other parts might be less biblical or not biblical at all. This is true if one measures 'biblical influence' by measuring the number of biblical quotations in the text, since certain parts of the *Summa Theologiae* do not contain many explicit quotations from Scripture; it is not true, however, at the level of theological reasoning behind the text, since it can be demonstrated that Scripture still functions as source and framework of theological *quaestiones* even where Aquinas does not make this visible in explicit quotations.[26] In order to see this, we are invited to read the *Summa* backwards: from its completion in the consideration of the Saviour and his benefits for humankind in the third part, to the presuppositions, both from the side of God (first part) and from the side of human beings (second part), for this salvation to be possible.[27] If Aquinas indeed deems holy teaching to be necessary for our salvation, his theological questions are meant to deepen the knowledge of his students concerning the mysteries of faith connected with this salvation. This is the reason why Aquinas inserts a sizeable section on the mysteries of the life of Christ (III.27–59) in the third part of his *Summa*, a section that is without precedent in medieval theology.[28] The reason why Aquinas inserted such a section in his *Summa*, absent in his earlier systematic works, is that his ongoing reading and explaining of Scripture as *Magister in sacra pagina* taught him to concentrate more on the soteriological meaning of the life of Christ.[29] Moreover, his own commentaries on the Gospels according to Matthew and John are the main sources not only for the wealth of biblical materials in the soteriological part of the *Summa*, but for its structure as well.[30] But, in order to understand the example that Christ taught us in his life, and the soteriological significance for us of what he did and suffered in his life, we need to know about the mystery of the incarnation, according to which God has become a human being for salvation; and this implies that we need to go back to learn about the ultimate goal of

---

[26] See Valkenberg, *Words*, 142–153.

[27] See III.*prol.* See also te Velde, *Aquinas on God*, 23–24: '... the student of theology cannot understand the proper *theo-logical* meaning of the life and deeds of Jesus Christ (*Tertia Pars*) unless he has previously obtained some knowledge of what God is (*Prima Pars*), and of how human life, in its moral and religious practice, is directed to God as its final goal (*Secunda Pars*).'

[28] Torrell, *Le Christ*, 26.

[29] Valkenberg, *Words*, 203.

[30] For Matthew, see Torrell, *Le Christ*, 18; for John, see the different contributions in Michael Dauphinais and Matthew Levering (eds.), *Reading John with St Thomas Aquinas: Theological Exegesis and Speculative Theology* (Washington, DC: Catholic University of America Press, 2005).

our lives, and finally about God who is the origin and the end of crea-tion.[31] In this manner, it is possible to see the parts in which Aquinas less explicitly refers to Scripture as preparatory questions that enable us to better understand the more explicitly 'biblical' questions about our knowledge of our salvation in Christ.

In the previous paragraphs, we have been looking for the connection between Aquinas' conception of holy teaching in relation to Scripture, and the structure of his *Summa Theologiae* as a work of holy teaching about the salvation brought by God incarnate. In this final paragraph we look for a similar coherence at the micro-level of specific considera-tions about Christ the Saviour. Our lead here is Corbin's insight that it is no coincidence that Aquinas quotes the same texts from Scripture at pivotal moments in his *Summa*.[32] In this manner, it is possible to con-nect different parts of the Christian faith in a meaningful way. Aquinas' most famous example (quoted in I.1.8) is how St Paul adduces the resur-rection of Christ to prove the resurrection of us all in I Corinthians 15, but elsewhere (Romans 4–6) he mentions the connection between crea-tion and resurrection as well. If we read the introductory questions to the different sections of the third part of the *Summa*, in which Aquinas searches for the fittingness (*convenientia*) of how God saved us through the mysteries of the life of Christ, we will see how attentive he is to this 'concatenation of mysteries' (*nexus mysteriorum*) that does not serve to prove our faith, but to show a certain beauty and coherence that strengthens our trust in God. So, when Aquinas investigates the neces-sity of the incarnation, of the passion, and of the resurrection of Christ, he finds multiple considerations for the fittingness for Christ to become incarnate, to suffer and to rise from the dead.[33] These considerations are guided by the idea that the life of Christ has in all its aspects, including his death and resurrection, a soteriological significance for us, which is one of the cornerstones of the theology of St Paul, condensed in the text that Aquinas often quotes from Romans 4: 25 'who was handed over for our transgressions and was raised for our justification'. Recently, Brian Johnstone has suggested that 'the resurrection may be called a theological structure of the *Summa*.'[34] Again, this suggestion can be strengthened by pointing to the fact that Aquinas does not only refer to the Pauline connection between the resurrection of Christ and our

---

[31] See III*prol*, and I.2 introduction.
[32] See Corbin, *Le chemin*, 877.
[33] See III.1.2; 46.1, and 53.1.
[34] Johnstone, 'The Debate', 198.

resurrection in I.1.8, but that he quotes the same text from Isaiah 64:4 linked with 1 Corinthians 2:9 in the very first article of the *Summa*, and again in his theology of the resurrection of Christ, in order to point out that the type of knowledge that we have concerning the mysteries of faith, transcends our common knowledge.[35] Because the resurrection of Christ pertains to the world of future glory, it was revealed only to the Apostles and transmitted through holy teaching; in the same manner, enjoying God *(fruitio Dei)* is a way of knowing God that radically transcends our natural capacities, but it is shared by the blessed in heaven and we may know about it as the salvation that is promised to us by holy teaching. That is the basic goal in Aquinas' *ST*, summarized in a quotation that is, in my opinion, most characteristic of Aquinas' theology on the resurrection of Christ: 'He will change our lowly body to conform with his glorified body' (Philippians 3:21).[36]

THEOLOGICAL EXEGESIS AND SCRIPTURAL REASONING

Although Scripture is not an important subject in most contemporary introductions to Thomas Aquinas, even if they explicitly refer to him as a theologian, one can no longer say that the role of Scripture in his theology goes entirely unnoticed.[37] Having edited a volume on *Aquinas on Doctrine*, Thomas Weinandy, Daniel Keating and John Yocum came to the conclusion that the many references to Aquinas' biblical commentaries in this volume justified a second volume on *Aquinas on Scripture*.[38] Although contemporary attention on Aquinas' use of scripture is directed primarily to his exegetical works, this attention will inevitably highlight the importance of Scripture in Aquinas' *Summa Theologiae* as well.

The most important relevance of this new attention to the Scriptural dimension in Aquinas' theology is that it may show us a way to overcome a disastrous compartmentalization in the contemporary study of theology between exegetical and historical approaches on the one hand, and systematic approaches on the other. While historical-critical approaches to the Bible still seem to be dominant in continental European theology, new approaches are gaining ground in the English-speaking theological environment. One or two of these approaches not

---

[35]   See I.1.1 and III.55.1.

[36]   For a more extended argumentation, see Valkenberg, *Words*, 206.

[37]   See Otto-Hermann Pesch, 'Thomas Aquinas and Contemporary Theology', in Kerr (ed.), *Contemplating Aquinas*, 185–216, here 196.

[38]   'Preface', in Weinandy *et al.* (eds.), *Aquinas on Scripture*, ix.

only have the potential to reintegrate the different academic procedures in holy teaching as a body of knowledge, but they do so while referring to patristic and medieval theological methods as well. First, some exegetes, historians, and systematic theologians retrieve some of the premodern approaches to Scripture in their endeavour to interpret Scripture theologically.[39] They not only draw attention to the theological status of the Bible as a canonical collection, but they explicitly want to read Scripture in continuity with the interpretative tradition in the Church.[40] Finally, they acknowledge that reading Scripture has consequences for one's life as a Christian.[41] The final approach to Scripture that appears to be congenial to Aquinas' approach, may be even more promising for the future of theology as holy teaching in that it develops its approach in an explicitly interreligious setting. Started as an explicitly Jewish movement to combine 'practices of text reading and of reasoning in response to the reading of texts', it began as 'textual reasoning' but soon transformed to 'Scriptural reasoning' in order to include Christian and Muslim participants.[42] In very different circumstances, 'Scriptural reasoning' seems to engage in a project very similar to Aquinas' project of *Sacra Doctrina*: to pass on the knowledge received through revelation to future generations with a view on our common future with God, in dialogue with the wisdom of human reasoning, whatever its origin.[43]

---

[39] See Stephen E. Fowl (ed.), *The Theological Interpretation of Scripture: Classic and Contemporary Readings* (Oxford: Blackwell, 1997). Also, Steven Boguslawski, 'Thomas Aquinas', in J. P. Greenman and T. Larsen (eds.), *Reading Romans Through the Centuries* (Grand Rapids: Brazos, 2005), 81–99.

[40] See A. K. M. Adam, Stephen E. Fowl, Kevin J. Vanhoozer, and Francis Watson, *Reading Scripture with the Church: Toward a Hermeneutic for Theological Interpretation* (Grand Rapids: Baker, 2006); Matthew Levering, *Participatory Biblical Exegesis: A Theology of Biblical Interpretation* (Notre Dame: University of Notre Dame Press, 2008).

[41] Stephen E. Fowl, *Engaging Scripture: A Model for Theological Interpretation* (Oxford: Blackwell, 1998).

[42] See the introductions by Peter Ochs in *Textual Reasonings: Jewish Philosophy and Text Study at the End of the Twentieth Century* (Grand Rapids: Eerdmans, 2002), 2–14, and *The Return to Scripture in Judaism and Christianity* (New York: Paulist, 1993), 3–51. The three religions are represented in David F. Ford and Chad C. Pecknold (eds.), *The Promise of Scriptural Reasoning* (Oxford: Blackwell, 2006).

[43] See Jim Fodor and Frederick Christian Bauerschmidt (eds.), *Aquinas in Dialogue: Thomas for the 21st Century* (Oxford: Blackwell, 2004).

Philosophy

KAREN KILBY

It is easy to form the impression that philosophy plays a dominant role in the thought of Thomas Aquinas in general and the *Summa Theologiae* in particular. Is not Aquinas after all the great follower of Aristotle within the Christian tradition? And does not the *Summa* practically begin with the *Quinque Viae*, the five ways, some of the most famous attempts ever written to prove the existence of God philosophically? And does not Thomas carry on from there to a philosophical account of God's nature, establishing divine simplicity, infinity, perfection, goodness, eternity, immutability and so on? Eventually of course he discusses God as Trinity, which he sees as beyond the purview of reason, but is not the controlling role of philosophy clear simply from the fact that he turns to the Trinity only *after* he has developed a pretty thorough philosophical account of what God is like?

Such an impression of philosophical dominance, however, begins to wobble under closer scrutiny. There is, first of all, what Aquinas himself says in the *Summa* about philosophy and how it relates to his task of *Sacra Doctrina*. In the very first question we find him describing *Sacra Doctrina* as more noble than the philosophical sciences, and insisting that it does not stand in any need of the latter; if *Sacra Doctrina* depends on philosophy, it is only for the sake of making its own teaching *clearer*, not for finding any justification or basis or foundation for it.

Even the role of helping to make things clear, indeed, is carefully circumscribed. It is not that *Sacra Doctrina* has any intrinsic lack of clarity, that it is in need, say, of the analytical gift of the philosopher to bring it into focus. In itself it is perfectly clear, but to us, because of the weakness of our intellect, philosophy can be of some assistance – because our intelligence is 'more easily led by what is known through natural reason ... to that which is above reason' (I.1.5*ad*2). One might think by way of analogy of a mathematician drawing pictures in the sand to illustrate a definition or theorem: the pictures in themselves are in fact far less clear than the mathematical formulae, but they may make things clearer to the audience. And just as the sketches in the sand do not themselves properly prove things, so the authority that Aquinas is willing to grant philosophers is very circumscribed: he ranks an argument based on the authority of a philosopher in some sense below not only those that appeal to Scriptures but also those that appeal to the Fathers.[1]

Aquinas is in fact very strong on what we might call the autonomy of theology. It takes its first principles from God's knowledge, Thomas insists, not from any other *scientia*, any other body of knowledge. It does not base itself even in part on philosophy. It is true that there are things about God that are accessible to human reason, that can be known to philosophy, but he does not suppose that these need first to be established philosophically before faith or theology can get off the ground. It would in fact be quite problematic if they did, because, according to Thomas, truths about God open to philosophy would only be known 'by a few, and that after a long time, and with the admixture of many errors' (I.1.1). Philosophy is in no position, in other words, to provide anything like a stable foundation. But in any case Aquinas is quite concerned to portray *Sacra Doctrina* as a coherent, integrated whole, a proper *scientia*, beginning from its own first principles, working by its own methods, not indebted to anything outside itself except to God's own knowledge. If some knowledge of God's existence and nature is available to philosophy, this does not so much mean that *Sacra Doctrina* begins from philosophy, as that there is a degree of overlap in the content (though not the methods) of *Sacra Doctrina* and philosophy.

On Thomas' own account, then, philosophy is a handmaid, a help to theology, but certainly not anything which provides its starting point, justification or guiding principles. And yet what of the *Quinque Viae*? Is he not here beginning precisely from a series of philosophical arguments purporting to justify belief in God?

It is interesting to consider the amount of space devoted to the five ways in the context of the *Summa* as a whole. They are not the focus of a part of the *Summa*, nor even a subsection of one part, nor even of a single question; in fact they make up the body of one article only.[2] It is worth considering, then, the possibility that these proofs may have had

---

[1]   Thomas deems arguments based on the authority of the doctors of the Church 'probable' (in contrast with the authority of the canonical Scriptures). Arguments based on the authority of the philosophers are not only 'probable' but also 'extrinsic' (I.1.8*ad*2).

[2]   The body, but not the whole of the article, for as usual there are the objections, the replies to objections and to the *sed contra* (here a quote from Exodus 3).

less importance in Thomas' mind than they do in our own.[3] We tend to suppose that apologetics or the rational justification of belief must be burning concerns: Thomas may not have done so.

Indeed, if one supposes the five ways to be Thomas' attempt, no matter how brief, to lay down a rational philosophical foundation for his theology, one would have to say that he goes about his business in a confused, sloppy, embarrassingly bad way. The proofs appear in Question 2 of the Summa. In Question 1, as we have seen, Thomas sets out the nature of *Sacra Doctrina*, and a huge amount is already presupposed here – God, revelation, salvation, the nature of God's way of knowing as differing from ours, and so on. Even if we set all this aside – perhaps question 1 is just a kind of methodological preliminary – and take Question 2 as the true beginning, we run into problems. First of all, before ever coming to the proofs, Thomas repeatedly invokes the authority of Scripture: he quotes from the Gospel of John and the Psalms in the first article, from Hebrews and Romans in the second, and, in the third article, immediately before listing the proofs, from Exodus ('I am who am'). And again, even if we were to set this quoting from Scripture aside – perhaps it is just a bit of sloppiness, a pious habit that he forgets to avoid when he is engaged in laying the foundations for his belief – what are we to make of the order in which he works through questions? For before article 3, in which Thomas asks 'Whether God exists' and sets out the 5 ways, comes article 2, in which he asks 'Whether it can be demonstrated that God exists?' and concludes that indeed it can. How can one pretend to know, before having established that God exists, that God's existence can be demonstrated? Why go about things in such a backwards way?

The sense that there is a great deal of clumsiness and confusion in Thomas' procedure disappears, however, if we can manage to abandon the supposition that his concern is to philosophically establish an independent basis for belief. But what else might the proofs be doing? One way to answer this question is to pay attention once again to their context in question 2, to the two articles that precede them. If we consider the movement of thought in this question taken as a whole, the issue to be resolved seems to be not whether God exists – as we've seen, this repeatedly seems to be presupposed, along with much else – but *how we know* of the existence of God. Should we suppose, as Anselm and many

---

[3] Presumably, had Thomas been at all concerned about establishing the validity of the proofs as arguments – at all concerned, that is to say, to establish that the proofs really do prove – he would have dealt with each in a separate article, allowing space for possible objections to each to be considered and refuted.

other Augustinians did, that the existence of God is self-evident, that we can know it immediately, or just by thinking about the concept of God? Or should we say that it is known only through faith? Or should we take a middle position, that we know it, but indirectly, that it can be inferred from the world around us? In the first two articles Aquinas sets out where he stands on these issues, and in doing so draws on a range of elements of his theology – not only the authority of Scripture (at a key moment Aquinas cites Paul that 'The invisible things of Him are clearly seen, being understood by the things that are made' [Romans 1:20]), but also the fact that God is simple, that God's essence is unknown to us, that the world is the effect of God, and so on. He grants that God's existence is, in itself, self-evident, but since we do not know God's essence, it cannot be self-evident to us. On the other hand, *even though* we cannot know God's essence, and this would seem to create a problem for any sort of argument for his existence, Thomas suggests in article 2 that there is a way around this problem, in that we can come to know God as cause by way of his effects – that is, by way of the world that he created. But if this is where we have arrived – if Thomas' conclusion is that while God's existence is not (for us) self-evident, he can be known by arguing from his effects – then it makes sense, almost by way of an appendix, to give some examples of how concretely such demonstrations of God from the world work. And so we have the five ways – examples confirming, after the fact as it were, that what Thomas says can be demonstrated can in fact be demonstrated. Thomas here gives, in other words, or begins to give, a theological account of how our reason stands in relation to God,[4] and then, as a kind of extrinsic confirmation of this, lists examples of philosophical arguments from the world to God.

This may not be the whole story. In fact a rather dizzying variety of proposals have been made as regards the real purpose of the proofs. Maybe their focus is not in fact so much on God as on the world – perhaps Thomas is trying to lead us to a perception of the world around us as fundamentally, ontologically dependent. Or perhaps the concern is to bring to expression a fundamental pre-philosophical intuition of being which we all share. Or perhaps the focus is really not so much on the existence of God as on taking the first steps in clarifying how we are to use and understand this term 'God'. Perhaps Thomas is in the proofs taking the first step towards a strongly negative theology.

---

[4] In the formulation of Denys Turner: 'there are reasons of faith for maintaining that the existence of God must be demonstrable by reason alone'. *Faith, Reason and the Existence of God* (Cambridge: Cambridge University Press, 2004), 14.

Perhaps, through the very fact that the proofs he lists are well-worn and completely unoriginal, he is trying to reassure readers that they need have no fear of dangerous novelties infecting his approach to theology.[5]

It is beyond the scope of this chapter to examine these and other, sometimes complementary, sometimes conflicting, ways of construing the purpose of the *Quinque Viae*. For our purposes it is enough to see that these philosophical arguments are not prior to, and foundational for, Aquinas' theology, but very thoroughly embedded in it, and that it makes far more sense to think of him as having theological reasons for granting a certain role to philosophy, than philosophical reasons for taking theological positions.

What then of Aristotle? If the place of the proofs in the *Summa* does not show that Thomas wants to provide philosophical foundations for his theology, does not his famous Aristotelianism suggest that his thought is fundamentally dependent on philosophy? Once again, closer examination raises doubts.

It would be wrong to go so far as to deny the importance of Aristotle and Aristotelian writers for Aquinas. Thomas lived at a time when the Latin West was, thanks to Islamic scholarship, becoming reacquainted with a range of forgotten Aristotelian texts, together with important Arabic commentaries on them. And he was by all indications very interested in getting to grips with this new, not yet fully absorbed, body of literature: he spent considerable effort reading and digesting Aristotle, as his commentaries on a range of Aristotle's texts, some written late in his life, attest. He cites him regularly in his works, including in the *Summa*. He refers to him as 'the philosopher', presumably to indicate some kind of pre-eminence to Aristotle among all those who might be considered philosophers. And he borrows or adapts from Aristotle widely, including the notions of matter and form (and of the soul as the form of the body), of potency and act, of substance and accident, of friendship, of happiness, and of the nature of knowledge.

All this, however, does not mean that we need to see Aquinas simply as a faithful disciple of 'the philosopher', as developing a theology which is essentially derivative from Aristotle. For one thing, Aristotle was by no means the only one from whom Aquinas borrowed. From Augustine, Denys the Areopagite and others he drew on Platonism and neo-Platonism, and through a variety of intermediaries, including Cicero and Boethius, he borrowed to a considerable degree from

5   Cf. the chapter 'Ways of Reading the Five Ways' in Fergus Kerr, *After Aquinas: Versions of Thomism* (Oxford: Blackwell, 2002), 52–72.

Stoic thought.[6] And then of course there were the Arabic thinkers such as Avicenna, who, though in a broad sense Aristotelian, went beyond Aristotle in significant ways that were very important for Thomas' thought. The precise balance of, and relationship between, these different influences may be a matter of dispute, but it is clear that the philosophical background to Thomas' thought is to some degree at least variegated. There were contemporaries of St Thomas at the University of Paris who were indeed wholly committed Aristotelians – the so-called Latin Averroists, of whom Siger of Brabant was the most famous – and to these Aquinas was clearly opposed.

A good deal of recent scholarship has in fact focused on disabusing readers of too philosophical a take on Aquinas, or any too simple assumption that he is an Aristotelian, and has attempted to rediscover and represent him as a theologian, a Master of Catholic teaching whose primary task was commenting on sacred Scripture.[7] That we tend to see his thought as philosophically dominated or controlled, or even to see him as chiefly a philosopher with perhaps a kind of theological supplement – this is quite widely regarded now as the result of several generations of misreading, a misreading inspired largely by the needs of Roman Catholic apologetics in the late nineteenth century and the first half of the twentieth. In the context of the Enlightenment's challenge to the rationality of belief, modern philosophy from Immanuel Kant on was seen as fundamentally threatening, and Thomas as the source of the necessary alternative, the provider of a distinctive philosophy of the Catholic Church, its answer to modernity. And if Thomas was to provide this, then naturally he needed to be read as a philosopher, or at least as providing a complete philosophical system as a basis for theology, and one, moreover, within which one could face and deal with the distinctive challenges of the Enlightenment.

And so in part at least we easily have the impression that Thomas' thought is largely philosophical in character because of the way his work has been mined for and presented as a philosophy over several generations. But it is not enough simply to point to historical reasons to account for the impression that Aquinas is somehow very philosophical.

---

6   Cf. Jean-Pierre Torrell, *Aquinas's Summa: Background, Structure and Reception* (Washington, DC: Catholic University of America Press, 2005), for a fuller account of what Aquinas borrowed from various sources.

7   One facet of this literature has been a retrieval of the importance of Thomas' trinitarianism, and a vigorous rebuttal of the notion that it is added as a kind of awkward after-thought to a philosophical concept of God. Cf. for instance Gilles Emery, *Trinity in Aquinas* (Ypsilanti: Sapientia Press, 2003).

Is there not also something about the *Summa* itself that gives rise to this impression, even if we don't just stop with the five ways? Is not a large part of the *Summa*, if not actually philosophical argument, something that looks rather *like* this? Consider the following passages, selected more or less at random[8]:

> As is clear from what has been said, our intellect, which takes cognizance of the essence of a thing as its proper object, gains knowledge from sense, of which the proper objects are external accidents. Hence from external appearances of things we come to the knowledge of the essence of things. And because we name a thing in accordance with our knowledge of it, as is clear from what has already been said, so from external properties names are often imposed to signify essences. Hence such names are sometimes taken strictly to denote the essence itself, the signification of which is their principal object; but sometimes, and less strictly, to denote the properties by reason of which they are imposed ... (I.18.2)
>
> Now it is evident that what is generically or specifically one with another, is one according to nature. And so everything loves another which is one with it in species, with a natural affection, in so far as it loves its own species. This is manifest even in things devoid of knowledge; for fire has a natural inclination to communicate its form to another thing, wherein consists this other thing's good; as it is naturally inclined to seek its own good, namely, to be borne upwards. (I.60.4).
>
> The intellectual soul is indeed actually immaterial, but it is in potentiality to determinate species. On the contrary, phantasms are actual images of certain species, but are immaterial in potentiality. Wherefore nothing prevents one and the same soul, inasmuch as it is actually immaterial, having one power by which it makes things actually immaterial, by abstraction from the conditions of individual matter: which power is called the *active intellect*; and another power, receptive of such species, which is called the *passive intellect* by reason of its being in potentiality to such species. (I.79.4ad4)
>
> Now man's final happiness, which is his final perfection, cannot consist in the knowledge of sensibles. For a thing is not perfected by something lower, except in so far as the lower partakes of something higher. Now it is evident that the form of a stone or of

---

[8]   These are taken from pages 100, 300, 400, and 600 of the edition that I happened to have with me when writing this passage.

any sensible, is lower than man. Consequently, the intellect is not perfected by the form of a stone, as such, but inasmuch as it partakes of a certain likeness to that which is above the human intellect, viz., the intelligible light, or something of the kind. (I-II.3.6).

These passages, as so many in the *Summa*, seem to be saturated with categories, concepts and contrasts derived from philosophers – form and matter, the sensible and the intelligible, actuality and potentiality, genus and species, essence, accidents, and so on. We find Aquinas at every turn making arguments, giving reasons, and in particular moving from very generalized, abstract kinds of considerations (e.g. 'a thing is not perfected by something lower', 'we name a thing in accordance with our knowledge of it', 'what is generically or specifically one with another, is one according to its nature'.) to the particular conclusions he wants to defend. It is not *just*, then, the legacy of an Enlightenment-shaped Catholic apologetics, nor is it just the misreading of the proofs or a too easy stereotype about Thomas' supposed Aristotelianism that makes us reach for words like 'philosophy' and 'philosophical' when reading the *Summa*. It is also something in the *ST* itself.

Another way to put this point is that one can get the impression of a dissonance in the *Summa* between theory and practice – between Thomas' programmatic comments on the status and role of philosophy which were outlined above on the one hand, and the way he actually proceeds on the other. There is, as we have seen, the clear insistence on the autonomy of theology (or to be more precise of *Sacra Doctrina*) over against philosophy, on its rootedness in revelation and God's own knowledge, on the superiority of Scripture and tradition (or Scripture and the Fathers) to philosophy, on the weakness of philosophy and the ancillary nature of its role; but on the other hand, even if we do not make too much of the five ways, we have vast swathes of the *Summa* which seem to be permeated by philosophical language and style.

One might of course simply decide that the programmatic statements about philosophy and its status in relation to *Sacra Doctrina* must not be taken at face value – perhaps we must say, in light of all that follows, that Thomas cannot really mean them. But is this conclusion forced on us? Is there any other way to make sense of the apparent dissonance?

A first approximation might be to distinguish between Thomas' dependence on the philosophy of others and his own philosophizing. What he carefully circumscribes in his programmatic statements, then, is the authority granted to the philosophy of others, while what we find him doing through so much of the *Summa* is philosophising in his own right. And, lest this account appear to make Thomas seem egotistical and self-privileging, setting his own philosophising above that of others, we should add that those whose authority he is so careful to limit are non-Christian philosophers, while his own philosophy is done within the larger context of revelation.

This approach immediately runs into a number of difficulties, however. The first is that Thomas would never place himself among the 'philosophers', a term reserved in his vocabulary for pagan think-ers, and so presumably would also not describe himself as engaging in philosophy.[9] And in relation to our use of the term in a contemporary context, too, there are questions to be raised. If we say that Aquinas is engaged in 'philosophising', how are we to distinguish this from 'theologising', given that even when Aquinas' writing seems most 'philosophical' in the *Summa* it is still interspersed with citation from Scripture and the Fathers, and occurs within a larger context which is clearly theological?

A different term, then, than philosophising is needed. We could per-haps more safely say that Thomas displays a tremendous confidence in the helpfulness of reason, or more particularly of reasoning.[10] The making of arguments, the dissecting and examining of the arguments of others, the deployment of general categories to illuminate a particu-lar situation, the drawing of comparisons with what is more familiar, the offering of reasons: one of the most distinctive things about the *Summa* is the way it is permeated by this calm, patient process of rea-soning, and it is this, perhaps, that makes us reach for the language of philosophizing.

Why engage in so much reasoning? Not, if we take seriously what Thomas says about the nature of *Sacra Doctrina*, for the sake of provid-ing rational foundations for faith. Why else then? There are at least three ends towards which all this reasoning is directed, I would sug-gest. First, Thomas is often involved in providing a kind of after-the-fact weak justification for that which is believed on the basis of revelation. Even though it is beyond the power of our reason to establish certain

---

[9] For a fuller discussion of this point see Mark Jordan, *Rewritten Theology: Aquinas after His Readers* (Oxford: Blackwell, 2006), 63–4.

[10] 'Reason' is not quite the right term here, because very often when Thomas refers to 'reason' as a kind of general capacity or faculty, it is closely associated with philoso-phy or with what can be known independently of revelation. It is, in other words, as Thomas uses it, too narrow a term for our purposes.

truths of the faith, it is, sometimes at least,[11] useful to do what one can to make sense of that which is believed, to gain a sense of its fitting-ness, of its coherence with other aspects of the faith, to gain a sense that it is not simply arbitrary, that it is part of some integrated whole. And so Aquinas will often offer arguments, even whole series of argu-ments, for a proposition which is in any case to be believed, even if it is clear (to him presumably as well as to us) that these arguments, considered abstractly, would not be sufficient to establish the truth of the proposition. And then secondly, there is the business of dealing with difficulties, or apparent difficulties, within the theological tradi-tion Thomas has received. If there are tensions between two aspects of the faith, or between two authorities, then some sort of reasoning process is deployed to resolve the tension, or, if necessary (and more rarely), to explain why one authority is to be followed and the other deemed in some way mistaken. Thirdly, there is the matter of thinking through the faith, thinking through the meaning of revelation, in the context of everything else one knows, or thinks one knows. Christian faith, while it may involve distinctive, non-negotiable commitments clearly does not, as Thomas conceives it, involve intellectual isolation. So for instance one may hold the doctrine of creation *ex nihilo* to be non-negotiable, and yet still need to work out how exactly to under-stand the relationship between this and Aristotle's beliefs about the eternity of the world. Just as a contemporary theologian will engage in some process of reasoning to explain how belief in creation is related to the theories of contemporary physics, or how theological anthropol-ogy is related to the findings and theories of neuroscientists, so one of the functions of Thomas' reasoning is to lead his readers to an under-standing of the relationship between revealed truth and all else that is believed or known.

Some such sketch of the overall function of reason, of reasoning, in the *Summa*, then, provides the broader context within which one can most fruitfully consider the role of philosophy as such. It is, I propose, two-fold. First, it is clear that Thomas finds in philosophy, and particu-larly in Aristotelian philosophy, a useful *language* with which to rea-son, a set of tools and concepts with which he can clarify issues, make

---

[11] Not always. See my 'Aquinas, the Trinity and the Limits of Understanding', *International Journal of Systematic Theology* 7 (2005), 414–27, for an argument that in some of the more technical aspects of his discussions of the Trinity, Thomas is trying principally to bring us to a recognition of our *lack* of understanding.

connections, get to the heart of a variety of matters. It is a language he makes his own, that he uses flexibly and freely, not one which should be seen as forcing his theology into predetermined categories: for the most part from philosophy he draws concepts which open up, rather than close down, the possibilities of his reasoning. But philosophy does not only function as a provider of a helpful language: it also, secondly, forms part of the broader intellectual context in relation to which the Christian faith must be thought through, in relation to which the process of reasoning must be undertaken. It is important to remember here that philosophy was not a narrowly delimited discipline in Thomas' time – it included what we would now call natural sciences, psychology, political science and more. So in large part the task of relating what we learn from faith to other things we know or think we know about the world meant, for Thomas, relating faith to philosophy. All this does not mean that Aquinas slavishly accepted Aristotle. But the rediscovery of Aristotle was the most exciting intellectual development of his time, and one of the things that Thomas was doing was working out how, concretely, the Christian faith was to be related to the new illumination of reality provided by the re-discovered texts of Aristotle.

What I am suggesting, then, is that the first thing to notice in Thomas is what seems to be a profound confidence in reason, or more precisely in reasoning, and that philosophy on the one hand provides useful tools *with* which to reason, and on the other hand substantive positions *about* which to reason. But it is important that the latter point is not misunderstood: Thomas' reasoning *about* substantive philosophical issues does not represent a second, philosophical agenda alongside the theological, nor does it indicate that he feels the need to sort out a proper philosophy as a basis for his theology. It is rather that an intrinsic part of theology is to work through our understanding of revelation *in relation to* other things we know or think we know about the world, and in Thomas' time this meant, in large part, in relation to philosophy.

If Thomas' confidence in reasoning is the context within which to make sense of the role of philosophy in his thought, what, one might ask, is the context in which to make sense of this confidence in reasoning itself? Thomas' endlessly patient, non-defensive engagement in reasoning is ultimately, I think, an expression of theological confidence. Trusting in the power of reasoning is not an alternative to, or a sort of check upon, faith, but rather its result. Thomas' fundamental attitude is that things generally ought to make sense – our minds ought to be able to see something of the truth of things, revelation ought to 'hang together', and the truths we know from elsewhere ought to fit, and certainly pose no threat, to revealed truths. All this is the case because God, the creator of our minds, the giver of revelation, the source of all truth, is intrinsically intelligible.[12]

---

[12] God's intrinsic intelligibility is also, of course, an intelligibility which is simply beyond us. On the face of it, the enormous patience in the process of reasoning that I have been discussing sits oddly alongside the sharply apophatic strand in Thomas' thought. This is a theme which takes us beyond the scope of this chapter, but it may well be that the best route to understanding these two sides of the *Summa* together is to see both as expressions of the same fundamental theological confidence.

Method

JOHN MARENBON

Aquinas' *Summa Theologiae* deserves to be placed on the shelf we might keep for Great Books of Philosophy – the shelf that holds, among other volumes, Plato's *Republic*, Aristotle's *Ethics*, Descartes *Meditations* and Kant's *Critiques*. But, much as Plato's elegantly turned dialogue, Aristotle's matter-of-fact prose, Descartes's lucid intimacies and Kant's tortured systematizings might differ from each other, none can approach in strangeness and apparent perversity the form in which Aquinas chose to write this *Summa*. Even untutored, the observant reader will notice that only in the middle section of each the articles into which the *Summa* is divided does Aquinas speak straightforwardly in his own voice. Each article is in the '*quaestio*-form': that is to say, it is framed as the answer to a question so posed as, at least on the surface, to be answerable by 'Yes' or 'No'. The structure is as follows:

Table 1. *Basic Structure of a Scholastic Quaestio*

Question: *p* or not-*p*? (Then, supposing that the answer that will be proposed is not-*p*: -)
A: Assertion of *p*, preceded by *Videtur quod* ... ('It seems that ...')
B: A series of arguments (*rationes*), based on authority or reason, in favour of *p*
C: A brief statement, usually from an authority, that not-*p*, preceded by *Sed contra* ('But against (this) ...')
D: A reasoned explanation by the author of why it is the case that not-*p* (This is often called the 'body' of the *quaestio*.)
E: Counter-arguments (*solutiones*) to each of the arguments proposed in B, explaining why they do not give grounds for believing that *p*

In the *Summa* and Aquinas' other *quaestio*-form works, this structure is unvarying, except that occasionally no counter-arguments will be offered under E, but it will just be said that, in the light of the explanation in D, 'the solution to the arguments is obvious' (e.g., I.16.2; I-II.31.7; II-II.109.4).

This chapter has three aims. The first is the limited and purely practical one, of providing users of the *Summa* with the information they need about its literary form in order to be able to read it properly. The second aim is to answer the historical question – which turns out to be complex and controversial – of how the *quaestio*-form came to exist, and why Aquinas chose it for this *Summa*. The third is to consider what is the connection between the *quaestio*-form used in the *Summa* and its status as a great work of philosophy.

THE *QUAESTIO*-FORM AND READING THE *SUMMA*

Table 1 gives the bare plan of a quaestio as found in the *Summa*, but it is only by looking at an example that the way in which this method works is made clear. To do so means looking, even if cursorily, at some of the individual arguments. Take, for instance, I.3.4. The point at issue is whether God's nature (*essentia*) is the same as his being (*esse*).[1]

The beginning (Part A), 'It seems that in God nature and being are not the same' indicates that the proposition (*p*) that Aquinas will defend is that they *are* the same. He immediately goes on (Part B) to give two arguments in favour of not-*p*, that is to say, of the view that nature and being are non-identical in God. One argument (B-1) is that, if God's nature were just being, God's being would just be being, with nothing added to it, and not the special, unsharable being which, as the Bible witnesses, is God's. The second argument (B-2) is that God's being must be different from his nature, because we know *that* God is, but not *what* he is. There follows (Part C) the *sed contra*, a statement from the church father Hilary that 'being is not an accident in God, but subsisting truth'. 'That therefore which subsists in God', Aquinas goes on, 'is his being.'

In (Part D) the body of the *quaestio*, Aquinas offers three arguments for the identity of God's nature and being, in brief: (D1) If God's being were not identical with his nature, then it would have, impossibly, to be caused by something outside God; (D2) God is completely actuality, and being is the actuality of any form or nature; (D3) If God merely *has* being, but is not himself being, then he would be a being only by participation and not the first being.

---

[1] The more usual translations are 'essence' and 'existence', but 'nature' explains more clearly what *essentia* means, whilst 'existence' determines the meaning of *esse* across all its uses too narrowly: see N. Kretzmann, *The Metaphysics of Theism: Aquinas's Natural Theology in 'Summa contra Gentiles' I* (Oxford: Oxford University Press, 1997), 121, n. 10.

Finally (Part E), Aquinas answers the two arguments for the non-identity of being and nature in God, in each case by making a distinction. For example, to (B-2), he replies (E-2) that 'to exist' (*esse*) can be used in two ways: to signify 'the act of existing' (*actum essendi*) or to signify 'the composition of a proposition found by the mind when it joins together subject and predicate': we cannot know that God exists when 'to exist' is understood in the first sense, but we can know, taking 'exist' in the second sense, that the proposition 'God exists' is true, 'and we know this, as has been said above, from his effects.'

This article also illustrates well some very general features of how Aquinas uses the *quaestio* form throughout the *Summa*:

- there are a small number only of *rationes* [Part B] and *solutiones* [Part C]: two, as here, or very commonly three, although sometimes there are five or six;
- even when the *rationes* call on an authority (as in the biblical citation in B-1), they usually involve rational argumentation;
- the *sed contra* (C) is brief and calls on authority;
- the discussion of the *rationes* is kept distinct from the presentation in the body of the *quaestio* (D) of the positive arguments in favour of the chosen answer. Not every article keeps them distinct – there are rare occasions, as noted earlier, where the discussion in D makes the answers to *rationes* obvious.
- the *rationes* are 'solved' not by refutation, but by a drawing a distinction, which shows that there is an aspect of what is argued that can be accepted, but does not constitute an argument against the answer ('yes' or 'no') chosen for the *quaestio*.

THE DEVELOPMENT OF THE *QUAESTIO*-FORM

Why did Aquinas use this strange format for his *Summa*? The simple answer is that, so far from being strange, the *quaestio*-form was 'the basic unit of (later) medieval theological (and philosophical, legal, and medical) inquiry.'[2] But this raises another question: *why* and *how* did such a complicated format become the main way of presenting intellectual discussions. A partial clue is to be found by looking at any set of 'Disputed Questions' (*quaestiones disputatae*). The basic plan of each

---

[2] I have added the 'later' to this excellent formulation proposed by Russell Friedman, 'The *Sentences* Commentary, 1250–1320: General Trends, The Impact of the Religious Orders, and the Test Case of Predestination', in G. R. Evans (ed.), *Medieval Commentaries on the 'Sentences' of Peter Lombard: Current Research* (Leiden: Brill, 2001), 41–128, at 85.

particular question discussed is the same (A, B, C, D, E) as that of an article of the *Summa*. But, in the case of Disputed Questions, there is an obvious reason for this argument and counter-argument structure. Disputed questions record, in polished form, the second of the two sessions which made up a disputation in a medieval university. The first session consisted of a fairly free exchange between pupils in which some put forward arguments against a thesis proposed by the Master, and others responded with counter-arguments. In the second session, the master summarized the various arguments and counter-arguments given by the pupils, and put forward his own considered analysis and solution of the question.[3] And so, by using the *quaestio*-form, the way Aquinas orders material in his *Summa*, it might be argued, reflects the practice of teaching by disputation in the later thirteenth-century universities.

This conclusion rests on a widely accepted view about the development of the *quaestio*.[4] According to this view, reading texts, exploring them by means of *quaestiones* and examining problems in disputations were three evolutionary stages for the *quaestio*-form. In their reading of the Bible, early twelfth-century scholars often found problems, especially those posed by apparently contradictory scriptural texts; discussion of these problems became independent of the business of exegesis, and so systematically ordered collections of *quaestiones* began to be made. And then – as first seen in the *Disputations* of Simon of Tournai (c. 1160–5) – difficult theological questions became the topics for scholastic debates, presided over by a Master. These disputations were the ancestors of the more formalized disputed questions in the universities, and it was in them, so it is held, that the *quaestio*-form reached its full development.

But this view should be questioned. There is good evidence that disputations went on in logic even at the turn of the twelfth century.[5]

3 See B. Bazàn, 'Les questions disputées, principalement dans les facultés de théologie', in B. C. Bazàn, J. W. Wippel, G. Fransen, D. Jacquart (eds), *Les questions disputées et les questions quodlibétiques dans les facultés de théologie, de droit et de médecine* (Turnhout: Brepols, 1985), 13–149, here 58–70.

4 See, for example M. Grabmann, *Die Geschichte der scholastischen Methode* (Graz: Akademische, [1911] 1957), II, 154–5, 203, 220–6, 424–30, 517–9; M.-D. Chenu, *Introduction à l'étude de Saint Thomas d'Aquin* (Paris: Vrin, 1955), 71–7; Bazàn, 'Les questions', 25–48; S. F. Brown, 'Key Terms in Medieval Theological Vocabulary', in O. Weijers (ed.), *Méthodes et instruments du travail intellectuel au moyen âge. Études sur le vocabulaire* (Turnhout: Brepols, 1990), 82–96, here 82–9.

5 Abelard, for example, engaged in logical disputations as a youth before he came to Paris, and there seems to have been a disputational character to his logical teaching in the early twelfth century: cf. J. Marenbon, *The Philosophy of Peter Abelard* (Cambridge: Cambridge University Press, 1997), 8, 11, 44.

And, although written *quaestiones* certainly influenced the form of disputations, the form seems to have developed towards its later thirteenth-century scheme more through a series of comprehensive *written* works: Robert of Melun's *Questions on Scripture* (1143–7), Peter Lombard's *Sentences* (1150s), the *Sentences* of Peter of Poitiers (c. 1167–70), Alan of Lille's *Summa 'Quoniam homines'* (?1170–80); and the early commentaries on one of these works, the *Sentences* by Peter Lombard. The over-emphasis on the role of disputations in the development of the form may derive from another widespread misapprehension: that the newly-available translation of Aristotle's *Topics* – which is indeed a handbook for a kind of disputation or argument game – was very influential.[6] In fact, Aristotle's *Topics* was little read; rather, it was Boethius's *'Topics'*, as it was called – that is, his *On Topical Differences* – which twelfth-century thinkers studied, and it clearly helped to give them a stricter, formal conception of the *quaestio*, which was not linked to disputation.[7]

By Aquinas' time, *quaestiones* were used in the Arts and Theology faculties both as a way of discussing texts, and for writing up disputations. The texts were, principally, the works of Aristotle in the Arts faculties, and the *Sentences* of Peter Lombard in the Theology faculties, where it had become the main text-book. As well as (sometimes) a short, literal discussion of the structure and basic meaning of the text, the problems raised by the text would be treated to independent, *quaestio*-form treatment which (especially in commentaries on the *Sentences*) often had little to do with the original author's ideas. Although the basic structure (ABCDE) of the *quaestio* was fairly stable, its proportions varied significantly between disputed questions and question-commentaries. In disputed questions there are usually numerous arguments for the position to be rejected, and correspondingly many 'solutions' of them, but often a few *sed contra* arguments too, and so B, C, and E form by far the greater part of a *quaestio*. In the commentaries, especially those by Arts Masters on Aristotle, the arguments and solutions are fewer and briefer and so the body of the *quaestio* (D) is much more prominent. The *quaestio*-form as used in his *Summa* is nearer to what Aquinas had used in his commentary on the *Sentences* than to that of his disputed questions, and even nearer to the way contemporary Arts Masters, like Siger of Brabant, use the form. Compare article 2 of question 7 of Aquinas' disputed questions *On Power* where he discusses almost exactly the same

---

[6] For example, Grabmann, *Geschichte*, 220–1, 430.
[7] See *PL* 64, 1177A-B.

problem as in I.3.4: instead of two arguments for the view Aquinas will reject, there are eleven, and therefore eleven replies: whereas the body (D) occupies about half of the *quaestio* in the *Summa*, in *On Power* it represents only about a fifth of the whole discussion.

Given the ubiquity of the *quaestio*-form, was it then a matter of course that Aquinas should have used it for his *Summa*? So it might seem, looking at the *Summa*s written by his close predecessors and contemporaries. For example, the monumental *Summa Fratris Alexandri*, composed by pupils of Alexander of Hales (1236–45) is in loose *quaestio*-form, and Philip the Chancellor's *Summa de bono*, although a little earlier, in a stricter *quaestio*-form, as are Albert the Great's early *Summa Theologiae* (c. 1246) and his late *Summa de mirabili scientia Dei* (c. 1270). But these works are based, much more closely than Aquinas' *Summa*, on actual university teaching, which they collect together. Whereas university teaching, whether disputation or text-based, was almost always written up in *quaestio*-form, practices were far more varied outside this context. And there are two important exceptions which show that it was perfectly thinkable at the time to write a *Summa* organized by chapters, rather than by *quaestiones*, both by pupils of Albert: Ulrich of Strasbourg's *Summa de bono* (1262–72) and Aquinas' own *Summa contra gentiles* (completed 1265).

Yet in fact there is a significance behind Aquinas' choice of *quaestio*-form for the *Summa*, which becomes apparent only in the light of the setting and aims of the work. Not only was the *Summa* not a record of Aquinas' university teaching: it originated outside the universities and does not seem to have been intended for university use. After his first period as Regent Master ended in 1259, Aquinas had no reason to expect that he would ever be teaching in a university again. He began the *Summa Theologiae* when he was at the Dominican convent of St Sabina at Rome.[8] Although Aquinas enjoyed great freedom in organizing the teaching there, his pupils were not the Dominicans specially selected because of their abilities who went to study at Paris University but more ordinary members of the order.[9] The course Aquinas introduced had many of the features of a university course: he conducted a set of disputations (the ones on power),[10] though perhaps at a more leisurely

---

[8] See J.-P. Torrell, *Initiation à saint Thomas d'Aquin. Sa personne et son œuvre* (Paris: Cerf, 1993), 207–15.

[9] See L. E. Boyle, 'The Setting of the *Summa Theologiae* – Revisited', in Stephen Pope (ed.), *The Ethics of Aquinas* (Washington, DC: Georgetown University Press, 2002), 1–16.

[10] See Torrell, *Initiation*, 234.

pace than the Parisian norm, and he seems to have begun lecturing on the Lombard's *Sentences*. The *Summa* was apparently designed as a way of providing a course in theology that was more direct and less confusing than those based on the *Sentences*, but at the same time offered a more comprehensive and theoretical grasp of Christian doctrine than the practically-oriented existing Dominican *Summae*, such as William Peraldus's *Summa vitiorum* and *Summa virtutum* (1236–1249/50) and Raymond of Peñafort's *Summa de casibus* (drafted 1224). Neither of these works was in *quaestio*-form. Aquinas' adoption of that form for this *Summa* seems, then, a deliberate move in his attempt to make the training of ordinary Dominicans nearer to that of the elite students who studied at university. But, bearing in mind his didactic purpose, he deliberately simplified the form from what would be found in disputed questions or even commentaries on Peter Lombard.

Not all Aquinas scholars would accept this conclusion: it has been argued recently that the *Summa* was not produced, as the historical context of its writing would suggest, for this audience, but rather for budding Aquinases and Albert the Greats.[11] But one of the considerations adduced for this view – Aquinas' ideas about pedagogy and the structure of the *Summa* – is perfectly compatible with the idea of an audience of well-educated, but non-elite Dominicans. The other main consideration, that among Aquinas' works the *Summa* is comparatively complex, is dubious, as will be seen in what follows.

THE *QUAESTIO*-FORM OF THE *SUMMA* AND PHILOSOPHY

How is the way in which Aquinas presents problems affected by the type of *quaestio*-form he uses in the *Summa*? The issue of being and nature discussed in I.3.4 provides a useful test-case, because almost exactly the same problem is treated by Aquinas not only in fuller *quaestio*-form, as already mentioned, in his roughly contemporary *On Power* (7.2), but also in brief treatise form in his *Compendium of Theology* (I.11) from the same period, as well as in longer treatise form in the *SCG* (1.22) written a few years earlier. The presentation in the *Compendium* is, as might be expected, much simpler than that in the *Summa*: two reasons are given for identifying being and nature in God, one the argument that God is pure act (= *Summa* D2) and one that God is non-composite. The treatment of the problem in the disputed questions *On Power* makes a

---

[11] J. I. Jenkins, *Knowledge and Faith in Thomas Aquinas* (Cambridge: Cambridge University Press, 1997), 78–98.

very different impression from that in the *Summa*. Although the two arguments and solutions used in the *Summa* are found here too, in somewhat different form (1.6), the body of the *quaestio* is devoted to a single argument, which attempts to show that God's nature must be to exist because he is the cause of all things existing. The profusion of other arguments and solutions bring up different ideas from those discussed in the *Summa*, including the notion of God's being as different from that of other things because it is just being (*ad*5), a discussion of how ordinary language relates to God (*ad*7), a much more elaborate consideration of potency and act than that in the *corpus* of the *Summa* article (*ad*9), and a distinction between different ways in which a proposition can be self-evident (*ad*11). The treatment in the *SCG* is different yet again. One of Aquinas's arguments here is an elaborate train of reasoning based on God's non-compositeness, but in a far more thoughtful way than in the *Compendium*; the other tries to show that there is no relation in which the nature of a necessary being could stand to being except for identity.

An even more obvious instance of the tendency of the *Summa*'s *quaestio*-form to simplify is found in I.2, the very first group of *quaestiones* after the introductory ones. The comparison between I.2.3 'Whether God exists' – the famous 'Five Ways' – and the discussion in the *SCG* is especially striking. In the *Summa*, Aquinas has two perfunctory arguments and solutions, and then fits the five proofs into a page and a half. In the *SCG* (I.13), he had concentrated on a detailed exposition of the Aristotelian proofs from motion. Any charitable interpretation of the first two Ways in the *Summa* needs to draw on the earlier work, where Aquinas sets out his reasoning fully. A little earlier, in I.2.1, Aquinas wants to show that the existence of God is not self-evident. The *quaestio* lends itself to a two-fold comparison, with the treatment of the same problem in the treatise-form *SCG* (I.12) and in a disputed question from the set *On Truth* (10.2). The body of the *quaestio* in both the *Summa* and *On Truth* is mainly concerned to distinguish the different ways in which something can be self-evident, but in *On Truth* the emphasis falls not here, as it does in the *Summa*, but on the series of no fewer than ten arguments (with solutions) and the same number of *sed contra* arguments. In the *SCG*, both the presentation of selected arguments that God's existence is self-evident, and of the reasons why they do not follow is fuller, subtler and clearer.[12]

---

[12] Jenkins (*Knowledge*, 82–3) makes a comparison between I.85.1 and *On Truth* 10.5 and 6, and the *SCG* II.77, in order to try to establish the *greater* sophistication of the way in which the same subject is treated in the *Summa* as against other works. But it is an odd juxtaposition, because the passages in the other two works do not deal

CONCLUSION

The *quaestio*-form of the *Summa* is often presented as initially distracting – it is not clear at first sight which views expressed are Aquinas' own – but 'dialectical', making the *Summa* into a work that does not dogmatically assert, but argues out each point. The received view of the development of 'the *quaestio*-form' adds to this impression, since it traces an evolution from reading of authorities, through to posing problems, and finally, to live disputations. The *quaestio*-form, it is suggested, acts as a vehicle for the harmonious combination of faith and reasoning which, it is often said, Aquinas' masterpiece achieves.

This story should not be accepted. There was not one '*quaestio*-form', that reached its prime in the *Summa*. Rather, Aquinas was using a special, simplified *quaestio*-form. And, within the two or three decades after his death, the form had changed, especially when used in commentaries on the *Sentences*, so that the main outlines of structure remained only barely visible and the body section became like an independent treatise. The type of *quaestio*-form Aquinas uses in the *Summa* was probably intended to bring it nearer than a bare compendium to university teaching, with its play of opinions and use of distinctions to reconcile differences, but the work lacks the emphasis on arguments and their solution found in disputed questions or the sustained questioning of a treatise like the *SCG*. Once grasped, the *Summa*'s format makes immediately clear exactly which are the main propositions Aquinas is asserting, and the usually short bodies of the *quaestiones* bring out with great clarity, sometimes compromised by brevity, why he is asserting them. Occasionally these positions are discussed in relation to other views – Aquinas expects the readers of the *Summa* to become familiar with certain key views of Plato, Avicenna and Averroes – but his concern is to establish, quickly and definitely, why they are not to be accepted.

Aquinas was both a great philosopher and a dedicated Christian and Dominican educator – roles which it was often not easy for him to reconcile, and nowhere more difficult than in his theological masterpiece. Although the type of *quaestio*-form found here owes something to the demands of each, it is at least a contributing factor to the dogmatism and simplification that makes us question whether *this Summa* should really go on the shelf of Great Philosophy Books.

in the main with the same problem as the *quaestio* in the *Summa* (Do our intellects understand by abstraction from *phantasmata*?).

Part II

God

BRIAN DAVIES OP

We do not know whether the title 'Summa Theologiae' derives from Aquinas himself. It is, however, utterly appropriate since the *ST* is just that. It is, from beginning to end, a theological survey, an extended treatment of what Aquinas calls *Sacra Doctrina* ('sacred doctrine' or 'holy teaching') and, therefore, a work of theology, or, more particularly, *Christian* theology.[1] Not surprisingly, therefore, its primary focus is on God, whom Aquinas calls 'the object of faith' (*obiectum fidei*).[2] Aquinas, of course, talks about more than God in the *Summa Theologiae*. In doing so, however, he always writes with an eye on what he takes to be truths about God. In this sense, the *ST* is just an enormously extended treatise on God, and a chapter on God in it could easily amount to a survey of the *Summa* as a whole.

The present chapter is not going to be that. Most of what Aquinas says about God in the *ST* rests on his account of God's nature as given in I.3–26. It also depends on his views about how we come to know about God's existence as presented in I.2. So I shall be concentrating (with occasional digressions) on these texts alone. They present what we might call 'Aquinas' philosophy of God' – something to be found in other works of his such as the *SCG* and the *De Potentia Dei*. They show us Aquinas reflecting on what can be said of God by reason alone.

GOD, REASON, AND REVELATION

To understand these texts, we need to recognize that Aquinas consistently distinguishes between (a) what can be affirmed of God by reason,

---

[1] The first question of the *Summa Theologiae* sets the scene for what follows by discussing the nature of *Sacra Doctrina*. For some discussion of this expression see Per Erik Persson, *'Sacra Doctrina': Reason and Revelation in Aquinas* (Fortress Press: Philadelphia, 1970) and Thomas Aquinas, *The Treatise on the Divine Nature*, translated with commentary by Brian J. Shanley OP (Indianapolis: Hackett, 2006), 153–175.
[2] II-II.1.1.

and (b) what can be asserted of God on the basis of revelation. He thinks that divine revelation teaches us that God exists and that certain things can be said of him, but he also thinks that reason can lead us to certain truths about God even though it cannot establish all that is taught in divine revelation. For Aquinas, one can be intellectually entitled to believe what one cannot show to be true merely by reasoned argument.[3] Indeed, believing what one cannot show to be true merely by reasoned argument is what he takes those with the theological virtue of faith to be doing.[4] He does, however, think that reason can explain why certain things said of God by believers are true. It cannot, he maintains, demonstrate the truth of, for example, the doctrine of the Trinity or the doctrine of the Incarnation.[5] But it can, he holds, tell us something about what he calls 'the divine essence' – what God must be whether or not he is three persons in one substance, and regardless of whether or not he became incarnate. The three divine persons are, for Aquinas, equally divine. So, he thinks, they share a nature. The son of God incarnate is, says Aquinas, as divine as God the father and God the holy spirit. So, he thinks, the son of God incarnate shares a divine nature with God the father and God the holy spirit. This divine nature is something that Aquinas holds to be knowable up to a point, and the purpose of I.2–26 is designed by him to say how and why that is so.

Some critics of Aquinas have accused him of wrongly dividing up the things that he has to say about God in the *Summa*. Here Aquinas has a lot to say about God before he ever comes to talk about the Trinity and the Incarnation. This, some have held, is disgraceful. For is it not just the case that God, for Christians, *is* the Trinity? And is it not true that God, for Christians, is one who has revealed what he is through the life, death, and resurrection of Jesus?[6] Yet Aquinas never denies (or even comes close to denying) that the best answers to 'What is God?' are 'Father, Son, and Spirit', or 'He who discloses himself in Christ'. He does, however, think that reason can tell us something about God and that what it tells us ought to govern our reflections or teachings when it comes to what we believe on the basis of revelation (such as

---

[3] For a famous twentieth-century defense of this conclusion, see Ludwig Wittgenstein, *On Certainty* (Oxford: Basil Blackwell, 1974).

[4] Cf. II-II.1.4.

[5] To see why Aquinas thinks this, look, for example, at I.32.1. Here Aquinas asks whether the trinity of divine persons can be known by natural reason (and argues that it cannot).

[6] For a critique of Aquinas along these lines, see Colin E. Gunton, *Act and Being: Towards a Theology of the Divine Attributes* (Grand Rapids: Eerdmans, 2002).

the doctrine of the Trinity or the doctrine of the Incarnation). Truth, thinks Aquinas, cannot contradict truth. And, since he holds that there actually are truths to be known about God (as opposed to being merely believed), he maintains that these need to be clearly expounded (and defended) at the outset. Revelation may tell us more about God than we can know without it, but, thinks Aquinas, what we know without revelation has to be kept in mind as we seek to explain what revelation amounts to. Hence I.2–26 (and comparable sections in the body of Aquinas' writings).[7]

Yet how might we acquire knowledge of God independently of revelation? Here we come to something else that we need to recognize in order to understand the texts with which I am concerned in this chapter. This is that Aquinas maintains that human reason can arrive at a knowledge of God only indirectly and by means of causal inference. Some have held that the existence and nature of God can be deduced from the concept of God.[8] Aquinas, however, holds that we cannot conclude that there is a God simply on the basis of a concept that someone might have (knowing what someone takes God to be does not, he thinks, allow us to conclude that God, therefore, exists).[9] Some have thought it possible to know God by something akin to our perception of other people.[10] For Aquinas, however, God is not something directly perceivable by us since he is incorporeal. According to Aquinas, human knowledge arises out of sense experience. For him, we know *that* something is, and *what* the something is, because the thing in question is an object with which we have bodily contact, or because it is something that we can infer to exist on the basis of what we know at the sensory level. Since God is not an object of sensory experience, says Aquinas, we cannot know him as we know things in the world (including people). 'The knowledge that is natural to us', he writes, 'has its source in our senses and therefore extends just so far as it can be led by sensible things. But our understanding cannot reach to a vision of God's essence from these'.[11] Aquinas believes that the blessed in heaven see

---

[7] Comparable texts include *SCG* I.10–102 and *Compendium Theologiae*, 3–32.

[8] Anselm of Canterbury (1033–1109) argues along these lines in his *Proslogion*. In Aquinas' day the position was defended by Bonaventure (c.1217–74). See, for example, his *Disputed Questions on the Trinity* I.1 and *Breviloquium* I.2.

[9] I.2.1ad2.

[10] For a relatively recent defense of this view see William Alston, *Perceiving God* (Ithaca: Cornell University Press, 1991).

[11] I.12.12. All my quotations from I.1–26 come from Brian Davies and Brian Leftow (eds), *Summa Theologiae: Questions on God* (Cambridge: Cambridge University Press, 2006).

the essence of God. But only by virtue of a special act of God, not by virtue of their natural powers of knowing.[12]

Aquinas, however, does not take all of this to entail that we have no knowledge of God by means of our natural human abilities. That is because he thinks that we can know something of what we do *not* directly encounter on the basis of what we *do* directly encounter. How so? By means of causal reasoning. Physicians at time 1 might not know of the existence and nature of a particular virus. Given the symptoms that people develop, however, they might reasonably come to conclude at time 2 that there is such a thing and that certain properties can be ascribed to it. Conscious of facts like this, Aquinas thinks it worth asking whether anything can be taken as an effect of God and whether it helps us to say what God is like. And his conclusion is that there are effects of God which can lead to some knowledge of him.[13] So now we need to see why he arrives at this conclusion – starting with his approach to the question 'Does God exist?'

DOES GOD EXIST?

People who ask whether or not God exists must be working with some understanding of the meaning of the word 'God'. And there is a sense in which Aquinas is no exception. When arguing for the truth of 'God exists' in the *Summa Theologiae* he says early on that 'God' signifies or is intended to refer to (a) the unchanged cause of all change, (b) the first cause of all other causes, (c) something not generable or perishable, (d) something which owes its existence to nothing at all, (e) something which accounts for all creaturely perfections, (f) something which accounts for the existence of everything other than itself, and (g) something which directs all natural things to ends.[14] As readers of the *ST* will quickly discover, Aquinas takes the word 'God' to mean a whole lot more than this. Given his theological inheritance, however, he takes it to mean *at least* this.

---

[12] Cf. I.12.5. In II-II.175.3 Aquinas, on the authority of Augustine of Hippo (354–430), and on the basis of 2 Corinthians 2:2, declares that Paul once saw God's essence. And yet, Aquinas quickly adds, this was not because of Paul's natural powers of knowing. Paul, says Aquinas, was given a foretaste of what the blessed in heaven enjoy only because of God's grace.

[13] Cf. I.2.2. Here Aquinas only explicitly argues that one can know from his effects that 'God exists' is true, not that one can know what is to be said about God other than that he exists. As the *ST* discussion continues, however, Aquinas takes 'God exists' to have a content that enables us to make other statements about God. More on this below.

[14] I.2.3.

Yet a presiding teaching of Aquinas is that we do not know what God is. In the *ST* this teaching first appears as early as the prologue to Question 3. Here we read: 'Having recognized that something exists, we still have to investigate the way in which it exists, so that we may come to understand what it is that exists. But we cannot know what God is'. So there is also a sense in which Aquinas does *not* claim to understand what 'God' means. His approach to the question 'Does God exist?' is not based on some prior grasp of God's nature. Rather, it is based on what Aquinas thinks that anyone can (at least in principle) come to know whether they believe in God or not. More specifically, it is based on the fact that, in Aquinas' view, the world in which we find ourselves (and do understand, at least to some extent) raises causal questions the answer to which we may rightfully call 'God'.

Aquinas draws attention to these questions in what is probably the most famous section of the *Summa Theologiae* – I.2.3, in which he presents five 'ways' of showing that God exists.[15] Here he asks, for example, 'How come that anything undergoes change?' and 'How come that things which lack awareness seem to behave in a goal-directed fashion?'[16] Above all, though, he asks how it comes to be that there is something rather than nothing. Suppose there is something which never came to be because something in the world produced it – something 'necessary', as Aquinas puts it. Unless it exists by nature, there would still, would there not, be a question about the cause of its existence? How come it exists at all?[17] And is not this question raised by the mere existence of what exists but does not have to exist?[18] In his five ways, as well as in many places in his writings, Aquinas takes these questions to be serious ones and, therefore, supposes that they have an answer. *Something*, he thinks, must causally account for there being things which do not exist by nature. Something which *does* exist by nature must, he thinks, bring it about that they are there at all and at any time (and that they change or are goal-directed).

These thoughts recur throughout Aquinas' writings, and they influence much that he has to say about God. The big idea running through

---

[15] Aquinas' five ways have generated a veritable mountain of expository and critical literature. Readers interested in working on them in some detail are best advised, I think, to start with chapter 12 of John F. Wippel's *The Metaphysical Thought of Thomas Aquinas* (Washington, DC: Catholic University of America Press, 2000). I offer a somewhat shorter account of the ways in my *Aquinas* (London: Continuum, 2002).

[16] These are the questions pressed in Aquinas' first, second, and fifth ways.

[17] This is what Aquinas is chiefly driving at in his third way.

[18] Aquinas' fourth way is effectively pressing this question.

them is that nothing that we encounter in the world can be thought of as existing by nature since knowing its nature does not guarantee knowing that it exists. I can know what my cat is by nature (feline), but a knowledge of what felinity is does not establish that my *actual* cat exists. And so on for any example you care to mention (even the last surviving member of a species).[19] Aquinas therefore concludes that the existence of absolutely everything in the world is dependent on, or given by, that which exists by nature – and not only when it *began* to exist, but for *as long as* it exists. In various places, including the *Summa Theologiae*, Aquinas asks if it can be proved that the world/universe had a beginning. He always says that it cannot be proved that it did, and that it cannot be proved that it did not.[20] He does not, however, take this conclusion to mean that the world does not require a cause that makes it continually to be. In his view, the existence of everything in the world has to be made to exist (to be *created*) regardless of *when* it exists and regardless of whether or not it ever *began* to exist.[21]

WHAT IS GOD?

For Aquinas, then, philosophical reflection concerning God primarily begins (or ought to begin) by noting that there is a need causally to account for things. It does not, for him, start with a preconceived and full-bodied notion of God. It starts with questions like 'How does it come to be that there is any world at all?' Obviously, therefore, Aquinas cannot countenance the suggestion that God is part of the world, and,

---

[19] Aquinas first presents this line of thinking in *De Ente et Essentia*, 4. As far as I can determine, he never abandoned it. It is, I think, definitely there in his five ways, as well as in what he goes on to say in the *Summa Theologiae* immediately following the text of the ways. For a trenchant attack on this aspect of Aquinas' thinking, see Anthony Kenny, *Aquinas on Being* (Oxford: Clarendon, 2002). For a response to Kenny (defending Aquinas) see my 'Kenny on Aquinas on Being', *The Modern Schoolman*, 82/2 (2005), 111–5.

[20] See I.44–46. For a more elaborate discussion, see Aquinas' *De Aeternitate Mundi* (*On the Eternity of the World*). For translations of texts of Aquinas on creation in general, see Steven E. Baldner and William E. Carroll (ed.), *Aquinas on Creation* (Toronto: PIMS, 1997).

[21] Drawing on the book of Genesis, and its teaching that 'in the beginning God created the heavens and the earth', Aquinas tends to predicate '___ creates/created' of God so as to say that God brought it about that the world came to be with nothing temporally prior to it. For Aquinas, however, God's making things to continue to be is no different from him making things to begin to be since it amounts to him making something to be (to exist). This is clear from, for example, what Aquinas says in I.44.1 in which he argues that everything other than God is from God just because it is real and not just because it had a beginning of existence.

as he goes on in the *ST* to ask what God is, he is mainly concerned to distinguish between God and everything in the world. He is concerned to note ways in which God is *unlike* things in his created order.[22]

Divine simplicity

For Aquinas, the most striking difference between God and his effects (i.e., his creatures) lies in the fact that God is simple, not composite. Here Aquinas means that certain ways in which creatures can be thought of as having parts cannot be attributed to God, so to follow him at this point we need to note some of the things that he takes to be true of creatures.

Forgetting about theology, Aquinas maintains that there is a particular, and rather commonsensical, account to be given in answer to the question 'What is there?'[23] For him, there are beings (*entia*) which can be distinguished into two kinds. There are *entia per se* – which Aquinas takes to be naturally occurring units (like people or trees). There are also *entia per accidens* – artificial units composed of parts with an independent existence of their own (like computers or houses), things with respect to which the parts precede the whole. According to Aquinas, *entia per se* are all *substances* – that is, distinct and self-contained individuals (some of which are alive and some of which are not).

In Aquinas' view (which is basically that of Aristotle) substances have distinct natures or *substantial forms*. But they can also possess properties or qualities which they can lose without altering what they are by nature. A cat, say, can become lighter or heavier without ceasing to be what it is by nature (i.e., a living cat). Aquinas calls these non-essential properties *accidental forms*, and he therefore distinguishes between substances and accidents. He also distinguishes between *substantial change* and *accidental change*. For him, something undergoes a substantial change when it ceases to exist as the kind of thing it is (as is the case with, for example, a cow that is slaughtered). An accidental change, by contrast, is a modification in something that does not prevent it from being what it is substantially (or 'by nature or essence', as Aquinas often says). In Aquinas'

---

[22] Having said in the prologue to I.3 that 'we cannot know what God is' Aquinas immediately adds that we can only know 'what he is not'. He then observes: 'We must therefore consider the ways in which God does not exist rather than the ways in which he does'.

[23] What follows is a very condensed account of Aquinas on this question. For a more detailed one, see my *Aquinas*, chapters 3 and 4. For a much more detailed account, see Wippel, *Metaphysical Thought*.

view, a cow, for example, would undergo an accidental change by getting sick (or even by moving from one field to another).

Yet what allows us to distinguish between two substances of the same kind? We can obviously distinguish between different kinds of substances simply by noting how they differ with respect to their substantial forms. We can say, for example, that cats are different from cows because cats are things of *this* kind (where 'this' can be filled in with an account of what cats are by nature) and because cows are things of *that* kind (where 'that' can be filled in with an account of what cows are by nature). Yet what about Lassie (the dog) and Rover (the dog)? How do we distinguish between them? How do we grasp that we are dealing with two things here, not one?

Aquinas' answer is 'at a sensory level'. We cannot, he thinks, distinguish between Lassie and Rover by noting their substantial form – for this is something they *share* (they are *both* dogs). Might we distinguish between them with reference to some of their accidental forms – by saying, for example, that Lassie is the brown one weighing twenty pounds while Rover is the black one weighing thirty pounds? Here Aquinas again says 'No' for, so he reasons, Lassie and Rover could not have acquired different accidental forms if they were not *already* distinct to begin with. Some philosophers have claimed that X is identical with Y if everything than can be affirmed of X can be affirmed of Y, but Aquinas rejects this claim.[24] He thinks that everything that can be affirmed of one thing could, in principle, be affirmed of something else. For him, what makes it that two things of a kind are distinct individuals sharing a nature is not anything that we can say or understand about them. According to Aquinas, we lay hold of individuality within a kind by means of our senses, by being able to point at or to rub up against things at a physical level, not a conceptual (formal) one. For Aquinas, as well as having intelligible or understandable forms, some things can have an unintelligible/non-formal factor with which we can only acquaint ourselves physically. This he calls *matter*, and he takes it to be the principle of individuation when it comes to things belonging to kinds.

Now with all that behind us we can return to God and Aquinas' claim that God is not composite. For part of this amounts to the insistence that God is (a) not something having form and matter, (b) not something capable of having accidental forms, and (c) not a substance belonging to a kind to which others can be thought of as belonging. There is no form and matter in God, says Aquinas, because God is immaterial.

---

[24] The claim is usually called the law of the identity of indiscernibles.

For Aquinas, material things are bodily things while 'God is in no way a body'.[25] There can, says Aquinas, be no accidental forms in God since there can be no change in God. And, holds Aquinas, God is no instance of a kind (or cannot intelligibly be thought of as such) since he is immaterial. Given that we distinguish between instances of a kind by virtue of their materiality, we cannot, Aquinas reasons, think of God as one of a kind if he is nothing material. In fact, Aquinas also wants to say, we cannot distinguish between the individual that God is and the nature that he has.

You can distinguish between me and my nature so as to say that they are not one and the same – for I am a human being and can perish without it being thought that human nature as such has passed away. But how are you able to make this distinction? Aquinas thinks that you can do so because you can single me out as one of a kind at a sensory level, and, since he denies that God is anything bodily (material), he therefore concludes that we cannot make a distinction between God and his nature. He writes:

> Things composed of matter and form cannot be the same as their natures or essences. For essence or nature in these things includes only what falls within the definition of a species ... But we do not define the species of anything by the matter and properties peculiar to it as an individual. We do not, for example, define human beings as things that have *this* flesh and *these* bones, or are white or black, or the like. *This* flesh and *these* bones, and the properties peculiar to them, belong indeed to *this* human being, but not to its nature. Individual human beings therefore possess something that human nature does not, and particular human beings and their natures are not, therefore, altogether the same thing. 'Human nature' names the formative element in human beings; for what gives a thing definition is formative with respect to the matter that gives it individuality. However, the individuality of things not composed of matter and form cannot derive from this or that individual matter. So the forms of such things must be intrinsically individual and themselves subsist as things. Such things are therefore identical with

---

[25] I.3.1. Apart from citing John 4:24 ('God is spirit'), Aquinas has three arguments in this article for God not being a body: (1) Bodies always undergo change while causing change; but God causes change even though he is himself changeless as being the cause of there being changing things; (2) bodies are always potentially divisible, but there is no possibility of change when it comes to God; (3) God is the most noble of things, but no bodily thing can be that.

their natures. In the same way, then, God, who ... is not composed of matter and form, is identical with his own divinity, his own life, and with whatever else is similarly predicated of him.[26]

In other words, for Aquinas it is just as true to say that, for example, God is goodness as it is to say that God is good. And, for him, this means that, though we use different predicates when speaking of God (though we say, for example, that God is powerful, wise, knowing, and so on), the predicates in question (though not synonymous considered as pieces of language) do not signify properties that are really distinct in God. For Aquinas, God just is, simply and in an undivided way, all that we truly say that he is insofar as we state what he is essentially. Aquinas thinks that all that is in God *is* God.[27]

To this conclusion, however, Aquinas wishes to add another. For, he says, there can be no distinction in God between essence and existence (*esse*). For Aquinas, God is 'his own existence'.[28] The meaning here is that God is *uncreated*. We may, thinks Aquinas, wonder what accounts for the (continued) existence of the universe, but such wonder is not in place when it comes to what actually does make things to be. This, Aquinas holds, must exist by nature. Its essence has to include existence. 'If a thing's existence differs from its essence', writes Aquinas, 'its existence must be caused by something other than the thing in question. But this cannot be so in God's case, for, as we have seen, he is the first efficient cause. So, we cannot say that God's existence is something other than his essence'.[29] Some readers of Aquinas have taken him here to mean that 'existing' signifies some property with which God can be identified – a view which they find erroneous on the ground that '___ exists' does not serve to describe anything.[30] Yet Aquinas is not suggesting otherwise. He never takes 'existence' (*esse*) to be a word telling us what something is. In saying that God's essence and existence are not distinct he is making a negative point. He is not purporting to *describe* God; he is saying that, whatever God is, he *cannot*

---

[26] I.3.3.

[27] This conclusion is not unique to Aquinas. Among others, Augustine endorses it. Cf. *De Civitate Dei*, XI.10. Cf. also Peter Lombard, *Liber Sententiarum*, I.8.28 and Scotus Eriugena, *De praedestinatione*, 2.

[28] I.3.4. Note that this teaching of Aquinas is what, for him, most radically distinguishes God from other things – for he holds that there are things other than God (i.e., angels) which are not constituted of form and matter and which cannot be distinguished from their natures.

[29] I.3.4.

[30] Cf. C. J. F. Williams, 'Being', in Philip L. Quinn and Charles Taliaferro (eds), *A Companion to Philosophy of Religion* (Oxford: Blackwell, 1997).

be something derived. Indeed, all of Aquinas' teaching on divine simplicity is first and foremost an essay in negative theology – an account
of what God is *not*.

Speaking positively of God

Much that Aquinas wants to say about God in the *Summa Theologiae*
takes the form of denying that God is something or other. He says, for
example, that God is knowing – yet by this he chiefly means that God
is *not* material.[31] Then again, Aquinas says that God is perfect, infinite,
eternal, and one. His meaning here, however, is that God does *not* lack
any perfection, is *not* limited, is *not* temporal, and is *not* multipliable.[32]
All of these teachings are viewed by Aquinas as accounts of what *cannot*
be true of God. Yet Aquinas does not think that all we say of God should
be construed only in negative terms. Indeed, in I.13 he explicitly rejects
the view that everything said of God means that God is not something or
other.[33] So how does Aquinas view positive talk about God?[34]

One will never understand Aquinas on this topic unless one grasps
that he works with a particular distinction in mind: that between
(a) knowing that a proposition is true and (b) knowing what it is that
makes the proposition true. I may know (or have excellent reason
to believe) that I have cancer. Yet (not being a medical expert) I may
know little or nothing about what cancer is in and of itself. In this
depressing situation I would know that a proposition is true ('Davies
has cancer') without knowing or understanding the reality that makes
it true (the actual cancer cells in my body). And, says Aquinas, it is
something like this when it comes to our positive talk about God.
This takes the form of propositions and, thinks Aquinas, we have reason for asserting them. And yet, so he also thinks, what makes them
true is the very being (essence) of God himself, which we do not know
or understand.

Aquinas develops this position in I.13. Here, as I have said, he denies
that all talk of God is to be construed as saying what God is not. He also
denies that it should be construed in a certain causal sense. He argues,

---

[31] For Aquinas, there just has to be understanding where there is immaterial existence.
For him, understanding occurs when non-material form exists. See I.14.1. For a brief
exposition of Aquinas on knowing in general, and God's knowledge in particular, see
my *The Thought of Thomas Aquinas* (Oxford: Clarendon Press, 1992), Chapter 7.

[32] See I.4, 7, 10, and 11.

[33] I.13.2.

[34] For a detailed answer to this question, see Gregory P. Rocca, *Speaking the
Incomprehensible God* (Washington, DC: Catholic University of America Press,
2004).

for example, that 'God is alive' cannot be thought to mean just that God
brings living things to be. After all, says Aquinas, God cannot be said to
be bodily even though it is perfectly true that he causes what is bodily
to exist.[35] And yet, so Aquinas goes on to argue, some of the things we
say about God are literally true of him. Take, for example, 'God is good'.
Clearly, says Aquinas, 'good' in this sentence cannot have exactly the
same meaning as it does in others we can think up (he means that God's
goodness cannot be just what, for example, that in which the goodness
of a good singer consists). But Aquinas does not therefore conclude that
its meaning has to be quite unrelated to other occurrences of it. For we
can, he thinks, employ the same word on different occasions without
meaning exactly the same by it and without meaning something entirely
different. In 'My money is in the bank' and 'The boat ran aground on the
bank of the river' the word 'bank' means something entirely different.
Not so, however, with 'love' in 'I love my job', 'I love my cat', 'I love
Indian food', and 'I love my husband'. Love of my job, my cat, and Indian
food is hardly quite the same as the love one may have for a spouse. But
we do not equivocate as we use the term 'love' with each of these objects
in mind. And, so Aquinas argues, we are not always equivocating (or not
always *purely* equivocating) when we apply to God words which we use
when talking of what is not divine.[36]

Why not? Because, thinks Aquinas, God must have in him all that
we can think of as creaturely perfection. Working on the principle that
you cannot give what you have not got, Aquinas suggests that there has
to be a sense in which any cause that acts so as to bring something about
(in Aquinas' language, any 'efficient' or 'agent' cause) must somehow
resemble its effect. He does not, of course, mean that it must *look* like its
effect. He means that an effect must be explicable in terms of the nature
of its cause, that a knowledge of the effect and cause together must leave
us seeing the effect as following naturally from what the cause actually is by nature, and, in this sense, resembling it. For Aquinas, causes
(efficient or agent causes) only cause insofar as they actually operate in

---

[35] I.13.2. In this connection, Aquinas also insists that some of the things we say positively about God relate to his essence and cannot, therefore, be construed only as
noting what God causes to exist since God is not compelled to cause anything to
exist. For Aquinas, what God is essentially cannot depend on what he freely chooses
to bring about. Rather, what God freely chooses to bring about depends on what he is
essentially.

[36] Responding to the idea that terms applied to God and other things are always used
equivocally, Aquinas observes that, if such were the case, there would be no point in
applying to God any particular word which we also use when talking of other things
(i.e., we would be saying nothing intelligible). See I.13.5.

the coming to be of their effects.[37] And, he thinks, when this happens, causes display what they are in their effects. Aquinas therefore reasons that, since God is the supreme cause of everything other than himself, his effects must somehow show him forth and, therefore, be such that we can name him after them insofar as the terms we use in so doing do not include in their meaning that which can only be thought of as primarily creaturely.

Take, for example, 'God is a mighty fortress'. Is that statement true? You might say that it is metaphorically true since God is a dependable refuge. Yet it cannot be literally true if God is incorporeal and not made of stone, and if 'mighty fortress' gets its metaphorical sense when applied to God because it has a primary sense as applied to castles and the like. But what about 'God is good'? Could this be said of God literally? Aquinas thinks that it can since he takes 'good' to be a word which has no essentially creaturely and primary connotation. For Aquinas, 'good' is equivalent to 'desirable', and he sees no reason why God cannot be thought of as desirable since, so he argues, God is the source of all that is desirable apart from himself and must therefore show himself forth in it. For Aquinas, the goodness of creatures, though taking different forms, is only there because God is making it to be. So we can, thinks Aquinas, take it to reflect what God is essentially – that is, good. Since Aquinas holds that God is not one of a kind, he does not suppose that God is a good X, Y, or Z. But his thinking, as I have just reported it, leads him to maintain that God can be literally said to be good. And in the *ST* this line of thinking also leads Aquinas to claim that other things can be said of God positively, essentially, literally, and without equivocation – such as that God is living, loving, wise, and omnipotent.[38]

GOD AND CREATURES

With all of that said, however, readers of the *Summa Theologiae* should never lose sight of the way in which it remorselessly insists on the distinction between God and everything else. We are often told that God is

---

[37] Aquinas does not think that as there are, for example, cats and cows, there are also causes. For him, something is only a cause insofar as it brings about a particular effect. I do not succeed in teaching unless someone learns because of me. So according to Aquinas there are only effects insofar as there are causes acting in them, and there are causes only insofar as there are effects in which they act. As he writes in his commentary on Aristotle's *Physics* (3.3), 'Action and passion are not two changes but one and the same change, called action in so far as it is caused by an agent, and passion in so far as it takes place in a patient'.

[38] Cf. I.18, 19, 20, 22, and 25.

a person – a center of consciousness alongside the rest of us. The author of the *Summa Theologiae* takes a very different line, however. For Aquinas, 'God' is not the proper name of some particular person. Rather, it is a *nomen naturae* (the name of a nature).[39] For Aquinas, God is what enables persons, in the ordinary sense, to exist from second to second.[40] Considered as such, says Aquinas, God is not an anything of any kind. Rather, he is the source of all diversity, change, and creaturely goodness. For Aquinas, God is *ipsum esse subsistens* (subsisting being itself).[41]

Does this mean that God, in Aquinas' view, is something distant and aloof when it comes to his creation? And does it mean that Aquinas takes God to be something static, inert, and impersonal? Casual readers of Aquinas might be tempted to suppose that the answer to these questions is 'Yes'. The God of the *ST*, they might think, is a kind of metaphysical abstraction and is something uninvolved with the created order. Yet nothing could be further from the truth. In the *ST* Aquinas certainly says that God is unchanging since he thinks that change ultimately requires a cause which is not itself subject to change.[42] But Aquinas' 'God is unchanging' no more implies that God is static than 'John is not German' implies that John is Swedish. For Aquinas it simply means that, whatever we say of God, we are bound to get it wrong if we ascribe real change to him.[43] And the account of God given in the *ST* hardly portrays him as something inert. Rather, it depicts him as the living source of all beings other than himself.[44] There is, indeed, a sense in

---

[39] Cf. I.13, 8.

[40] Aquinas applies the term 'person' (*persona*) to God in his discussions of the Trinity. Here he speaks of God as being three persons (cf. I.27–32). Note, though, that Aquinas never suggests that the three persons of the Trinity are three centers of consciousness.

[41] Cf. I.4.2, I.11.4, and I.12.4. Cf. also I.13.11.

[42] Cf. I.9.1.

[43] Aquinas allows that change can be ascribed to God *in a sense*. If my daughter has a child it could be said of me that I have become a grandfather. Yet it does not follow from this, of course, that I have therefore actually undergone any modification. With that kind of thought in mind, Aquinas is happy to say that changes can be ascribed to God. He thinks, for example, that we can say that if Fred starts worshipping God, then God *comes to be* worshipped by Fred. Aquinas has a similar take on the use of tensed statements used of God. Since Aquinas thinks that change comes only with time, he says that God transcends time and is eternal (I.10.2). Does this mean that we cannot truly speak of God using tensed statements? 'No', says Aquinas. We can, for example, say that God led the Israelites out of Egypt at such and such a time. But not, Aquinas adds, because God exists in time. We should, he thinks, say that God led the Israelites out of Egypt at such and such a time since at such and such a time the Israelites were led out of Egypt by the God who transcends time (cf. I.13.7).

[44] Aquinas ascribes life to God since he thinks that living things are, primarily, things with a power of movement lying in themselves. So he holds that, for example, cats

which God appears in the *ST* as something abstract. For, as we have seen, Aquinas thinks that we cannot categorize God or take him to be literally like the things with which we are familiar as beings who know what things are at a sensory level. Yet if 'abstract' is taken to mean something like 'hypothetical', 'non-concrete' or 'disengaged', Aquinas never takes God to be abstract. For him, God is the most real of things since everything apart from him owes its existence to him and reflects him insofar as it is good. For him, too, God is closer to everything created than any created thing can be to any other. I can be close to you by holding you to me. For Aquinas, however, God is actually wholly present *in* everything he makes to be. God, Aquinas writes, 'is in everything ... as an efficient cause is present to that in which its action takes place ... During the whole period of a thing's existence, therefore, God must be present to it, and present in a way that accords with the way in which the thing possesses its existence'.[45] Pursuing this thought Aquinas adds that God is *wholly* in everything since he not something composite. God, he says, is 'essentially' in everything.[46]

One arresting conclusion that Aquinas derives from this thought is that God is causally present where many have sought to exclude him – in the free choices that people make. It is often said that when we act freely God is standing back from us and letting us do our own thing. What can this thesis amount to? It seems to be stating that a free human choice is not caused by God. Yet can there be something created which is not caused to be by God? Aquinas thinks not, so he takes God to be so present to us as to be causally active even in what we do freely. God, says Aquinas, 'is the first cause on which both natural and free agents depend'.[47] In Aquinas' view, human free actions are as real as anything else. So he concludes that they have to be made to be (i.e., created) by God.

Given that Aquinas is of this opinion, you might suppose that he takes all human action to be determined – determined by God. Yet if 'to be determined' means 'not to be free', Aquinas would disagree with you. That people can (sometimes) act freely is something he never denies. Indeed, he argues to the contrary.[48] For Aquinas, however, my freedom is

are alive while stones are not. And he takes God to be living since he believes that God (and without anything acting on him) is able to bring about effects – the first of which being the existence of anything other than God. Cf. I.18.3.

45 I.8.1.
46 Cf. I.8.3 and I.8.4.
47 I.83.1.
48 Cf. I.82 and 83. Cf. also Aquinas' *De Malo*, question 6.

threatened insofar as something in the world is having its way with me –
acting on me as the kind of thing it is so as effect a change in me which
is not of my choosing. And God, Aquinas thinks, cannot be anything like
this. For Aquinas, God makes no difference to anything.

In the *ST* Aquinas develops this thought while saying that God's act
of creating is not the bringing about of a change in anything. One can
only change what is already there to be altered, so God's causing creatures to exist cannot, Aquinas reasons, be thought of as a modification
of anything.[49] For Aquinas, God's making to be of things is not a matter
of him *tinkering* with them or acting on them from *outside* (as I might
act on you from outside as I force you to do something). Aquinas takes
God to make things to be exactly what they are and can be understood
to be even by those who have no belief in God. So, he notes, some things
are things which act freely while others are not. Or, as he says in I.83.1:

> Free decision spells self-determination because people, by their free
> decisions, move themselves to action. Freedom does not require
> that a thing is its own first cause, just as in order to be the cause of
> something else a thing does not have to be its first cause. God is the
> first cause on which both natural and free agents depend. And, just
> as his initiative does not prevent natural causes from being natural,
> so it does not prevent voluntary action from being voluntary, but,
> rather, makes it be precisely this. For God works in each according
> to its nature.[50]

In the *Summa Theologiae*, as throughout his writings, Aquinas consistently holds that nothing we might come up with as a true account of
what is in the world is remotely compromised by any truth of theology.
He therefore thinks that any decent defense of the thesis that people act
freely is completely compatible with the claim that God exists and is the
cause of everything other than himself. In this sense, Aquinas holds that
God makes no difference to anything – though, of course, he also thinks
that God makes all the difference: that between there being nothing and
something (only God and a world created by God).

I am sure that accounts of Aquinas on God in the *Summa Theologiae*
might well draw attention to matters that I have passed over in what
I have had to say on the topic. But any such account has to emphasize
the way in which the *Summa Theologiae* needs to be read as offering a

---

[49] Cf. I.45.1 and 1.45.2.
[50] I quote here from *Blackfriars* 11. For a notable passage in which Aquinas makes the
same point, see his commentary on Aristotle's *Peri Hermeneias*, lecture 14.

sustained critique of idolatry, by which I mean 'the failure to recognize the difference between God and creatures'. Many theologians and philosophers have spoken of God as if (in the language of Matthew Arnold), he lived on the next street.[51] Following what he took to be the teachings of the bible, and using his philosophical skills, Aquinas effectively argues against such thinkers – not only in the *Summa Theologiae* but throughout his writings. And his view is that we can only appreciate what divine revelation has to offer insofar as we recognize how different from creatures God is. Contemporary theologians might be well advised to learn from Aquinas here. And contemporary philosophers might, from Aquinas, get a sense of what belief in God might amount to – so that they might engage with it more usefully than they have sometimes done.

---

[51] Cf. *Literature and Dogma* (1873) and *God and the Bible* (1875).

Eternity

HERBERT MCCABE OP[†]

Aquinas is famous for having brought together Aristotelianism and Christianity (a project about as surprising and popular in the thirteenth century as, say, bringing together Marxism and Christianity today).[1] Yet Aquinas was not simply a disciple and commentator on Aristotle. He went well beyond him in a variety of fields, and his thinking about eternity is one of them. This is because, as we shall see, talk about eternity is, for Aquinas, talk about God, and Aquinas' philosophical discussion of God goes well beyond anything to be found in Aristotle.

For Aquinas, God is the Creator, and the notion of creation (or rather the *attempt* to have a notion of creation) was not available to Aristotle. Perhaps I should say straight away that it seems to me that philosophical thinking about God reached a certain high point in medieval times, just as logic did. With the renaissance, I think, both philosophical theology and logic declined disastrously, but whereas logic was miraculously rescued and revived by Frege, Russell, and others at the beginning of the twentieth century, no such rescuer has yet been found for philosophical theology. What passes for thinking about God these days is of a crudity and naivety that would have astonished Aquinas. This is just so you know where I stand.

For Aquinas, strictly and properly only God is eternal, but he allows that we can use the word 'eternal' in a derivative sense of other things. We can speak for example, as St John does, of the eternal life of the blessed in sharing God's life. We can even speak of the 'eternal punishment' of hell, though that for Aquinas is not really eternal but merely unending. He himself even wrote a short book called *On the Eternity of the World* discussing whether the world could have existed for ever (i.e., without a beginning). The Bible, as he notes, even speaks of the 'eternal hills', but that he says is pure metaphor.

[1] Herbert McCabe died in 2001. This contribution is an edited version of a lecture given by him during the 1980s at the University of Bristol.

I had better begin, then, by saying something about Aquinas' concept of God – though strictly speaking he did not think we could have a concept of God; all we have is a use for the word 'God'. Ordinarily, these two would coincide. Normally, to know what an X is *is* to know how to use the word 'X'. If you know what a horse is, then you know the meaning of the word 'horse' – you may not have a very clear idea of what a horse is but, if you have some idea, then you have some idea of how to use the word. But Aquinas holds that we know how to use the word 'God' not because of any idea we have, even a hazy one, of what *God* is, but because of what we know about *other* things. In other words, we use the word 'God' not because we have noticed God but because we have noticed something about the world. What we have noticed, according to Aquinas, is its radical questionableness. Let me explain that as briefly as I can.

In the course of our life we are struck from time to time by what Aquinas calls *admiratio* (surprise). We come across the unexpected, the puzzling. Ordinarily, we can only be surprised in this way if we already have expectations. We are surprised when these expectations are disappointed. Such expectations are part of our understanding of the nature of things. If you know what a rabbit is, if you are familiar with the nature of rabbits, you will expect a rabbit to run away from a dog – you do not necessarily formulate this to yourself as a proposition, it is just what Aquinas would call a habitual or dispositional understanding. Now if you come across a rabbit that does not run away from a dog, but perhaps turns and bites it, you will have *admiratio*. It seems unnatural and unexpected for the rabbit to behave like this, so you look for some factor in the situation that will explain what is going on. What you are looking for is a factor which will make it clear that in these circumstances it is after all quite natural for the rabbit to act as it does. You discover, let us say, that the rabbit has been drinking heavily, and then your *admiratio* disappears. The unexpected has become what you would expect. Inebriated rabbits naturally do odd things.

When you have an explanation you say 'Oh yes, I see; that was how it had to be.' For Aquinas, an explanation or *causa* (you could translate that as cause, but you might be misled) is anything which accounts for the naturalness of an event. It shows that the event or situation was after all only to be expected. Of course, there are several senses in which you 'explain' something, and Aquinas discusses some of these. But he always concludes that what you are doing in each case is showing how what happened was to have been *expected*. You know the *causa*, the cause, when you know what would naturally bring something about. Saying that your flu is due to a virus depends on your conviction that if you look into the nature of viruses you will see that they are just the sort of thing that would bring about flu. If you say that the popularity of some political party or other is not due to serious political thinking, you are suggesting that such serious thinking would not be of a nature to bring about this result.

For Aquinas, there are two familiar cases in which we look for explanation. And they are both changes. But they are changes of different kinds. When something new has come about we ask 'Why?' or 'How come?' But there are at least two senses in which something new can be said to come about. First of all there is a change in some subject, as when, for example, my nose goes red. There is the subject, me, and the going red of my nose. You may ask 'How come?' and offer the answer: 'He has a cold, or has been riding his bike in a keen wind, or drinking a lot of whiskey'. This is what Aquinas, following Aristotle, calls 'accidental change', a modification of some kind in a subject. He contrasts this with the more fundamental change which takes place when something comes into existence in the first place, as when a kitten is born, or when I die and a brand new corpse comes to be. This kind of change Aquinas calls 'substantial change'.

According to Aquinas, the big difference between the kinds of change now in question is that the first is an alteration taking place in some already existing subject while the second is not. In the first case there was first of all me with my pinkish grey nose, and then there is still me, but with a red one. In the second case it is not that some subject has been *modified* but that a quite new thing has come into existence. Sure, things have to be modified in order that, say, a kitten should be born (things have to happen between the father and mother cats, and something has to be *turned into* the kitten), but the kitten is not itself a modification of some subject. It is a *new* subject, made out of what was previously something else that has now perished.

Still, there is a kind of modification in something when a kitten is born, though it is not the modification of a subject. It is a sort of modification of the world. Previously, the world did not contain this kitten, and now it does. Previously, there was stuff about the place which could be made into this kitten, but it had not yet been (all the food that the mother cat was to eat and so on). Now Aquinas thinks that we can and do ask how come that a nose which previously might have been red, but was not, became actually red, and we can ask how come that a world which previously contained merely stuff that could be, but was not yet, made into a kitten, now actually contains a kitten. And, of course, we have answers to these questions. That is what scientific investigation is for. Note, though, that asking how a kitten came newly into existence out of a world that did not have it is a more radical question (is digging down further) than asking how an already existing nose became red.

Yet suppose we ask a third and still more radical kind of question: not just how come this subject is modified in a new way, or how come a kitten exists when previously the world lacked it, but how come there is *anything* instead of nothing at all. The first kind of question is asked against a background of a subject which may or may not be modified. The second kind of question is asked against the background of a world which might or might not have this kitten in it. The third kind is asked against a background of there not being anything *at all*. We can imagine the nose that is not yet red. We can imagine, or even remember, the world without this kitten. We cannot imagine nothing at all. And yet, Aquinas notes, we can ask the question 'After all, how come anything instead of *nothing*?'

To ask this question is to suffer a kind of vertigo. It is to try to think what is for us unthinkable: that there should not be anything at all. It is, of course, a matter of debate amongst philosophers whether we can legitimately ask the question. Aquinas thought we could, and his famous 'five ways'[2] for proving the existence of God are simply five ways of trying to show that this is a legitimate question. In his view, our exploration does not have to stop at asking questions within our world, and in terms of the nature of things in it (why this or that happens or comes into existence). We can go on to ask about the whole world, how it exists instead of not existing. One needs to note, however, that, though Aquinas thought we could ask this question, he was quite clear that we could not *answer* it. The nose is red instead of being pink, the kitten exists instead of what it was made out of, and in each case we can give explanations of how this has happened by reference to causes, to things whose *nature* it is to make noses red or to make kittens. But if it occurs to us that everything there is might not have existed but does, then we have no explanation in terms of something whose nature it is to make this happen. We have no explanation at all. That sense of vertigo is a sense of an unanswerable question, a sense of *mystery*.[3]

For Aquinas, then, there is a question here to be asked, but we do not and could not know its answer. The label we give to this answer we

---

[2] I.2.3.

[3] Cf. Ludwig Wittgenstein, *Tractatus Logico-Philosophicus* (London: Routledge and Kegan Paul, 1922), 6.44: 'Not *how* the world is, is the mystical, but *that* it is'.

do not know is 'God'. To say that God exists is, for Aquinas, simply to say that the universe really does present us with a valid question: how come it exists instead of not existing? It is a valid question, so it has an answer, and this answer is called 'God'. But we do not understand the answer, we do not know what God is, God remains absolute mystery, we use the word not because of anything we know about God but because of the question that the world puts to us.

Now although we have not the faintest idea what the answer is to our question, which we may call the question of creation ('How come the world instead of nothing?'), we can at least say what would *not* count as an answer. For example, nothing which is part of the universe could be the explanation of how it is that the universe is at all. God, then, cannot be an inhabitant of the universe. God cannot be a thing alongside other things – it is precisely things that we are asking about. Concerning God, (if by God we just mean the mystery that would be the answer to our question), it must not be legitimate to ask 'How come God is instead of not being?' It must be quite impossible for God not to be.

May I just try to clarify that? Of course, the sentence 'God does not exist' makes perfectly good sense in English. It is not like 'This circle is square'. But the fact that we can sensibly say 'God does not exist', and thus envisage the possibility of God not existing, is merely the consequence of the fact that we do not know what God is. The meaning we have for the word 'God', the way we are taught to use the word, does not correspond to any understanding at all of what God is. If we did know what God is we would no doubt see that he could not *not* be, just as when we know what circles are we see that they cannot be square. But our language does not express an understanding of God as it does express an understanding of circles. It is thus not *obvious* to us that God has to exist. We therefore do not see or understand what we may call the *necessity* of God – I mean that it is simply not possible that he not be in the way that, for example it *is* perfectly possible for me not to be (I did not exist before 1926 for example) or it is perfectly possible (though improbable) that my nose should not be red.

For Aquinas, it is not just that God is *imperishable* – he thought there were lots of imperishable things (he calls them 'necessary beings') that are not subject to decay and thus cannot die. In the material world, as Aquinas saw it, things come into existence by the perishing of other things, and every death is the production of some new thing. In *that* world things are, as Aquinas put it, *contingent* upon other things. But he thought that there were other beings which were not in this way generated from the perishing of other things and which themselves were not turned into other things (immaterial beings that he identifies with the angels and of which we shall see more in a moment). But even of such necessary imperishable things we can say: 'OK they do not, like us, owe their existence to other *things*; but how come they exist instead of simply not existing?' Now of God (simply because what we refer to by 'God' is the answer to our question), we know that *that* question cannot be legitimately asked. So, for Aquinas, God brings about everything that exists, sustains in existence everything that exists. We raise the question of God not because of the *way* the world is but because it exists *at all*.

I shall not go into Aquinas' intricate line of reasoning from this point on, but he claims to show that although we know nothing of what God is, we do know that, for example, he cannot be changed, that change has no place in God, for, of course, if there were a change it would be legitimate to ask 'How come this new feature or factor?' And this we know is never a legitimate question concerning God. There can be nothing in God which might be but is not; there can be no actualising of a potentiality, a might be. God cannot but be purely and simply actual without any incompleteness of any kind.

And it is for this reason that Aquinas denies that God can be in time. It is for this reason that he says that God, and only God, is eternal. 'Eternity in the true and proper sense', he says, 'belongs to God alone, for eternity follows upon unchangeableness, and God alone is entirely unchangeable.'[4] Notice that to say that God is eternal, as Aquinas understands the statement, is to say something *negative*. It is to say, and only to say, that God *cannot* be in time. So in order to understand this we shall need to look at Aquinas' notion of time, something we might do by turning first, and by contrast, to Newton.

According to Newton, 'Absolute true and mathematical time, in itself, and from its own nature, flows equally, without relation to anything external; and by another name is called duration. Relative apparent and vulgar time is some sensible and external measure of duration by motion, whether accurate or unequable, which is commonly used instead of true time; as an hour, a day, a month, a year.'[5] For Newton, absolute space and time were what he called the 'sensorium' of God – that is, not how you or I or anyone experiences the world but how the world is from God's point of view. As he says in his *Opticks*: 'There

---

[4] I.10.3.
[5] Isaac Newton, *The Mathematical Principles of Natural Philosophy* (New York: Daniel Adee, 1848), 77.

is a Being incorporeal, living, intelligent, omnipresent, who in infinite Space, as it were in his Sensory, sees the things themselves intimately, and thoroughly perceives them, and comprehends them wholly by their immediate presence to himself ... a powerful ever-living Agent, who being in all Places, is more able by his Will to move the Bodies within his boundless uniform Sensorium, and thereby to form and reform the Parts of the Universe'.[6]

It will, I hope, be clear that Newton's God is totally different from Aquinas'. Newton's God is the principal being, the privileged spectator and operator upon things, and to know as this Being knows is the ultimate aim of scientific investigation. For Newton the scientist aims at, though he does not attain, a God's eye view of the world. For Aquinas, Newton's God would be a creature. For Aquinas, the aim of science is not to know as *God* knows but to know as *human beings* can know.

Aquinas' notion of time is as different from Newton's as is his notion of God. For Aquinas, time is the terms in which we compare two motions with each other, not in respect of their intensity or anything else, but their *succession*, what comes after what. In other words we speak of time because we speak of one thing or event coming before or after another. For Aquinas, time is what clocks are for, as space is what tape measures are for. In this respect the pre-Newtonian Aquinas is in agreement with what I take to be post-Newtonian physics. For Newton, if we get away from vulgar and relative times, there can be only one absolute time for the universe, the time of God. But both Aquinas and the modern physicist, who both think that all time is fairly 'vulgar', can envisage the possibility of there being more than one time. Aquinas does, in fact, ask whether there is only one time, and he answers that there is, not because of the nature of time as such but because of what he believed to be the actual structure of the physical universe. According to the medieval astronomy that he inherited, the universe consists of concentric spheres centring on the spherical earth. This central position of the earth did not, however, imply some superiority for our domain. On the contrary, the earth region (the sub-lunar area) was the dregs of the universe. It was the area where things perished and changed, the area of contingency and chance, where nothing is permanent and nothing is perfectly intelligible. There is, however, a certain element of order in the sub-lunary world. There are physical laws, and there are the natures of things, and it is the scientist's business to discern these amidst the

---

6 Isaac Newton, *Opticks, Or, A Treatise of Reflections, Refractions, Inflections, and Colors of Light* (4th ed., London: Dover, 1730), 370 and 403.

confusion. These elements of intelligibility and order are derived, in the medieval view, from the causal influence of the higher spheres that rotate around the earth and affect it. So, for example, the fact that we have these particular species of animals and these particular elements, things with these natures, is due in some way to the operation of various heavenly bodies. These spheres, in their turn, are regulated by yet higher spheres until you come to the *primum caelum*, the first and highest heaven, the outermost sphere whose rotation governs all the rest.

The relevance of what I have just been noting to our purposes is that this *primum caelum* provides Aquinas with a privileged clock. Because the movement of the *primum caelum* is causally related to every other movement in the universe, every clock in the universe can in principle (you might say) be set by the *primum caelum* and there is, therefore, only one time for the material universe. Having rejected various opinions to the effect that there must *necessarily* be only one time scale Aquinas says that 'the true ground of time's unity is … the unity of the most fundamental process in the world, by which, since it is the simplest, all others are measured'.[7] In some ways the revolving heavens in the medieval world view were rather like the revolving electrons of more recent theories. In both cases the changes and chances of our world are to be explained by reference to changeless incorruptible spinning bodies. The medievals made them macroscopic. Nineteenth-century physics made them sub-microscopic.

I do not want here to go into the complex details of Aquinas' view of time because my brief is to discuss eternity. I just want to establish that, for him, time and change are inseparably connected. Time is the measure of motion and of moving things, though it is also the measure of that kind of rest which is simply privation of motion – when something which can move happens not to be doing so while other things are. When the things that change belong to a single causally related system then there will be one single time for them all, the movement of the fundamental process, the rotation of the *primum caelum*, which sets the time to which we can compare the movements of the rest. Whereas for Newton there is a single absolute time belonging to *God*, for Aquinas there is a single time belonging to the created ultimate stars.

Now it will be clear that for Aquinas there can be no sense in speaking of God changing or moving. So, Aquinas thinks, we have to deny of God that he is in any way in time, that he can be measured by time, that

7 I.10.6.

he has a life or activity that could be dated or successive in any way. This is for God to be eternal.

It will be obvious then, I hope, that eternity (for Aquinas) is not a very long time, nor an endless or infinite time. It is not time at all. For Aquinas, God could not have existed *before* the world was created, or before or after anything. You cannot say that God existed before last Wednesday. What you can say is that the statement 'God exists', made before last Wednesday, was true when it was made, just as it would be true whenever it is made. But this is not because God endures through all time. God, for Aquinas, does not exist *at* any time. It is merely true at any time that *he exists*. For Aquinas, therefore, what is interminable (without beginning or end) is not thereby eternal, for eternity implies a total absence of succession. Or, as Aquinas himself puts it: 'In any change there is successiveness, one part coming after another, and by numbering the antecedent and consequent parts of change there arises the notion of time, which is simply this numberedness of before and after in change. Now something lacking change and never varying its mode of existence will not display a before and after. So just as numbering antecedent and consequent in change produces the notion of time, so awareness of invariability in something altogether free from change produces the notion of eternity. A further point: time is said to measure things that begin and end in time, as Aristotle points out, and this is because one can assign a beginning and an end to any changing thing. But things altogether unchangeable cannot have a beginning any more than they can display successiveness. So two things characterize eternity. First, anything existing in eternity is unending, that is to say, lacks both beginning and end (for both may be regarded as ends). Secondly, eternity itself exists as an instantaneous whole lacking successiveness.'[8]

Thus Aquinas himself thought that the created world might have had no beginning or end, that it might have been interminable, but this would not make it strictly eternal. He argued that there were no valid philosophical or scientific reasons for thinking either that the past has been finite or that the future will be.[9] To put it in terms of his world picture, he could see no reason why the number of revolutions of the *primum caelum* should have been finite or why they should ever cease. Note, however, that this view is in no way incompatible with Aquinas' theory of creation. For him, the question as to whether the world began

[8]   I.10.1.
[9]   He does so especially in his work *De Aeternitate Mundi* ('On the Eternity of the World').

a finite time ago is a quite different one from the question 'Is it created?' There is no reason, in his view, to suppose that God could not have created a world of interminable duration, since he held that whatever is not logically impossible must be possible to God. (According to Aquinas, the reason why God could not, for example, make a square circle has nothing to do with any limitation on the power of God; it is simply that, since the words in the phrase 'square circle' cancel each other out, the phrase cannot be used to name anything God might make because it cannot be used to name *anything*.) Now the notion of an interminable world does not seem logically impossible in the way that a square circle is. Hence God might have made it. For Aquinas, a world with no beginning would be just as much created (dependent on God for existing instead of there not being anything) as a world with a beginning.

Although Aquinas thought that there were no valid arguments for thinking either that the world had a beginning or did not have a beginning, he also thought that the Bible happens to tell us that the world *did* have a beginning and will have an end. But if you think this, he said, you should be clear that you do so out of faith in what the Bible says not out of philosophical reasons. (Just in passing I think Aquinas was here wrong about the Bible. I don't think a biblical scholar would accept that the authors, say, of the beginning of Genesis were intending to answer the question as to whether the world began a finite time ago. They just took it for granted, which is a very different thing.)

So, as Aquinas puts it: 'Time and eternity clearly differ. But certain people make the difference consist in time having a beginning and an end while eternity has neither. This however is an incidental and not an intrinsic difference. For even if time had always existed and will always exist, as those hold who think the heavens will rotate for ever, there will still remain the difference ... that eternity is an instantaneous whole (*tota simul*) while time is not, eternity measuring abiding existence and time measuring change'.[10]

Besides eternity and the time of our material world, Aquinas allows for other time systems. So I think you might just be interested now to hear a very little about *aeon* or *aevum*, the time of creatures outside the sublunary sphere, a measure which Aquinas places somewhere between eternity and time. He makes what I believe to be an interesting distinction between *ageing* and *the order of events of your life*.

If you go to Paris in January, and then go to London in September, your visit to London will be *after* your visit to Paris. Also, you will be

---

[10] I.10.4. (*Blackfriars* 2, 145).

older on your visit to London than you were when you went to Paris. For these two things, an event occurring after another, and our being older or younger, coincide. Nevertheless, Aquinas suggested, they are distinct, for being older or younger has to do with our perishability and contingency. If you are perishable then you have a lifetime. Every plant and animal has a lifetime, an approximate amount of time available to it. No tiger could exist for less than a hundredth of a second, nor could any tiger exist for more than two hundred years – not at any rate in the usual run of things. To be older is to have used up more of your *lifetime*. As you get older, more of your lifetime is in the past. By contrast, the sequence of past and future in the events of your life does not in the same way have to do with your perishability. It simply has to do with the fact that things can happen to you, or that you can do things that you have not yet done. We *age* because we carry in us the potentiality to perish, to cease to exist, to be turned into worms and what not. We have a successively *varied* life because we carry in us the potentiality to different accidental modifications. Ageing is connected with substantial change, succession with accidental changes.

Now it is logically possible to conceive of a being which had the second of these without the first: an imperishable being which changed in this or that respect. The life of such a being could be measured by the succession of different modifications; it could not be measured by ageing; it could not get any older or ever have been younger. Aquinas thought that examples of such beings, which he called necessary beings, were the heavenly bodies, the stars, and also immaterial angels.

A word about medieval notions of stars. I can and will perish because what Aquinas calls my materiality, my potentiality, which is fulfilled by my being a human being, could also be, and will be, fulfilled by becoming worm food, and when I die this is what happens: the potentiality which was actualised as a human being now becomes actualised as a corpse. That is why we say that the corpse is *my* corpse. It is made *out of* me, just as I was made out of other things originally. If I did not have this material factor in me, this capacity to lose my own form and have it replaced by another, I could not be turned into anything else. I would be imperishable along with the angels. The stars are a more complex case. They are visibly material things that exist, for example, in place, and yet they were thought by medieval authors to be imperishable. (This of course was pure superstition, but it was the inherited 'wisdom' of the ancients – and it was superstition, though in a way that talk about angels is not, for that [at least in the hands of Aquinas] is a discussion of logical possibilities, whereas medieval talk of the stars purported to be about an observable world that people had not observed enough yet.)

The stars were supposed to be imperishable because, although they were material and, thus, potential, their potentiality was completed, satisfied, and fulfilled by the form they had, and thus they had no real possibility of changing into anything else. They were thought of rather as we think of the inert gases such as helium or argon, which are incapable of chemical reaction because their outside electron rings are completely and satisfactorily filled with the right number of electrons. Thus, since neither angels nor stars were perishable, they could not be said to age. Yet they have succession. The stars, for example, move across the sky, are first potentially in one place and then actually in it, and so on. The angels, Aquinas thought, had an intellectual life, made choices, and could be related to place (not by being in it – an angel can no more have a position than a quadratic equation can – but by acting on what is in place). Such beings, then, are in a kind of time, but not a time which measures age. And this is what Aquinas, in Latin, calls *aevum*, which tends, rather oddly, to be translated into English by the Greek word *aeon*. Since angels are not part of the causal system of the material world, their time systems do not correspond with and cannot be checked against our clocks. Aquinas asks whether there are many angelic time systems or only one, and he says this must depend on whether the angels themselves form one system or whether they are each independent units. For rather obscure biblical reasons he opts for the idea of them forming a hierarchical system in one aeon.

I would like to conclude this brief survey of Aquinas on eternity by looking at an interesting text from Aquinas to show how he employs his notion of eternity to solve a classical problem. It is this: If God does not know from eternity everything that is to happen, then he learns things about the world and is thus affected by the world and thus cannot be the source of all that exists. Rather, the world would be the cause and source of some of his knowledge and he would, therefore, not be God. If however God *does* know from eternity (and still more if from eternity he brings about everything that happens), then it would seem that everything happens determinately, that everything that happens is fated, and there cannot, for example, be any genuinely free and spontaneous human actions, there cannot be what are known as 'future contingents'.

The puzzle about God's knowing arises because it is true before an event happens that God knows of it, and if it were true before an event happened that *I* knew of it, then it certainly *would* be necessitated. But this puzzle, says Aquinas, arises not from knowledge itself but from the *way* that I know things. It is not my *knowledge* of future events that imposes necessity on them. It is just that the only way *I* could have knowledge of future events would be if they are already necessitated. If I am right in claiming that I know today what will happen tomorrow, it can only be because what will happen tomorrow is already determined by causes that are there today. But this, Aquinas argues, is because my knowledge is restricted to what is contemporary with me, or antecedent to me, and, since nothing could be either contemporary or antecedent to God, it would be a mistake to attribute this restriction to him. As always with Aquinas, he shows that theological puzzles arise because we unthinkingly attribute to God features which we take for granted in our world but which we have no right to attribute to him (which it would make no sense to attribute to him, indeed). The idea that God's foreknowledge of events implies that they are necessitated events arises from the uncritical (and usually unconscious) assumption that God acquires his foreknowledge in the way that we do, by knowing the antecedent causes of things.

For Aquinas, I can know what is *contemporary* with me, present to me, and I can know what is past; for these things are there to know. Of course I do not know *everything* that is present or past because some of them are too far away, and anyway I cannot be bothered; but in principle I *could* know any event that is present or past. I can have no such knowledge of the future because future events have not happened, they are not there. I can only know that something is going to happen if its happening is already determined by some cause or other that I know in the present or past. I cannot know that you will ever tell a lie in the future because that is a matter for your choice; it is not determined. On the other hand I can know that you will die, for that is determined by factors I know in the present or past – such as the chemical structure of your body and so on. Of course, even the future things we *think* we know (like that you will die) we may not actually know – perhaps you will not die but be taken up to Heaven in a fiery chariot like Elijah. But we can only be *said* to know the future *in so far as* it is determined by the present or past.

So if we *do* know that something will happen tomorrow then this is a sure sign that it is already determined or necessitated, for how else could we know it? The necessitation does not arise from our knowledge. On the contrary, our knowledge arises from the necessitation. If God were to know future events in some other way than by knowing them in their causes, then there would be no need to conclude from *God's* knowledge to their being necessitated. God could then know future contingent events as well as future necessitated events. He could know *both* what lies you will tell and that you will tell them freely. For us there is a contrast between those rather rare occasions when we know what will happen in the future and knowing what is going on in the present or what has gone on in the past. If you tell a lie in the present and I know that you are lying, this in no way implies that your lying is necessitated; for I am knowing the lying *itself*, not something that necessarily caused it. It is only events that are future to me that we have to know (if we know them at all) in their causes. Now Aquinas argues that it could make no sense for an event to be future to God since God does not belong within a time series. Nothing can be future to him since he cannot himself have a date. Or, as Aquinas says at one point: 'A mind contained in some way within time relates differently to the knowing of what happens in time from a mind altogether outside time ... Since our knowing occurs within time ... things are known as present or past or future. Present events are known as actually existing and perceptible to the senses in some way; past events are remembered; and future events are not known in themselves (because they do not yet exist) but can be predicted from their causes: with certainty if their causes totally determine them, as with things that must happen; conjecturally if they are not so determined that they cannot be obstructed, as with things that happen usually; and not at all if they are only possible and not determined either to one side or the other, as with things that *might be either* ... God's knowing, however, is altogether outside time, as if he stands on the summit of eternity where everything exists together, looking down in a simple glance on the whole course of time. So in his one glance he sees everything going on throughout time, and each as it is in itself, not as something future to himself and to his seeing and visible only as it exists within its causal situation (although he sees that causal situation). But he sees things altogether eternally, each as it exists in its own time, just as our own human eye sees John sitting there himself, not just as something determined by causes. Nor does our seeing John sitting there stop it being an event that might not have been when regarded just in relation to its causes. And yet while he is sitting there we see him sitting there with certainty and without doubt, since when a thing exists in itself it is already determined. In this way then God knows everything that happens in time with certainty and without doubt, and yet the things that happen in time are not things that must exist or must come to exist, but things that might or might not be'.[11]

One thing that I hope will be clear from all of the above is that, for Thomas, eternity is a notion we arrive at by a negation of what we understand, a negation of time (itself a sufficiently mysterious idea). Eternity, like God himself is not intelligible to us. And if you now find after all this that you do not understand what I have been talking about, then that is entirely as it should be.

---

[11] *In Aristotelis Librum Peri Hermeneias*, 1.14. The present translation of this text is taken from Timothy McDermott (ed.), *Aquinas: Selected Philosophical Writings* (Oxford and New York: Oxford University Press, 1993), 281f.

Trinity

EUGENE F. ROGERS JR.

In the Trinity, God is always on the move, and God's movement is love.[1] The Trinity enacts perfect love already in itself, and gives it to rational creatures without cost or cause – an act unnecessary but characteristic. In the *ST* Aquinas broadens those ideas to the utmost: they structure, finally, anything that moves. The persons of the Trinity perfect their love in 'real relations' and share their love with rational creatures in 'missions.' 'Relations' and 'missions' involve analogous aptitudes toward another (*respectus ad aliud*) – a readiness for love that goes all the way down.

HOW THE TRINITY ENACTS PERFECT LOVE

The Trinity first enacts perfect love in the 'procession' of the persons: God's internal life proceeds with love (I.27.1). These movements are not local, physical, or directed to the outside, but most intimate. Does that make them imaginary – all in our human heads – or do they really take place among individuals whose movement pushes one another around? Thomas avoids both difficulties in his teaching about 'real relations' (I.28).

'Real relations' define the trinitarian persons as neither imaginary nor individualized. If relations are 'real', they are not imaginary; if the *relations* have reality (attenuated, analogous thinginess), then the persons are not individuals standing *over against* or *apart from* one another. Rather they face *toward* one another: the whole exposition rests on the preposition *ad*, 'toward' or 'for'. 'Things called "toward something" [*ad aliquid*] properly signify only "regarding another" [*respectus ad aliud*]'

---

[1] Even if 'motion' is analogous in Trinity, and God's motion remains pure act, not from potency, I.27.2. See Simon Oliver, 'Trinity, Motion, and Creation *Ex Nihilo*' in Janet Martin Soskice, David Burrell, Carlo Cogliati, and William R. Stoeger (eds), *Creation and the God of Abraham* (Cambridge: Cambridge University Press, 2010), 133–51.

(I.28.1). The Trinity does not consist first of free-standing 'things' (*aliquid*) or even 'others' (*aliud*) who then initiate relations among themselves. Rather the Trinity first involves a 'toward,' a 'regarding'. Aquinas sees the persons of the Trinity as not *pushing*, but at most *looking* at one another. They look not with need, but love, admiring the good. They see only occasions of joy. If among human persons the loving regard of another can transform one's life, among divine persons the loving regard of Another can *found* their life. So Aquinas renders the persons neither imaginary nor pushy, and makes love the fount of the real. As Rowan Williams has written, the Trinity's 'whole life is a "being-for," a movement of gift.'[2] So Aquinas finds 'real distinction' in God, not as individuals who prize independence, but in real regard (I.28.3), because God's moves do not push but give. Otherness in God does not *oppose* the persons, but *relates* them.

So far Aquinas unfolds his doctrine from love *among persons*. But he also unfolds it from love *within the mind*. This indicates why the Trinity might be *three*. Just two occasions of joy, he thinks, bring love without neediness: understanding truth and willing good. In love, the Father regards the truth with joy, generating the Son; in love, the Father wills the good with joy, breathing the Spirit. Love completes itself in three persons, no more no fewer, and all God's moves come from gratuitous love.[3]

Love in the mind prepares the whole salvation-structure of the *Summa*, whereby the Trinity embraces additional, unneeded, gratuitous sharers in the divine life. To do that, it patterns them on its own diversity-in-unity, its own looking-toward-another. Yet that diversity in unity does not stand still, but moves into love. So the Trinity also patterns them on its own *agency*, its own movements of understanding and will: it creates rational creatures in God's image.

HOW THE TRINITY SHARES ITSELF IN CREATED DIVERSITY

No creature represents the Trinity by itself, but only 'multiply and diversely' (I.47.1) and 'by degrees' (I.47.2). Thus to represent the Trinity

---

[2] Rowan Williams, 'The Body's Grace', in Eugene F. Rogers Jr (ed.), *Theology and Sexuality: Classic and Contemporary Readings* (Oxford: Blackwell, 2002), 310–21, here, 317; so too 'occasion of joy,' 'loving regard of another,' 312.

[3] For other accounts of God's threeness, try Pavel Florensky, *The Pillar and Ground of the Truth* (Princeton: Princeton University Press, 1997), 37–8 (giver, receiver, and gift), and Eugene F. Rogers Jr., *After the Spirit* (Grand Rapids: Eerdmans, 2005), 139–40 (the kingdom of heaven is like a wedding feast with two spouses and a witness).

more perfectly means to relate to, even to love, others. In loving, the creature better fulfills its vocation to represent the Trinity, and thus itself. To receive or participate 'more perfectly' in trinitarian relations enables a creature to be more itself, to move more characteristically (I.47.2). God differs from us, in lying deeper in us than we are to ourselves. God does not rival or compete with us – only things on the same level do that. But God works on us and in us, not against us. This ability of God's to work from within and without violence – since God created us and holds us in being – is what distinguishes God from creatures. And this very *distinction* from creatures at the same time assures God's 'direct and intimate relation' to creatures.[4] God can be closer to us than we are to ourselves, and that is how God is different.

Conversely, what unites creatures to God – the Word's structuring them and the Spirit's leading them – is precisely what distinguishes us from one another and as well as from God, since it takes diversity to represent divine goodness (I.47.1). This movement 'communicates God's goodness to creatures' precisely in their distinctiveness (I.47.1 and *ad*1), even as it also 'deifies' ('bestowing a partaking of the Divine Nature by a participated likeness,' I-II.112.1) because the Trinity differentiates the participated likenesses. The persons of the Trinity can make creatures more distinctive and more deiform at the same time, because they themselves move that way. Within God, the Word expresses the mind and the Spirit desires the will of the Father. None other than God's own internal movement, sharing itself with creatures by analogy and by grace, fuels and furnishes them. The Trinity is not just the farthest out in theological speculation: it is also the deepest in.

The more diverse are human movements, the more they receive the Trinity's impetus and form, the more God expresses infinity through them. Humans image God best when they vary most in their ways. Most creaturely among them is Jesus, because *his* humanity can vary the way of life and death: 'it is fitting that a creature which by nature is mutable, should not always be in one way' (III.1.1). His elevation of human nature also marks Jesus as divine, since 'the very nature of God is goodness,' and 'it belongs to the essence of goodness to communicate itself to others,' so that 'it belongs to the essence of the highest goodness to communicate itself in the highest manner' in the Incarnation (III.1.1). Thus Jesus does

4 Richard Norris, *God and World in Early Christian Theology* (New York: Seabury, 1965), 84-86, as developed in Kathryn Tanner, *Jesus, Humanity and the Trinity* (Minneapolis: Fortress, 2001), 2–5, 11.

divine things humanly and human things divinely. 'This is proper to a divine person, on account of its infinity, that there should be a concourse of natures in it' (III.3.1). Here unity and diversity do not oppose but join one another, both in the Incarnation, and our participation in it, since we come to join an infinite regard for others. Although the Incarnation happens in the Person of the Son, its effect is trinitarian, since the Father's mind expresses itself in his body (III.20), while the Spirit's love conceives and illuminates him (III.32.2, III.39.6). Our adoption as sons in the Son involves us in the whole Trinity: the Father as author, the Son as its exemplar, and the Holy Spirit as the likener (III.23.2).

HOW THE TRINITY SHARES ITSELF IN CREATED UNITY

The unity of the Trinity and the deification of creatures share the same reason: the good unites. The Spirit who (as Love) grounds the divine koinonia also (as Gift) joins us to it. This joining does not violate, coerce, or reduce us, because 'the distinction and multitude of things come from the intention of the first agent, who is God' (I.47.1), and because relations in God – *ad aliud* or *respectus ad alterum* – are *real* (I.28.1 and *ad*1). 'Love is a binding force, because it aggregates another to ourselves', but not reductively, because the one who loves 'puts the other in the place of himself' (I.20.1*ad*3). What founds the Trinity – that relations in God are real - is what founds creatures – that 'in creatures there is real relation to God' (I.28.1*ad*3). Because God's goodness involves real relation, it follows not by necessity, but by God's 'intellect and will' (God's character) that God makes creatures; and because God's goodness involves real relation, God can appropriately *mobilise* creaturely difference to bring us into the Trinity, even when that difference arises from finitude. God can use even finitude to bring creatures to the infinite, as long as the infinite is *good*.

> The distinction and multitude of things come from the intention of the first agent, who is God. For He brought things into being in order that His goodness might be communicated to creatures, and be represented by them; and because His goodness could not be adequately represented by one creature alone, He produced many and diverse creatures, that what was wanting to one in the representation of the divine goodness might be supplied by another ... and hence the whole universe together participates the divine goodness more perfectly, and represents it better than any single creature whatever (I.47.1).

This reasoning applies not only to the creation of creatures and their representation of the divine goodness, but also to the end of creatures and God's communication of the divine goodness to them:

> If the means be equal, so to speak, to the end, one only is sufficient. But the creature is not such a means to its end, which is God; and hence the multiplication of creatures is necessary (1.47.1*ad*3).

The Trinity makes creatures distinct in order to reunite them: they differ in order to love.

HOW THE TRINITY SHARES ITSELF IN AGENCY, OR MOVEMENTS INTO LOVE

The Trinity makes human beings in its image to communicate itself to us, to bring us to share in its activity. It makes us in its image to grow us over time into fellowship with itself. The Trinity *needs* no fellowship with us, since it enjoys perfect love and companionship already in itself. But for that very reason, the trinitarian persons *want* to share their fellowship, their very selves, also with us. Their fellowship is for Father, Son, and Spirit to enjoy, and for us to join. Our sharing is nothing they need, but something they desire; they want to celebrate their fellowship, by extending it to us. To express the gratuitous superfluity by which God, without need, creates, loves, and gives Godself to creatures anyway, Aquinas calls God's relation to the creature real not in God but in us: we depend on God, but not God on us (I.28.2). Both God's love and its gratuity are built into us. God's love builds into us not just dependence but also structure: reason and will make us human, so that Christ and Spirit can make us divine. The parallel goes all the way down, because Christ is God's reason, the Spirit God's love. Christ informs our reason with his sight, while the Spirit enlarges our hearts with its love. Aquinas imprints human form with God's relations and human destiny with God's desire.

Such thoughts structure the entire *Summa*. It helps to hold the whole pattern in mind at once. By necessity we read Aquinas piecemeal. Thomas famously makes distinctions: he also sweeps large programmes together. Read the following passages all at once, two or three times over. What follows then tries to keep them together.

> The human being is directed to God as to an end that surpasses the grasp of his reason: 'The eye hath not seen, O God, without Thee, what things Thou has prepared for them that wait for Thee'

(Is. 64:4). But the end must first be known by human beings, since to be human is to direct their thoughts and actions to their goal ... which is in God (I.1.1.).

God is in all things by His essence, power, and presence, according to His one common mode, as the cause existing in the effects which participate in His goodness. Above and beyond this common mode, however, there is one special mode belonging to the rational creature wherein God is said to be present as the object known is in the knower, and the beloved in the lover. And since the rational creature by its operation of knowledge and love attains to God Himself, according to this special mode God is said not only to exist in the rational creature, but to dwell therein as in His own temple. (I.43.3)

The gift of grace surpasses every capability of the created nature, since it is nothing short of a partaking of the Divine Nature, which exceeds every other nature. And thus ... it is necessary that God alone should deify, bestowing a partaking of the Divine Nature by a participated likeness, just as it is impossible that anything save fire should enkindle (I-II.112.1).

That whereby things are heated must itself be hot. Now the human being is in potentiality to the knowledge of the blessed, which consists in the vision of God, and is ordained to it as to an end; since the rational creature is capable of that blessed knowledge, inasmuch as she is made in the image of God. Now human beings are brought to this end of beatitude by the humanity of Christ ... And hence it was necessary that the beatific knowledge, which consists in the vision of God, should belong to Christ pre-eminently, since the cause ought always to be more efficacious than the effect. (III.9.2)

Because Aquinas makes God's being God's act, the Trinity shows how God is and acts, how God 'moves.' God moves; creatures *are* moved; thus the Trinity also tells how God moves creatures. Because Aquinas calls the human in God's image a *mover* – a *moved* mover – the Trinity even tells how creatures move themselves. The Trinity shows both how God moves creatures, and how creatures move themselves – not as God's instruments, but as what engages and gives life to them, in whom they live and move and have their being, and thus their final environment, their habitat or home. The Trinity moves human beings to itself through itself. In the process, it engages their powers to make them more active and free.

Now, this is no longer the Trinity in itself: it is the Trinity bringing humanity into Godself. Still, God can save or elevate us only because God is Trinity: something to join, something to share, the community of love. The Trinity is not only a concept to explain how God can accommodate others in God's life. The Trinity is also the real reason or deepest relation for that – the cause, the mover, the draw, the love. Aquinas uses various metaphors for God's love: community, friendship, kingdom, marriage, even 'republic.'⁵ The loves and moves of human beings, among themselves and into God, find their source in those of the Trinity. The Trinity needs no human being, but the love of the trinitarian persons for one another explains why they might love us *freely*, why they might enjoy us. Because the Trinity loves out of regard for others, God's transcendence does not separate God from the world, but draws God to it.

> God is not transcendent in the sense that he needs a difference [from the world] to be the unique one he is. God is not different within a certain genus, on the basis of a common similarity ... God is 'outside' of any genus, and thus God is not different from creatures the way in which creatures mutually differ. God differs differently ... Such an account undermines the difference between transcendence and immanence, because God is not transcendent in such a way that he is simply 'outside of' or 'above' the world, and thus not transcendent in such a way that it would exclude his 'descent' into the world.⁶

Because the Trinity loves that way, God's very difference from the world allows unlimited engagement with it, closer to the world than the world is to itself.

The missions of the persons articulate as broadly as possible *how* God indwells things more intimately than they are to themselves (I.46). God underlies the structure and bestows the goal of every created thing. For every created thing, God supplies both *how* it moves (its way) and *where* it heads (its end). Thus Thomas makes the pattern as deep and universal as he can. God knows no limits of extent or depth. Whatever I am, God engages and attracts me, because my very form takes part in God the Word, my goal in God the Gift. My form, my way of being most myself, is a goodness that God speaks; the gift I most deeply desire is the beauty that God radiates. That goes for all things, from rocks to plants to animals to us. God is what created movers move *by* and *to*. God moves the rock by its structure (heaviness) and its love of

---

⁵ I-II.99.2, I-II.100.2, 5.
⁶ Henk J. M. Schoot, *Christ the 'Name' of God: Thomas Aquinas on Naming Christ* (Leuven: Peters, 1993), 144–5.

the earth, its *amoris pondus*, its weight of love. God moves the plant by its heliotropic structure, and the love by which the sun draws it up. God moves the dog by its ownmost reasons, its deepest instincts, and the gift it most desires, meat. In a higher way God also moves us by what is most deeply human, our reason, toward what we most love, community. This power of pursuing the good (Spirit) by reason (Word) is called freedom.

The missions of the persons impose that intratrinitarian pattern on creation in general and in particular on God's image in us. The Son becomes the known in the knower, the Spirit the love in the lover (I.43.3). A statement more sweeping and intimate is hard to imagine.

In the mission of the persons, Thomas shows how the Trinity most comprehensively and intimately joins the world to God's own self. It is as broad as structure and desire, as deep as form and heart. Every created thing owes its origin to the Father, its structure to the Word, its goal to the Spirit. Remotely, partially, and gratuitously, every created thing shares in the intratrinitarian movement whereby the Father generates, the Son images, and the Spirit draws. Every created thing gives off God's triune goodness from its deepest interior, its own internal word or form, its love or heart. Remotely, partially, gratuitously, every created thing lives from the Trinity more than from itself. That is how God moves any created thing from the inside, without violating it, according to its own deepest principles. Those deepest principles are the Father, the Son, and the Holy Spirit. Aquinas appropriates to the Father the push that moves the creature into being, to the Word the form whereby the creature moves itself, to the Spirit the pull whereby God draws the creature to its end. So the Trinity describes the technical mechanics – better, the personal character – by which God does not rival but empowers the world. The Trinity tells how God does not compete with things but engages them, how God does not violate nature, but perfects it.

Any created thing is, by definition, *moved.* To call God Unmoved Mover does not place God merely at the end of a series of causes, the Last Push. Nor does it merely reverse the perspective, so that God attracts, although that is an improvement. Rather, it distinguishes God from creatures, *moved* movers. God alone is unmoved. Aquinas applies Aristotle's dictum, 'everything moved is moved by another,' strictly to *creatures.* This difference – God moves, creatures are moved – does not separate creatures from God, it relates them to God. Aquinas now *shares* God's internal relationality with creatures, because God places God-relatedness into creatures. Their very being is being God-moved.[7]

---

[7]   See Oliver, 'Trinity, Motion'.

When God moves creatures, God does not force or stop them. Because creatures are God-moved by definition, all the way down, God moves them most interiorly, or *'sweetly'* (*suaviter*, I.22.2). When God moves creatures, they move with the music. The more God moves them, the more they are themselves, the more they like it. The more God moves them, the more they move themselves. If to be a creature is to be God-moved, then to be *more* God-moved is to be more creaturely, not less. In creation, to be more creaturely is to receive more from the relations by which God is God, and the creature most capable of participating in those relations is human.

The doctrine that the human being is created in God's 'image' and 'likeness' reflect the missions of the persons in giving the human being a Trinity-welcoming structure, the image, and a Trinity-directed goal, the likeness (I.35). The *Summa* treats the image of God in humanity by name (I.35, *'de imagine'*) only within the discussion of the Trinity.[8] The image reflects God's creation of the human being as master of her own knowing and doing. Humans identify their good by reason (rather than by photo-sensitivity or hunger) and seek it by choosing (rather than by heliotropy or instinct). Thus they resemble God more than plants and animals do. God has truth and liberty absolutely and infinitely and can cross any limit to reach them. Human beings have truth and liberty historically and finitely and receive them by depending on God. The Son is God's Reason, Word, or Logos. The Spirit is God's Gift, Life, or Liberty. Because the persons interact, attributions shift; because they act inseparably toward creatures, attributions overlap. The Spirit leads into all truth, and the Son also liberates. But the Trinity so comprehends and pervades creation that Aquinas can sweepingly ascribe to the Son the knowledge in the knower, to the Spirit the love in the lover. The Trinity moves us as we know and love. It moves us, that is, as we do our own thing.

Our taking part in God's movement might remain distant and still. God might hold it at arm's length. God might have created us barely good enough, with nothing better in view. That would be creation without consummation, nature without glory. But Aquinas thinks God did not do that. God made creation for glory, good with more in store, dynamic and destined for friendship with God. God would draw us close. Human power – finite in freedom – could not cross the boundary between Creator and creature. But the Trinity's freedom acts across boundaries, love drawing us over. The Trinity is always coming to us – in

8 Victor Preller, *Divine Science and the Science of God: A Reformulation of Thomas Aquinas* (Princeton: Princeton University Press, 1967), 255.

itself it faces another – and in the mission of the persons, grace on grace, it does. Son and Spirit enter time to be with us and catch us up into their life with the Father. They do so not by any taking – this catching up is hardly rapture, and never rape – but by engaging precisely our ownmost knowing and loving. And they do so by a movement not new to the persons, who always face another, but to us, because their eternal movement reaches us in time.

Therefore the Son comes to share beatitude and the Spirit to share grace with us. Aquinas works out the implications of those missions far from the questions on the Trinity, in questions about the knowledge of Jesus and the grace of the New Law. The discussions seem technical unless you keep in mind that divine and human power do not compete, but the divine supports the human. How, in Jesus, do divine omniscience and human ignorance not conflict but coincide? (Over time, by teaching and learning.) How do divine freedom and human agency not rival but cooperate with one another? (Over time, through empowerment and habituation.) Those are the issues Thomas faces if it is to come true, in the *Summa*, that the Son is the known in the knower and the Spirit is the love in the lover.

The pattern remains dynamic all the way down, never reducing to bare possession – because it remains a *movement*. The human being could never image God by standing still and holding a pose. 'In order to designate the imperfection of the image in man, man is not said *to be* an image, but is said to be *to the image*, through which is signified a certain movement tending toward perfection' (I.35.2*ad*3). The image sets the human creature in God-drawn *motion* toward perfection. No accident that Aquinas stresses the same preposition here, '*to the image, ad* imaginem,' as in trinitarian relations: the persons look *toward* one another, and we image them in looking and loving toward them. The image provides structures after the pattern of the Son through which the Spirit engages us, so that we come to share God's own activity. The more we do our own thing, the more godlike God can make us, because God brings us into the trinitarian fellowship from the inside, most interiorly, by what God has given us as most our own. Indeed, this dynamism *just is* the fellowship, in advancing degrees always appropriate to the growing creature. This is an analogy of activity, or an *appropriate* equivocation.[9] We do not resemble God by *possessing* an image to hold still, but by *undergoing* the divine movement that the Son and Spirit make toward the Father – the same movement that they, of their own

---

9   Ibid., 243.

power, undertake. When we undergo what Son and Spirit undertake, God is *already* bringing us, by grace and by anticipation, into the trinitarian life. For the life of the Trinity does not keep to itself, but shares and spreads itself, by degrees fit for creatures. The Trinity makes time for those in time, to *move* them from knowledge to knowledge, from love to love, from glory to glory, in a way more their own than they are to themselves (since the Trinity created them for itself), and in a way appropriate to them, over time (since the Trinity created time as their way of stretching out knowledge and love). So the Trinity works, and the human being images its work, not by standing still and apart from each other like two mirrors, but in the very process whereby on one side Son and Spirit pursue their missions and on the other the human being conceives knowledge and love. 'The divine image is attained in man insofar as there is conceived in him a word derived from God's own knowing and a love derived therefrom. Therefore, the image of God is present in the mind insofar as the mind is *carried into God'* (*fertur in Deum,* I.93.8). The Son expresses the Father, and the human being receives it in her own, active knowing. The Holy Spirit creates *koinonia,* communion, and the human being receives it through her own, active loving. The moves by which the Trinity is and enjoys Itself extend, by grace, also to human beings.

The questions on grace bring together two springs of human acting, outer and inner. Thomas calls the outer principle 'law' (I-II.90 *proemium*), the inner 'virtue' (I-II.49 *proemium*). Law is a wise ruler's public prudence, *leading* the human being to the good (I-II.91.1). Virtue is a wise subject's interior disposition, *exercising* her powers for the good. In grace, the Holy Spirit writes the *law* on the *heart* (I-II.106.1 and 2*ad*3) to plant the 'external' principle inside. God's prudence becomes my desire, and God's desire is to sway, to move *suaviter,* courteously, delicately, sweetly, according to Wisdom 8:1, a verse the *Summa* drums upon to correct the misimpression that God and creatures must be at odds (I.22.2, I.103.8, I.109.2, I-II.110.2, II-II.23.2, II-II.165.1, III.44.4, III.46.9, III.55.6, III.60.4). God's suasion is a dance of love, full of courtesy and deference, even its raptures are nonviolent. In grace, the Holy Spirit works both *on* the human being externally, by law, and *in* the human being interiorly, by heart. Thus the Spirit does not isolate either pole of any contrast, but occupies both: inner and outer, law and habit, structure and flow, love drawn forth and love coming running. The Spirit is love in the lover, on earth as it is in heaven, in the heart as it is in the Trinity. That way the heart no longer languishes far from the Trinity, but is actually enjoying fellowship with it.

Knowing follows a similar pattern. The questions on the knowledges of Christ (III.9–12) bring together two ways of human knowing, learning and enjoying.[10] Thomas calls learning 'acquired knowledge' (III.9.4, III.12); enjoying he calls 'beatific vision' (III.9.2, III.10). Learning lays down a followable structure over time, stepwise, whereby reason takes apart and puts together. Beatitude sees everything at once with God's own joy. Learning and enjoying perfect two different skills, like practicing a piece of music on the piano and hearing it in the orchestra. Jesus hears the music – then acquires the skills of playing it on the piano.[11] Why? To teach it in a way we can make our own. We take the playing and listening as rivals by mistake. The question is malformed, how Jesus could both learn and already know. It imagines that the knowing whereby Jesus knows everything is the same as comes from learning. But it is not. The question also imagines that learning leads to knowing. Here it is the reverse. In some cases, we learn to play the music, to know what it sounds like. But here we have a teacher. Jesus doesn't need to play the music, to know what it sounds like: he needs to play the music, to teach it to us. Thus Jesus does a divine thing by human means and a human thing with a divine result. The two internalizations coincide: The Trinity both draws the creature into its own life, and the Trinity pervades or inhabits the creature.

---

[10] Actually four ways.
[11] This example differs from Aquinas', who compares beatitude to seeing rather than hearing, and takes the example of music as *scientia* in I.1.2 in a different direction.

Holy Spirit

GILLES EMERY OP

Staggeringly, the *Summa Theologiae* does not include a treatise on pneumatology properly speaking; but Thomas' teaching about the Holy Spirit is spread throughout all the major treatises of this work. So, to grasp properly the place and role of the Holy Spirit in the *Summa*, one must undertake a complete reading of the work, considering especially the sections dedicated to: the distinction of the divine persons, creation, anthropology and the image of God, the New Law and grace, Christian activity and the organization of the virtues, the gifts of the Holy Spirit, charisms, the incarnation of Christ, the life of Christ and his work of salvation, as well as the sacraments. One should also know the doctrinal structure of the *Summa* so as to appreciate its internal connections.[1]

SUBSISTENCE AND THE PERSONAL PROPERTY OF THE HOLY SPIRIT

In *ST* I.27–43, which expound the distinction of the divine persons, Thomas considers the Holy Spirit in the intratrinitarian life (God the Trinity 'in himself'), under the aspect of the subsistence and personal distinction of the Spirit. These questions presuppose and integrate the preceding questions (2 to 26), which treat 'what concerns the divine essence': since the divine person subsists in the divine essence, it is thus necessary to ascribe to the Holy Spirit all of the essential attributes common to the three persons. And since Thomas considers the divine person to be a 'subsisting relation' (I.29.4), the study of the Holy Spirit focuses first of all on the relation of origin that constitutes the person of the Holy Spirit, as well as on the procession that our mind conceives as the foundation of this relation.

---

[1] For a more developed insight, with bibliography, see Torrell, II, 153–224; Gilles Emery, *The Trinitarian Theology of Saint Thomas Aquinas* (Oxford: Oxford University Press, 2007), 62–9 and 219–97.

To offer an account of the personhood of the Holy Spirit, Thomas thus first seeks to make clear the nature of his procession. It concerns an 'immanent' procession, according to which the person that proceeds remains in his principle, or originator, being consubstantial with that principle. In order to make the Christian faith in the Holy Spirit clearer in the minds of believers, here Aquinas follows the 'way' of Augustine who looks to the analogy of love in the mind.[2] He shows that in God the procession of love is distinguished in reality from the generation of the Word, because generation takes place through the mode of a *similitude* (by definition, a word represents the thing known), while love proceeds as a dynamic *principle of impulsion* toward the being that is loved, whereby this beloved being is made present within the will of the lover (I.27.3–4). This makes it possible to manifest a real origin that gives rise to two real 'opposed' relations: spiration (the relation of the Father and the Son to the Holy Spirit) and procession (the relation of the Holy Spirit to the Father and the Son). The name 'procession' (*processio*) is employed here for lack of another word to designate the *personal relation* of the Holy Spirit, that is, the *relative property* that distinguishes and constitutes the person of the Holy Spirit.[3] According to his doctrine of subsisting relations, Thomas thus considers the Holy Spirit as the relation (relative property) of 'procession', insofar as this relation subsists in the divine being with which it is identical: 'The procession *is* the Holy Spirit' (I.40.1*ad*1). These explanations offer an account of the distinct personhood and the divine subsistence of the Holy Spirit.

The study of the personal property of the Holy Spirit, that is, the study of the person of the Holy Spirit, focuses on *three names* that signify him properly: 'Holy Spirit', 'Love', and 'Gift'. The theological explanation of the name 'Holy Spirit' makes use of the theme of love: 'For among corporeal beings the term "spirit" appears to denote a surge and a movement; we give the name *spiritus* to breath and to wind. Now it is distinctive of love that it moves and impels the will of the lover towards the beloved' (I.36.1*corp*). It is thus the study of the name 'Love' that will make it possible to grasp the profound sense of the name 'Holy Spirit'. Nevertheless, before treating the name 'Love', Aquinas shows that the Holy Spirit proceeds from the Father *and the Son*, the Father and the Son being *one single* principle of the Spirit.[4] The doctrine of relative opposition according to origin obliges the recognition that if he did not proceed

---

[2] Cf. I.32.10*obj*2.
[3] See I.28.4; I.32.2–3.
[4] I.36.2.3–4.

from the Son, the Spirit would not be distinguished personally from the Son (Sabellianism). For this reason, to Aquinas, who has multiplied arguments on this point and devoted long elaborations to the question, the Byzantine doctrine that the Spirit proceeds from the Father alone and not from the Son appears to be profoundly incomprehensible.[5] Aquinas recognizes the value of the formula, 'the Holy Spirit proceeds from the Father *through* the Son': this formula shows that it is from the Father that the Son receives the power to spirate the Holy Spirit along with him, in virtue of the one single 'power to breathe forth the Holy Spirit' that he has with the Father. Nevertheless, this formula necessarily implies the procession of the Holy Spirit from the Son, because every relation of distinction of divine persons reduces to a relation of origin. For Thomas, who finds this teaching in Scripture itself (not literally, but in the sense of Scripture, especially in John 16:14),[6] the doctrine of the procession of the Holy Spirit from the Father and the Son is necessary for the faith. At the basis of this doctrine we find the correspondence between the mission of the Holy Spirit and his eternal procession.[7] The Spirit is sent to the Church by the Father and the Son: this mission expresses and reflects, at the level of the economy, the eternal origin of the Holy Spirit from the Father and the Son.

Aquinas emphasizes the property of 'Love' in order to manifest the personal identity of the Spirit.[8] By 'love', in analogical fashion, he does not mean the act of loving but the 'affection' that is found in the human will at the beginning of the act of loving, that is, what 'moves and impels the will of the lover towards the beloved' (I.36.1*corp*). So, here love designates the 'imprint (*impressio*), so to speak, of the reality loved' that proceeds from the will and in the will when this will loves, that is, the affectionate surge according to which the beloved is present in a dynamic way in the will that loves (I.37.1).[9] The imprint that Thomas discerns at the origin of love, as impelling the will of the lover towards the beloved, makes it possible by analogy to manifest a fecund act of spiration in God who loves. This 'impression' or 'affection' possesses a relation of origin to the will from which and in which it proceeds: this relation of origin, distinct from the relation of the Word, makes it

---

[5] See Gilles Emery, *Trinity in Aquinas* (Ypsilanti: Sapientia Press, 2003), 209–69.

[6] See I.36.2*ad*1.

[7] See I.43.1.2, 7, and 8.

[8] See Yves Congar, *I Believe in the Holy Spirit* (London: G. Chapman, 1983), vol. 3, 116–27; Anthony Keaty, 'The Holy Spirit Proceeding as Mutual Love', *Angelicum* 77 (2000), 533–57.

[9] See also I-II.28.2*corp* and *ad*1.

possible to manifest the Holy Spirit as a distinct person in the Trinity. It is thus this 'imprint' that Aquinas signifies analogically, by a kind of concession of language (for lack of a more precise word), when he speaks of the Holy Spirit as Love in person. On this basis, Aquinas completes his explanation in taking up again the Augustinian theme of the Spirit as the mutual Love of the Father and the Son, which he reinterprets in a personal way. This theme of mutual Love does not signify the Spirit as an intermediary person between the Father and the Son but as *proceeding* from the Father and the Son who love each other with one same and single love (I.37.2). These explanations also clarify the work of the Holy Spirit in the economy of creation and grace. In effect, it is *by the same Love* that the Father and the Son love each other and their creatures. In summary: 'The Father and the Son love each other and us by the Holy Spirit, or Love proceeding' (I.37.2*corp*; cf. *ad*3).

It is also by means of Love that Aquinas shows that the Spirit is Gift, because 'love has the property of being the first gift' (I.38.2*corp*). As Love proceeding from Father and Son, the Holy Spirit is eternally inclined toward being given. This name *Gift* means the aptitude, congruence or disposition for being given to rational creatures: 'The name Gift conveys the idea of being givable' (I.38.1*corp*). When Aquinas considers the Spirit as Gift in person, he does not signify a Gift that the Father makes to the Son and vice versa, but he shows that in virtue of his property of Love, it belongs properly to the Spirit to be given by the Father and the Son to angels and men in grace, so that the saints 'possess' and 'enjoy' the Holy Spirit himself. This accounts for the gift of the Holy Spirit that occurs in the economy of grace. For that reason, the first thing requested in Christian prayer is the Holy Spirit, because he is the 'principal gift' (II-II.83.9*obj*3). This is also the reason why the Father and the Son are given to us in the Holy Spirit. And it is by way of this first Gift that all other gifts are bestowed (I.38.2*corp* and *ad*1).

Today it is common to criticize the understanding of the Holy Spirit as Love for offering a 'psychological speculation' detached from the economy of salvation that does not give enough weight to a starting point in the history of salvation.[10] Such a judgment, as far as concerns Aquinas, is not correct. On the one hand, the concepts of Love and Gift make it possible to highlight the economic action of the Holy Spirit from creation to final beatitude. Aquinas is not content to describe the action of the Holy Spirit but offers a genuine *economic*

---

[10] See Karl Rahner, *Foundations of Christian Faith: An Introduction to the Idea of Christianity* (New York: Seabury, 1978), 135.

doctrine of the Holy Spirit by means of two main themes, as we will show briefly below: firstly, the property of the Holy Spirit as Love and Gift; secondly, his procession *a Patre et Filio*, from the Father and the Son. On the other hand, the starting point of this doctrine is closely linked to the economy of salvation. It is through charity that the Holy Spirit dwells in the saints: 'In it (namely, charity) the Holy Spirit is given specially, as in his proper likeness' (I-II.70.3*corp*). The charity poured out by the Holy Spirit (Rom. 5:5) is 'a participation in the Holy Spirit' (II-II.23.3*ad*3), that is, a participation in the sanctifying Love of the Father and the Son.[11] Thus, the personal property of the Spirit is manifested to us through his action, in particular through the charity with which the Spirit is given in person. Aquinas' reflection on the Holy Spirit as Love and Gift is tied from its very starting point to the economy. We touch here on a difficulty of method. The *Summa Theologiae*'s exposition follows a movement that goes from the first and enlightening reality (the eternal personhood of the Spirit) toward the second and enlightened reality (the creative and sanctifying action of the Spirit). In other words, although Aquinas *presupposes* the path of our discovery that begins with the revelation of the Holy Spirit in the economy, he follows rather an order of exposition that conforms to the reality itself, that is, an order that begins with the eternal personhood of the Spirit in order to then manifest his action and effects. Thomas' teaching on the Holy Spirit as Love is not detached from the economy but is, on the contrary, intimately linked to it.

The mission of the Spirit

The mission of the Spirit consists in his eternal procession *a Patre et Filio*, as well as in a new mode of presence in the just through grace. Aquinas first examines the 'invisible mission', that is, the sending of the Holy Spirit into souls. The mission of the Son and that of the Holy Spirit (the two missions are inseparable) are made possible through sanctifying grace, but they are formally accomplished through the operative gifts of wisdom (mission of the Son) and charity (mission of the Spirit: 'enkindling of the affection'[12]), which are the formal effects of sanctifying grace and are always given with this grace. Aquinas consistently explains the sanctifying action of the Spirit through charity and the *inclination of the will* that this charity procures. The sending of the Holy Spirit produces an *operative conformation* of souls to the Holy Spirit himself: the souls

---

[11] See II-II.24.2*corp*; II-II.24.7*corp*.
[12] See I.43.5*ad*3.

of the saints are conformed to uncreated Love. 'Since the Holy Spirit is Love, the likening (*assimilatio*) of the soul to the Holy Spirit occurs through the gift of charity, and so the Holy Spirit's mission is accounted for by reason of charity' (I.43.5*ad*2). The created gift of charity *disposes* one to receive the uncreated person of the Holy Spirit, who comes to dwell in the saints.[13] This is divinization. The same teaching is found in anthropology in the doctrine of the *imago Dei*. The image of God finds its fulfilment (image of grace and glory) when the human being is likened to the Trinity. This assimilation is brought about through 'the word conceived from the knowledge of God' (conformation of the soul to the divine Word), and through 'the love flowing from this word' (conformation to the Holy Spirit as Love).[14]

The 'visible missions' of the Holy Spirit reveal his invisible mission through tangible signs (I.43.7). Thomas counts four 'visible missions' of the Holy Spirit. The two visible missions made to Christ (under the sign of a dove at Christ's Baptism and under the sign of a luminous cloud at the Transfiguration) manifest the fullness of the Spirit who indwells the humanity of Christ from the first instant of his conception. They show Christ as the giver of grace 'by spiritual regeneration' and by his teaching. The two visible missions made to the apostles (the Spirit breathed on the apostles by the risen Jesus in John 20 and given to them in the form of 'tongues of fire' in Acts 2) manifest the abundance of grace given to the apostles to 'plant the Church' through the sacraments and the proclamation of the word (I.43.7*ad*6), that is, to pass the Holy Spirit on to others (III.72.2*ad*1). Thus the Holy Spirit is the source of Jesus' human activity and the source of ecclesial activity. He guarantees the continuity between Jesus and the Church. The explanation of the 'visible missions' of the Holy Spirit rests on his personal property of Love and Gift. The Holy Spirit is sent visibly in signs that manifest his identity as *sanctifying Gift* in person, because he is Love. While the Son is sent in the flesh insofar as he is 'the author of sanctification' (the giver of the Spirit), the Spirit is sent insofar as he is 'the Gift of sanctification' (the Gift itself: I.43.7*corp*). We encounter here the correspondence between the eternal property of the Spirit and his action in the economy as well as the soteriological import of the doctrine of the procession *a Filio*: the Holy Spirit is the Gift poured forth by Christ to sanctify the Church and lead her to the Father.

---

[13] See I.43.3*corp*., *ad*1, and *ad*2. See Anna N. Williams, *The Ground of Union: Deification in Aquinas and Palamas* (Oxford: Oxford University Press, 1999).

[14] See I.93.8*corp*.

CREATION AND PROVIDENCE

The action of the Holy Spirit is not exercised only in the order of grace but first of all in the order of nature. The Holy Spirit is the 'reason' for all the effects that God accomplishes by his loving will. 'God the Father wrought the creature through his Word, the Son, and through his Love, the Holy Spirit' (I.45.6corp).The Holy Spirit acts in conformity with his personal property, that is, insofar as he is the Love of the Father and the Son. This personal and proper dimension of the action of the Spirit concerns his eternal relation to the Father and the Son. As it is *proper* to the Holy Spirit to be the Love proceeding from the Father and the Son, so does it fall to him *properly* to be the one through whom the Father and the Son act in the world.[15] This proper mode of acting grounds the appropriation of the works that manifest divine love, to the Holy Spirit. These works are common to the whole Trinity; they are not proper to the Holy Spirit, but they are appropriated to him by reason of their affinity to his personal property of Love proceeding from the Father and the Son. That is why the creation and government of creatures (the exercise of Providence) are appropriated to the Holy Spirit.[16] Following Augustine, Aquinas discerns the personal presence of the Holy Spirit in the 'breath of God' that hovered over the waters (Gen. 1:2) and in the pleasure with which God considered the goodness of his works (Gen. 1: 'and God saw that it was good').[17] So, to know the Holy Spirit is 'necessary' in order to have a right view of the creation of things: 'For by maintaining that there is in God the procession of Love, we show that he made creatures, not because he needed them, nor because of any reason outside him, but from love of his own goodness' (I.32.1ad3).

THE GIFTS OF THE HOLY SPIRIT

The structure of virtues developed by Aquinas accords a central place to the seven gifts of the Holy Spirit: understanding, knowledge, fear, wisdom, counsel, piety, and fortitude. Aquinas expounds the role of these gifts in the *Prima Secundae* (q68) and then studies them individually in the *Secunda Secundae* where he associates each gift with a theological or cardinal virtue. The gifts of the Holy Spirit are thus at the heart of the

---

[15] See Gilles Emery, *Trinity, Church, and the Human Person: Thomistic Essays* (Naples, FL: Sapientia Press, 2007), 115–53.

[16] See I.45.6ad2.

[17] See I.74.3ad3 and ad4.

architecture of the virtues. They perfect the human soul that is formed by the theological virtues (these theological virtues 'unite man to the Holy Spirit who moves him'), and they are the principle of the Christian exercise of the moral virtues (I-II.68.8). 'The Gifts of the Holy Spirit are *habitus* by which man is perfected so as to obey the Holy Spirit readily' (I-II.68.3*corp*). These gifts, which remain in eternal life, are stable dispositions for following 'the prompting and moving of the Holy Spirit' (*instinctus et motio Spiritus Sancti*); and since human beings need this superior 'instinct' of the Holy Spirit in order to reach their ultimate and supernatural end, these gifts are necessary for salvation.[18] They are a 'participated likeness in the Holy Spirit' (II-II.9.1*ad*1). Between the Holy Spirit and the human being, they establish a coordination similar to the communion of wills that forms a friendship, a communion so close that it becomes connatural. These gifts, both speculative and practical, represent the receptive face of Christian activity under the motion of the Holy Spirit such that the deeds of graced human beings are effects of the Holy Spirit at work in them and order these saints to eternal life.

THE NEW LAW AND GRACE

The Holy Spirit is at the heart of Christian life. Aquinas explains this especially when he treats of the New Law: 'That which is preponderant (*potissimum*) in the law of the New Testament is the grace of the Holy Spirit, given through faith in Christ' (I-II.106.1*corp*). This law is engraved on hearts interiorly by the Holy Spirit. All other aspects of the New Law are elements which either 'dispose us for the grace of the Holy Spirit', or 'pertain to the use of that grace' (ibid.). Since the New Law is inseparably the 'law of Christ' and the 'law of the Holy Spirit', Aquinas challenged Joachimism, which was waiting for a new age of the Spirit: 'We are not to look forward to some future state in which the grace of the Holy Spirit will be received more perfectly than it has been until now, above all by the Apostles, who received the first fruits of the Spirit, that is to say, received it prior to others in time and more abundantly too' (I-II.106.4*corp*).[19]

Aquinas constantly attributes grace to the Holy Spirit, because he is Love and Gift in person. 'The justification of the unrighteous takes place through the grace of the Holy Spirit justifying us' (I-II.113.7*sed contra*). Acting at the depths of the human being whose creator he is, the Holy

---

[18] See I-II.68.2*corp*, and 3*ad*1.
[19] This mention of the apostles recalls the 'visible missions' of the Holy Spirit.

Spirit arouses the free welcome of his grace, as well as the free mode of human acts animated by this grace under the motion of the same Holy Spirit. The law of the Spirit is the 'law of perfect freedom' (I-II.108.1ad2). The active presence of the Holy Spirit is also the fundamental reason for merit. If one considers human good works insofar as they originate from free will, there can be no equivalence with eternal life, but only some fittingness (*congruitas*). 'But if we consider the meritorious work in so far as it proceeds from the grace of the Holy Spirit, then it is meritorious of eternal life by equivalence (*ex condigno*). For now the value of the merit is assessed by the power of the Holy Spirit moving us to eternal life, according to John 4:14: *It will become in him a spring of water welling up into eternal life*' (I-II.114.3corp). Aquinas clarifies: 'By grace the Holy Spirit dwells in man; and the Holy Spirit is the sufficient cause of eternal life, and so he is called *the pledge of our inheritance* (Eph. 1:14)' (I-II.114.3ad3). The charity of the Holy Spirit, which is always given with grace, is the *root* of a holy action. The grace of the Holy Spirit is intrinsically bound to faith in Christ: 'No one has ever had the grace of the Holy Spirit except by faith in Christ, whether this faith be explicit or implicit' (I-II.106.1ad3).

CHARITY

Charity is found at the very heart of the Holy Spirit's presence in the economy. The theological virtue of charity is a created gift that is given through the Holy Spirit, that is put into action by a motion of the Holy Spirit, and that is 'a *participation* in the Holy Spirit' (II-II.23.3ad3),[20] that is, a participation in the Love of the Father and the Son (II-II.24.2corp). Charity, which conforms saints to the Holy Spirit and disposes one to receive the Holy Spirit, has the Holy Spirit himself as its uncreated model. 'Through charity, the Holy Spirit dwells in us' (II-II.24.11corp)[21] Thus the charity by which human beings love God and their neighbor is a participation in the personal property of the Holy Spirit; this participation is inseparable from the indwelling of the Holy Spirit in person. Concerning charity, Aquinas also constantly repeats that sins are forgiven by the Holy Spirit insofar as he is the Love and Gift of the Father and the Son.[22] By his charity, the Spirit liberates from sin and procures the freedom of the children of God.[23] Aquinas associates the virtue of charity with

[20] See also II-II.24.5ad3; II-II.24.7corp.
[21] See also III.7.13corp.
[22] See, for instance, III.3.8ad3.
[23] See, for instance, II-II.183.4ad1.

the gift of wisdom. This gift of the Holy Spirit procures a 'connaturality with divine things' that comes from charity (II-II.45.2*corp*), and it joins its beneficiaries to Christ: 'The Holy Spirit is called the *Spirit of adoption* because we receive from him the likeness of the natural Son who is Wisdom Begotten' (II-II.45.6*ad1*). Adoptive filiation, which is a participation in the divine filiation of Christ, is procured 'through the Holy Spirit, as the Love of the Father and the Son' or 'as the Bond common to the Father and the Son' (III.3.5*ad2*). Adoptive filiation – becoming children of God by grace – is appropriated 'to the Holy Spirit as the person who imparts to us the likeness of the model [the Son]' (III.23.2*ad3*).

CHARISMS

Charisms (*gratiae gratis datae*) are procured through the Holy Spirit for the benefit and building up of the Church. 'The Holy Spirit sufficiently provides the Church with all that is needful for salvation' (II-II.178.1*corp*). Since the Holy Spirit is Love and Gift, 'charisms are attributed to the Holy Spirit as their first principle' (II-II.172.2*ad2*). The place of the Holy Spirit is especially underscored in the study of the charisms of prophecy and speech. The Spirit of truth lifts up the prophets' minds and enables them to see hidden mysteries and communicate them by oral and written word. Just as he inspires the authors of sacred Scripture, the Holy Spirit also guides the interpreters of Scripture, 'because the Scriptures are expounded by the same Spirit from whom they originated' (II-II.176.2*obj4*.). The same goes for the preaching of the gospel: 'The Holy Spirit uses the tongue of a man [the Christian preacher] as a sort of instrument, and it is the same Spirit who completes the work inwardly [in the hearers]' (II-II.177.1*corp*). Aquinas notes also that the unwritten apostolic traditions (such as the veneration of icons) come from 'the inward instinct of the Holy Spirit' (III.25.3*ad4*).

CHRIST AND HIS SPIRIT

The Holy Spirit is omnipresent in the christology of the *Tertia Pars*. Without entering into the details, we must observe the structural placement of the Holy Spirit in Aquinas' christology. Firstly, the Holy Spirit forms Christ's body, because he is the Love of the Father and the Son (the incarnation is sovereign manifestation of the love and grace of God), and because he is the Spirit of holiness and filiation: through the Spirit 'Christ was conceived in holiness to be the natural Son of God' (III.32.1*corp*).

Secondly, the Holy Spirit fills the human soul of Christ completely from the first instant of his conception (III.39.2*corp*). The Father gave the Spirit to the Son 'without measure' (John 3:34).[24] Aquinas' commentary on Matthew makes it very clear: 'In Christ, God poured out not only "from his Spirit" (*de Spiritu*) but his whole Spirit (*totum Spiritum effudit*)..., and that [he did] insofar as Christ possesses the condition of a servant.'[25] According to Aquinas, Christ's soul thus possesses an infinite habitual grace and is endowed with the fullness of virtues and charisms as well as with all the gifts of the Holy Spirit: 'The soul of Christ was perfectly moved by the Holy Spirit' (III.7.5*corp*).[26] Under this aspect, Christ in his humanity is considered as the *beneficiary* of the Spirit. The Spirit is the principle of Christ's habitual grace, and he dwells in fullness in Christ's soul through charity (III.7.13*corp*). This action of the Spirit in Christ is distinct from the hypostatic union. The fullness of grace by which the soul of Christ was sanctified (invisible mission of the Holy Spirit in Christ) was derived from the very union of the Word (mission of the Son: hypostatic union).[27] The 'visible missions' of the Spirit to Christ (Baptism and Transfiguration) manifest the fullness of the Spirit with whom Christ was filled from his conception, so that Christ might communicate his grace to others through his teaching and through the mysteries of his life in the flesh (III.39 and III.45). The motion and charity of the Holy Spirit in Christ's humanity are the reason for the salvific value of Christ's human action: 'The passion of Christ derives its efficacy from the Holy Spirit: *The blood of Christ, who through the Holy Spirit offered himself to God* (Heb 9:14)' (III.66.12*obj*3).[28]

Thirdly, Christ pours out the Holy Spirit with the instrumental collaboration of his humanity filled with grace and perfected by the Holy Spirit (III.8.1*ad*1). Under this third aspect, Christ in his divinity *and* in his blessed humanity is the *giver* of the Spirit: 'The Holy Spirit is dispensed by Christ to all others' (III.39.6*obj*4).

THE SACRAMENTS OF THE CHURCH

The sacraments apply the redemptive work of Christ to believers. On one hand, the sacraments have their efficacy from Christ 'and from the

---

[24] See III.7.11*ad*1.

[25] *Super Evangelium S. Matthaei lectura*, cap12, lect1.

[26] See III.7.1–2, 7–12.

[27] See III.7.13*corp* and III.34.1*corp*.

[28] Although this statement is found in an objection, it is Aquinas' own thought. See *Super Epistolam ad Hebraeos lectura*, cap9 lect3.

Holy Spirit, as their first cause'.[29] Aquinas does not neglect to recall this aspect as regards the Eucharist: transubstantiation takes place through the power of Christ and the action of the Holy Spirit (III.78.4ad1).[30] On the other hand, the sacraments communicate the grace of the Holy Spirit that is the grace of Christ himself. The central role of the Holy Spirit is particularly present in the teaching on confirmation, since this sacrament (which Aquinas closely associates with the visible mission of the Spirit at Pentecost), confers 'the plenitude of the Holy Spirit' (III.72). At the center and summit of the sacramental system, the Eucharist reinforces and strengthens the unity of the Church in charity. Now, this unity is precisely the work of the Holy Spirit who sanctifies the Church. Through the charity that he pours out, the Holy Spirit unites the faithful to Christ and the Trinity, and in so doing is the source of the mutual union of the members of Christ (the communion of the saints).[31] The Holy Spirit is in some way the 'heart' of the Church (III.8.1ad3). Faith in the Church is included in faith in the Holy Spirit (II-II.1.9ad5).

ESCHATOLOGY

The *Summa Theologiae* was not finished and does not include the treatise on the resurrection and immortal life that Aquinas announces in the prologue to the *Tertia Pars*. The eschatological dimension of the Holy Spirit's action is nevertheless present in the preceding questions. One can observe this particularly in the discussions of grace and merit, on the theological virtues and on the gifts of the Holy Spirit, which order human beings directly to eternal life. In conforming the faithful to Christ (adoptive filiation), the Holy Spirit is the life-giving principle of souls, by grace in this world and by glory in eternal life. He is also the principle of the glorification of the body, that is, the source of the body's glory that is a bursting forth of the soul's glory.[32] Aquinas sees the announcement of this especially in Christ's Transfiguration where the Spirit is manifested (III.45.4ad2), as well as in the Eucharist that gives life to souls and bodies. The believers who 'spiritually eat' the Body of Christ become participants in the Holy Spirit; the Holy Spirit enables them to prepare themselves actively for the resurrection that he will

---

[29] III.66.11*corp* and *ad1*. The statement made here concerns baptism, but it applies to all the sacraments.
[30] See also III.82.5*obj2* and *sed contra*.
[31] See II-II.183.2*ad3*; III.68.9*ad2*; III.82.6*ad3*.
[32] See III.8.2*corp*; III.25.6*corp*.

confer on them when he joins them fully to the life of glory and the resurrection of Christ.[33]

CONCLUSION

The huge range of the Holy Spirit's action in the *ST* shows that for Aquinas it is hardly possible to put together a treatise on pneumatology as distinct from the rest of theology. In effect, the Holy Spirit's action is intrinsically tied to the action of the Father and the work of Christ: to speak of the Holy Spirit is to speak of the Father and the Son, of their mutual love and their love for their creatures, that is, to display Christian teaching (*Sacra Doctrina*) in its full extent. In other words, the doctrine of the Holy Spirit does not constitute a 'chapter set apart' in the exposition of the Christian mysteries but rather plays an integrating role in the teaching on the Father's plan and its accomplishment in Christ. On the one hand, having prepared humanity for Christ, the Spirit fills Christ's sacred humanity so that Christ's human life reveals God and actively assists in the gift of salvation. On the other hand, Christ saves the human race through the Spirit that he communicates in order to lead men to the Father. Aquinas offers an account of the economic activity of the Holy Spirit by means of two main themes that are directly linked to his speculative manifestation of the eternal person of the Spirit: (1) the Spirit is Love and Gift in person; (2) the Spirit leads to the Father and the Son from whom he proceeds eternally and by whom he is given. The work of the Spirit, in the *ST*, is constantly seen as the work of Love who is the Gift of the Father and the Son.

---

[33] See *Super Epistolam ad Romanos*, cap8 lect2 and lect3; *Super Evangelium S. Ioannis lectura*, cap6 lect7.

Creation

KATHRYN TANNER

In accord with the *exitus-reditus* scheme of going out from and coming back to God that organizes the whole work, Thomas' treatment of creation occurs in the first part of the *Summa*, that part devoted primarily to the one and triune God and secondarily to creatures as they proceed from and so find their beginning in God (I.2*prol*). Given this context for the discussion of creation, the interpreter of Thomas is well advised to avoid isolated attention to the questions in this part that have creation as their explicit subject matter (questions 45–9). These questions are properly understood only in light of the treatment of God that came before.

Especially important for understanding God's creation of the world are of course the earlier questions that concern God's general operations, irrespective of their object, that is, whether they are employed in the creation of the world or not: the knowledge, will, and power of God (14–26). But equally important are the questions that concern the existence and nature of God (2–11) and the particular properties of the persons of the Trinity (33–43).

Consider, first of all, one major issue raised in the former block of questions (2–11): the question of divine transcendence, God's difference from everything else, the heart of Aquinas' effort in these questions to tell us something about God by telling us what God is not, by excluding from God the manners of existence characteristic of everything else. Two ways in particular that Aquinas makes the point have a significant bearing on creation. God is different from everything else, Aquinas says in I.3.4, because existence and essence are identical in God; and because, Aquinas goes on to tell us in I.3.5, God is not contained in a genus, and is not a kind of thing. The two claims are closely related.

One might take the former claim to be saying simply that a metaphysical distinction between essence and existence, which holds everywhere else, is absent in God. Thomas, following Arabic commentators on Aristotle such as Avicenna, believes that what gives something its essence, what makes it the sort of something it is – its form – does not bring existence with it; like matter, which is actualized only by receiving a form, form too must be actualized, by receiving an act of existence. To define God as existence itself as Aquinas does is just to say that God does not receive existence: God *is* that existence and does not have it from another. And for that very reason essence and existence are not distinct in God but identical. The difference between God and everything else appears in this way to be a difference in kind: God is simple – in this respect as in every other – in contrast to everything else that is metaphysically composite.

But given that in the very next article Aquinas says God is not a kind of thing, Aquinas must mean something more. If one thought of God as a particular sort of thing, one might think the claim that God's essence is existence simply means God has an essence of some kind or other that does not require actualization, an essence existing of itself. If God is not a kind of thing at all, however, the claim that God's essence is God's existence makes the stronger point that God has no essence at all like other things: being itself, to be, the very act of being, is instead all that God's essence is. God is not defined by any particular form or set of forms that might allow for a simple contrast in kind between God and the world, but is set off from everything else by identification with what is not a form at all – being itself.

In making such a claim Aquinas would be going along with a very common strategy in the history of Christian theology for distinguishing God from everything else: God does not have God's predicates but is them; and therefore the meaning of those predicates can be exhaustively identified with God. I may be righteous in the sense of having righteousness as a quality, but righteousness cannot be identified with me as it can with God who alone therefore is properly termed righteousness itself. Aquinas is innovative here by substituting for a quality that which is not a quality at all – being itself. And in so doing – by saying that God is being itself – he suggests that God transcends all differences in genus (I.4.3*ad*2).

The primary import of this discussion for an understanding of God's creation of the world is methodological or procedural. Negatively, God's transcendence so defined becomes a limit that must not crossed, a simple test for any proposed account of God's creation. The account of creation must not, for example, suggest that God is contained within a genus by making God one agent among others of a distinctive kind or by implying that divinity is a general quality or class term in which other things can share in different degrees. But more positively, this discussion directs the way that one can incorporate accounts of ordinary productive causes when attempting to come up with a theologically elaborated interpretation of God's creation of the world. No one such account should have a *prima facie* privilege over another in such an interpretation; God's creation of the world is not to be overly closely associated with a single kind of causality. Thomas is in this way freed to mine any and all such accounts of ordinary productive causes for their usefulness, as far as it goes, in elaborating how God creates the world. Besides not being a particular kind of thing, God is beyond differences among kinds and therefore the mutual exclusion of what are ordinarily thought to be contrasting kinds of productive cause also need not be respected: the account of creation can incorporate what would ordinarily be thought of as opposed forms of causality. When utilized for theological purposes the ordinary implications of all accounts of productive causality need to be severely modified and in doing so they become compatible with one another, patient of incorporation within a single, complex treatment of God's creative activity.

In what follows, I would like to show how this works with respect to the two major forms of productive causality that Aquinas, following very common historical trends within Christian theology, incorporates within his treatment of creation: natural causality, operating according to what a thing is, and artisan causality, operating through intelligence and will. Exhausting the field of productive agents for Aquinas are, on the one hand, natural causes which produce things according to the respective forms that constitute their natures (which they cannot do anything about), and, on the other hand, artisan causes which produce things according to intellectual forms they freely devise and act upon – that is, according to the ideas of whatever those things are that they then decide to make. Natural causality is predominant in Neo-Platonic influenced Christian treatments of God's creation of the world by emanation; the world comes forth from God in the way light streams from a source or the way water bubbles from a spring. Artisan causality figures prominently in Christian treatments of God's creation with a more personal cast: God enters into a loving relationship with the world by freely willing its good in creating it. Despite the ease with which one might identify Aquinas with the latter perspective, he masterfully combines the two, as we will see.

Our previous discussion of God's transcendence in the early questions of the *Summa* bears directly on this matter of what Thomas himself does with ordinary accounts of productive causality and is therefore not merely of methodological interest: these early questions are one place where natural causality, in particular, seems to be coming to the fore in Aquinas' account of how things find their source in God. As Aquinas makes clear in succeeding questions, God is beyond every genus by including them all and for that reason may be the source of all: all other things seem to be declensions, processions in some imperfect fashion, from what God is perfectly and primordially.

If God does not exist after any particular mode or manner but is being itself, this is to say, Thomas affirms in question 4, that God includes all such manners and modes of existence in a preeminent, perfect way. The argument here depends in part simply on the account of God as being itself. The being of being itself is not a minimal condition for having all other perfections, a simple prerequisite for added perfections, in the way one might think one cannot also have life or be wise if one does not first exist. The being of being itself is instead an intensive perfection inclusive of all others (I.4.2ad3). 'Every perfection is a perfection of existing, for it is the manner in which a thing exists that determines the manner of its perfection. No perfection can therefore be lacking to God,' if God simply exists by being being itself (I.4.2*corp*). In the same way that heat if it could subsist on its own – and not simply imperfectly and partially in hot things – would contain within itself the full perfection of heat, so being itself by subsisting on its own in God contains the full perfection of being found impartially and imperfectly in all existing things (ibid.).

But the reasoning here is also based on attributing a certain productive causality to God. All the excellences of every genus under which creatures fall are to be found in God in the most perfect possible fashion, because God is the effective cause of those excellences of every genus in ways suggestive of a natural cause such as the sun. Like the sun, God gives rise to diverse qualities and substances by already possessing all of them in a higher and more perfect manner within the unity of God's own nature. With Dionysius, the primary early Christian proponent of some form of emanationism, Thomas can therefore say, God is not 'this and not that' but 'everything, inasmuch as he is everything's cause' (ibid.). The perfections of everything must pre-exist in God in a higher manner since God gives rise to them.

Because God contains them all in supreme fashion, all the perfections possessed by created things 'flow out' from God (I.6.2*corp*). God's perfection is so full and replete that it radiates or spills out in the creation of inferior things, which come to be by sharing in that way in what God is. This would seem to be the clear implication of the fact that

Aquinas consistently talks in these early questions about the productive agency of God in terms of natural causes, particularly the sun. In creating them, God shares with or 'communicates' to others in a variety of ways, and therefore imperfectly, what God already is in supreme fashion, the closest example being the sun that diffuses itself – its light and heat – in generating things different from itself (I.4.3corp). Aquinas will not hesitate therefore to use the language of emanation explicitly in later questions: 'the emanation of the whole of being from the universal cause which is God; it is this emanation that we designate by the term "creation"' (I.45.1corp, translation modified).

In keeping with an emanation viewpoint, the efficient or productive causality of God, especially in these early questions, brings with it a stress on God as the formal and final cause of creatures. As Aquinas' fourth way of proving God's existence in particular suggests (I.2.2), it seems here that God produces creatures by being their formal cause, by being in the most perfect fashion what they are. As the hottest of all things – fire – produces the less hot, that supreme perfection that all things resemble is for that very reason their cause. Things other than God come forth from God insofar as, and in order to be, some kind of reflection or resemblance of what God is. And because what they are exists most perfectly in God, God is the final cause of the creation of those things, that for the sake of which they exist. The end or object of God's creation of things is the communication of what God already is most perfectly. The end of those things – the reason they exist – is to share in what already exists in the most desirable fashion in the one who creates them (see I.6.1).

The great virtue of an emanation account of God's creation of the world is how easily it suggests the universal reach of God's agency as a creator. Everything unrolls from God because God contains everything to come in some virtual fashion. God includes what everything else is in the most perfect imaginable fashion and therefore everything that exists in imperfect fashion must come forth from God. If God is being itself, understood in the fulsome and replete way that we have discussed, then 'everything that is at all real is from God.' In much the way all hot things must get their heat from what is hot by nature – fire – all the different ways of sharing in existence that comprise the created world have their source in the 'one first being who simply *is* in the fullest sense of the word' (I.44.1corp).

This universality of extent is in keeping with the character of natural causes which provide the model for emanation. Natural causes need not presume for their operations a multiplicity of independent causal factors, thereby restricting the range or extent of what it is about their effects that they are responsible for. They do not necessarily work on anything, for example. Instead they can give off something proceeding wholly from themselves, in the way light streams forth from a light source. Their productive influence can therefore extend to the whole of their effects. Considering God's agency along the same lines suggests that God is not one agent among others responsible for some part or aspect of world – say, the rational arrangement of matter that has some other source or none at all. Every dimension of things owes its existence to God. 'To be the cause of things in that they are beings is to be the cause of all that belongs to their existence in any way whatsoever, not merely as regards what they are like by the properties which shape them or what kind they are by their substantial forms' (I.44.2*corp*).

Emanation accounts of God as a productive agent often, however, suggest that God's production of things is not equally direct in all cases. God directly produces only the highest rung of being most like itself, with lower beings proceeding from that being, in like fashion, on down a successive chain of beings until the lowest rung is reached. Aquinas in I.65.3 explicitly modifies an emanation account to avoid this suggestion by insisting that God alone creates whatever is created. Productive causes that are themselves created by God do not have the capacity to create other things, because they must always presuppose something they haven't created – in every case, the being that all creatures must receive from God (I.65.3; I.45.5*corp* and *ad*1). Only God has the power to bring something into being without any presuppositions – to bring it to be from nothing, in short – because that manner of making requires infinite power (I.65.3*ad*3; I.45.5*ad*3). Given the fact that nothing else has the capacity to create, everything included in an emanation account, whatever its ontological character, however high or low on the ontological scale, must have its existence immediately from God. The proof of God's omnipotence is that God's creative action requires no intermediary instruments or powers to reach even those things most distant from, because most unlike, God; lacking all intermediaries God's agency must be in direct contact with everything, whatever its character (I.8.1*ad*3).

An emanation account suggests God's productive agency is not equally direct in all cases because the natural causes that are its model imply a certain restriction of scope. Natural causes act according to that single form that makes them what they are, and therefore they usually have the capacity to produce only one thing like themselves: fire gives off only heat; the sun produces nothing but light, and so on (I.47.1*ad*1). Although natural causes can give rise to the whole of what they produce, the sort of things that they are able to produce is often therefore limited. And rather severely so: they can produce only one kind of thing. While a help in explaining the way all the dimensions of any particular thing are created by God, natural causality is therefore not as useful for making clear that the causality of God covers the many kinds of things in the world in all their specific differences from one another, that 'the causality of God, who is the first efficient cause, covers all existing things, immortal and mortal alike, and not only their specific principles but also the source of their singularity' (I.22.2*corp*). Multiplicity of kind and individual particularity within an emanation account of God's creation of the world would seem to require a multiplicity of creative agents: below God there must be others.

The fact that God does not have a particular nature to restrict God's operations is one way around this problem. God is not a kind of thing but an all-encompassing perfection, and therefore God does not give rise to one kind of thing but to all of them. Indeed, God's nature could not be effectively communicated to creatures if they were to take only a single form. Because God includes within the unity of his undivided nature all sorts of different perfections, only a multiplicity of creatures of different sorts could hope to do justice to it (I.47.1).

By suggesting things come out of God, an emanation account of creation might also not seem properly to respect the difference between God and the world. The world is not some quasi-divine entity – a part of God, becoming itself through simple division of God's nature, or some thinned out version of God, God's own light dimmed as it recedes from its origin, the torrential stream of water as it exists at its source in God having become a trickle the further it proceeds from God. Aquinas' efforts to bring non-univocal causes under the rubric of natural ones in the early questions of the *Summa* would be one way around this (I.4). Natural causes communicate themselves but what is communicated does not always exist in the way it exists in its cause, as is the case, for example, in biological reproduction where a human being gives rise to another human being of the same nature as itself. Natural causes, like the sun, contain in a higher way in themselves what they communicate to others; so much so as to be unlike their effects for all their effects' resemblance to them (I.4.2). Cause and effect in the case of natural causes are not necessarily then of the same sort, even when the effect bears some likeness to the cause. Cause and effect may be of the same species, as when a human being produces another human being. But, as in the case of the sun's generation of other things by its heat, cause and effect may be of different species (the sun doesn't give rise to another sun) and therefore share only a generic resemblance. So, if there is an agent that is not contained in any genus – God – its effects will still more distantly reproduce the form of the agent; the likeness will be that much more remote – neither a specific nor a generic resemblance (I.4.3).

It is hard to see however how the character of God's own agency would not bleed onto the character of the world if God's creation of the world is understood along the lines of a natural cause. Natural causes like the sun always act to bring about their effects unless hindered or weakened internally. Absent such restrictions on God's agency, God's acting in the way a natural cause does would suggest that the world is as eternal and necessary as God is. God is always successfully acting to communicate God's nature to other things and therefore those other things must always exist. God's creative powers are necessary to God; God cannot be without them. And since God's acting according to those powers cannot be hindered, the effects of God's agency would be necessary too. This shared character between God's own agency and the world would in effect restrict the scope of God's agency. God could not create a world that is as a whole contingent nor one that contains contingent things or contingent causes within it. God could not create a world that began or ceased to be, as the teachings of the church, following Genesis 1 affirm.

Again, the all-inclusive perfection of God's own nature helps here. Because the perfection of God's own nature is complete, God has no need to create anything else. Since God already has all perfection, God, unlike all created natural causes, is not acting to acquire any perfection, and therefore God's action in creating the world is by definition a perfectly free one (I.44.4*corp* and *ad*1). God already contains everything that might be gained from creating the world; indeed the world itself is always less than what God already is. Self-sufficiency is suggested for all God's natural diffusiveness; God can perfectly well make do with himself. And therefore God's creation of the world becomes an act of majestically disinterested largesse.

God's diffusion of Godself may be something God naturally does – a necessity of God's nature in that sense – while remaining an optional matter in another, in that God retains the full perfection of God's nature without it. Indeed, the two things go together here. It is because God is so full that God naturally diffuses Godself. But God is freely self-diffusive for the same reason – because God is already so full that what God creates by self-diffusion can contribute nothing to that fullness.

The primary way, however, that Aquinas avoids all these problems with the emanation account of God's productive agency – all suggestions of indirection, restriction of scope, and shared character between God's agency and the world – is to talk about God's productive agency in terms of an artisan cause. God is still communicating or diffusing to the world the perfection of God's own nature in creating it, but now God is said to do so through knowledge and will (I.19.2). More specifically, God knows all the different ways that the perfection of God's own nature could be shared by creatures (I.14.6) and wills to bring into existence all those particular manners or modes of God's own perfection that God forms the intention of creating (I.14.8). In short, the knowledge of God is the cause of things when the will is joined to it (I.14.9ad3).

The form that artisan causes follow when acting is not the form of their natures but the idea of what they want to make and therefore the causality of an artisan is not limited by its nature. An artisan cause is not constrained by its own singularity of nature to produce only one sort of thing. Conceiving a complex idea of what it would like to produce, it can instead produce many different things. If God's productive agency is like that of an artisan, the intention that God forms in creating the world can be as complex as God wants it to be, and therefore God's causal agency can extend to everything in the world without any of the conceptual difficulties an emanation scheme suggests for God's creation of multiplicity.

For the same reason, what an artisan cause chooses to make need not correspond to its own nature, in a way that suggests only indirect influence, at best, over what is not like itself. A human being as a natural cause can only reproduce itself; human beings give birth only to human beings. But working according to an idea of what it would like to make, the same human being can choose to produce effects different from itself – a house, a book, a cloned mouse, and so on. Unlike an emanation scheme, an artisan account of God's causality therefore does not suggest a progressively indirect, sequential production of things by God. It does not suggest, specifically, that God brings about only that one thing most like itself which has the task, in turn, of creating things less like God. God instead can directly intend to bring about the world in all its differences from God's own being.

Artisan causality does allow for a certain indirection in God's very intention for some things in the world. In much the way a created artisan cause produces things sequentially, deciding to produce other things on account of things produced earlier, one might imagine that God creates one thing and then chooses to create something more on that basis, given the fact of what already exists in virtue of God's prior intention.

God would will to create some things only because of a previous intention to create others; to that extent God's will for the former would be indirect, mediated by a more direct intention for the latter. To get around this, Thomas maintains that God creates the world according to a single, all encompassing idea of what God would like to create; within that single intention things are ordered to one another, but God does not intend to produce one thing because of another (I.19.5). God's will for everything is in this way equally direct.

Because God creates the world by forming an idea of the sort of world God wants to create, the character of God's own agency is not transferred as a matter of course to the character of the world created, as we saw to be the case when considering God's agency in terms of natural causality. The content of the intention is what determines the character of what an artisan cause produces; not the character of its own agency. What the will intends rather than the character of the willing is what the object produced turns out to be like. So even though God's will is itself eternal, what God wills could very well be a world that comes in and out of existence. God's eternal will just means, let's say, that whatever God wills God always wills, but that fact doesn't stop what God wills from being a world that comes in and out of existence. In that case God's eternal will is just for a world of that sort. The 'always' of God's willing does not translate here into an 'always' of the world's existence for the same reason that my always wanting to receive a pony on my twelfth birthday does not mean, were I to get my way, that I always have one. As Aquinas makes the point in I.46.1 *ad* 10: 'Given the action, the effect follows according to the thrust of the form which is the principle of action. In causes that act through will the concept ... [is] such an operative form. Therefore an eternal effect does not result from God's eternal action, but only such a one as God has willed, namely an effect possessing existence after non-existence.'

The same thing would seem to hold for necessity: God's will for something might be itself necessary and yet what God wills might be a world contingent as a whole, meaning by that a world that does not have to exist, and containing at least some specifically contingent things (and meaning by that things that do not necessarily exist, given their own existence or that of other things). At least that lack of a corresponding necessity between the will itself and what it wills holds for created agents operating by knowledge and will: I may have to will something, say, because of the intensity of my own desires. But that does not mean that what I want is something that has a necessity to match the character of my own intention. I may indeed have to will

– because that is the only thing that would satisfy my desires – something I know and want because of its very contingent, non-necessitated character – say, the free love of another. One complicating factor for saying the same thing about God is that God's own agency is necessarily efficacious: God's will is always fulfilled (I.19.6). God's intentions bring about their effects in necessary fashion; if God, unlike me, wants something to happen – say, the love of another – it has to happen. Aquinas, however, does not think this is a serious problem, in and of itself, since what God wants extends to the mode in which it is to happen: 'Since God's will is of all causes the most effective, the consequence is that not only those things come about which God wills, but also that they come about in the manner that God wills them' (I.19.8). What God wants necessarily happens therefore in just the way God wants it to. If God wants the world to be contingent, then the world necessarily exists in that contingent manner. A more serious problem arises, however, if (following the analogy with human willing that I provided) God has to will what God wills. The world as a whole simply cannot be contingent if God has to will that it exist. It must exist in the way it exists if God must will it to be that way and God's will is necessarily efficacious. The simple fact that God acts according to an idea and not by nature is therefore not enough to ensure the non-necessary character of an infallibly effective cause: God's will for the world must also not be necessary.

Aquinas therefore insists that God's will for the world is free: God is not necessitated to choose to create the world. God is free not only in a way compatible with natural or necessary self-diffusiveness (as we saw before), but God is self-diffusive by free choice and therefore God need not be self-diffusive at all. The argument here is an intensified version of the one we looked at earlier which depended upon God's self-sufficient perfection: the world is not necessary for God's perfection if that perfection is all inclusive, and therefore God does not have to will its existence in willing God's own good. The will is required to will only what is necessary for its own happiness; anything without a necessary relation to that happiness is a matter of free choice, because one can be happy without it (I.82.2). But God includes within God's own nature the complete perfection of all goods; therefore God necessarily wills only himself. Nothing short of God is required for God's happiness and therefore God's decision to create any of that is free and not necessitated. God's will is 'necessarily related to his own goodness, which is its proper objective. Hence he wills his own good necessarily.' But 'since God's goodness subsists and is complete independently of other things, and they add no fulfillment to him, there is no absolute need for him to will them' (I.19.3).

Because it is free in this way, God's creation of the world becomes a loving act of unconstrained generosity for what is other than God. Without any intention of profiting himself, God freely chooses to give creatures a share in what God is (I.19.2). What God intends is for creatures to enjoy in the limited, imperfect ways appropriate to them the goodness of God's own perfect being. The object of God's action is God himself as something now sharable beyond God's own existence and nature. God's intent, when diffusing God's own goodness in creating the world, is only to give and never to acquire (I.44.4).

This free generosity of God in creating the world can easily find expression in trinitarian terms. The Trinity, Thomas thinks, simply enforces the point. 'To know the divine persons [gives us] a right view of the creation of things. For by maintaining that God made everything through his Word we avoid the error of those who held that God's nature compelled him to create things. By affirming that there is in him the procession of Love we show that he made creatures, not because he needed them nor because of any reason outside himself, but from love of his own goodness' (I.32.1*ad*3).

Moreover, if God creates by way of knowledge and a loving will, the formal and final causal dimensions of God's productive agency that we looked at before can also be a given an explicitly trinitarian treatment. God is the formal cause of all things because the ideas of all those things reside in the divine wisdom (I.44.2). God in knowing himself in his own Word knows all the different ways in which his own perfections could be shared by created things. God therefore produces all things through his own Word which contains in itself the exemplars of everything created. 'The name the 'Word' connotes a reference to creatures. The reason: in knowing himself God knows every creature ... [B]ecause by the one act he understands both himself and all else, his single Word expresses not only the Father but creatures as well. Moreover ... the Word of God is purely expressive of what is in God the Father, but he is both expressive and causative with respect to creatures. This is why we have in the Psalm, 'He spoke and they were made,' that is, the causal plan of all God's works is contained in the Word' (I.34.3).

And in loving himself God loves all created things. The Spirit proceeds in the manner of the love by which God loves his own goodness, and it is out of that love for God's own goodness that God extends a share in it to others. '[E]ven as the Father utters himself and every creature by the Word he begets, inasmuch as the Word begotten completely expresses the Father and every creature, so also he loves himself and every creature by the Holy Spirit, inasmuch as the Holy Spirit proceeds as Love for the primal goodness, the motive of the Father's loving himself and every creature. Obviously, too, the Word and the Love proceeding include ... a reference to creation, inasmuch as the divine truth and goodness are the grounds of God's knowing and loving any creature' (I.37.2*ad*3).

All the persons of the Trinity together, in virtue of their common essence, create the world but the Word and the Holy Spirit provide the reasons for it to the extent they may be identified with the knowledge and loving will of God, respectively. The Word, because it includes the ideas in accordance with which God creates the world, is the reason why the world exists the way it does. And the Holy Spirit provides the motive: love, as that is expressed in the communication of his own perfection to another. Artisan causality is what makes this sort of trinitarian discussion of the creation of the world possible: 'causality concerning the creation ... answers to the meaning of the [processions] each Person implies. For ... God is the cause of things through his mind and will, like [a maker of artifacts]. An [artisan] works through an idea conceived in his mind and through love in his will bent on something. In like manner God the Father wrought the creature through his Word, the Son, and through his Love, the Holy Ghost. And from this point of view, keeping in mind the essential attributes of knowing and willing, the [processions] of the divine Persons can be as [reasons of the production of creatures]' (I.45.6, translation modified).

For all that it has going for it, however, artisan causality has certain distinct disadvantages for talking about God's creation of the world. Aquinas therefore rather severely modifies its usual implications in ways often suggestive of the natural causality favoured in an emanation account. Thus, artisan causes work on materials given to them; God instead creates the whole of what exists including the material that constitutes it (I.44.2). Rather than presupposing what is given a form that either alters its accidental properties or turns it into something new, as in artisan causality, creation involves 'emanation from the universal source of being' and therefore not even the matter worked on is left out (I.44.2*ad*1, translation modified).

Artisan causes use tools that make their own contribution to the character of what is produced. These also have to be excluded from the idea of God's creating like an artisan since God creates the whole of what exists. Indeed, all means of creation must be excluded if God's creation of the world is always immediate and perfectly direct. Unlike artisan causes, God must therefore be creating the world apart from any intervening process or movement at all. In order to produce something, a human being needs to do something: make some decision and then take some steps to realize it. But God's knowledge and will are unchangeable (I.14.15; and I.19.7) and therefore God does not have to come to a decision to create the world: if that is God's intention, it is always God's intention. Nor need God put some process into motion in order to bring about the existence of anything according to that intention; created things are never in the process of being created by God in the way artisan causality suggests. Creation is instead an instantaneous happening in the way 'there is no interval or time between becoming lit and being lit' (I.45.2ad3). God produces things without movement (I.45.3) in much the way that fire and sunlight produce their effects immediately, without their having to do anything else but be themselves. Absent all movement or change, creation simply means a relation of direct dependence upon God as the source for one's whole being.

Contrary, finally, to what artisan causality suggests, this relation of dependence holds for however long a creature exists. After a building is made it does not continue to depend for its existence upon the one who made it. For this reason artisan causality suggests things exist independently of God once they have been created. Aquinas explicitly brings natural causes back into the picture to correct this impression. 'Now since it is God's nature to exist, he it must be who properly causes existence in creatures, just as it is fire itself [that] sets other things on fire. And God is causing this effect in things not just when they begin to exist, but all the time they are maintained in existence, just as the sun is lighting up the atmosphere all the time the atmosphere remains lit' (I.8.1). Creatures do not have the capacity to retain what they get from God in the way it exists in God; they therefore remain dependent upon God for it. They are in this respect like air, which lacks the capacity to retain light in the way the sun does, the principle of light. Just as air loses its illumination when the sun ceases to shine, so every creature would sink back into nothingness if God ceased granting existence to it (I.104.1).

Providence

DAVID BURRELL CSC

> God not only gives things their form, but He also preserves them in existence, and applies them to act, and is moreover the end of every action (I.105.5ad3).

Nothing exhibits the centrality of creation in Aquinas so much as his reflections on providence. Indeed, his insistence that *conservation* and *creation* are but notionally different sets the stage for his treatment of divine providence, forcibly reminding us that whenever God acts, God acts as creator. And that axiomatic statement will help loosen many a conundrum regarding 'divine acting in the world'. Furthermore, Aquinas' ongoing discussion with Avicenna (Ibn Sina) and with Moses Maimonides on the subject of God's knowledge of and care for individuals in the world will tease out further clarifications of the meaning of *providence* for his creation-centered philosophical theology. The corollary that God's knowing in these recondite matters is best modeled on 'practical knowing' will point us to the unique 'distinction' of creator from creation as well as their singular relation, with crucial implications regarding prayer. So attending to these metaphysical peculiarities will help to explicate a *providence* at the very heart of – rather than merely 'compatible with' – creaturely *freedom*.

In the course of his explicit treatment of *providence* in I.103–5, Aquinas will employ key terms signaling his reliance on the initial questions of the *Summa* on God and creation (I.2–49), notably 'good', 'cause of being', 'participation'. Rather than try to tell us 'why God lets bad things happen to good people', Aquinas plunges us into a rich biblical-metaphysical field of force, to equip us to neutralise our spontaneous construal of the relation between creator and creatures, which Maimonides reminds us will inevitably lead into idolatry.[1] I say

---

[1] Moses Maimonides, *Guide of the Perplexed*, tr. Michael Freidländer (New York: Dover, 1956), 1.58.

'biblical-metaphysical', for a proper understanding of *providence* will require an active appreciation of 'the distinction' of creator from creature, which Robert Sokolowski shows to be implicit in revelation, precisely in order to construe their *sui generis* relation appropriately.[2] So rather than march readers through those key questions of the *Summa*, I suggest that they peruse them first (I.103–5), to appreciate the elegant way in which Aquinas expounds what can be vexatious issues, thereby allowing this commentary to expose the structure of that elegance. In that way, certain apparently preposterous assertions, like that of the epigraph to this treatment, can be shown to follow as a matter of course from his overall 'biblical-metaphysical' scheme.

GOD ACTS AS CREATOR

Aquinas opens the *Summa Theologiae* by reminding the reader of its subject: 'God, as the beginning and end of all things, and especially of rational creatures' (I.1*prol*). This simple identification places him firmly in the field of force of the 'Abrahamic faiths', as his continuing interlocution with Moses Maimonides and with Avicenna will imply.[3] The 'god' who is the subject of this inquiry is the free creator of the universe. Otherwise, there would be no way for us to identify 'god' as the One we worship, God, primarily in gratitude for our very existence. This may sound redundant, yet as Wittgenstein reminded us, the most reliable guidance that discourse can have in these reaches will be grammatical (or 'analytic') in nature.[4] Whoever neglects this animadversion can easily be seduced by the grammar of our ordinary language into thinking that the 'god' of which we speak is but another item within our universe. Indeed, examples abound, so Aquinas presciently heads them off from the outset. John Inglis has also reminded us how the Cathars' propensity to adopt a bipolar (good/evil) principle, reminiscent of Augustine's flirtation with the Manichees, also motivated Aquinas to employ his philosophical skills to bolster the presumption of revelation that the God we worship is One.[5] As history testifies, mere inculturation into

---

[2] Robert Sokolowski, *The God of Faith and Reason* (Notre Dame: University of Notre Dame Press, 1982).

[3] See my *Knowing the Unknowable God: Ibn-Sina, Maimonides, Aquinas* (Notre Dame: University of Notre Dame Press, 1986)

[4] That 'essence is expressed by grammar' is the leitmotif of *Philosophical Investigations*, tr. G. E. M. Anscombe (Oxford: Basil Blackwell, 1959), cf. §371.

[5] John Inglis, 'Emanation in Historical Context: Aquinas and the Dominican Response to the Cathars', *Dionysius* 17 (1999), 95–128.

'monotheism' has never sufficed to neutralize the pagan lure to reduce the Abrahamic God to 'god'.

The opening formula, introducing God 'as the beginning and end of all things, and especially of rational creatures', is initially reinforced by question two: 'whether god exists?', which locates this God firmly within the human quest to ascertain whether the universe is intelligible.[6] Indeed, if we take what have often been considered (in an isolated manner) as 'proofs', we find them to be exemplary probings exhibiting a schematic structure: any attempt to offer a complete explanation for the universe will prove to be deficient in one way or another, so each example will at best point to a free creator who surpasses any ordinary explanatory scheme, any recognizable notion of *cause*.[7] And though all this will not be spelled out until Aquinas explicitly treats creation (I.44–46), an alert reader will recognize that the very notion of free creation suffuses the entire *Summa*, so much so that Josef Pieper has contended that Aquinas' title should be 'Thomas *a creatore*'.[8] Yet as this treatment will explicitly undergird his understanding of *providence*, it will also corroborate the 'grammatical' exposition of 'God' in I.3–11, in the wake of question two. For as we shall see, none other than an eternal divinity, identified uniquely as the One whose very essence is to-be (I.3.4), could be creator in the comprehensive and intentional manner demanded by Abrahamic revelations. This complex assertion offers a sterling example of the way Aquinas invokes metaphysical theorems to delineate the coherence of revelation. Let us consider it piecemeal.

Careful to distinguish 'eternal' from 'everlasting', Aquinas reserves *eternity* for God alone (I.10.3). For God's 'singularity', if you will, cannot be assured by setting God apart from everything else in the normal way by which individuals are identified, but it can effectively be assured by a unique attribution: the One whose very essence is to-be. There can be only one such, but as Plotinus reminded us, this One cannot be identified as 'one' in the ordinary way. For to do so would be to follow the contours of ordinary grammar to make of this One an item in the universe it creates. Or in Islamic terms, to 'associate' things with God

---

[6] Denys Turner, *Faith, Reason and the Existence of God* (Cambridge: Cambridge University Press, 2004); see my review in *Modern Theology* 21 (2005), 686–88.

[7] Nicholas Lash, 'Ideology, metaphor and analogy', in Brian Hebblethwaite and Stewart Sutherland (eds), *Philosophical Frontiers of Christian Theology: Essays Presented to D. M. MacKinnon* (Cambridge: Cambridge University Press, 1982), 68–94, and Fergus Kerr OP, *After Aquinas: Versions of Thomism* (Oxford: Blackwell, 2002).

[8] Josef Pieper, 'The Negative Element in the Philosophy of St Thomas', in Idem, *The Silence of St Thomas: Three Essays* (New York: Pantheon, 1957), 47–67.

by 'associating' God with things. That God is available solely as creator entails what Robert Sokolowski has deftly called 'the distinction' of creator from creatures, a 'distinction' unlike any we know between creatures. We shall have occasion to explore this in greater detail, but for now let us simply register how the 'formal features' by which Aquinas uniquely identifies divinity (in I.3–11) follow from, as well as support, what God must be to be creator of all-that-is.[9] Put in terms of *eternity*, it could not be the case that the creator of temporal beings would itself be temporal, for it would have to initiate temporality itself in originating temporal beings. Why? Because the mode of originating which is creating must clarify the ambiguity in the phrase: 'bringing things to be', since an artist or artisan can also be said to bring something to be by making it. Yet in creating *ex nihilo*, the One creating something brings about the very conditions of that thing's existing as the thing it is. Nor can we avoid such a convoluted construction to distinguish *creating* from *making*, as we may also use the grammatical reduplication: in creating something, God makes it to be the case that it exists, where 'making it to be the case that' alludes to 'bringing about the very conditions of that thing's existing as the thing it is'; while ordinary *making* operates within those conditions. By having recourse to such reduplicative expressions, we can remind ourselves that what brings something to be (in this radical way) cannot be of the same genre as the things brought about. So while temporal beings are generated by their predecessors, they can only be created by One who is eternal, and not only in the minimal sense of atemporal, but in the maximal sense, as well: the One who enjoys the 'full possession of unending life', since the creator is the source of anything's existing (I.10.1).

Yet we have no way of simply asserting that the creator must be *eternal*, as though 'eternal' were a property one could assert of anything.[10] For as Aquinas notes, *eternity* is proper to God; that is, we have no way of understanding an object to be eternal other than as a 'formal feature' of divinity. For that One whose very essence is to-be cannot be measured by time, since change is in no way germane to it. And even more, what makes that to be the case is the metaphysical status which attends the uniqueness of divinity: the One whose essence is to-be.

---

[9] For a consideration of the shaping 'divine attributes' (I.3–11) as 'formal features', see my *Aquinas: God and Action* (London: Routledge & Kegan Paul, 1979), with credit to Edy Zemach, 'Wittgenstein's Philosophy of the Mystical', *Review of Metaphysics* 18 (1964), 38–57.

[10] David Braine, *The Reality of Time and The Existence of God* (Oxford: Clarendon Press, 1988); see my review in *Faith and Philosophy* 13 (1996), 163–78.

For that One alone could be the requisite 'cause of being' demanded by the Abrahamic assertion of free creator presupposing nothing, a status which also confers maximal *eternity* to God, since 'existing is measured, not by time, but by eternity' (I.10.2), as the 'full possession of unending life'. Aquinas is appropriately silent regarding the manner of the creator's causing things to be, yet it should be clear that none of Aristotle's four causes will suffice, for the most likely – efficient cause – presupposes something on which to work. The most salient feature of God's causing things to be, however, is that it takes no time; there can be no process involved (I.45.2ad3). And for a closer look at such a modality of causation, we are led to his commentary on the *Liber de causis*, an Islamic adaptation of Proclus, which veers towards *emanation*.[11] Yet in the *Summa* itself, after having rendered the Avicennian scheme of mediated emanation redundant, Aquinas gives a lapidary definition of creation as 'the emanation of all things from the universal cause of being' (I.45.1). So apparently he could find no better metaphor than *emanating* for *creating*, once logic forced him to eschew a direct description of this *sui generis* activity bereft of any process. So we have a prime example of Aquinas' judicious recourse to metaphor in order to assert what cannot properly be articulated, to remind us that what cannot be asserted in a properly constructed statement can nonetheless be asserted metaphorically.[12] Aristotle had introduced a similar strategy in searching for the way to affirm grammatically an act of understanding which culminates inquiry by an activity which itself requires no time. Yet as we shall see, while God's eternity is a necessary condition for removing any competition between the acting of creatures and the creator, it is not sufficient to do so; that will have to await a richer articulation of divine creating activity.

THE CREATOR KNOWS INDIVIDUAL CREATURES BY 'PRACTICAL KNOWING'

Now since the activity of creating asserted in the Abrahamic traditions is free, it must be intentional, yet discussions of the appropriate mode of knowing have notoriously generated conundrums, especially with regard to God's knowing 'what will happen'; or as some innocently put

---

[11] See my 'Aquinas' Appropriation of the *Liber de causis* to Articulate the Creator as Cause-of-Being,' in Fergus Kerr (ed.), *Contemplating Aquinas* (London: SCM, 2003), 55–74.

[12] Olivier-Thomas Venard OP, *Littérature et théologie: une saison en enfer* (Geneva: Ad Solem, 2002); see my review in *The Thomist* 68/4 (2004), 651–3.

it: 'the future', as though that were an identifiable item. To avoid such conundrums, Aquinas takes a page from Avicenna's treatment of these matters, to differentiate the knowing that creates radically from creaturely knowing, since things themselves derive from the creator's knowing them, whereas our knowledge derives from those very things (I.14.8 especially *ad*3). In other words, the paradigm for a knowledge which creates will be taken from practical knowing, as differentiated from speculative knowing. Yet in fact, our use of 'know' invariably suggests what Aristotle calls 'speculative knowing', while practical knowing seldom employs the term 'know', settling rather for 'plan', organize', and so on.[13] In another idiom, speculative knowing must be 'knowing that' while practical knowing is more 'knowing how'. So knowing that something is the case need not be part of God's knowing what God is doing in creating something. And even though a plethora of 'knowings-that' will doubtless contribute to the works of human artisans or planners, the decisive doing or making will not itself be one of those. And to make matters worse, contemporary philosophers can hardly be faulted for trying to model what we call (following Aristotle) 'practical knowing' on some form of 'speculative knowing' plus motor skills, since the notion itself quite resists further analysis. Artists or planners are understandably reticent to try to articulate what goes into a stunning product or a superb conference. They rightly say: here it is; if I could talk about it I would not have had to do it! As Aristotle remarks, what is required in each case is a specific know-how, or 'virtue', which can only be developed through apprenticeship.

So the best we can say is that God knows what God is doing in creating. This radical contrast with 'knowing that' can be illustrated by a notorious thesis of al-Ghazali, exquisitely delineated by Eric Ormsby: that the world God creates is 'the best possible'.[14] Ghazali's assertion, which Ormsby traces through the Islamic commentary tradition, and later formulates succinctly, is regularly confused with Leibniz' contention that 'God creates the best of all possible worlds'. Indeed, contemporary philosophers will inevitably take both formulations to presume that we can inspect an array of 'possible worlds' to determine

---

[13] For a probing of Aquinas on 'practical knowing', see my *Freedom and Creation in Three Traditions* (Notre Dame: University of Notre Dame Press, 1993).

[14] Eric Ormsby, *Theodicy in Islamic Thought: The Dispute over al-Ghazâli's 'Best of all Possible Worlds'* (Princeton: Princeton University Press, 1984) and his later clarification, 'Creation in Time in Islamic Thought with Special Reference to al-Ghazali', in David Burrell and Bernard McGinn (eds), *God and Creation* (Notre Dame: University of Notre Dame Press, 1990), 246–64.

which one is best; whereas Ghazali's way of putting it is a flat-out faith assertion: since God creates it, we must insist that the world-as-it-is is the 'best possible', as we have no criterion allowing us to assess putative alternatives. Divine wisdom is inscrutable, so even if our understanding of the freedom with which God creates will lead us to think of God's having alternatives, neither those 'alternatives' nor the criterion of 'divine choice' lie within our purview. So it is pointless to think that our model of human freedom, which presupposes deliberation, might offer some insight into free creation.[15] Instead, we must say that God knows what God is doing in creating the universe, and in so acting is guided by divine wisdom. That is why Aquinas will insist that God's knowing in creating, while practical in mode, is also speculative, 'for as much as He sees all things other than Himself in Himself, and He knows Himself speculatively; so in the speculative knowledge of Himself, he possesses both speculative and practical knowledge of all other things' (I.14.16ad2). But of course, Aquinas here stretches Aristotle's notion of 'speculative knowledge' which, humanly speaking, will derive from things, to a divine example of pure knowing-by-identity, a knowing which will exemplify the divine wisdom which guides creating. This will be more explicitly exemplified, in his *Commentary on John*, by the 'Word, through whom the universe is made', to show that a 'proper understanding of creation' will require the revelation of God's triunity (I.32.1ad3).[16] Correlatively, as we have noted, Aquinas will invoke the *Liber de Causis* to formulate this activity which escapes comparison with human knowing and acting.

Aquinas' move to 'practical knowing' as the master-metaphor for creating helps him corroborate Maimonides' criticism of Avicenna, adding some precisions of his own, and yet in the end veering more closely to Maimonides' position than his own explicit criticism of 'rabbi Moses' suggests. In criticizing 'the philosophers', often identified as Aristotle but usually referring to Avicenna, Maimonides baulked at the suggestion that the One who originates the universe could not know individuals, as though it were beneath the dignity of that One (*Guide*, 3.16–18, 20). What is at stake, of course, is providence. And Maimonides' objections offered a variant on those of al-Ghazali, who cited this contention as one

---

[15] On God's singular freedom in creating, see James Ross, 'Real Freedom', in Jeff Jordan and Daniel Howard-Snyder (eds), *Faith, Freedom and Rationality* (New York: Rowan and Littlefield, 1996), 89–117.

[16] See my 'Creation in St. Thomas Aquinas's *Super Evangelium Joannis*', in Michael Dauphinais and Matthew Levering (eds), *Reading John with St Thomas Aquinas* (Washington, DC: Catholic University of America Press, 2005), 115–26.

of the three reasons for considering 'the philosophers' to be unbelievers.[17] Yet in explicating his own position on God's attending to individuals, Maimonides registers what he calls a 'personal opinion': that it may
be that the creator attends to individual human beings yet not to other
creatures. Aquinas objects to this 'personal opinion' of Maimonides,
noting that (in general) God's knowledge extends to the reaches of God's
power, and certainly the creator's power extends to each individual
(I.14.8). Yet on the Aristotelian perspective which Aquinas certainly
espouses for natural things, individual subhuman animals have no destiny apart from serving to continue the species, so that providence as we
understand it – attending to each individual – need not be part of God's
knowledge of them. But the general point has been made: knowing individuals cannot be below the dignity of the creator, or any personal relation with God would be impossible. Moreover, so long as the model
for divine knowing is practical rather than speculative, such knowing
terminates in individual actions of making or of doing, so is oriented to
individuals.

But does not the paradigm of practical knowing raise the even more
threatening image of God making happen what one thinks to be the
result of one's own free action? As the epigraph relates: 'God not only
gives things their form, but also preserves them in existence, and applies
them to act.' (I.105.5*ad*3). So must we not say that God makes me do
what I do? Now any such direct causal implication will be blocked, of
course, by our earlier remarks that a 'cause of being' *makes it to be the
case that* what happens happens. Or as Barry Miller suggests, 'God sees
to it that (my action happens)', where the parentheses signal indirect
discourse to forbid any direct competition.[18] Indeed, to fail to employ
this strategy is to inadvertently consider the creator to be a creature. Yet
we observe these grammatical tactics because we have recognized it to
be axiomatic that whenever God acts, God acts as the creator acts; and
that creating *ex nihilo* cannot be assimilated to a process, so we cannot
entertain the question: how? Indeed, anyone asking '*how* it is that God
makes it to be the case that what happens happens?' would show they
had overlooked 'the distinction' in failing to grasp the need for the very
grammatical strategies we deliberately introduced. The same would be
true were anyone to describe God's providential guidance as 'controlling'

[17] For Ghazali's critique, see Sherman Jackson, *On the Boundaries of Theological
Tolerance in Islam* (Karachi: Oxford University Press, 2002).
[18] Barry Miller, *A Most Unlikely God* (Notre Dame: University of Notre Dame Press,
1996); *From Existence to God* (London: Routledge, 1992); *The Fullness of Being*
(Notre Dame: University of Notre Dame Press, 2002).

what happens, for that very expression presumes the 'cause of being' to be a cause within the world of causes. So the manner of providence must escape us, yet some may find it unseemly to assert what we cannot properly formulate or even imagine. That may be the motivation of those who find themselves constrained to speak of creaturely and creating activity in a competitive mode, yet anyone who asserts free creation ought to see that the act of creating can in no way interfere with actions of a creature. Given their utterly distinct *modus operandi*, they simply cannot compete. Yet non-interference hardly bespeaks distance here; in fact, creatures can only act by virtue of the sustaining activity of the creator, which in bestowing the very to-be of things [*esse*] 'is more intimate to them [than anything else]' (I.8.1).

Harm Goris has traced the inner connection of providence with creation in the careful manner which exemplifies Utrecht scholarship on Aquinas, so anyone fascinated with the intricacies of Aquinas' deft maneuvering will find them amply exposed there.[19] Moreover, this axial study is complemented by Rudi te Velde's exploration of the role which *participation* plays in Aquinas' philosophical theology, as he tries to articulate the link between creator and creatures, having emphasized 'the distinction'.[20] Leaving a fuller treatment to these studies, I nonetheless call attention to the obvious here: the strategic moves which Aquinas makes will appear to be devious legerdemain to readers whose philosophical *ethos* studiously avoids attention to analogous discourse, and especially that form of discourse which Aquinas elucidates in his treatise on the 'divine names' (I.13). There he expounds the linguistic implications of his careful metaphysical delineation of God as object of study in the axial questions 3–13, whose import he had clearly articulated in the prologue to this entire set of questions:

> because we cannot know what God is, but what God is not; we cannot consider how God is, but rather how God is not [*quia de Deo scire non possumus quid sit, sed quid non sit, non possumus considerare de Deo quomodo sit, sed potius quomodo non sit*] (I.3prol).

So those averse to 'negative theology' have been duly warned that they will find the *Summa*'s treatment of divinity unintelligible, yet anyone so averse will also tend to pay little or no attention to its axial presumption: free creation. Correlatively, anyone inattentive to the implications of free creation will also prove tone-deaf to linguistic strategies suffusing

---

[19] Harm Goris, *Free Creatures of an Eternal God* (Leuven: Peeters, 1996).
[20] Rudi te Velde, *Substantiality and Participation in Aquinas* (Leiden: Brill, 1996).

the *Summa*, only a few of which we have noted, yet which Olivier-Thomas Venard OP amply illustrates in his exposition of Aquinas' 'poetics,' the linguistic complement to Harm Goris' commentary.[21] So with those references to further reading, let us now consider the practical implications of this exposition of divine providence

HOW CREATURES RELATE TO THE CREATOR

We have seen how introducing a free creator into Hellenic philosophy demands that we learn how to speak of the One from whom all things freely flow *not* as an item in the universe – even an 'infinite' such item. For this One is indeed 'beyond being' as we know beings, suggesting a secret link between Aquinas and Plotinus in a domain where they are regularly contrasted.[22] As a result, our relation to this One who speaks the universe through the divine Word cannot be on a par with our relation to any other thing. Many a philosophical appropriation of Aquinas has failed to appreciate this crucial corollary of the 'distinction' enshrined in Aquinas' analogical semantics, which we can find eloquently expressed in Meister Eckhart's arresting paradoxes. Furthermore, a recent set of reflections on Aquinas in relation to Shankara offers that quality of 'mutual illumination' which intercultural perspectives can often bring to familiar formulations. Sara Grant's 1997 Teape lectures, subtitled 'Confessions of a Non-Dualist Christian', offer a narrative of the journey of this Religious of the Sacred Heart to India and her subsequent life of study and prayer in the context of a Hindu-Christian ashram in Pune.[23] Pondering the manner in which Aquinas characterizes creation in things as a *relation* to their source, she observes how malleable is the maverick Aristotelian category of *relation*, so that this relation (of creatures to their creator) can hardly be assimilated to relations among creatures themselves – lest we fail to distinguish creator from creatures. Her prolonged study of Shankara, with the subtle language he introduces of 'nonduality', helps her to see what many Thomistic commentators have missed: how Aquinas' insistence that the *esse* of creatures is an *esse-ad-creatorem*, their to-be is to-be-towards-the-creator, utterly transforms Aristotle's world, where the hallmark of *substance* is to 'exist in

---

[21] *La langue des choses: fondements théologiques de la métaphysique* (Geneva: Ad Solem, 2004).

[22] Lloyd Gerson, *Plotinus* (London: Routledge, 1997).

[23] Sara Grant, *Towards an Alternative Theology: Confessions of a Non-Dualist Christian* (Bangalore: Asian Trading Corporation, 1991; University of Notre Dame Press Press, 2001), 35–36.

itself'. Yet ironically enough, the reason why we may miss Aquinas' transformation of Aristotle is that the relation is so *sui generis* that it does not alienate the creature from itself. Since God cannot be 'other' in the sense in which different things must be other – as God remains the very source of anything's being, anything's to-be [*esse*] is at once a participation in the very being of God – so 'more intimate to things than anything else' (I.8.1*corp*).

So we begin to see how a proper articulation of the mystery of creation structures any 'spiritual' discourse regarding our intentional relations to our creator. For if Jews, Christians, or Muslims think they are praying to 'someone else' in addressing their praise and thanksgiving to God, they will be distracting themselves from the One who is the very source of their being. Only by properly distinguishing this One from all other things can we hope to relate to that same One, for if we think God must be separate from us, then we must *be* separate from God. But that is the self-defeating notion of *autonomy* concocted by a modernity which found it necessary to renounce a creator. Anyone who employs those outmoded categories cannot help but misconstrue the God whom they wish to elaborate.[24] Yet once we appreciate how radical is the act of faith in a free creator, then it becomes clear that we cannot *be* separate from God. Moreover, we will fail to understand that corollary of free creation – perhaps even mistake it for 'pantheism' – if we have not seen how the unique character of the *relation* called 'creation' also demands that we learn how to think the creator *not* as an item in the universe, but as its One free creator! Yet engaging in that mode of thinking, which Kathryn Tanner dubs 'non-constrastive', will also demand that we appreciate how to employ language analogously.[25] So proficiency in philosophical theology will require poetic sensibility as well, since all analogous speech – whether used of divinity or used to evaluate human situations, as in ethical discourse – will invariably display a touch of metaphor.[26] For employing and grasping metaphors elicits an acute awareness of the tension between our perspective and the one we are endeavoring to elucidate – a tension which God-talk should exacerbate and which is ever in evidence in Aquinas, as Robert Barron's *Thomas Aquinas: Spiritual Master* shows so well,[27] and as Olivier-Thomas Venard, OP shows

---

[24] See my 'Creation, Metaphysics, and Ethics', *Faith and Philosophy* 18 (2001), 204–21.
[25] Kathryn Tanner, *God and Creation in Christian Theology: Tyranny or Empowerment* (Oxford: Blackwell, 1989).
[26] See my *Analogy and Philosophical Language* (New Haven: Yale University Press, 1973).
[27] Robert Barron, *Thomas Aquinas: Spiritual Master* (New York: Crossroad, 1996).

by comparing Aquinas' lapidary forms of expression in the *Summa Theologiae* to Rimbaud's poetry.

All of this culminates in the realization that 'relating to God', as in 'praying to God', should take no effort, as there can be no 'gap' to be bridged. For if our very being is a 'being to the creator', then the interior path to one's own self will lead us invariably to the One who sustains us in existence. Aquinas' rich presentation of providence is the corollary of free creation: a thoroughly metaphysical yet eminently personal relation to the creator in whom 'we live, move and have our being', so that relating to this One, by faith, constitutes our 'life in Christ', for our relation to the creator as creatures is modeled on that of the Word to the Father.

The human person

DENYS TURNER

You could say – indeed you should – that Thomas' anthropology, his account of the human person, body and soul, is essentially christologically based, and that if you want to find it in the *Summa* look in the third part on Christ.[1] This, of course, would thus far set Thomas' anthropology in line with the likes of Karl Barth for whom any concretely grounded Christian anthropology ought to begin from our historically actual human condition, as creatures hopelessly fallen into the mire of sin but redeemed by grace, which grace is formative of our return to the perfect image, at once of humanity and of God, an image that is to be found in Christ alone. That being the case you might say that for Thomas there are three anthropologies, all three intersecting in the historical Christian person: that of the human condition of innocence before the fall; that of human nature fallen; and that of human nature fallen but redeemed and exalted to a condition now in degree immeasurably greater than the extent of that fall from innocence. What there is for Thomas and isn't, indeed can't be, for Barth is a fourth anthropology: an account of human nature that appears to abstract entirely from any considerations of this context of salvation history.

Yet just that is what we get in the first part of the *ST*, questions 75–89. What are we to make of this lengthy exposition in which Thomas sets out a purely philosophical account of human nature abstracting not only from the historical condition of human beings as redeemed sinners, but also from that complete and completely visible human person that is Christ? Within these pages is Thomas' account of the human soul (I.77), its powers of sense (I.78.3, I.81), imagination (I.78.4) and intellect (I.79) and the relations between them, the soul's relation to the body especially in reference to the identity of persons (I.76.8), the soul's survival of death as the necessary but insufficient condition of a person's survival of death (I.89), all of which and nothing less are to be found

[1] III.1–19.

discussed in Aristotle's *De anima* with which Thomas was both then and now in a much disputed degree of agreement. There is not a single theological reference to be found within the fifty-six thousand words of his discussion of these topics. How are we to understand either the epistemic standing of this discussion within an explicitly theological work, or its purpose – that is to say, why does Thomas think that the aspirant theologian needs not only answers to these purely philosophical questions but also philosophical arguments in defense of those answers, when to any of these questions that mattered theologically (at any rate in the view of many of his contemporaries) theological answers were to hand as a matter of faith?

You cannot just say: Thomas thinks it is important to know what a human being is in principle before you get into the discussion of any specifically Christian doctrines about the human condition, when, as he knows as well as anyone, what human beings are 'in principle' is not how they are in actuality, since what actually exists is human nature fallen and redeemed. So what is this theologian doing rehearsing a (not uncontroversial) reading of Aristotle's *De anima* when either Aristotle can look after himself or he cannot, but either way that is up to him – or, if it is up to anyone else, then to the philosophers in the Faculty of Arts at Paris or Oxford or Bologna. Either way how is it any business of the theologian with feet on theological terra firma?

Manifestly the philosophical discussion *does* matter to Thomas, and not just philosophically. It matters theologically. One of the certainties that can be easily maintained about the *Summa* is that there is nothing in it at all that, in Thomas' view, does not have its place for good theological or pedagogical reasons. It would in fact be possible to run through the eighty-nine articles that this stretch of the *Summa* contains, in each case with a view to demonstrating what the theological consequences would be of differing from Thomas' philosophical positions. Examples are easy to proliferate. Get the relationship between body and soul right, as Thomas argues for it in questions 75 and 76, or else we are bound to get the doctrine of the resurrection post-mortem of persons wrong, starting with that of Christ himself;[2] get the sense right in which we share with coyotes, cabbages and carrots a common nutritional life or else we will have no grounds in what we are as humans for eating and drinking being the sacrament that for Thomas it is, containing the deepest mysteries of creation and redemption themselves. Get the sense in which human beings are animals wrong (for Thomas they are real,

---

2 III.50.5.

not pretend, animals) and you will never get right the sense in which they are rational, for it is only animals that can have rational intellects. Angels can't construct inductive inferences, and can't because they have no need of such roundabout methods. Thomas' point – the point, that is, of composing fifty-six thousand words of philosophical psychology (as we would now call it) within a work of theology – is not that you have to know all that Aristotelian argument in order to believe what you should: you can be a person of the fullest and firmest faith without being a philosopher at all. The point is that if you do the philosophy and get it wrong and then mediate your theology through it, you will either get your theology wrong as a result or else end up with an inconsistent conceptual muddle, as one finds in Bonaventure from time to time. In short, there is no call on Christian believers to be philosophers at all. But there is a call on Christian theologians where they play to their own theological standards not to find themselves in philosophical positions that are plainly muddled or wrong-headed and indefensible. A theological opinion is *theologically* indefensible if it entails philosophical positions that are demonstrably false.

And fair enough, it really is not easy to see how Bonaventure can reconcile his Platonist account of the nature of the soul and its sufficiency unto personal identity (I am my soul with or without a body) and at the same time maintain the centrality of the body's resurrection for the survival of persons. For if death is to be seen as the liberation of the soul from the body, thus to release the person from entrapment in it, what is the 'sting of death' that the resurrection is supposed to remove? Thomas, of course, did not complete his *Summa*, and there is no account to be found in his work of the resurrection of persons, for which we have to turn to the notes taken from his lectures on I Corinthians 15, delivered, according to Torrell, in much the same period (1265–1268) as the composition of the first part of the *Summa*. There Thomas is adamant: my soul is not I and if only my soul were to survive death then I would not – adding that in his own view Platonising Christians get it all the wrong way round, for my survival as a person requires, but does not as they think consist in, the survival of my soul. It is rather, he says, the other way round: the survival of my soul after death depends logically on the resurrection of my body and without that bodily resurrection there would be no I to survive. In that example alone, and there are many others, one can see how theologically important for Thomas it is not to allow philosophical muddles to intrude upon the articulation of faith. And if there are reasons for those fifty-six thousand words of philosophical psychology, they are of just that sort: philosophical muddles will translate into theological mix-ups, as here. Even if, as he avers, you need both doctrines, of the immortality of the soul and of bodily resurrection, it is the Christian's resurrection of the body that is central for Thomas, not the Platonist's immortality of the soul. And even if, as he thinks, the immortality of the soul does need to be demonstrated (and can be) it is not the Platonist's account of the nature and powers of the surviving soul that will supply the theological need.

II

As with so many other apparently discrete stretches of the *Summa*'s long argument, it is first of all important to understand exactly what this discussion of the psychology of human nature is doing just there within the work's structure as a whole. So vast is the *Summa* that few read it through from beginning to end, tending rather to dip in and out, trawling for Thomas' views on this or that topic at will or as needed. Just how misleading a procedure this can be is dramatically illustrated by the inconclusive nature of the argument contained in this group of questions. It begins in I.75 with the discussion of the nature of the soul and ends at I.89 with a question concerning what kind of knowledge is possible for a soul separated from the body by death. What shows that this section of the *Summa* does not even remotely represent anything like a complete account of Thomas' arguments for personal survival is the absence, as noted, of a single word here about the Christian teaching of the resurrection, and silence about death itself – except, that is, a single reference to the bare fact that the soul survives it.

That said, if you start at the end of this group of questions, at I.89, and read back to I.75, you get a much clearer picture of a subtle, and distinctly theological strategy at work precisely in the argument's incompleteness, even if there is not a single word of theology throughout its eighty-nine articles. That strategy is simple: it is to demonstrate that you do not get anywhere near to a coherent position concerning the survival of persons if all you have got to work with is the philosopher's arguments, even the good ones, Aristotle's in his view being as good as you will get.[3] In fact the specific reason why Thomas prefers an Aristotelian

---

3 Though what exactly Aristotle is arguing in *De anima*, III, concerning personal immortality was a hotly debated issue in the late thirteenth century. Thomas entered the ill-tempered fray as hotly as anyone, furiously rejecting as irresponsible the reading of Aristotle much influenced by the Arabic philosopher Ibn Rushd (known in the Latin world as 'Averroes') that prevailed in the Faculty of Arts at Paris in the late 1260s.

anthropology to a Platonist one is that while both construct arguments for the immortality of the human soul, it is Aristotle's account in *De anima* of the soul's survival that, for Thomas, yields the theologically right conclusion: nothing that shows the bare survival of my soul is sufficient to show my survival as a person – whereas on Plato's account my soul's survival *is* my survival. And that, you could say, is the whole point of the argument between I.75 and I.89: for my survival of death to be secured you would need grounds for believing that I will be raised post-mortem body and soul. And only faith in Christ's resurrection, not philosophy, can provide those grounds.

The eight articles that form the argument of question 89, therefore, demonstrate the insufficiency of what philosophy can supply by its own means if we are to secure a foundation for our hopes of personal survival. The questions go like this: suppose bare naked souls, bodiless minds, survive death, what sort of rump of a person have you got post mortem? What can bodiless souls understand? What can they know? What can they remember? What can they feel? In what way, if at all, can bodiless souls relate to still living embodied persons? The answers are depressingly negative for all those Platonists whose hopes lie in the soul's immortality alone. True enough, surviving bodiless souls can retain some powers of understanding, but only in a deficient, residual form. For what is natural and best for human beings is that they should live in a world they can understand and otherwise relate to only in and through the images of things that their embodied senses provide them with. Human beings are animals. They are environmentally dependent in multiple ways, not just for bodily food, but also for food for thought. Otherwise than as thus embodied, the only understanding they can have of anything by means of their natural powers is, he says (I.89.1*corp*), 'general' and 'undifferentiated' (*in quadam communitate et confusione*). He seems to mean that separated from their bodies, souls cannot ground their knowledge in any instances of anything, their cognitive condition being perhaps like my knowledge of Japan – never having been there I have no experience of anything I know about the country: which is fair enough, for you need a body to *visit* Japan and see for yourself.

That said, Thomas asks, can my surviving soul get to know other surviving souls (I.89.2)? Yes, he replies, indeed surviving soul-mates are pretty much all that surviving souls can know with any degree of adequacy, because in that one case knower and object known are in possession of some sort of common form of existence, a condition which

Thomas maintains is required for a subject's knowledge of an object. Not so as regards either the natural world (I.89.3), of which a separated soul's knowledge, once again, lacks grounding in any bodily experience, or with their knowledge of individual people as yet still alive, this being confined to what they have pre-mortem experienced and can still remember of them, especially of people they have loved and still love. Otherwise, their knowledge is confined to such as God 'infuses' them with (I.89.4). The same holds of what knowledge of general principles (I.89.5) or of such knowledge applied (I.89.6) as a person pre-mortem had possessed: such knowledge is not lost, but it cannot increase, except, again, by divine infusion. In short, a dead person is a soul surviving but intellectually, imaginatively and emotionally disabled, hardly recognizable as a person at all, a quasi-entity stuck in a condition of memory stalled and incapable, by means of any powers of its own, of experiential refreshment. At any rate, such, paradoxically, is the dismal anti-climax you would have to envisage the post-mortem outcome of life to be if all you could count on was the post-mortem survival of the soul. By comparison with the experientially undernourished and intellectually static condition of disembodied human souls, there is a rich and vibrant complexity whether of knowledge or of feeling, of agency or of relationship, of a pre-mortem embodied person. And it is with that account of pre-mortem personhood that the questions from 75 to 88 are concerned: tactically, they show just why a Platonist account of the soul's immortality will not do whether pre- or post-mortem.

It is for this reason that it is not after all so odd to start the exposition of Thomas' episode of philosophical anthropology at the end, at I.89. As an account of the human person it is demonstrably incomplete: and that demonstrated incompleteness seems deliberate, tactical. For it seems as if Thomas' intention is to show that the survival of the human person is not secured by anything the philosopher could demonstrate, and the incompleteness of the argument, its downbeat conclusion, is designed to show that the bare survival of the soul is the survival of but a person-fragment, for 'I am not my soul' and 'were only my soul to survive then I would not, nor any other person.' The demonstrable insufficiency of a purely philosophical account of personal survival *is* the theological point of this part of the *Summa*.

Thomas' philosophical account of the human person is, therefore, by no means a merely incidental side-show. It is indeed Thomas' belief that we need to know what it takes to be a human being *tout court* if we are to know what the Christian doctrine of post-mortem existence is the survival of – more simply put, if truly it is I who survives death then we need to know what is essential to my identity. But this does not mean that for Thomas it is the philosopher who makes the running, by laying down the conditions that a Christian doctrine of resurrection must meet if it is to count as the survival of persons, even if the order of Thomas' exposition in the *Summa* might seem to suggest this. On the contrary, it is fair to say that a theological purpose directs and motivates the argument of questions 75–89 even though there is not a single theological proposition appealed to at any point in the argument. Thomas says as much, making the logical priorities clear in his commentary on I Corinthians, 15: 'It would not be easy, indeed [it would be] difficult, to defend the immortality of the soul without the resurrection of the body.'[4] And questions 75–89 of the first part of the *Summa* are designed from end to end to show that the human soul is naturally immortal but that to have shown this is not at all to have demonstrated the Christian doctrine of the resurrection. What it has done of theological relevance is to have cleared the conceptual space for that Christian teaching: *if* human persons are to be said to survive death you need more than a good argument for the immortality of the soul. To that end Aristotle is worth all the trouble of questions 75–88.

III

That said, Thomas' position is far from being in the clear. Indeed it is just because of his acceptance of an Aristotelian form of anti-dualism that the serious conceptual problems begin for him. The first bit has been all too easy, and all the easier in our day than in his. For in our times it is the theological orthodoxy, as little supported by argument as it is ever challenged, that there is no case for the immortality of the soul dependent upon a dualistic platonist anthropology. What is less easily stomached is almost the opposite problem that Thomas' Aristotle presents you with. For while Plato will give you the immortality of the soul at the excessively high price of a dualist anthropology, it can seem close to impossible to make anything of the soul's immortality consistently with the non-dualist anthropology that Thomas finds in Aristotle. Thomas thinks that it can be done, though the point of his comment just cited, that it is not easy to do so without the resurrection of the body, is worth taking more seriously than most readers of Thomas do. You might almost conclude that the carefully constructed philosophical

---

4   *Super I ad Corinthios*, 14, 5.

psychology set out in questions 75 to 88 is designed specifically to create maximum difficulty for any doctrine of post-mortem survival, not just for the immortality of the soul, so remorselessly anti-dualist is it.

Thomas' grammar of soul-talk is carefully tracked through a mine-field of potential errors. There is nothing since Descartes quite like it, and we have to set aside arguments both for and against Cartesian accounts of the soul if we are to get near to understanding Thomas'. As we have seen, Thomas says that it is wrong to maintain that I *am* my soul. Does he therefore think it right to say that I *have* a soul? No he does not. For without a soul there is no I to have one, and there is no such thing as a body that either has or does not have a soul: 'have' is the wrong word. For where there is no soul there is no body to lack one, just as, if I lack the brain I once had, then there is no longer any Turner to miss it. The reason you shouldn't say that bodies 'have' souls is that their being bodies just is their being matter alive in certain typical ways. And what you mean by 'soul' is what accounts for those typical ways in which a body is alive, alive, in the case of humans, as human bodies are alive – eating celebratory meals together, having sex, solving cross-word puzzles, or in the case of cabbages and carrots, as cabbages and carrots are alive – germinating, growing and dying. Putting it simply, for Thomas my death is the end of me. It is not properly said, as it is by Platonists, that it is the end merely of my body.

Does Thomas say I have a body? Again he does not, as we have seen, since properly speaking without a body there is no I to be in possession of one. Once more following Aristotle, he maintains that a dead person's body is only 'equivocally' said to be a body at all. It is a corpse, and it is called 'Gertrude's' because that is what it once was, her body, though now it is not and cannot be, there being no Gertrude any more. Moreover, even as to the corpse itself, there is no longer an 'it' of which 'it is rotting' is true, because, the person being dead, what was her body when she was alive is now nothing but a congeries of dissolving chemicals. Again, strictly speaking (and Thomas does like to speak strictly) 'a dead body' is an oxymoron. For bodies are living matter.

How does Thomas find himself saying such things? Because he is following Aristotle in his account of the relationship between body and soul: they relate, he says, as matter and form. Now on the standard and basic account of that relationship such as Thomas found in Aristotle, there is no such possibility as that of matter existing without form, though for maintaining the impossibility of formless matter Thomas found himself posthumously in trouble with Stephen Tempier, the bishop of Paris who, on March 7, 1277, three years to the day after

Thomas' death, condemned the proposition as heretical. For Thomas it was as obviously true that you can't have matter that doesn't fall under some description of what it is the matter of, a cauliflower, a cat or a capitalist, as that you can't have a lump of stuff that isn't any kind of stuff, that has no shape at all, no dimensions, no position, no weight, in short, (as we would say today) matter with no properties. That being so, however, it would seem that Thomas is in trouble and not only with bishops, for on the ground of his own Aristotelianism, it would seem just as unlikely that you can have any form without matter as that you can have matter without form. After all, would it not seem that you can no more have clay that doesn't occur in any lumps at all, an occurrence of clay that isn't *this* bit of it, than you can have lumps of matter that aren't clay or any other kind of stuff? This, for the most part, is how Thomas works with the concepts of matter and form in respect of human persons: formless, soul-less matter is not a human body; matterless souls are not human persons.

It would therefore seem that in the general case of the reciprocity of matter and form you would be forced into what, for Thomas the theologian, would be a strict dilemma: you can have your doctrine of the soul's immortality at the price of a body-soul dualism; or you can have a non-dualist account of the body-soul relationship at the price of abandoning the doctrine of the soul's immortality. It is fair to say that for Thomas becoming impaled on either prong of the dilemma's fork is equally to be avoided. In fact the principal goal of Thomas' argument in this part of the *Summa* would seem to be to negotiate a way between the dilemma's horns, to find arguments for the natural immortality of the soul without appeal to any form of body-soul dualism.

IV

The argument in this bit of the *Summa* goes roughly like this. A human being is a species of living being, and whenever you talk about something's being alive you are talking about it insofar as it is informed by a soul. Or you can put it the other way round: the only thing you refer to in speaking of a thing's 'soul' is whatever it is that you cease to talk about when that thing is dead. Now for Thomas some living things are alive only in one sort of way – generically, that is. Cabbages are just vegetables, alive in that they germinate, grow and wither away. Other living things are animals and are alive in every way that a cabbage is, but also in that they can move themselves from place to place, can sniff and hunt, they hunger and thirst and are motivated to slake them both, some want sex, and in some cases they live together as sexual partners or even larger herding groups, some see and hear, some remember routes to hunting grounds and places of safety. In short, animal life is immeasurably more complex than vegetable life, but includes everything that counts as life in a cabbage in a higher, that is, more complex and differentiated, form: cabbages and coyotes both grow, but growth in a coyote is a biologically, ecologically and psychologically far more complex affair than that of a cabbage, above all in that a coyote has a conscious life of sorts and a cabbage none of any kind. Now both cabbages and coyotes being alive, Thomas will speak of their souls, and will do so for the following reason.

Living things have powers that are attributable to them as agents, that is to say, as identifiable sources of action in their own right. A meteorite is not an agent: it is a reaction. A cabbage is likewise subject reactively to most of what causes it to survive, but it has some powers of agency that are attributable to its own action in its own right, like growing; and the description of what a cabbage can *do* as distinct from what it merely reacts to, is the description of its life, a 'life of its own', as we say, its soul being the source of that life. In that case the living cabbage and the cabbage's soul are one and the same, they begin to exist and cease to exist at one and the same time.

Why, then, is there any need to talk of a cabbage's soul at all, since it would seem to be merely circumlocutory, or, as Hobbes was later to say about 'soul-talk' generally, it would seem to do nothing more than to unnecessarily invent entities out of platitudes? Why not just do botany and biology, as you don't need souls in the study of organisms? As I understand what little Thomas has to say on the matter, he thinks that talk of a cabbage's soul is ineliminable because one of the ways in which animals are alive (if in many another ways besides) is as vegetables are, for animals, as vegetables do, germinate, grow, feed and, after a roughly fixed life-span, die; and animals have souls. And if you push the line of questioning further and ask, why bring soul-talk into the description of animals, the answer will be along the same lines: everything that counts for being alive in an animal is true of what it takes to be alive as human, for human beings are animals, if also more besides, just as animals are all vegetables, if more besides. Hence, if you need to talk about human souls as accounting for how humans are alive, then you need to talk about animal and vegetable souls because any talk about forms of life is talk about souls.

At this point, however, Thomas ran into trouble with nearly all of his contemporaries, many of whom maintained that, being as Thomas agreed, alive in generically distinct ways (as between any vegetable and any animal) or in specifically distinct ways (as between rational and non-rational animals), human beings must have three distinct principles of life, three distinct souls, a vegetative, an animal and a rational soul. Moreover, Bonaventure argued, given that the vegetative and animal souls in a human being are so immersed in matter as not to survive the demise of the body, it follows that upon my death what survives is only my rational soul. Thomas disagrees: had I three souls I would be three entities and three sources of agency, not one. For, he had argued in an opusculum of his early maturity, the *De ente et essentia*, I am not in part a vegetable, in part an animal, in part rational. As he puts it, if it were correct to say that I am partly vegetative, partly animal, partly rational, then you would be compelled to say that these parts belong to me as my leg or my heart or my brain belong to me. But for Thomas this is to make a grammatical and substantive mistake: a brain and a heart and a leg are parts of me; but you cannot say being an animal is part of the human being I am. An animal *is* what I am. For Thomas I am from top to toe a vegetable, feeding, growing, ageing, dying as a whole; I am from top to toe an animal, hunting, desiring sex, seeing danger, feeling heat and cold as a whole, the *same* whole; I am from top to toe rational, constructing strategies of means and ends, marrying, playing chess, devising strategies of a good social life. I am all three, in mutual interaction, one and the same whole, the same existent. I am rationally vegetative: I arrange banquets for my friends; I have an animal's reaction to danger, for my hair stands on end at its prospect, but it is only a *rational* animal's hair that stands on end at the threat from Al Qaeda. I am definitively rational, that is to say, my whole life, vegetative and animal as it is, is an expression of *meaning*, my body, material as it is, is at once language, as only a human index finger can point a direction, wordlessly saying 'over there,' as a kiss, which signifies love, can mendaciously enact a betrayal. Thomas, of course, puts it otherwise (and in 1277 was condemned for his pains): 'I have but one soul and it is intellectual.' Innocent enough as the formula might sound, his contemporaries felt the sting in its tail: for it means, as they saw, that my intellectual life is inseparable from my life as an animal and as a vegetable: my life as a fully functioning human person involves my insertion into a world, into an eco-system along with animals and vegetables. That is where human persons by nature belong, as rational animals.

Hence, 'if only my soul survives, then I do not.' For a surviving soul would be a human fragment in waiting to be a person. But why is there a case for my soul's surviving, as Thomas nonetheless maintains it does? The argument in the *Summa* is brief and to the point. Seeing is essentially organic: it is not just that you cannot see without an eye, an eye is what you see with. So too with hearing: it is I who hear, but the ear is the organ with which I do so. In general, where there is no body there is no sensory *subject* to which these and the other senses belong, so that though the powers remain as such, they remain incapable of their characteristic exercise (I.77.8*corp*). Not so with the intellect, says Thomas: the brain is not what thinks and judges as to good and bad, true and false: it couldn't be, any more than a tennis racquet could be what serves an ace. And even though the quality of your racquet will affect how well you can play, and even if in the same way a brain damaged by injury or disease will affect how well you can think; and though it follows that human powers of thinking, feeling, or remembering would be all the more seriously impaired if, altogether lacking a body I lacked a brain, nonetheless, it is not and cannot be the brain that thinks. I think. And even if I need a brain to be an I who thinks, I am not my brain.

In fact the agent of thought in a human has to be an immaterial power, because thought itself has to be immaterial. For just as the power by which we see a patch of yellow cannot be a yellow power, else anything red we would see as orange, so that by which we can understand this to be such and such and not that, cannot itself be either, and that is true for any values of 'this' and 'that' whatever. Hence, Thomas concludes, intellect, which is precisely our human power of distinguishing this from that, cannot share any of the characteristics of any of the things it knows, it has to be materially nothing at all if it is to know anything at all material. And being immaterial, it follows it is not naturally subject to decay and death. Qua intellect, I am, therefore, immortal.

But because human intellects are in their nature embodied, *my* surviving death is not secured by my intellect's survival. We are, then, back where we started, with a demonstrably inconclusive outcome. The human person's natural condition is embodied and though my soul may be naturally immortal and its survival a necessary condition of my survival, it is not, for Thomas, a sufficient condition; only my bodily resurrection can guarantee that, and no philosophical anthropology, but only faith, can provide that guarantee. It is at that point that I.89 ends, and since the *Summa* itself is incomplete, falling short of the discussion of the resurrection of the body, we are left with a doctrinal torso which we could complete only by appeal to other works of Thomas, in particular to his commentary on I Corinthians 15. It is from that commentary that we can see how the incompleteness of the account of human immortality as it stands in the *Summa* is purposive and strategic, and is the demonstration neither of the concrete actuality of the *perfectus homo* in Christ, nor of the concrete actuality of historical human beings as fallen, but rather of the need for a revealed ground for the certainty of our personal survival of death, given 'how hard it is to defend the immortality of the soul without the resurrection of the body.' This passage of the *Summa* is, in short, the demonstration simultaneously of the philosophical necessity and of the theological insufficiency of a non-dualist account of himan nature, pushing philosophy as far as it can go, because you need it to go that far in order to demonstrate that it cannot go far enough.

Happiness

JEAN PORTER

In the introduction to the *Prima Secundae*, Aquinas says that he will
begin by considering the final end of human life, and will then discuss
the way in which that end is to be attained. 'And because the final end
of human life is said to be happiness,' he adds, 'it is necessary first to
consider the ultimate end in general, and secondly, to consider happiness' (I.2.1*intro*). This remark has surprised many of Aquinas' readers,
and is often ignored, or interpreted in such a way as to minimize its
significance.[1] Yet by this point, Aquinas has already indicated that the
concept of happiness, regarded as the final end of human action, is central to the rationale and structure of theology itself. He begins the *ST* by
asking why it was necessary that God reveal certain truths to us, beyond
what we could discern through the use of human reason. He replies that
besides philosophy, we stand in need of 'another teaching' stemming
from divine revelation because 'the human person is ordained to God as
a specific end which exceeds the comprehension of reason ... yet the end
must be known in advance to human persons, who ought to order their
intentions and actions towards it' (I.1.1). The critical point is that in
order to count as fully rational, action must be oriented, directly or indirectly, towards some overarching goal or final purpose, which the agent
grasps as such and knowingly pursues. At the same time, salvation,
which is our true final end, consists in a kind of direct communion with
God that exceeds our natural capacities for comprehension and choice.

---

[1] Among contemporary moral theologians, Servais Pinckaers is almost alone in insisting on the significance of the concept of happiness for Aquinas' moral thought;
see *Les Sources de la morale chrétienne: Sa méthode, son contenu, son histoire*
(Fribourg: Éditions Universitaires, 1985), 28–33, and more recently, *L'Évangile et la
morale* (Fribourg: Éditions Universitaires, 1990), 103–116. While I agree with much
of what he says, I do believe that Aquinas gives greater weight to a conception of terrestrial happiness conceived as the practice of the virtues than Pinckaers recognizes,
and correlatively, that Aquinas' position is more in line with classical antecedents
than he allows; see *L'Évangile et la morale*, 108–109.

For precisely that reason, this end must be revealed to us, in such a way as to transform and go beyond anything that we could have grasped or hoped to attain through our natural powers – hence, the necessity for revelation, and for the systematic science of theological reflection built on that revelation. Almost in passing, Aquinas goes on to specify this end as 'the perfect knowledge of God, in which eternal happiness consists' (I.1.4). This clearly implies that the concept of happiness, far from being an awkward addendum to Aquinas' theological synthesis, both motivates and structures that synthesis.

Aquinas' identification of happiness with the perfect knowledge of God – that is to say, the Beatific Vision – goes some way towards answering possible objections to his approach. Certainly, he does not identify happiness with a subjective state of good feeling, still less does he claim that one's self-interest, narrowly construed, should be the over-arching aim of human life. Nonetheless, we might still wonder whether Aquinas' focus on happiness, even construed as the perfect knowledge of God, reflects a problematic tendency to privilege the desires and satisfactions of the individual. We might understand why it is important to give some place to individual well-being in this way, but can we really regard happiness as an objectively worthwhile aim? Alternatively, it might seem that Aquinas' identification of happiness with the Beatific Vision is too abstract and too clearly stipulative, to be persuasive. How can we possibly identify such a remote and incomprehensible end with happiness, on any plausible, experientially grounded account of what happiness means?

In order to address such questions, we must place Aquinas' analysis of happiness in a twofold context. Aquinas' analysis stands within a long-standing classical tradition of reflection on happiness, considered as the proper aim of human life, which he appropriates through the framework of the broadly Aristotelian metaphysics and philosophy of nature that inform much of his theology. When we place Aquinas' remarks in this context, we see that the key to understanding his complex conception of happiness lies in his analysis of happiness as a kind of perfection: 'by the name of happiness is understood the ultimate perfection of a rational or intellectual nature; and hence it is that it is naturally desired, since everything naturally desires its own perfection' (I.62.1; cf. I.12.1). Happiness thus represents the distinctively human (and angelic) form of a universal desire for fulfillment, understood as the complete development and expression of the proper capabilities of a specific kind of creature. Once we appreciate this point, we can more clearly see why the concept of happiness should be so central to Aquinas' theology, and we can more readily trace the inner logic of this complex idea.[2]

HAPPINESS IN CLASSICAL AND PHILOSOPHICAL CONTEXTS

The philosophers of Greek and Hellenistic antiquity would not have been surprised by Aquinas' focus on happiness, because as Julia Annas says, 'The question 'In what does my happiness consist?' is the most important and central question in ancient ethics.'[3] In pursuing this question, these philosophers presuppose that happiness is not equivalent to subjective good feelings or even with sustained personal satisfaction. Rather, it is identified with whatever constitutes the final and defining aim of human life, an aim which, it is assumed, is an objective reality, grounded in whatever it means to be human. The idea of happiness thus carries connotations of worth and value, suggesting a life that is in some way admirable as well as enjoyable – the ideal invoked when we say that someone's time on earth has been well-lived, meaningful, rich, and full. At the same time, ancient philosophers, or some of them at any rate, also knew that 'Happiness implies a positive view of one's life. If our final good is happiness, this does at least rule out conspicuously miserable or frustrated ways of life.'[4] They attempted, therefore, to offer an account of the final good of human life which was both defensible in broader philosophical terms, and plausible as an attractive and satisfying way to live.

Much of what we take to be distinctive in Aristotle's account of happiness actually reflects the consensus view of his time.[5] His account is

---

[2] In what follows, I draw on and expand an interpretation of Aquinas' conception of happiness set forth in my *Nature as Reason: A Thomistic Theory of the Natural Law* (Grand Rapids: Eerdmans, 2005), 141–230.

[3] Julia Annas, *The Morality of Happiness* (Oxford: Oxford University Press, 1993), 46; in what follows, I largely rely on her account of ancient debates over the nature of happiness and its normative significance, as set forth in 27–46. In addition, for a most helpful overview of the concept of happiness as developed by Aquinas' immediate predecessors and contemporaries, see George Weiland, 'Happiness: The Perfection of Man,' in Norman Kretzman, Anthony Kenny, and Jan Pinborg (eds), *The Cambridge History of Later Medieval Philosophy From the Rediscovery of Aristotle to the Disintegration of Scholasticism, 1100–1600* (Cambridge: Cambridge University Press, 1982), 675–686.

[4] Annas, *Morality*, 46.

[5] The main source for Aristotle's account of happiness is the *Nicomachean Ethics*, especially books 1 and 10. I have not attempted to document the following interpretation in detail, but at any rate I do not believe it would be controversial, except perhaps in its emphasis on the metaphysical underpinnings of Aristotle's views. Annas

distinctive, however, insofar as it reflects his wider metaphysical analysis of existence and identity. Admittedly, Aristotle is not always explicit about the metaphysical presuppositions of his moral theory, but what follows appears to be a defensible construal, and to reflect Aquinas' own interpretation. For Aristotle, something can only exist as an individual of a specified kind, in accordance with structured principles of activity. Correlatively, every entity naturally operates in such a way as to exercise these principles, to develop them as fully as possible, and to sustain them through some degree of resistance or engagement with its surrounding environment. And since Aristotle construes the good as a terminus of activity or desire, this line of analysis further implies that the creature's good, the purpose intrinsic to its proper operations, is nothing other than the full, sustained expression of the formal principles constituting it as this or that specific kind of creature. Human happiness, understood as the objective good towards which we are naturally oriented, can thus be construed as the fullest possible expression of the principles of activity specific to us as individuals of a specific kind, that is to say, a 'human being'. As is well known, Aristotle goes on to offer two accounts of what the full expression of humanity comprises – philosophical contemplation of divinity itself, an end which he describes as more than human, and on a more properly human level, the practice of the civic virtues in a well-ordered political community.[6]

AQUINAS' ACCOUNT OF HAPPINESS

Aquinas' metaphysics and philosophy of nature are clearly indebted to Aristotle, although it is difficult to say how far, or in what ways, he transforms Aristotle in the process of adapting him. At any rate, Aquinas clearly appropriates an Aristotelian account of perfection as the fullest possible development of one's active powers, taking this as the cornerstone for his own analysis of happiness. This is apparent in the first question of the *Prima Secundae*, which takes up the question of the final end of human life abstractly considered. After establishing that it is proper to the human person to act for an end and drawing out some of the implications of that claim (I-II.1.1–3), he goes on to argue that human life has an ultimate end, at least in a minimal sense that would rule out an indefinite series or a

offers a helpful overview of Aristotle's overall theory, with special emphasis on the ways in which he relates virtue to the development of natural tendencies or capacities; see Annas, *Morality*, 142–158.

[6] Specifically, see the *Nicomachean Ethics* Book 10, 7–8 (1177a10–1179a35).

plurality of ends (I-II.1.4). Clearly, this claim is only plausible if the end is formulated in general terms, and so it is not surprising to read further that each person has one ultimate end, namely perfection understood as the fullest possible development and exercise of one's active powers (I-II.1.5). What is more, each person desires and does everything on account of this end (I-II.1.6). All human beings share in the same final end, insofar as each person naturally desires his or her perfection, even though individuals differ widely in their conceptions of what it would mean to enjoy a perfect, or complete or fulfilled, human life (I-II.1.7).

So far, what we have is an extended application of the Aristotelian idea that perfection – that is to say, the full development and expression of one's natural capacities and inclinations – constitutes the final cause, the architectonic aim, for the operations of every substantial creature. What does this have to do with happiness? We have already observed that Aquinas defines happiness as the ultimate perfection of a rational or intellectual nature (the latter referring to the angels; again, see I.62.1). On this basis, he moves from his analysis of the end of human life, generally considered, to a more focused analysis of the concept of happiness (I-II.2–5). He sets out, first of all, to give a substantive meaning to the formal concept of happiness as perfection, and after rejecting various alternatives (I-II.2.1–7), he concludes that the final end of human life can only be God, attained through contemplation – an answer which could have been given in pre-Christian antiquity, except for the further qualification that the mode of attainment in question utterly transcends the natural capacities of the human (or any other kind of) creature (I-II.2.8; cf. I.12.4, I-II.5.5).

In the following question, 'What is happiness?' Aquinas further develops this line of analysis. He argues that properly understood, happiness is an operation, because it is the ultimate perfection of the human creature, and to be perfect simply means to be in act (I-II.3.2). Further, it is an act of the highest and most characteristic human faculty, the intellect, although this act is necessarily conjoined with delight, which is an act of the will (I-II.3.4). But not any act of intellect will do. Rather, true happiness can only consist in the fullest possible exercise of the intellect and will, through contemplation of a supremely intelligible and lovable object – which is to say, God, grasped as fully and comprehensively as it is possible for a creature to do (cf. I.12.1). And this brings us back to the point just noted, namely, that happiness in its fullest sense can only consist in the direct vision of God, that is to say, the Beatific Vision. Yet we must keep in mind that the Beatific Vision, the direct comprehension of God as a personal and Triune reality, exceeds the natural capacities

of any creature (including the angelic intellects; see, among many relevant texts, I.12.4, I-II.62.2, I-II.109.5). If we are to attain true and complete happiness, therefore, God must bestow a principle of action that
is supernatural, in the sense that it goes beyond our natural principles
of action – grace, in this life, and what Aquinas describes as the light of
glory in the life to come (I.12.2).

So far, the identification of happiness with the Beatific Vision may
strike us as too austere or abstract to be persuasive, but it does at least
provide a straightforward and cogently argued account of what happiness
is. But as we continue reading in the *Prima Secundae*, it becomes apparent that Aquinas' conception of happiness is after all not so straightforward as we might have assumed. The happiness of the life to come
consists in the direct Vision of God, through which we will see God as
God most essentially is, a Triune, personal reality, comprehending but
infinitely exceeding an intellectual grasp of God as initiating cause and
final goal of all created beings (I-II.3.8). Happiness at this level is thus a
kind of contemplation, which engages and fulfills the human faculties
for rational comprehension and love to the greatest extent possible, in
such a way as to meet and transcend every conceivable human desire.
Only this deserves to be called happiness in a full, unrestricted sense.

Yet Aquinas also recognizes that we can legitimately speak of happiness in another, qualified sense, referring to the happy state of the
individual whose life has been transformed by grace. Not only does the
graced individual anticipate the happiness of the Beatific Vision through
faith and hope, which are themselves aspects of happiness, she may be
said to participate in that happiness already, through the graced activities through which she will ultimately attain the complete happiness of
the life to come (I-II.5.1, I-II.69.1,2). This kind of happiness falls short of
the unqualified happiness of the Vision in many respects, not least that
it is not completely secure, since it can be lost through serious sin. More
surprisingly, the happiness of the life of grace, unlike the happiness of
the Vision, is not identified with those forms of philosophical reflection
or contemplation available to us here and now. Aquinas insists that for
the pilgrim, the truly happy life includes the comprehensive practice of
all the virtues, including both the theological and the infused cardinal
virtues (I-II.4.5,6; I-II.55.4). What is more, Aquinas identifies another
legitimate yet qualified sense in which we might speak of happiness,
namely, the connatural happiness that we can attain through the appropriate development of the natural powers inhering in us as creatures
of a given kind. This kind of happiness consists in the practice of the
acquired virtues (I-II.5.5, I-II.62.1), and since Aquinas believes that we

are capable of attaining genuine virtue on a properly human level without grace, presumably he regards this kind of connatural happiness as a real possibility (I-II.65.2).

Aquinas thus recognizes that there is more than one legitimate sense in which a man or woman may be said to be happy, but it would be a mistake to conclude that these diverse kinds of happiness have no relation to one another. Rather, each represents a distinctive way of attaining happiness understood as perfection. As Kevin Staley puts it, 'Thomas does not argue that man has two ends, the one natural and the other supernatural. Rather, he speaks of a single end which is twofold, which is realized at both a natural and a supernatural level, and which he describes in the *Summa Theologiae* as imperfect and perfect beatitude respectively.'[7] This ultimate end, we should recall, is formally understood as perfection, that is to say, the fullest possible development of one's potentialities in accordance with one's specific form. This implies that different senses of happiness represent diverse levels or modalities of perfection. Admittedly, this would seem to imply, paradoxically, more and less perfect kinds of perfection itself. We can make sense of this line of analysis, however, if we formulate it in terms of different stages or levels of perfection (cf. I-II.4.6–8, I-II.5.3–5). Thus, the imperfect happiness that we enjoy through grace would be regarded as imperfect in the sense of incomplete, even though oriented and actively moving towards the complete perfection of the Beatific Vision (I-II.69.1,2). The kind of happiness that is connatural to us as creatures of a specific kind, in contrast, is imperfect by contrast to the greater possibility revealed to us, yet considered on its own level it represents (at least ideally) the complete perfection of the human creature in accordance with its natural principles of operation (I-II.62.1, I-II.63.3).[8]

---

7 Kevin Staley, 'Happiness: The Natural End of Man?', *The Thomist* 53/2 (1989), 215–234, at 227; Weiland makes a similar point in 'Happiness', 678–680. I would add, however, that Aquinas does in fact recognize the existence of a kind of natural happiness which could be experienced and enjoyed as a limited but distinctive kind of happiness even if we had not be called to any further end; on this point, I agree with Steven Long, 'On the Possibility of a Purely Natural End for Man', *The Thomist* 64 (2000), 211–237.

8 Of course, this kind of happiness would be transitory and limited at best, and we would be aware of those limitations – yet as Long suggests, this does not necessarily imply that we would not find natural fulfillment to be satisfying, or that we would be tormented by unfulfilled longings, if we had not in fact been called to the higher happiness of direct union with God. See 'On the Possibility', 226–229. In my view, the natural desire for happiness should not be equated straightforwardly with a natural desire to see God; however, it would take us too far afield to pursue this complex and much-debated topic.

HAPPINESS AS ORGANIZING PRINCIPLE, IDEAL
AND ASPIRATION

Once we realize that Aquinas identifies happiness in every proper sense with some modality of perfection, we can more easily understand why this concept is so central for him. His analysis of happiness as perfection unifies central strands of his moral/theological synthesis, so much so that it plays a key role in the structure of the *Summa* itself. We recall that Aquinas structures the *ST* in accordance with the trajectory of all creatures, which come forth from God as Creator and return to God as Final End, mediated through God's providential sustaining power and direction (I.2*intro*). This trajectory begins with God's creation of entities in accordance with intelligible principles of existence and activity, reflecting the specific kinds that they instantiate. Generally speaking, it ends in the creature's attainment of its final end through the (more or less) complete development and expression of these intelligible principles, which is to say, its perfection, in and through which it attains its fulfilment as a distinctive expression of God's wisdom and goodness (I.6.4). The universal desire for happiness is nothing other than the distinctively human expression of this broader metaphysical tendency, and that is the sense in which we and all of creation are joined together in a common journey towards one and the same final end (I-II.1.8).

At the same time, the rational creature participates in this process in a distinctive way, that is to say, consciously and deliberately, guided by a self-reflective conception of what it means (at least for the individual), to attain the perfect fulfilment of happiness (ibid.). For this reason, our pursuit of happiness can go wrong, in a way that it cannot go wrong for any non-rational creature. Our conception of happiness may be corrupt, or we may be unable to act consistently in accordance with a sound conception, and in either case, our happiness will be undercut by sin. But by the same token, we have the possibility of pursuing happiness of a kind that is unavailable to non-rational creatures, and which we ourselves could not have envisioned apart from God's revelation of the personal, Triune reality that God most fundamentally is (I-II.109.3 and 5). Thanks to God's initiatives, we are capable of pursuing and attaining direct union with God as a personal reality, to respond to a God who befriends us, in a way that comprehends and infinitely exceeds our natural orientation towards God as the first and final cause of all things (I.12.4, I-II.3.8, I-II.62.1). Clearly, happiness understood on this level meets the classical criterion of a worthwhile and admirable state. At the same time, the more limited kinds of happiness available to us through grace, or through the proper development of our natural dispositions, are likewise objectively admirable, since each consists in the practice of the (infused or acquired) virtues, which are as such praiseworthy.

So far, we have focused on the way in which Aquinas' analysis of happiness allows him to bring together his overall metaphysical theology of creation and providence with the moral theology of the *Secunda Pars*, which, we recall, focuses on the way in which the rational creature returns to God through its own proper mode of activity, that is to say, through the agent's own intentional acts. Aquinas' identification of terrestrial happiness, in both graced and connatural forms, with the practice of the virtues tethers his moral theology to his broader synthesis in another way. That is, the virtues are integral to happiness, because they are themselves perfections, which is to say, stable dispositions towards the full and proper development and exercise of the distinctive faculties of a rational creature. Thus, each of the faculties of the human soul has its own proper virtues – the intellectual virtues, including both faith and prudence, perfect the various faculties of the intellect; justice, hope and charity perfect the will, and the virtues of fortitude and temperance perfect the spirited and desiring passions, respectively (I-II.58.1, I-II.61.2 and 4). What is more, Aquinas' insistence on the connection of the virtues implies that in the case of someone in possession of genuine virtue (even on the level of acquired virtue), the virtues operate together in such a way as to integrate the inclinations and activities of the rational creature (I-II.65.1).

Given his account of the virtues as perfections, we see that when Aquinas identifies the genuine forms of terrestrial happiness with the practice of the virtues, he is not imposing a preconceived set of values, stipulating that true happiness just is a life of moral goodness. On the contrary, the overall logic of his analysis of both happiness and the virtues in terms of perfections requires this identification. It holds true, in a qualified sense, even with respect to the supreme happiness of the Beatific Vision. Recall that the Vision too is an activity, reflecting the fullest possible engagement and development of the agent's rational faculties for knowledge and love, as these are transformed through grace and glory (I-II.3.1,2). Like every other fully developed rational activity, this activity can only take place through the operation of virtues, especially charity, through which the blessed love God. What is more, since Aquinas takes the virtues as the organizing motif for the concrete moral precepts and ideals discussed in the *Secunda Pars*, his analysis of happiness connects his broader theology to the specific content, as well as the formal principles of his moral theology.

There is thus a good case to be made for the cogency of Aquinas' analysis of happiness as perfection, understood as the practice of the virtues. We may still ask how well this analysis can be squared with a further classical criterion – that is to say, is it plausible as an attractive, satisfying, and desirable way of life? Admittedly, this is not so clear. For most people today, references to the virtues are likely to evoke images and associations that may well be admirable and inspiring, but will probably also be somewhat depressing, even repellent. Probably few of us would want to be virtuous, in the terms understood by our peers – that is to say, emotionally subdued, always under control, not disposed to spontaneity or fun, perhaps a bit smug and censorious.

In addressing this issue, we must first of all simply acknowledge that we cannot really even imagine what it would mean, subjectively, to attain the Beatific Vision, and for that reason, if no other, we cannot convey the attractiveness of final beatitude. Indeed, the logic of Aquinas' analysis, particularly taken together with his doctrine of God, leads him to an account of beatitude that is in many respects unattractive. God offers the supreme, comprehensive and unchanging fulfilment of our capacities for knowledge and desire, and while Aquinas argues that it thereby fulfills and infinitely exceeds more mundane desires, the fact remains that the happiness of the Vision seems to lack much that we would naturally regard as components of a humanly satisfying life (I-II.4.7). Most disturbingly, it does not require the society of other people, although Aquinas does say that communion with associates in beatitude will contribute to its 'good estate' (I-II.4 and 8) Nonetheless, it is doubtful whether any kind of happiness that we can now imagine would genuinely be desirable, considered as an everlasting activity. No matter what we most value or enjoy, would we really want to continue doing it for ever and ever? Arguably, only a timeless and comprehensive Vision, in which we rest in the perfect love and fellowship of the Trinity, would be tolerable, let alone attractive, as the object of a literally unending consciousness – and in this life, we simply cannot imagine such a condition.

Initially, Aquinas' construal of terrestrial happiness as the practice of the virtues might seem to be no more persuasive, for the reasons just mentioned. Recently, some Aristotelian philosophers have defended similar claims on the grounds that the virtues are necessary, or at least reliable and proper means to attaining other kinds of goods, more clearly related to happiness as we normally understand it – for example, we are more likely to stay healthy over time if we practice temperance in food and drink.[9] But this argument is notoriously problematic, and in any case Aquinas seems to reject it out of hand (I-II.2.4 and 8). Nonetheless, these philosophers are right to remind us that for Aquinas, the practice of the virtues is connected to the attainment of the ordinary necessities and pleasures of life – only, the link in question is conceptual, not instrumental. Let me explain.

Recall that the virtues, properly understood, are perfections of the natural capacities of the human soul, including both cognitive and affective faculties. As perfections of a rational animal, they reflect processes of (increasingly) self-reflective formation in the light of ideals of human goodness or nobility or rectitude – they are thus dispositions of reason, as Aquinas repeatedly remarks. But at the same time, they are also perfections of the capacities of an animal (albeit a very sophisticated social animal), including natural inclinations to desire and pursue a range of objects and activities proper to organic life and social existence. Thus, precisely because the virtues are perfections of natural appetites, they will necessarily be dispositions to pursue and to enjoy a wide range of objects and activities in an appropriate and harmonious way. For example, the virtue of temperance comprises a family of rational dispositions, through which the agent pursues the basic aims of our sensual, animal life in a reflective, appropriate way – but the reasonable character of temperate desire and enjoyment should not obscure the fact that the temperate person, considered as such, really does desire and enjoy the sensual goods of human life. A temperate woman does not just eat whatever comes to hand when she is hungry, or pursue sexual relationships with any attractive and willing stranger who turns up when she feels in the mood – but she does eat, and (probably) she participates in sexual relations, in the appropriate ways, and normally she enjoys herself while doing so.

My point is this. The Thomistic ideal of happiness, considered as the practice of the virtues, does not simply equate happiness with the well-being of the human organism, understood in terms of physical health and vitality, reproductive success, and the like. Certainly, he does not regard the virtues as instrumental to the attainment of organic well-being or (much less) specific desiderata such as health or security,

---

9 These would include most notably Philippa Foot, whose program is set forth most recently in *Natural Goodness* (Oxford: Oxford University Press, 2001), Rosalind Hursthouse (with some qualifications), *On Virtue Ethics* (Oxford: Oxford University Press, 1999), and from a more theological perspective, John Bowlin, *Contingency and Fortune in Aquinas' Ethic* (Cambridge: Cambridge University Press, 1999).

as contemporary Aristotelians tend to do. But neither does he sever all connections between the practice of the virtues, and the pursuit of the more fundamental components of a naturally good human life. Rather, the virtues are dispositions through which characteristically human desires and capacities, naturally directed towards a wide-ranging set of pleasant objects and activities, are disposed in such a way as to pursue these in rational, appropriate, and harmonious ways. Thus, in order to count as perfections of the relevant capacities, the virtues must also preserve and even strengthen the agent's orientation towards the natural goods, without which human life could not be sustained or developed. Once this point is appreciated, an ideal of happiness as the practice of the virtues begins to be more persuasive. Under normal circumstances, the life of virtue will be a life devoted to the fundamental aims that inform everyone's life, to some degree at least – including basic aims such as nutrition and security, and (probably) sexual pleasure and reproduction, as well as more distinctively human and rational aims. It will include most of the activities that nearly everyone would regard as enjoyable – the basic activities of animal life, marriage and child-rearing, productive work, and much else. The virtuous individual pursues and enjoys these activities, just as nearly everyone else does – but she will do so in a particular way, exercising her capacities in a rational, self-reflective way, in accordance with some overall sense of what it is to live a good, decent, praiseworthy human life. And even when circumstances are not favorable, when the individual cannot attain or securely enjoy some aspects of basic well-being – due to sickness or adverse circumstances – he can still find satisfaction in the practice of the virtues, both through enjoying those basic goods that are still within his grasp, and through reflective participation, in some way or other, in ideals that he regards as attractive, compelling, or beautiful.

In addition, in his discussion of the Beatitudes (I-II.69), Aquinas offers a further perspective on the happiness enjoyed by those whose practice of the virtues stems from grace and is oriented, through its own inner dynamism, towards fulfilment in direct union with God. While those transformed by grace cannot yet be said to have attained complete and secure happiness, nonetheless they anticipate full happiness, and in a sense begin to enjoy it, through hope (I-II.5.3, I-II.69.1). Hope is a theological virtue of the will, but in its exercise it draws support and substance from the individual's sense of herself as someone whose activities are already oriented towards charity and final union with God, which is to say, her sense of herself as someone leading a life of virtue informed by grace. Understood in this context, the Beatitudes, which

Aquinas insists we begin to enjoy even in this life, reflect the distinctive joys and satisfactions that stem from the practice of the infused virtues. In particular, they reflect the serenity and inner freedom that comes to someone disposed, through charity, to find security and joy in his union with God. Even in this life, we can begin to develop a kind of detachment and security proper to the reign of God, by placing our own affairs in the perspective of God's providential care; we begin to possess the land through self-possession, as our desires and fears are brought into some alignment with that care; and we accordingly find that our hunger and thirst are satisfied as we begin, however imperfectly, to see God. We cannot imagine what final beatitude will be like, but we can experience and enjoy some anticipations of that beatitude through the serenity, fearlessness, and wisdom that come through the experience of God's grace. This experience, in turn, gives us further grounds to hope that our final beatitude, while exceeding all that we can imagine, nonetheless will represent the fulfillment of our deepest longings – a life of joy, lived in the freedom of children in the household of God.[10]

---

[10] I would like to thank Joseph Blenkinsopp for his comments on an earlier draft of this essay. Needless to say, any remaining mistakes or infelicities are my own.

Virtues

JAMES F. KEENAN SJ

This essay is divided into three parts. First, we consider Thomas' teaching about the virtues in his anthropological and moral epistemological frameworks, concluding with its evident place in the natural law. Second, we turn to his distinct understanding of the acquired cardinal virtues and the infused moral and theological virtues. We conclude by addressing the matter of each of the four cardinal and three theological virtues.

THE VIRTUES AND NATURAL LAW

In order to understand Thomas on the virtues we must presume to use his own concepts. He argues that the human being is made up of a variety of powers (I.77–78). When speaking of the virtues, he focuses on two general powers of the soul: the intellectual and the appetitive. While the first is about the practical and speculative intellect, the latter is more complicated and prompts him to break it down into three specific powers: the intellectual appetite or the will, and two sensitive powers, which he names the concupiscible and irascible powers. Thomas notes that these latter two represent first that we seek to acquire what seems necessary for us and second that we resist that which seems to corrupt us (I.81.2corp).

Thomas notes that these powers have no determined ends in themselves (I-II.50.5; I-II.51.3). Therefore each power needs to be realized or developed through appropriate habits or dispositions. These particular habits dispose the particular power to act well or to not act well. In a manner of speaking these habits or dispositions mediate a power's ability to be realized into action (I-II.49). But these mediations are not toward neutral actions, for inevitably whatever we intend to do aims to better or worsen us.

These mediations are then toward right or wrong practices. For this reason we need to choose right habits that mediate the powers of the soul to their right realization. Here, then, is where the virtues enter, that is, as good habits that dispose a power toward proper or right actions. Conversely, vices are bad habits that dispose a power toward improper or wrong actions.

These virtues then direct the power by disposing it to performing sets of actions, that is, practices which in turn further realize the power (I-II.54.4*corp*). In a manner of speaking, these habits develop precisely as they are habitually practiced. A good way of understanding this is to recognize that Thomas uses the word '*exercitio*' that is, exercise or practice, in order to discuss how we acquire a habit. With clear appreciation for the athleticism of the term, Thomas instructs us that by exercising ourselves through right practices we train ourselves into being disposed virtuously to act rightly (I-II.65.1*ad1*; I-II.65.3*ad2*; II-II.47.14*ad3*; II-II.47.16*ad2*).

Virtues are therefore the right habits or dispositions for mediating the powers of the soul. Simply put, they are right habits that develop our capacities to live and act rightly. These virtues inhabit our powers; they enter into the fiber of our powers, funneling our capacities toward right practices. They become our second nature.

The virtues fit into Thomas' anthropological profile of powers and their 'perfection.' We should not take this word 'perfection' to refer to some utopic ideal. Rather for the scholastics, the word 'perfect' functioned often as a verb, as in 'the virtues perfect powers,' and today 'perfect' would mean 'rightly realize' (I-II.54.4*corp*; I-II.55.2*corp*; I-II.56.1*corp*; I-II.57.5*corp*; I-II.59.5*ad1*; I-II.64.4*ad2*; I-II.65.1*ad1*). The good habits then perfect or rightly realize the powers within us.

Not only do these virtuous habits 'perfect' our powers, but they perfect our intentionality as well. Intention for Thomas is not simply the willing of this or that action, but rather the seeking of a particular end (I-II.12.1*corp*). In order to intend an end, the intention needs to receive from reason some worthy object to intend. For Thomas, the object ought to be one of virtue (I-II.19.1*corp*). Intending a right or virtuous object leads the person into virtuous, intended activity. Indeed, the acquisition of virtue is precisely by the habitual intentional realization of the virtuous objects of the will.

Thomas therefore helps us to see immediately a rather strikingly dynamic moral agenda. Morality is not primarily about doing right actions and avoiding wrong ones. Rather morality is primarily about acquiring virtues for the moral life through practices and then further growing into those virtues by further practices. Morality is then a life project and Thomas gives us the building blocks or the virtues for constructing that life.

In Christian history this is a welcome development. Much of the history of moral theology is written, as John Mahoney correctly argues, in the sin manuals from the sixth until the twentieth century and found extensively throughout the history of Christianity in general, and Roman Catholicism in particular. These manuals were originally meant to help abbots settle on fair penances when absolving monks and others from their sins. Later, when in the thirteenth century all Christians were mandated to make a yearly confession, more elaborate confessional manuals were developed. In those manuals, the moral life is simply the avoidance of sin and, if sins are committed, the absolution of sin through the sacrament of penance. In these sin manuals, the virtues make an appearance but only as auxiliary to the strategy of avoiding sins: virtues exist not for our right realization or for doing the good, rather they simply help us to avoid sin.

In this light, like other thirteenth-century scholastics who wrote *summas*, Thomas gives us a moral agenda that is extraordinarily *positive, comprehensive, human, and hopeful*. The moral agenda is no longer simply and entirely about sinful actions. The moral agenda is not singularly about actions to avoid, but rather about virtues to pursue, acquire, and realize. The moral agenda then aims positively at moral development and growth.

The virtues are no longer primarily restraints against sinful action; rather they are the embodiment of the character traits for how the human person can become fully alive. In this *positive* agenda not only do virtues function differently, sin does as well. Sins are defined now as that which diminishes human growth (I-II.74–89). The result is that even the notion of human sin expands because it is now not simply the action that we should avoid but, more importantly, the vice we dare not acquire. Worse than performing an isolated action is to engage in a vicious habit that will subsequently engender a plethora of subsequent vicious actions.

The agenda is *comprehensive* because it encompasses the virtues and their contraries, that is, the vices (I-II.71–73), as well as virtuous practices and actions and vicious practices and actions or sins. Both the person's interiority and the exterior actions and practices which emanate from the acting person are subject to moral consideration. The interiority of the person, let us remember, concerns both the powers being formed by the virtues and the intentions being shaped by the virtuous objects.

The moral agenda is also more *human* because now what is evaluated as 'moral' are not generic classes of actions, but rather classes of virtuous habits that are embodiments of the characters we ought to develop. Indeed when we examine the cardinal virtues of Thomas we see the profile of the type of person we ought to become, yet that profile only becomes expressed when it perfects a particular person's powers. The humanity of the virtues is that they provide a certain 'second nature' to the individual person and they really are only virtuous when they perfect one particular person's particular powers.

Above all, the structure is remarkably *hopeful*. The entire structure of the *Secunda Secundae* is based on seven sections each encompassing one of the seven virtues. That the entire matter of moral theology comes down to the virtues is, in itself, an affirmation of the human being as competent to be master not only of her or his actions, but of her/his very self.

In conclusion, we should note that Thomas Aquinas' understanding of the virtues is within the framework of the natural law. Thomas discusses the natural law having outlined his entire anthropological profile of powers, inclinations, intentions, ends, habits, virtues, etc. (I-II.94). Thomas has already explained that the good we intend by the habitual exercise of virtuous practices is the perfect: it is good because it is its perfection, its right realization, its end (I.4–6). This is the natural law, then, to pursue through the virtues the right ends of our own natural inclinations or powers. Thomas tells us that every inclination of every part of ourselves, for example, the concupiscible and irascible powers, belongs to the natural law inasmuch as it belongs to the rule of reason (I-II.94.2*ad*2). Thus whatever in us that can be ruled by reason is contained under the law of reason (I-II.94.2*ad*3).

Naturally Thomas moves to asking whether all virtuous acts are prescribed by natural law. (I-II.94.3). He confirms that all virtuous acts belong to the natural law. The human is, by nature, inclined to act according to reason and this is to act according to virtue (I-II.94.3*corp*). In short, since reason rules the other powers, similarly all the inclinations belonging to these powers must be directed according to the order of reason (I-II.94.4*ad*3).

The insistence that the virtues belong to the natural law does not compromise our understanding of Thomas' ethical agenda as positive, comprehensive, human, and hopeful. Rather, on reflection, the reverse is implied, namely that Thomas Aquinas' natural law theory was itself more positive, comprehensive, human, and hopeful than others might have interpreted it as being.

BECOMING VIRTUOUS

How do we become virtuous? We saw above that Thomas uses the concept *'exercitio'* to talk about repeated practices which train the powers toward their right realization. This is how we acquire the cardinal
virtues. But Thomas acknowledges that we become virtuous in two
very different ways: by acquisition and by grace (II-II.49.1ad2). When
Thomas turns to how the virtues are caused in us (I-II.63), he begins
to unfold a fairly complicated and elaborate system of connections
between the virtues. First he claims that inasmuch as virtue perfects us
to the good, we should realize the good is defined as such by two rules
(referring back to I-II.19.3 and 4). First there is the good defined as such
by human reason, but there is also the good ruled by divine law. Now
virtue as the good defined by reason is acquired through rightly willed
and intended practices. To the extent that these practices are coherent
with human reason, to that extent they make us more rightly ordered.
But when virtue ordains us to the good as defined by the divine rule,
then those dispositions cannot be acquired by us, but only infused into
us by God's power. Here Thomas describes God as the efficient cause of
such virtues and argues that only by God's free gift do we receive these
infused virtues.

Thomas identifies the acquired virtues as the cardinal virtues
(I-II.61). The cardinal virtues are made up of the three moral virtues, justice, fortitude, and temperance that perfect respectively the three appetitive powers, the will, and the irascible and concupiscible powers. In
turn these three virtues are, as we will see, perfected by the intellectual
virtue, prudence. Prudence perfects practical reason. Inasmuch as these
virtues are governed by the rule of reason, prudence then directs these
virtues by this rule.

Thomas distinguishes the infused virtues as the theological virtues
(faith, hope, and charity). Faith perfects the intellect, and hope and charity perfect the will. Together they bring reason and will under the rule of
God, and empower these powers with the grace of God.

Just as Thomas assigns these sets of virtues as acquired or infused,
he also asks whether the moral virtues of justice, temperance or fortitude can also be in us by infusion. Thomas replies that they can, but
that when infused these moral virtues are not like the acquired ones
which enable us to work and live well in the natural world. Rather these
are infused in us so as to endow us with additional capacity to achieve
the supernatural end won by the theological virtues (I-II.63.3*corp*). These
infused moral virtues do not have, then, the same matter as the acquired

virtues. Acquired justice is about observing what is due in human affairs, while infused justice is about observing the due among the communion of saints (I-II.63.4*corp*, *ad*1, *ad*2).

Beside these two articles from question 63 of the *Prima Secundae*, Thomas rarely refers again to the infused moral virtues, but by highlighting them he reminds us that God's direct activity in our moral lives simply is multitudinous. God is constantly empowering us. First, Thomas presupposes that God always fundamentally works within us. What really differentiates infused from acquired virtues is not that God is the cause in one, but not in the other. On the contrary, Thomas says quite clearly that God causes both infused and acquired virtues because, even in those latter virtues, God 'works in every will and in every nature' (I-II.55.4*ad*6). What differentiates the two is that the acquired virtues require our agency; the infused require only our assent. Second, regarding the infused theological virtues, Thomas argues that the virtue of charity is the beginning and end of Christian virtue ethics (II-II.22–27). It is nearly impossible to divorce the infused virtues from the moral life of the Christian. Third, in addition to the infused theological virtues, Thomas discusses the gifts of the Holy Spirit (I-II.68) which are also infused and make us more amenable and receptive to divine inspiration. In short God infuses us with the gifts to prepare us for the infusion of the theological virtues. Thomas is so interested in the gifts (a topic mostly overlooked by scholars) that throughout the *Summa* II-II, he returns to each of the gifts (II-II.8–9, 45, 52, 121, 139). Fourth, Thomas also treats the fruits of the Holy Spirit by which we delight in what we do, having been moved by the gifts of the Spirit (I-II.70). Thus grace manifests itself throughout the economy of virtue in the *Summa Theologiae*.

Still these claims must be seen within the context of a development that Thomas makes in the moral tradition. It occurs when he asks whether the traditional definition of virtue (attributed to Augustine, but more likely a later scholastic compilation) is suitably defined. The definition is: 'Virtue is a good quality of mind by which one lives righteously, of which no one can make bad use, which God works in us without us' (I-II.55.4*ob*1). Thomas claims that the definition 'comprises perfectly the whole notion of virtue,' but then adds that the phrase 'which God works in us without us' is applicable only to the infused virtues of which God is the efficient cause (I-II.55.4*corp*) He reiterates this modification again in the response to the sixth objection in the same article.

What has Thomas done? Effectively he has broken from Augustine. In the *City of God*, Augustine argued that virtue is ordered love (15.22).

This is based on the simple insight that an ordered will is a good love, and a misdirected one is a bad love (14.7). From that he adds that passions are evil if the love is evil and good if it is good (14.7.2). Still because of the need for our will to be ordered by God's grace, Augustine insisted in *De Trinitate*, that virtues without charity were not true virtues (XV.18.32) and that no one could have charity without first having faith. Basing his argument on Paul's claim that everything not from faith is sin (Rom 14.23), Augustine held that all true virtues were rooted in charity without which they were false and not true (*City of God*, XIX.25).

Thomas does not hold this. Thomas allows us to speak of the cardinal virtues under the rule of human reason. Certainly, for Christians, these cardinal virtues could be formed by charity. But, unlike in Augustine, were they not formed by charity, they could still be cardinal virtues. For instance, Thomas considers how virtues are affected by mortal sin. A mortal sin is incompatible with a divinely infused virtue; a mortal sin is our rejection of charity. When we commit a mortal sin, we automatically lose charity. But by a mortal sin, though we lose charity, we do not lose any acquired virtue, because these virtues are in us by the cultivation of habitual practices and one act cannot sufficiently undo an acquired habit by a single act (I-II.63.2ad2).

Thomas develops his position of the acquired virtues not needing faith or charity by discussing the theological virtues as being united in charity and the cardinal virtues being united by prudence. In short, he establishes two ambits for the virtues, following from his first designation, that is, that the theological virtues come under the divine rule and the cardinal virtues come under the rule of reason.

Certainly for the Christian, and in speaking as a Christian one would say that this holds for all human beings inasmuch as we believe that we are made by God, the virtues are only perfectly virtues when they are perfected by charity (II-II.161.1ad4). Thomas believes that if all people are called to attain the fullness of humanity, then we need both the theological and cardinal virtues. Without charity one lacks that which finally perfects us and puts us in union with God (II-II.184.1corp). Still, the absence of the theological virtues does not mean, as Augustine believed, that one automatically lacks the cardinal virtues. On the contrary, Thomas insists that they are cardinal virtues if they have been acquired.

This means that the non-Christian can acquire the cardinal virtues just as the Christian can. Now Aristotle, Plato, Moses, Avicenna, Averroes, and Maimonides can be considered virtuous. Moreover human reason alone becomes the arbiter of what belongs to the cardinal virtues and what does not.

Here then Thomas accords a highly elevated role to prudence because by prudence, the cardinal virtues can observe the rule of reason. Whence then is the rule of reason established? Thomas expressly says that without prudence the moral virtues are not virtues but merely habits or dispositions. Only by prudence, uniting the moral inclinations under the rule of reason, do these habits become virtues (II-II.47.5ad1).

In this light Thomas further articulates these parallels between charity and prudence: the connection of the moral virtues results from prudence; the connection among the theological virtues results from charity (I-II.66.2corp; I-II.68.5corp). Thus all the matter of the moral virtues come under the one rule of prudence (I-II.65.1ad3; see I-II.66.2corp).

In the thirteenth century Thomas gives us then a way of studying ethics with an eye toward comparative study. While Augustine could not imagine a contemporary Confucian or Moslem as virtuous, Thomas could. Different cultures and different religious traditions have veritably true virtue systems just as Christianity does. That premise allows, for instance, Lee Yearly to compare Thomas' understanding of courage with Mencius'.

We can conclude then by asking whether the moral virtues need prudence and prudence needs the moral virtues (I-II.65.1), the cardinal virtues need the theological virtues (I-II.65.2)? The question is important because charity's end (union with God) is more important than prudence. But Thomas answers that without charity the acquired virtues are still virtues, though not perfectly or simply so. Though they can only attain their natural end, even as they were in many Gentiles, they are still virtues. To be disposed for the last end, however, we need charity. Charity does not in itself need the acquired moral virtues, though it does need the infused moral virtues (I-II.65.3), in order for us to be well disposed for whatever helps us toward maintaining union with God.

DIGGING INTO THE CARDINAL VIRTUES, DIGGING INTO THE THEOLOGICAL VIRTUES

In question 57 of *Summa* I-II, Thomas discusses the intellectual virtues and notes that there are two for the practical intellect which guides us in matters about this life. Art, he defines, as right reason about things to be made (I-II.57.3). Prudence, however, is distinct from art; it is right reason about things to be done (I-II.57.4). In order to act well, the agent needs to act as a whole person; the agent needs rectitude of appetite.

In order to highlight the ambit of each, Thomas retrieves a difference in activities which he developed earlier while addressing happiness. There he argued that either we make something in which our energy passes into another thing or we do something by which our energy redounds to ourselves and immanently perfects ourselves. Happiness can only be known in this latter activity (I-II.3.2ad3). Now in writing about the virtues he notes that the creative energy of an artist passes transiently into the object that is made; the creative energy of the prudent person redounds immanently onto the agent as the prudent person acts or does. Through prudence, we become what we do: people only become dancers by dancing, runners by running, and just persons by doing justice (I-II.57.4corp). Prudence then is for the doer. It is about right reason for things to be done and its ambit is enormous: Prudence is of good counsel about matters regarding our entire living (I-II.57.4ad3).

Prudence is then what puts the order of reason into the appetites: it makes our will and our passions subject to reason. But Thomas also helps us to see that the virtue of prudence needs the moral virtues just as the moral virtues need the rule of prudence (I-II.58.4–5; I-II.60.1). Without the moral virtues we would not have the moderated appetites to take and give prudent counsel.

Among the moral virtues, the most important is justice. While fortitude and temperance perfect the passions, justice perfects the will. He defines justice as being the constant will to give to each one his due (II-II.58.1). He adds that justice is the same as making things right, not essentially, but causally; for it is the habit which makes both the deed and the will rightly ordered (II-II.58.1ad2).

Thomas takes a decidedly 'other' orientation when speaking about justice. Asking whether our own dealings with our very selves need to be governed by justice, Thomas argues that our dealings with ourselves are sufficiently made right by temperance and fortitude (II-II.58.1ad4). Justice, instead, is about external affairs (II-II.58.3), though it emanates from the interior will made just by just practices (II-II.58.4).

Thomas differentiates justice as belonging to two types: general or legal justice and particular justice. The first allows us to see that the good of any virtue ought to refer itself to the common good (II-II.58.5–6). He calls this justice general or legal justice. As a particular virtue, justice puts us in right relationship with each person giving to each their specific due (II-II.58.11). According to his hierarchy, legal justice stands, then, above all the moral virtues by disposing us to the common good, while particular justice is superior to all other acquired virtues by putting us into right relation with other individuals, which is always greater than putting ourselves in right relation to ourselves (II-II.58.12*corp*; I-II.66.4).

Prudence perfects the passions as well. Of course, underlying this premise is the presupposition that the passions are capable of becoming good. Earlier, Thomas asks whether good and evil can be found in the passions (I-II.24.1). He answers that in themselves, there is no moral good or evil in the passions since good or evil depends on the reason; however, if they are subject to the command of reason, then they are good (I-II.24.1*corp*). He adds that the passions are found in and are common to the human and the animal, but only the human's passions can be commanded by the human's own will and reason (I-II.24.1*ad1*). He therefore denies that our passions are evil (I-II.24.2), though he does acknowledge that if a passion is contrary to the order of reason, it will incline us to sin; but if it is controlled by reason, it pertains to virtue (I-II.24.2*ad3*). Moreover, he also claims that passions can make our actions better (I-II.24.3), for since our good is founded on reason as its root, passions help spread the reasonableness throughout our very selves. It belongs to the perfection of the human good, therefore, that passions should be controlled by reason.

Prudence directs the moral virtues by determining the mean as their specific end. For instance, Thomas argues that in order for the passions to be virtuous they must observe the mean between too much and too little (I-II.64.1*corp*). Prudential reason sets this mean (I-II.64.1*ad1*).

Thomas then distinguishes between the rational and real mean. Justice needs the real mean; temperance and fortitude require the rational mean. The rational mean is not the real mean but only the mean in relationship to the agent. The norm for temperance and fortitude is then self-regulated. A temperate amount of sleep, nourishment, affect, leisure, etc., depends on what constitutes the extremes of excess and defect in an acting person. For some people eight hours of sleep is the norm; for others it is too much; for yet others, not enough.

Being about right relations among one another, justice observes a more objective mean, one that needs to be articulated for all, and not just the agent, as the due. All of distributive justice therefore depends on prudence directing us to this real mean.

Whether speaking of the rational or the real mean, prudence reflects on and then sets the mean. Certainly that we can prudently determine the rational mean to know the sleep we need is not a guarantee that we will prudently determine the real mean to distribute goods justly (I-II.64.3). And certainly the prudence to regulate temperance depends upon the virtue of temperance in the agent, just as the prudence to regulate distributive justice depends on the virtue of justice of the agent.

Interestingly Thomas insists that for the divine rule which governs the theological virtues, the summit and not the mean is the end. Theological virtues do not need nor observe the mean (I-II.64.4). The mean is a created rule; the divine, uncreated rule of the theological virtues is always exceeding. Here then we see how dynamic faith, hope and charity are. In a manner of speaking, our love, belief and hope is never, in this world, enough.

On this note then we turn to the theological virtues. It is central to understand that Thomas believes the theological virtues to be in sequence: faith, hope, and charity. Without faith there is neither hope nor charity: the first begets the second, the second begets the third (I-II.65.4–5; II-II.17.8).

Faith is an infused virtue that perfects the intellect (II-II.4.1–2). It enables us to believe in the truth of God and revelation. It is the foundational theological virtue (II-II.4.7). Still, if faith does not have the virtue of charity, it is lifeless. While lifeless faith is nonetheless faith, if there is no charity, it is not a virtue (II-II.4.5*corp*).

Given the arduousness of the pilgrim's journey, God gives us the infused virtue of hope that perfects our will. It enables us to maintain along the way the divine rule (II-II.17). Like faith, it only exists in the pilgrim and not in the blessed, who in seeing God no longer need to believe or hope in God, nor in the damned, who have no grounds for hope (II-II.18.2–3).

While all three are about the divine rule and all three concern God, charity is the one virtue that is proximate to God. Faith and hope are precisely about God as not yet; whereas charity is about union already (*iam*) being possessed (I-II.66.6*corp*; II-II.24.12*ad5*). Though Thomas considers charity as friendship with God (II-II.24.1), his preferential definition for charity is simply union with God (II-II.23.6*ad3*; II-II.27.4*ad3*; II-II.82.2*ad1*; II-II.184.1*corp*; see also I-II.67.6*corp* and *ad1*). Inevitably the end of the union is to be dissolved and to be in Christ (II-II.24.9*corp*). Echoing charity as union with God, Thomas frequently quotes *Psalm* 72. 28: My good is in adhering to God (I-II.109.6*corp*; I-II.114.10*corp*, II-II.23.7*corp*; II-II.27.6*ad3*).

Appreciating that charity is union, we ought not be surprised at the prominence that peace enjoys in the treatise on charity. As an effect of charity, peace results from a two-fold union, with God and with our neighbor (II-II.29.3). It is salutary not for what it offers, but for how Thomas situates it against a host of contradictories. For with respect to charity, we find as its contrary effects: discord (II-II.37); contention (II-II.38); schism (II-II.39); war (II-II.40); strife (II-II.41); and sedition (II-II.42).

What does it mean to be in union with God, the last end that we seek, in whom we hope to be dissolved? As proximate, charity becomes the virtue of privileged place, not because it is the first of the theological virtues: it is not, faith is. Rather, in the order of perfection, charity by being in union with the last end, can, as form, direct all subsequent virtues to a meritorious end (I-II.62.4corp; I-II.65.2corp; I-II.114.4corp, ad1, ad3; II-II.23.8). What does this mean? I find that Thomas consistently when discussing charity speaks of it as that out of which we act. In the *Summa*, when discussing a virtue he uses the structure of '*de temperantia*' or '*de justitia*' that is, 'about temperance,' or 'about justice,' but when he discusses charity he always uses the grammatical form, '*ex caritate*,' that is, that something is done out of charity. The structure is relevant.

When we say 'out of charity,' we are talking about so being in union with God that we can direct any worthy action not only toward its end, but also toward the supernatural end of justice. But intending a just action out of charity not only achieves the end of justice, but the just action is meritorious by the charity which motivates us. Merit for Thomas is only possible as the fruit of freely given grace, for no action can be meritorious unless it is done out of charity.

The virtues then allow us to be well and do well in the natural and supernatural order. They help us to grow in reason and in grace and they inevitably lead us to a life of being fully alive. In this way, then, virtue is its own reward.

Grace

PHILIP MCCOSKER

One could be forgiven for thinking, on reading the so-called 'treatise on grace' within Thomas' mature *Summa* (I-II.109–114), that the thirteenth century Dominican would agree with the twentieth century Carmelite, Thérèse of Lisieux, when she said shortly before dying that *'tout est grâce'* ('all is grace').[1] There is a strong sense in these questions that one needs grace to do anything whatsoever: thinking, knowing, willing, acting, loving. And, as we shall see below, there is a real sense in which this is true: for Thomas here we do indeed need God's grace to do anything, just as it is only by God's continuing act of creation that we are in existence at any moment. Absent God and God's grace and we would neither exist nor do anything. Granted that we have been created and do indeed exist, there is not much we can do without reliance, in some way or other, on God's grace.

God's grace then, whatever it may be, is central to the *Summa*. So central in fact that one's study of the theme should not really be restricted to the five questions under investigation here. A longer study would look at how Thomas' understanding of grace flows out of his treatment of predestination earlier in the *Summa*, and then how his treatment of grace is christologically shaped in his account of our graced adoption as children of God. It is important to read the *Summa* in the round.

But even if grace is one of the permeating themes of the whole *Summa*,[2] Thomas, a master of apposite distinctions, would not be happy without further differentiating this picture. In this way he eats his cake and has it in a variety of ways. In particular we will note how he is at great pains to maintain both the primacy of God and God's action – his

[1] See Thérèse of Lisieux, *Novissima Verba: The Last Conversations and Confidences of Saint Thérèse of the Child Jesus, May – September 1897* (Dublin: M. H. Gill and Son, 1953), 16.

[2] For one argument for this, see Thomas O'Meara, 'Grace as a Theological Structure in the *Summa Theologiae* of Thomas Aquinas', *Recherches de théologie ancienne et médiévale* 55 (1988), 130–53.

grace – as well as to assert humans' proper natural action. These two, although inconceivably different, are *not* related as a zero-sum. Thomas is able to maintain this point absolutely consistently in his mature *Summa* much more effectively than in some of his earlier writings because of his ever greater understanding of the nature of God's transcendence as well as his astute deployment of Aristotle's philosophy of nature.[3] A longer account would have to consider how the teaching presented in questions 109–114 on grace differs from his earlier writings on the topic. This would reveal much work by Thomas in the intervening years on the Letters of Paul and certain works of Augustine.

What then *is* grace for Thomas? In these questions in the *Summa* he gives a initially bewildering variety of answers and this variety reflects, I think, the fact that grace is for Thomas a way of denoting and grouping together the myriad effects on humans of God being God and imposing some theoretical order on them. Thus in these questions in I-II Thomas talks of grace as 'the principle of good acts' (111.1*corp*), as 'something supernatural' (110.1*corp*), as 'the effect of God's gracious will' (110.2*corp*), as 'God's love' (110.1*ad*1), as a 'movement' (111.2*corp*, 113.8*corp*), as a 'formal cause' (110.2*ad*1), as something which 'makes us formally pleasing to God' (113.2*corp*), something which 'makes us worthy of eternal life' (113.2*corp*), as a 'participation in the divine nature' (110.3*corp*, 112.1*corp*). Notice how many of these descriptions are dynamic and to do with verbs rather than nouns: grace is much more to do with God's action and ours than it is a special kind of thing. In many ways, in Thomas' optic, grace might best be seen as a kind of divine adverb to our human verb, whatever that action might be. Or, to put it in more Aristotelian terms, grace is accidental to our substance. Grace is that which enables us to do what is beyond us, to be more than we are: to be gracefully.

Thomas' thoroughly dynamic understanding of God as self-diffusive good means that God cannot but be grace. It is important to note early that in order to eat his cake and have it Thomas wears what one might call stereovisual spectacles. By means of stereovision – holding together two different perspectives at the same time – Thomas brings together a divine perspective and a creaturely one. Thus from the point of view of God there is nothing that God does or is which is not God and which is

---

[3] For the best account of Thomas' deployment of Aristotle's philosophy in his theology of grace, see Simon Francis Gaine OP, 'Aristotle's Philosophy in Aquinas's Theology of Grace in the *Summa Theologiae*', in Gilles Emery OP and Matthew Levering (eds), *Aristotle in Aquinas's Theology* (Oxford: Oxford University Press, 2015), 94–120. I am grateful to Gaine and Levering for allowing me to see a pre-publication copy of this article.

not gift or grace, and this is what Thérèse was on about. But from our point of view as creatures *in via*, travellers on the way to our divinely ordained end or goal, that simple active unity which is God plays out in our creaturely context in a textured, differentiated way. Thus it can appear from Thomas' account of grace, and especially in the accounts of some of his overly-slavish commentators and followers, that there are many different kinds of grace, reified as various special kinds of stuff, or tool, that one might need to solve different problems, much as one needs a whisk to beat eggs or breath to play the flute. Grace is much more like electricity which can achieve many different effects in different contexts: lighting a bulb as well as powering the internet. Grace is differentiated by its effects.

There are a number of general points which need to be borne in mind in coming to the questions on grace so as not to get the wrong ends of several sticks. Crucially for Aquinas, drawing on the recently translated works of Aristotle, especially his philosophy of nature, all entities which exist do so as particular natures and as such have capabilities coordinate with those natures. What we are determines what we can do, and likewise what we can do indicates quite a bit about what we are. Thus thinking and writing are capabilities consonant with the nature of being rational animals, they are natural abilities for us. They are not, however, natural for sunflowers. Were sunflowers given the ability to think and write those abilities would be super-natural which is to say beyond or without their natural capabilities, super-icing added on top, as it were, of the natural cake. Similarly, the *telos*, goal or destiny of a nature is consonant or proportionate to that nature. Thomas, a thoroughly teleological thinker like Aristotle, thinks that the ends or goals of natures are also important for telling us about those natures. So, for Thomas, it is absolutely crucial that our end or *telos* is to enjoy the plenitude of happiness in God. As humans, as plants, or as geese we have, as it were, our own stories within which to live. In the normal course of events we can only live within those narratives. We live out our narratives actualising the potentialities or possibilities within us according to our natures, tending towards the goals or ends of those natures. We should note that for Aristotle, as for Aquinas, this is decidedly not a static vision as our contemporary understanding of 'nature' might suggest, some abstracted collection of properties which a certain kind of thing has or exhibits. Rather, for Aristotle and Aquinas, this talk of 'natures', 'actuality', and 'potentiality', is a way of trying to understand the world as it is in all its dynamism and change. How is it that an oak tree grows from an acorn to full size, dies and decomposes as one entity? It lives out the narrative of its nature, 'oak-tree-ness', actualising the potential of the acorn to the full, constantly changing within the confines of its nature. Aquinas is extremely careful in his account of the operations of grace to preserve the integrity of our nature. Any action of God does not threaten that integrity or its actions at any point.

For Thomas, however, there is *another* narrative for rational animals like humans (and perhaps other animals) which is stretched out between creation and the eschaton, between an origin with God and an end of blissful happiness with God. As humans we are located in the middle of this narrative, looking backwards and forwards: more stereovision. We discover this second narrative from revelation: in the scriptures and paradigmatically and most fully in Jesus Christ. Once we know of this second narrative we live as it were straddling two narratives, as human natures within the created world around us, with all that goes with our nature: the joy of sex, the pain of childbirth, the boredom of homework, the inevitability of work, the frustrations of old age, the decay of the grave and much more. But our natural narrative is now situated within another narrative, that of a life created by God and which God wishes to consummate with us in Godself in the future. We have, as it were, to tell two stories about ourselves at the same time. These stories are dynamically intertwined and they are most definitely not mutually exclusive, as if, on entering the narrative of a life from and to God one suddenly escapes one's nature. They do not operate on the same 'level'.

How then does one coordinate or link up these two levels of existence? This is where grace comes in: it is God's many ways of bringing us to Godself without interfering or destroying our own nature. As we will see several times, Aquinas' understanding of the operations of grace allows him to emphasise both God's underlying and omnipresent action as well as our own natural freedom and action. The theologies of divine grace and human freedom are written on sides of the same coin.[4] Again he is able to eat his cake and have it. Thomas is always keen to avoid the twin dangers of any form of Manichaeism (a dualistic devaluation of the material and creaturely) or Pelagianism (an optimistic over-confidence in the abilities of humans to save ourselves without divine aid), by always emphasising *both* the full integrity, goodness, and

---

4 For a stimulating account of Thomas' theology of grace which focuses on these questions as the culmination of his account of the human as moral agent, and thus as the summit of his account of freedom, see Theo Kobusch, 'Grace (Ia IIae, qq 109–114)', in Stephen Pope (ed.), *The Ethics of Aquinas* (Washington, DC: Georgetown University Press, 2002), 207–18.

freedom of human nature and creation, *and* the ubiquity and constant
need for grace.

Turning then to the five questions which deal explicitly with grace
we find, as usual, a mass of careful distinctions which give the impression of a Linnaean taxonomy of different kinds of entity. We need to
remember our stereovisual spectacles: the multiplicity comes from our
creaturely perspective, from grace's several and various effects, the different kinds of grace are really ways of our conceptualising God's constant and simple action of self-diffusing goodness. Above all we must
avoid thinking of Thomas' distinctions between different kinds of grace
as divisions between different kinds of stuff, different kinds of godly goo
which do this or that. Rather Thomas' distinctions are ways of highlighting the way God's constant gracious action appears to us in different
contexts. Light appears differently as it illuminates different objects.

Question 109 sets the stage for Thomas' subsequent intricate distinctions in a startling way. The question concerns the grace of God and
proceeds by way of a series of questions, one for each article, in the form
of 'can one do x without grace?'. In all but one of these the answer is a
resounding 'no', and in the one exception it is a case of a hypothetically
qualified 'no'. Thus Thomas affirms that we need grace to know the
truth (109.1), to will and do the good (109.2), to love God (109.3), to ful-
fill the commandments (109.4), to merit eternal life (109.5), to prepare
for grace (109.6), to rise from sin (109.7), to avoid sin (109.8), to do good
or avoid sin after grace (109.9), and to persevere in grace (109.10). The
one exception with an equivocal answer is to the question of whether
one can love God without grace and the affirmative answer relates to
the pre-lapsarian human-being – from our point of view a hypothetical.
Loving God is natural to human beings, that is to say it is a capability
inherent in its nature, but it is the fall which damages this capability.
This is an important distinction throughout Thomas' treatment of grace:
between the human before the fall and the human after the fall, incor-
rupt and corrupt. Although Thomas doesn't focus his treatment of grace
around the issue of sin as much as Augustine does – and his creative use
of Aristotle's philosophy of nature is key here – nevertheless he returns
again and again to this distinction.

With this one notional exception Thomas' position is clear: we need
God's grace to do just about everything. Indeed he explicitly says in
the first question of article 109 that 'it is clear that just as all physical
movements are derived from the movement of the heavenly body as primary physical mover, so all movements, both physical and spiritual, are
derived from what is the primary mover simply speaking, which is God.

And so, however perfect a physical or spiritual nature is taken to be, it cannot proceed to actualize itself unless it is moved by God.' This is a remarkably radical statement: any nature, of every kind, cannot actualise itself without the movement of God. This is not to deny that the nature itself, once moved initially in some way by God, does not move itself – change, grow, sing – as well, but in some fundamental sense every nature's movement of itself is grounded in God's prior movement of it. And, crucially, these two kinds of movement do not compete, as we saw above.

Thomas helps us understand this further by differentiating the two movements. He is clear that natures can exercise their natural capabilities, for instance in our case we can know 'such intelligible things as we can learn through sense', in other words we can carry out the actions proper to our own natures under our own steam. But when it comes to doing things of a higher order, beyond our natures, it is then especially that we need the 'light of grace', for instance, as he puts it, the human intellect 'cannot know intelligible things of a higher order unless it is perfected by a stronger light, such as the light of faith or prophecy, which is called "the light of glory" since it is added to nature' (109.1*corp*). Here we see very clearly, as we shall see again below, how Thomas is keen to safeguard the integrity of our natures and yet also maintain that we can at the same time be capable of reaching beyond those natural capabilities with the illumination of grace. The choice of metaphor here and elsewhere is important: light leaves the objects it illuminates – the faculties of our natures – intact, it does not destroy or replace them but enhances them, dilating and expanding their capabilities. Not for nothing is Thomas known for the maxim which he frequently quotes in various forms: grace perfects nature but does not destroy it.

Again and again in the bulk of this question a repeated pattern emerges. Thomas relies on the distinction between our natures considered before and after the fall. Generally speaking in the now hypothetical pre-lapsarian state when our natures were not corrupted by the effects of sin – which Thomas sometimes calls the 'state of pure nature' (eg 109.4*corp*) – we were naturally capable of doing good and loving God (109.3), fulfilling the commandments (109.4), avoiding sin (109.8), actions 'natural' to our natures; and yet we would still need the initial gracious movement of God. In our actual case of natures corrupted by sin we still need God's initial gracious movement, but also need God's healing grace to overcome the effects of the corruption of sin, that our natures 'may be healed' (109.3*corp*).

But more than that, and in a sense regardless of sin, the actions of a nature are commensurate with that nature, according to its principle and end, and proportionate to its powers. This is the micro-narrative we mentioned above. Once this nature is situated within the macro-narrative of which God is the principle and end, the origin and goal, the landscape broadens and other possibilities beckon, ones which exceed the capabilities of the nature considered solely within the micro-narrative. Grace is the means of getting into, and staying in, the bigger narrative – exceeding our natures – which puts our existence on a journey which leads out from God in creation and returns to God in the eschaton. And further, any action which draws us further along the journey of that bigger picture – rising from sin, meriting eternal life, persevering in the good – also needs grace. Again one can distinguish between these two by noting that the former grace, which expands us as it were, has been called *elevating* grace (*elevans*), whereas the latter grace which is tied to the story of sin, its consequences, and their attenuation or remission, has been termed *healing* grace (*sanans*). Now, as I have emphasised, these are not to be thought of as two different kinds of thing, but different ways of looking at God's action in different contexts. It is Thomas' virtue to have used Aristotle's philosophy of nature to resituate the theology of grace on the cusp between what is natural and what is beyond nature. In so doing he does not ignore sin and its effects, but zooms out as it were to the broader metaphysical context.[5] The two contexts do not negate each other. In doing this Thomas is able to hold together Augustine's earlier emphasis on grace as healing the effects of sin, God's medicinal action in us to cure us and lead us back to himself, with Aristotle's philosophy of nature with its emphasis on the integrity, rationality, and dynamism of each nature. One might say Thomas' theology of grace enables him to hold together both the transcendence of our natures and the immanence of those natures.

---

[5]   Bernard Lonergan argued in a version of his doctoral thesis that Thomas was enabled to relocate the theology of grace by Philip the Chancellor's delineation in his *Summa de bono* of the 'theorem of the supernatural': the idea that human beings are called to that which is beyond their nature. See Bernard Lonergan, *Grace and Freedom: Operative Grace in the Thought of St Thomas Aquinas* (Toronto: University of Toronto Press, 2000), especially 17–18, 162–92. He relied in this on the historical work of Artur Landgraf's *Dogmengeschichte der Frühscholastik: Die Gnadenlehre* (Regensburg: Pustet, 1952). Subsequent theology has seen virulent battles over the term 'supernatural' sparked off by Henri de Lubac's *Surnaturel: Études historiques* (Paris: Aubier, 1946). We cannot go into that controversy here, but suffice it to say that my reading of Thomas suggests that both de Lubac and his fierce neo-Thomist detractors are both right and wrong.

In the short question 110 Thomas moves on to consider in greater detail just what grace might be thought to be. To be sure he doesn't give what appear to be straight answers and as usual considers the topic in response to some fairly narrow questions: is grace something in the soul; is it a quality of the soul; is it the same as virtue; is it the subject or power of a soul? These are not obvious questions for us today. Thomas starts out by analysing the workings of the Latin word for grace, *gratia*, in common usage and sees that it can be used in three related senses. First it can indicate someone's 'love' for another, as 'we might say that this soldier has the king's grace and favour' (I suppose 'grace and favour mansions' are a mark of the sovereign's love or grace in this sense); secondly it can indicate a gift which is given freely, *gratis* as we still say, with no expectation of payment; thirdly it can indicate the gratitude shown for such a free gift (gratitude coming from the same Latin root as grace). Why are these distinctions important for Thomas? They serve for him to highlight the differences between God's love and ours. Whereas our love for another presupposes something pleasing in the one we love, God's love conversely creates that which is pleasing in the one loved: God makes us lovable in loving us. God loves us by creating us but also by willing for us the eternal goodness which God is, and turning us towards him. We are back to the macro narrative. In doing all this God 'raises a rational creature above its natural state, to share in the divine good ... to say that someone has the grace of God, therefore, is to say that there is something supernatural in them, which God bestows.' How does this love take the form of a gift? Thomas tells us that God gives human beings the gift of 'habitual grace'. What is this? In addition to moving natures in the initial way described above, getting them going, God also gives them the graced disposition of acting beyond their natures, that is the wherewithal to act themselves in ways beyond their natural capabilities. This means giving natures the forms, powers and principles to advance beyond themselves. They allow a nature to form habits (persistent dispositions) to perform regular actions, hence habitual grace, beyond those of which it is naturally capable. This is why Thomas says grace is an accidental quality of the soul, so as to emphasise that the nature is not destroyed or displaced but rather that its capabilities are enhanced and expanded. For this reason grace cannot be the nature's substance for that would be to fundamentally change the nature such that it no longer itself exists. If grace were to act in this way it would be acting as a material or efficient cause and God would be the sole, invasive, agent. Thomas insists in this article that grace acts more in the way of a formal cause, luring, as it were, the nature to act in enhanced ways, with expanded habits and virtues. In this delicate balance, Thomas manages to describe how both we and God act in concert. This is enabled by the groundwork Thomas laid in the early questions of the first part of the *Summa* exploring the nature of God's transcendence such that God's primary causality does not displace, but rather enables and enhances, the secondary causalities of creatures, as well as his judicious use of the Aristotelian philosophy of nature.

Thomas' skill in making illuminating distinctions is brought to the fore in question 111. This question is the source of the many 'kinds' of grace which have often been reified into separate entities by Thomas' proximate and not so proximate commentators. Importantly he notes here that grace 'is ordained to the bringing back of humans to God' (111.1*corp*). That is what grace is doing overall. As I have stressed, the different kinds we will encounter here should be seen as different only from our side of the 'stereovision', that is to say grace in x or y context looks different because it is operating in that particular context, on particular natures in particular states. Thus, in the first article Thomas distinguishes between sanctifying grace (*gratia gratum faciens*) and freely given grace (*gratia gratis data*). It is important to see the pleonasm here: surely all grace is 'freely given' and all grace 'sanctifies'. What differs is the context of operation. The first kind of grace is one which heals us and makes us lovable or 'graceful' before God (undoing the effects of sin) and by which a person is 'united to God'. It is that which 'justifies' us and does so formally not efficiently (it is still I who am justified; I am not changed into another). The second kind of grace, for Thomas, is the grace which enables us to help make others graceful before God, a second, outward-looking, stage of grace, helping the recipients of grace to help others. As Thomas notes, this kind of grace is over and above the working of our nature (just like all grace) but it is also over and above any merit we might have earned ourselves: in both these senses it is 'freely given'.

Next, building on this inward/outward pairing, Thomas draws a crucial distinction between operative and co-operative grace in the second article. An effect is attributed to the agent or cause of that effect, so for Thomas grace is the movement of God in us and in this sense grace is considered 'operative', we might say from the side of the agent of grace. On the other hand, when considered from the point of view of the nature or soul which is moved and goes on to act outwardly in a graced way, this is termed co-operative grace. In the first case God alone is the mover, the 'gracer', in the second we are enabled to also be graced movers alongside God. It is tempting to divide these up into separate entities or movements but they are one grace, the one activity of the one gracious God. Thomas' next distinction is not dissimilar. He distinguishes between prevenient grace and subsequent grace, again based on grace's differing effects. Thomas describes the different stages of the working of grace in different contexts of our macro-narrative: grace heals us from the effects of sin, it moves us to want to do good, it helps us actually do that good, it helps us to continue wanting to do that good (persevering), and finally it aids us in reaching the glory of eternal bliss. Straightforwardly, Thomas says that each of these different 'snapshots' of the working of grace is relative to the others, so some come before others and vice versa and this is how some are prevenient (coming before) and others subsequent (coming after). Thomas crucially emphasises that these are 'not numerically different' – they are the same grace.

In the next question the Dominican turns to the 'cause of grace'. Thomas draws a striking link here between the operation and bestowal of grace and deification. Grace is, he says, 'none other than a certain participation in the divine nature' (112.1*corp*).[6] Grace gives a real access to God. For this reason he explains God alone can bestow grace. Even when we are cooperating with grace to lead another person back to God we are precisely *co*-operating with God who is the prime mover. As he has emphasised time and again in these questions: nothing can act above its nature. Otherwise put: a cause must always be 'higher' than its effect. If the effect is deification it cannot be worked by human nature alone. To be sure we can help the working of grace and we do this by being instrumental causes rather than principal causes – God is always the principal cause. The same idea underlies Thomas' understanding of sacramental causality.

Can we prepare for grace? 'Yes and no' is Thomas' careful, stereovisual or paradoxical response. Given that grace relates to human nature as form to matter, that matter needs to be prepared; we need to prepare ourselves. This is the affirmative side of the paradox. We must of course balance this simultaneously with the other side: every action of our free will is such only as a result of the movement of God. Thus our preparation for grace, which is really ours, is also God's. We are, as it were, partners, albeit at different 'levels', in a common task. God graces us to act in our own return to him. Thomas strives in his theology of

---

[6] For an account of Thomas' theology of grace from the perspective of union, which emphasises connections with Thomas' theology of the Trinity and draws on his whole *corpus*, see Bernhard Blankenhorn OP, *The Mystery of Union with God: Dionysian Mysticism in Albert the Great and Thomas Aquinas* (Washington, DC: Catholic University of America, 2015), chapter 6, 249–95.

grace, and indeed his theology *tout court*, to establish us theologically as God's co-operators by God's grace. One might say he wants to get us to see ourselves as God's friends, or family (which amounts to the same thing).[7] As I have emphasised earlier, God's action and our own are not exclusive. We both prepare ourselves and are prepared by God: this is the paradox of grace. God's action has priority, however – it is a lopsided or asymmetrical paradox. No matter how much we may prepare ourselves, God's grace is not necessarily bestowed. God's grace always 'exceeds any preparation by human power' (112.3*corp*). Viewed from God's point of view the bestowal of grace is uniform, but viewed from the human perspective, with varying degrees of preparation and cooperation, the effects of grace differ (112.4*ad*1). And, in any case, we cannot know whether we have grace or not for several reasons. Grace's principle, object and goal, namely God, is beyond our natures and therefore our power to know. God's light is so immense, Thomas tells us, that we cannot be certain that we have grace, but we can know 'conjecturally by means of signs' (112.5*corp*).

What are the effects of grace, if we receive it? Here Thomas uses the distinction between operative and cooperative grace again but adds into the mix a distinction between the godly and ungodly. He is especially preoccupied in question 113 with the justification of pagans: how does it happen? Thomas thinks this happens through a movement of the ungodly towards justice (another central Aristotelian category) and this happens by remission of sins which involves the bestowal of grace. Even the ungodly need grace, whether they realise it or not. Sin blocks that effect of divine love which is grace leading us to eternal life of happiness. The remission of that sin involves the bestowal of that blocked grace. As before Thomas strikes a paradoxical balance. The movements towards justice and away from injustice (sin) – Thomas insists that both are needed – which lead to the justification of the pagan are, as should by now be clear, both the work of the pagan and of God. God moves the pagan to will justice but that willing is nevertheless the pagan's own free willing. Because God and humanity operate with different causalities which do not exclude each other this is not a contradiction but a paradox of grace. Likewise, although the bestowal of grace occurs

---

[7] For a fresh account of Thomas' theology through the lens of friendship see Denys Turner, *Thomas Aquinas: A Portrait* (New Haven: Yale University Press, 2013), especially 152–68. For a philosophical analysis of Thomas' inflection of Aristotle's understanding of friendship see Daniel Schwartz, *Aquinas on Friendship* (Oxford: Oxford University Press, 2006), with my review in *Reviews in Religion and Theology* 15/1 (2008), 112–16.

instantaneously or without succession, from God's point of view as he is grace's principle, object and goal, nevertheless, from our point of view, from the perspective of the effects of that grace, there is temporal succession, so one can point to different 'stages' of grace such as the infusion of grace, the turning away from sin and towards justice, the remission of sin and the attainment of eternal life. As Thomas says 'there is nothing to prevent us from understanding two things at the same time provided that they are in some way one' (113.7*ad2*) – two apparently contradictory perspectives can be held simultaneously because they are grace. In the order of nature they appear successive, but in the order of grace they are simultaneous.

Interestingly, Thomas thinks that with respect to achievement, the justification of the ungodly is a greater work than that of creation for it effects the eternal participation in the divine nature. But when viewed from the perspective of the way this is done, the work of creation is greater, for it is done not out of anything at all (113.9*corp*). Similarly the justification of the ungodly is not a miracle because 'the soul is naturally capable of receiving grace' (113.10*corp*). This must mean that we are in some sense pre-ordained, as created in the image of God, for union with that God.

Our final question, 114, turns to the question of merit, the effect of cooperative grace in which we cooperate with God in the diffusion of grace. As Joseph Wawrykow has admirably noted, this question mirrors what has gone before.[8] The question of the meriting of grace is of course one which was made controversial in the period of the reformations but we must be careful not to read later disputes back into Thomas' text. He in fact presents, not surprisingly, a most nuanced position.

Thomas emphasises the absolute inequality between God and human beings which might lead one to argue that a human being could never merit anything from God, there being such an incommensurable difference, 'a very great inequality', between them (114.1*corp*). All the good in us is due to God. But of course God's difference is such that he can in fact establish his creatures in a kind of justice from which they can relate to God in a relative way according to the proportion and mode of what is done. Given that all good is God's in the first place, human beings can merit from God only by the good which they have received

---

[8] See Wawrykow's admirably lucid accounts of Thomas' theology of grace and merit in his *God's Grace and Human Action: 'Merit' in the Theology of Thomas Aquinas* (Notre Dame: University of Notre Dame Press, 1995), as well as 'Grace', in Rik van Nieuwenhove and Joseph P. Wawrykow (eds), *The Theology of Thomas Aquinas* (Notre Dame: University of Notre Dame Press, 2005), 192–221.

from him beforehand by divine ordination. By moving our wills towards good, following on from God's initial movement as discussed above, rational creatures can exercise their free will to do good and it is this which is meritorious. Notice how hard Thomas has worked to ensure that we realise God's major role in this – that merit is only ours in quite a qualified, relative, sense, but it is nevertheless really our merit achieved by our free will. As usual he has struck a careful paradoxical balance in which God plays the major, and determining, but thoroughly enabling, role. Our work, as Thomas goes on to say, is rewarded according to the grace by which we are 'made partakers of the divine nature and adopted as a child of God to whom the inheritance is due by right of adoption' (114.3*corp*). A person cannot merit the 'first grace', that grace by which we are made lovable to God, both because, as we have seen, grace is above the order of nature but also because, in our unlovable state, sin gets in the way of any merit (114.5*corp*). Once a person has that first grace however, and is lovable before God, they can merit for another person that same grace, because that is what friends do, it is 'congruous with the relation of friendship', and this is congruous merit. What we can't do is merit for another by 'condign merit' which God alone, or God acting in Christ, can do (114.6*corp*).

Interestingly, Thomas insists that merit is more closely involved with the exercise of charity or love than the other two theological virtues, faith and hope. This is because the principle of grace is God's love, just as its goal is the enjoyment of God's love in eternal life. Charity leads the other virtues in seeking that goal (114.4*corp*). Similarly, but somewhat surprisingly, because temporal goods of various kinds may help in attaining that goal, by leading us to virtue, they can be merited by someone who has the first grace. Perhaps we can think of this as an argument for meriting to receive inspiring books or the money to do good works.

One might think – and some have done so – that Thomas' account of grace in these questions is insufficiently theological. Where are the references to Christ, to the Spirit? The fact that Thomas in the questions is relocating or re-expressing the theology of grace from within the framework of the language of natures, habits, powers and ends – an Aristotelian framework – does not mean his theology is less than Christian. Far from it. At strategic points in these questions he indicates that although he is using Aristotle's philosophy as primary currency here, what he is saying could be perfectly well expressed in more familiar Christian guise. Thus what has been emphasised above about his efforts to safeguard the natural, to establish us as cooperators with

God, as friends and family of God is directly related to Thomas' christology. As Cornelius Ernst rightly notes, a theology of grace is fundamentally an account of the relation between God and creation and the
paradigm for such a relation is Christ.[9] Thus it is no wonder that there is
an isomorphism between Thomas' christology and his account of grace.
You could say grace is christomorphic: in human, creaturely, form grace
takes a Christic shape, and so, to advance from grace to grace we need to
be and to act ever more like Christ. Thomas is clear that our access to
grace is through Christ *via* the Church. It is the 'grace of Christ' which
we receive (109.10ad3); by receiving that Christic grace we are 'created
anew out of nothing' in Christ Jesus, that is to say we become Christic,
take on Christ's filial relation to the Father: we are adopted as children of
God (110.2ad3). Grace comes through 'spiritual regeneration by Christ'
(113.3ad1): we become new, recreated, precisely by taking on the form
of God's children, God's relatives (110.4corp). This is the effect of grace,
how we are drawn back to God.[10]

It is true that the trinitarian, christological strand through these
questions is thin. Why does Thomas emphasise the Aristotelian matrix
here so much? We must remember that Thomas is writing a text for the
instruction of Dominican students, those who are themselves going to
preach and teach. The Christian narrative would be a given for them
and thus we can speculate that Thomas thinks they need to be given the
tools to reason with the faith, and shown how to do it. Aristotle's philosophy is his main interlocutor in these questions, but not to the exclusion
of other theologians, especially Augustine. And of course, precisely as a
Dominican text by a Dominican for Dominicans, Aristotle's philosophy
of nature was – and remains – a very useful tool for Thomas in arguing
against any kind of Manichaean dualistic devaluation (or worse) of the
goodness of creation.

Understandably these features have led to a variety of ways of reading these questions in the *Summa*, each with their own fundamental logic but rarely exclusive of each other. There are those like Theo
Kobusch, who emphasise the philosophical influences and moral context of these questions.[11] Others wish to stress how Thomas' theology

---

[9] See Cornelius Ernst, *A Theology of Grace* (Notre Dame: University of Notre Dame
Press, 1974), 62. This short, quirky, but highly stimulating text is well worth reading
in its entirety.

[10] The best study of filiation, how we are regenerated as children of God, and how
that relates to Thomas' christology is Luc-Thomas Somme, *Fils adoptifs de Dieu par
Jésus-Christ* (Paris: Vrin, 1997).

[11] See Kobusch, 'Grace'.

of grace is a complex, historically evolving, interweaving of earlier sources (Aristotle, Paul, Augustine) combined with novel insight, paradigmatically Joseph Wawrykow, building on Henri Bouillard and Bernard Lonergan.[12] Yet others choose to emphasise the theological, evangelical, and Dominican nature of the *Summa Theologiae* and read these questions through those lenses, and here one thinks of Nicholas M. Healy and now Frederick Bauerschmidt.[13] All of these readings are possible and it is a mark of a 'classic text' to be generative in this way and inspire many interactions with itself.

What has been most striking in Thomas' theology of grace? What can we take from this reading? What might be worth reflecting on in our construction of a theology for today and tomorrow? Thomas' theology of grace is thoroughly dynamic, pervaded by the Aristotelian concepts of *motus* and *motio*, a theology of action, an expression of Thomas' thoroughly active understanding of God. Our world is one of globalisation and change: it could well be that Thomas' highly nuanced ways of understanding (and thus also of *mis*understanding) the multiple coordinations between God's action and ours, as well as the many facets of change, might well be helpful in forging a theology for the future.

Central to that analysis would be the feature of Thomas' theology of grace that I have been most at pains to emphasise: his efforts to safeguard the integrity of created nature and its actions, precisely by underwriting those with his understanding of God's transcendence such that it does not displace but rather enhances the natural, such that God and creature can be co-operators in grace, indeed even friends. This drives, as we have seen, a theology of grace which emphasises its 'omni-applicability' and which militates against the reification of different kinds of grace into different separate entities. The prolix variety of Thomas' names for grace, along with his frank admission of its ultimately unknown nature, is an important reminder that we will not be able to comprehend grace completely in this life. Thomas, despite some appearances to the contrary, always eventually reminds us of the intrinsically and necessarily apophatic nature of theology.

This article has suggested that it is vital not to read Thomas' understanding of grace through subsequent doctrinal disputes, reading later

---

[12] See Wawrykow, *God's Grace*, and 'Grace'; Henri Bouillard, *Conversion et grâce chez S. Thomas d'Aquin: Étude historique* (Paris: Aubier, 1944); Lonergan, *Grace and Freedom*.

[13] See Nicholas M. Healy, *Thomas Aquinas: Theologian of the Christian Life* (Aldershot: Ashgate, 2003), 107–19; Frederick C. Bauerschmidt, *Thomas Aquinas: Faith, Reason, and Following Christ* (Oxford: Oxford University Press, 2013), 246–58.

hard divisions into his merely conceptual distinctions. Likewise we have noted how it is important to see how Thomas' views themselves changed over the course of his career, reacting and engaging with the different literatures he was reading. Methodologically this should remind us of the incarnational nature of theology: theology is always done in a context, in a particular place and time. Thomas' theology of grace reminds us of this supremely. Moreover in his use of Aristotle in this area of his theology as with so many others in the *Summa*, Thomas was using the best philosophy and science of his day and wrestling to produce a theology which integrated the best of other disciplines of the day: this too is a (huge) task that we cannot ignore as theologians if we are to follow Thomas today.

Person of Christ

SARAH COAKLEY

INTRODUCTION

Thomas treats of the major theological and philosophical issues of the person of Christ in the major opening sections of the Third Part of the *ST*: questions 1–26.[1] One of the most striking features of the introduction to the *Tertia Pars* is Thomas' acknowledgement (retrospectively enunciated) that the incarnation represents the heart of his whole theological endeavour: '. . . we must bring the *entire theological discourse* to completion by considering the Saviour himself', he writes (III*prol*, my emphasis). But such a belated placing of his christology in the complex structure of the *ST* does not, for Thomas, imply any sort of demotion of its significance – as it would, for instance, to a modern Barthian. On the contrary, it is intrinsic to the *exitus/reditus* scheme of the whole work that christology be left thus till the last book of the *ST* – precisely as climax, and as the unique means and access of salvific 'return': for 'Our Saviour, the Lord Jesus Christ . . . showed in his own person that path of truth, which, in rising again, we can follow to the blessedness of eternal life' (III*prol*). Any 'abstract' theological account of the incarnation, or philosophical clarification of its possibility, thus lies firmly within the narrative of an unfolding salvific event, with vital existential implications for all Christian life; and this entirely pastoral contextualization must be kept in mind throughout any discussion of the christology of the *ST*, abstract as it may seem at times. What Thomas' chosen structural arrangement does mean, nonetheless, is that the success or failure of his particular account of the intricacies of the relation of the human and

---

[1] Thomas' decision to divide his treatment of christology between 'person' (semantic and ontological issues: questions 1–26) and 'history' (the narrative of Christ's life: questions 27–59) is distinctive to him and part of the subtlety of his presentation. The latter account, however, relies crucially on the former: on this, see Paul Gondreau's chapter, 'Life of Christ', *infra*. See also I.2*prol* where there is a fleeting, but significant, anticipation of the climatic nature of the christology to come.

divine in Christ potentially affects the coherence of the *Summa*'s project as a whole. Either his construal of the unique intersection of the human and the divine convincingly sustains and infuses his more general vision of creation, providence, grace, virtue, freedom and salvation – or it does not. That contemporary interpreters of Thomas' christology should be so divided on the success or otherwise of his metaphysical strategies in propounding it is thus of no little significance, as we shall indicate. *Either* the sophisticated (but highly paradoxical) account that he supplies is one of the most philosophically-nuanced renditions in the Christian tradition of the person of Christ, albeit one that stretches attempts at analogous explanation to their limits; *or* it is a resounding failure, dogged from the outset by an impossible ambition to bring incompatible divine and human characteristics into one 'personal' expression.

In what follows, then, I shall choose to focus particularly on the notable theological and philosophical conundrums which arise in trying to explicate Thomas' unique account of the 'hypostatic union'. In fact this discussion only takes up part of the relevant sections of the *Tertia Pars* (principally questions 2–6 within the broader discussion of questions 2–15: this is the section which Thomas calls in the *Prologus* 'the manner of union between the Word and flesh'). But it will be necessary also to probe some elements of what Thomas calls the 'consequent implications', which follow in questions 16–26, and which not only display one of the first, and keenest, understandings of the later Greek ecumenical councils manifested in the Latin scholastic West,[2] but also opt for some quite radical opinions about the mutability and perfectibility of elements of Christ's human nature within his own incarnate life. Thomas' christology is, as we shall see, distinctive and daring even within the boundaries of an unshakeable commitment to historic conciliar 'orthodoxy'. In large part this is because of his scriptural acuity and his insistent concern to avoid any hint of 'docetism' (any mere 'appearance' of authentic humanity in Christ). In other ways it results from Thomas' fearless acknowledgement of the metaphysical *uniqueness* of the event he seeks to explicate: whilst philosophical reasoning can clarify this mystery up to a point, and certainly help to ward off doctrinal error, there is no better example in the *ST* of a revelatory doctrine which finally exceeds even the best attempts at analogical explication. No wonder, then, that Thomas changed his mind several times in his

---

[2] A useful recent discussion of Thomas' unusually acute knowledge of Greek conciliar materials is to be found in Marcus Plested, *Orthodox Readings of Aquinas* (Oxford: Oxford University Press, 2012), chapter 1.

career about how best to express this mystery.[3] If we are not ready for this 'scandal' element in his christology we shall find Thomas' account frustrating from the outset.

THE METAPHYSICS OF THE INCARNATION ACCORDING TO THOMAS

It is not insignificant, then, that Thomas opens his discussion of christology in the *Summa* (III.1), not with any ambition rationally to *demonstrate* the 'manner of union', but in *pedagogical* vein, with a section on the incarnation's 'fittingness'. This strategy reminds his readers at the outset that *convenientia* (theological 'appropriateness': the 'fittingness' of divine salvific condescension in Christ) is what governs this topic overall, more than abstract philosophical speculation; and this is a *trope* that is re-expressed sporadically throughout Thomas' christological exposition. In the course of this introduction to his christology Thomas also discloses his mature opinion that the incarnation would not have needed to happen had Adam not sinned (III.1.3*ad*5). Here he parts company not only from his own earlier (agnostic) assessment, but more decisively from that of several other leading scholastic authors. It is specifically the work of the Christ to rescue humanity from the ravages of sin, and this is the heart of the incarnation's 'appropriateness', as understood by Thomas.

For the purposes of a succinct exposition, I shall focus here on four related issues which Thomas tackles within the crucial sections of the *Tertia Pars* (qq2–26) which now follow. None of them is without exegetical or philosophical intricacies or difficulties, as we shall chart.

The semantics of the incarnation

The first, and tangled, issue is one of sheer christological semantics. Much difficulty is enshrined in the technical language in use here; but Thomas is never one to shirk exacting linguistic and philosophical distinctions. On the one hand he has of course inherited from the Greek conciliar

---

[3] A helpful introductory account of consistency and shifts in Thomas' christological thought can be found in Wawrykow, 'Hypostatic Union' in Rik van Nieuwenhove and Joseph Wawrykow (eds), *The Theology of Thomas Aquinas* (Notre Dame: University of Notre Dame Press, 2005), 222–251. In contrast, Richard Cross offers a trenchant critique of Thomas' apparent inconsistency and incoherence: see Cross, 'Aquinas on Nature, Hypostasis, and the Metaphysics of the Incarnation', *The Thomist* 60 (1996), 171–202, and idem, *The Metaphysics of the Incarnation* (Oxford: Oxford University Press, 2002), chapter 2.

heritage of Chalcedon (451 CE) the normative insistence that Christ is to be understood as an *hypostasis* (usually translated *persona* / 'person' in the West) into which two *phuseis* ('natures'), human and divine, in the language of Chalcedon, 'concur'. On the other hand Thomas is also adding Latin translations and philosophical definitions of his own, which do not always map exactly onto the Greek conciliar categories; and the understanding of that heritage had in any case become contested and refined through the later decisions of Constantinople II (553 CE) and Constantinople III (680–81 CE).[4] As already noted, Thomas shows an extraordinarily acute understanding in his discussion in *ST* III of that Greek trajectory; but he is also aware of puzzles that remain even after the conciliar refinement. Let me explain further.

First, take the term 'nature'. Thomas immediately raises the issue in III.2 of whether the 'kind of union the Incarnation is' could occur *in* a 'nature'. The answer is no, not only because the Chalcedonian definition explicitly denies it, but more specifically because of the way 'nature' should, as Thomas initially proposes, be defined – as 'the "whatness" of a species'.[5] The location of the christological union in just *one* of such would thus deny the necessary duality in Christ's 'person', in which are uniquely conjoined *two* ' "whatnesses" of species' – the human and the divine.

So what then is a 'person', if this, rather than 'nature', must form the point of unity in Christ? This is trickier, because the Latin *persona* does not have quite the same semantic overtones as the more abstract

---

4   Constantinople II clarified an issue left just slightly ambiguous in the Chalcedonian Definition: the point of final identity in Christ (the *hypostasis*) *is* the pre-existent divine Logos, the second person of the Trinity; and thus that identity prioritizes and personalizes one of the natures (the divine one) – the *hypostasis* is not ontologically 'confected' *out of* the two natures at the incarnation, as one 'nestorianizing' reading of Chalcedon could have it. Constantinople III took on the further problem of the two wills in Christ, after the so-called 'Monothelite' controversy (in which the hypothesis of only one will in Christ was entertained, but then rejected). It might then be said that Constantinople II newly intensified the personal unity of Christ (against remaining possible forms of 'Nestorianism'), whereas Constantinople III returned to clarify a significant aspect of the duality. It is a moot point whether the Western scholastic discussion at the time of Lombard's *Sentences* (and their immediately reception) had sufficiently understood the metaphysical implications of Constantinople II: certainly Thomas in *ST* III thinks not.

5   Thomas here appeals to both Aristotle and Boethius (III.2.1*corp*). A little later on he glosses nature as 'the essence of the species which the definition expresses' (III.2.2*corp*). For a detailed probing of the philosophical issues raised by Thomas' decision for a 'definitional' understanding of 'nature' in this context, see J. L. A. West, 'Nature, Specific Difference, and Degrees of Being: Metaphysical Background to Aquinas's Anti-Monophysite Arguments', *Nova et Vetera* 3 (2005), 39–80, especially 41–57.

Greek, *hypostasis*, as Aquinas is well aware: in the classic definition of Boethius, a 'person' (whether human or angelic) is 'an individual substance of a rational nature' (see III.2.2*ad*3; III.2.3*corp*). But in Christ's case, we are talking about a different sort of 'person', one who pre-exists as the divine Logos, and at the incarnation 'assumes' all the rational characteristics of a (Boethian) human person, and with that the 'soul/body' conjunction which Thomas, following Aristotle, takes to have the relation of a 'form' (the soul) to an individuated physicality (the 'body'). Herein, then, lies the special difficulty of explaining quite what the word 'person' might mean *vis-à-vis* Christ. Following Chalcedon, there must just be *one* 'person', not two; yet if we must constantly remind ourselves that this 'person' is unlike any other (is not, that is, merely a human 'person', but first and foremost a 'person' of the Trinity),[6] how can this reminder best be achieved linguistically?

It is here that Thomas tends to prefer his own term 'supposit' (*suppositum*) as a less misleading synonym of the Greek *hypostasis* than the Latin *'persona'*. A 'supposit' is simply an individual substance, existing in itself (III.2.2*corp*) As such the word has wider application than the normal rendition of 'person', which (as we have seen) points specifically to intelligence and will; it is also nicely distinguishable from 'nature', since, whilst a 'supposit' may concretize characteristics of a 'nature', it cannot be reducible to them. Nor indeed – and this is crucial for the incarnation – need it only concretize the features of *one* nature. As Thomas puts it, 'the supposit is taken as a whole, which has a nature as a formal or standard part' (III.2.2*corp*). 'Supposit', then, is a suitably abstract term which helps us to think away from the distracting overtones of human 'personality' when reflecting on the unique metaphysics of the incarnation; it thus does good work standing duty for the Greek *hypostasis*, which Thomas defines as 'a particular substance, particular not in just any fashion, but as rounded off and complete' (III.2.3*ad*2). That is why, for instance, the 'human nature' in Christ cannot be *identified* with the *hypostasis*/supposit/'person' since the nature cannot stand alone but 'comes into union with something more complete' (III.2.3*ad*2).

So far so good. But a problem has already crept in which is going to have to concern us in the next section. Note that in order to distinguish semantically here between 'nature' and 'person' *in the particular*

---

[6]   Important here is the earlier discussion in I.29.3*corp* on divine 'persons' in the Trinity: technically the term 'person' pre-eminently belongs to God, according to Thomas, but in a 'higher sense' than that applied to humans.

case of Christ, Aquinas has introduced a slightly different definition of 'nature' from that with which we started in III.2.1. There it was a generic ' "whatness" of a species' which 'nature' connoted; now, in the particular case of Christ, we have an *'individual* human nature' which the Word is said to assume in the incarnation: this is *not* a 'common species ... thought of in the abstract from the individual, or ... as existing in all individuals' (III.2.5*ad*2), but something which Richard Cross, commenting on this passage, glosses as 'a *particular* individuated substance'.[7] And in the use of an analogy which has caused much exegetical and philosophical probing, and to which we must shortly return, Thomas had slightly earlier likened the 'hand of Socrates' to such a particular individuated substance which is only *'in a way* individual'; whereas the 'person Socrates' represent the more perfect 'whole' in which the 'hand' must be instantiated: it simply could not exist by itself, since it is only a 'part' (III.2.2*ad*3 [my emphasis]). And it is likewise so in the relation of the human 'nature' to the 'person' of Christ, or so Thomas implies.

Why is this particular move *definitionally* troubling? The answer, surely, is that the newly individuated understanding of 'nature', here described in the context of the 'hypostatic union', seemingly begins to blur back towards what Thomas has just set off against it as 'supposit'/*hypostasis*, declaring the distinction vital.[8] Yet if the human 'nature' is itself an individuated 'substance' of some sort, does that not mean that it also has *'esse'* (individual being), and thus that there are two *'esses'* in Christ, not one? And is this then not perilously close to 'dividing the person'? Or is such a duality of essence, in contrast, vital for preserving the integrity of the human? As we shall see, Thomas retained an uneasiness throughout his career about whether to attribute one or two *'esses'* to Christ, and many have accused him of equivocation, if not outright confusion, on this point.

There is however one last and crucial semantic distinction which is going to prove vital for Thomas when moderating the problem just noted, and that is the difference which he draws between 'accidental union' and 'assumption'. Early in the *Prima Pars*, Thomas had already argued that nothing 'accidental' can happen to God: God is by definition *actus purus*, and thus not subject to any contingent changes such as happen to those in the created realm of time and space (I.3.6*corp*;

---

7 See Cross, 'Aquinas on Nature', 177 (my emphasis).
8 See again Cross, ibid., 177: it is just a 'negative' condition that distinguishes the nature and supposit here.

see I.9.2).[9] By the same token, then, the 'union' with the human into which the divine Logos *enters* in the incarnation cannot have the quality of an 'accident' either – it cannot change God; it must involve something more subtle and precise, not exactly identical with the generic idea of 'union'. This is what the notion of 'assumption' supplies: whereas the 'union' in Christ points to the (achieved) 'relation itself' between the divine and human, 'assumption' refers to the unique 'action' by the Word of 'taking up' human nature into itself.[10] Much hangs on this manoeuvre, as we shall see: the idea of the human nature being 'taken up' into a higher principle ultimately means (at least in the *ST* III account) one (personal) *'esse'* in Christ, not two. It also resists all suggestions of *contingency*: Thomas remains insistent that the two natures cannot belong together merely in some form of accidental conjunction.[11]

This quick survey of the crucial semantic definitions present in this part of *ST* III already suggests how demanding it will be for Thomas to give a completely coherent account of the 'hypostatic union': given his particular philosophical presumptions and his refined understanding of the conciliar discussions, how is he going to do equal and simultaneous justice to what Michael Gorman has called the 'unity principle' (the indissoluble unity of Christ's person) and the 'integrity principle' (the uncompromised integrity of both the divine and human natures in that person)?[12] And yet the distinctions already rehearsed are going to be precisely the crucial ones utilized in that attempt. Now that the main concepts with which Thomas is dealing have been provisionally defined, we must explore in somewhat greater detail the deeper difficulties that he faces in providing his fuller metaphysical account. Three problems are particularly bothersome, and take us to the heart of the distinctiveness of the account of the hypostatic union in *ST* III; for they are also the three issues on which Thomas either deepened his understanding or changed his mind in the course of his career, as his christological thinking became more refined and subtle.

---

[9] See III.2.1*corp*: nothing 'happens to' God in the hypostatic union, as would occur in any created union.

[10] See III.2.8*corp*, where Thomas supplies three subtle distinctions between 'union' and 'assumption'. III.5 and 6 go on to discuss details of the body and soul thus 'assumed'.

[11] III.2.5*ad*1: the 'conjoining' of human nature to the higher principle of the Logos 'increases power and dignity' rather than signalling accidental change. See Cross, *Metaphysics*, 51–62, for a critical account of this argument and Thomas' decision for a one *'esse'* view in the *ST*.

[12] See Michael Gorman, 'Christ as Composite according to Thomas Aquinas', *Traditio* 55 (2000), 143–57, here 143–4, 156–7.

The metaphysics of the hypostatic union

The first issue is that of whether a 'Chalcedonian' christology allows of a variety of different legitimate explications. Thomas had written on this question long before he wrote *ST* III. In his relatively early work, the commentary on Lombard's *Sentences* (usually dated to the 1250s), he had discussed three variant renditions of the metaphysics of the incarnation (three 'opinions') already laid out by Lombard: the theory associated with Abelard (elsewhere termed the *'assumptus-homo* theory'), which, in its zeal fully to protect the human nature appeared to separate it substantially from the person of the Word; the theory proposed by some of Abelard's followers (the so-called *'habitus* theory') which allowed Christ's soul and body to be separately united to the Son of God, as if he were donning his clothes; and then, in contrast, the *'subsistence* theory', which Thomas endorses as the only one of the three which properly expresses the goals of Chalcedon and avoids the taint of Nestorianism to which the other two alternatives, in his view, fall prey.[13] By the time he came to write *ST* III, however, his criticism of erroneous understandings of the Chalcedonian heritage had sharpened even further, in part because of his now-deepened knowledge of the Greek patristic heritage in general, but more especially because of his new understanding of the implications of Constantinople II and its clarification of the Chalcedonian heritage. Thus in III.32.6 (when considering the question of whether the human nature is united to the Word only 'accidentally'), Thomas briefly recapitulates his rejection of the two 'opinions' in Lombard which make this mistake, and this time explicitly cites the 'Fifth General Council' (twice, in quick succession) in support of his position: 'Catholic teaching' must subscribe to the non-accidental union of the natures in the *hypostasis*. Any other 'opinions', which lurch either towards a division of the natures (Theodore and Nestorius), or towards a fusion (Apollinarius and Eutyches), are to be firmly rejected (III.2.6*corp*).

---

[13] Lombard's discussion is to be found in his *Sentences*, III, distinction VI, and Thomas' first sustained analysis of Lombard's three christological alternatives was undertaken in his own Commentary on the *Sentences*. (For a detailed account of this discussion, and a comparison with the later *ST* treatment, see J.L.A. West, 'Aquinas on Peter Lombard and the Metaphysical Status of Christ's Human Nature', *Gregorianum* 88 (2007), 557–586, especially 558–569.) Thomas also mentioned the three alternatives, in the context of a more historical survey of patristic christological heresies, in his *SCG*, IV.37–38, composed between the time of the *Sentences* Commentary and the *ST*. There is a useful introductory discussion of the *SCG* material in Thomas Weinandy, 'Aquinas: God *Is* Man – The Marvel of the Incarnation', in Thomas G. Weinandy, Daniel A. Keating and John P. Yocum (eds), *Aquinas on Doctrine: A Critical Introduction* (London: T&T Clark, 2004), 67–89, here 69–73.

But if on this point Thomas is now completely clear, it leaves him little room for defensive manoeuvre in two other related and contested areas which immediately loom. The second problematic issue is that of *how*, exactly, the human nature is 'assumed' into the *hypostasis* of the Word and what, if any, analogy best expresses the relation of that human nature to the divine person who assumes it. The third, and related, issue – already noted – is whether there are two *'esses'* or only one in the *hypostasis* of the Word. We recall from our earlier discussion that Thomas is insistent that the human nature in Christ is not simply generic but individuated; this conviction, combined with his Aristotelian presumption that in any *ordinary* human being there is simply an integrated soul and body, leaves him with an intensely paradoxical state of affairs to explain in the incarnation. As he puts it in III.2.5*ad*1: 'in other men the union of body and soul constitutes the person ... In Christ, on the other hand, they are united in such a way as to be conjoined to another and higher principle ... Because of this, no new person or hypostasis is set up in Christ through the union of soul and body; instead the composite comes to an already existing person or hypostasis.'

There are at last two glaring issues to be addressed here. The first is the oddity of a soul/body which in this case does *not* have its own subsistence (is not a *hypostasis*/supposit) but needs to be taken up into another, higher entity in order to be assumed into 'personhood'. It seems that Thomas just asks us to accept this mysterious state of affairs and to acknowledge its complete uniqueness. Assuming that this nettle can be grasped (it is of course demanded by Constantinople II), the second problem relates to what is actually going on in this 'assumption'. To put it in Aristotelian terms, *how* can a supposit (here, the pre-existent Logos) assume a 'kind nature' that is not its own, whilst only one personal *'esse'* still pertains? Would not the outcome be some sort of subsumption of the 'kind nature' (in this case, humanity) *into* the (divine) nature of the supposit, thus implying a covert form of Monophysitism? This, at any rate, is Richard Cross's charge against Thomas: either he is an undercover Monophysite or he has lapsed into complete incoherence.[14] Is there a way through this dilemma?

Let us for the moment do our best to explicate Thomas' position in *ST* III in his own terms, whilst acknowledging his own evident uneasiness, across his career, about the best way figuratively to express this unique and paradoxical mystery. Speaking wholly abstractly, Thomas insists repeatedly from III.2 onwards, as we have charted, that the

---

[14] For this criticism see again Cross, 'Aquinas on Nature', and, *Metaphysics*, 51–64.

personal union of the incarnation is achieved by a non-accidental assumption of a (fully integrated) human soul/body, which *in Christ's case alone* has no independent personal *'esse'*. When he comes back to the issue of the 'unity of Christ's existence' somewhat later, in III.17.2, Thomas makes one further clarification. He explicitly raises the question of whether there are two *'esses'* ('acts of existence') in Christ or not, first citing John of Damascus's view that 'whatever follows on nature is in Christ *two*-fold' (III.17.2.1 [my emphasis]). But this time he is able to clear up the difference between the meaning of *'esse'* as applied to a nature, on the one hand, and as applied to a supposit/person, on the other: 'Now the act of existence pertains both to nature and to the subsisting subject. It pertains to the subject as to *that which* possesses existence. It pertains to the nature as to that *by which* something has existence; thus the nature is considered as a form which belongs to the order of existence inasmuch as by it something exists' (III.17.2*corp*). In other words, there are different senses of *'esse'* as applied to the person and nature; and in the incarnation Christ therefore does not acquire a 'new personal existence' but simply 'a new *relation* of his already existing personal existence to the human nature' (III.17.2*corp* [my emphasis]). In terms such as these, an apparently inconsistent shilly-shallying by Thomas on the number of *'esses'* in Christ is a charge that can be averted.[15]

But it is his attempts to come up with helpful analogies for this mystery, whether in terms of a 'whole/part' analogy or not, that tend to lead Thomas into trouble and result in repeated accusations of inconsistency or incoherence (or both). As we saw above, Thomas' first attempt to supply such a visual analogy in the *ST* III account (III.2.2) suggested that the human nature might be compared to Socrates's hand – not an accidental part of Socrates, nor a mere instrument either, yet in principle separable from the existence of the person Socrates (as his head would not be):[16] 'for the hand is not a complete substance but part of it' (III.2.2*ad*3). Already, however, Thomas is displaying nervousness about

---

[15] Unfortunately this is not the end of the story about different meanings and types of *'esse'* in Thomas' writings, but it is sufficient for our purposes here. In different writings Thomas distinguishes different forms of *'esse'*, which is why both Christ's person and his natures can have different types of it. For a fuller probing of this exegetical problem (and, in my view, a completely satisfactory answer to Cross on this point) see Michael Gorman, 'Questions Concerning the Existences of Christ', in Kent Emery Jr., Russell L. Friedman and Andreas Speer (eds), *Philosophy and Theology in the Long Middle Ages: A Tribute to Stephen F. Brown* (Leiden: Brill, 2011), 709–735, especially 724.

[16] The point about the head is not made until later: III.17.2*corp*.

the notion of a 'part' as an analogue for the human nature, even while seemingly recommending it – for he wants to avert the idea of bits put together to make something out of them, especially as relating to God (who of course cannot be divided).[17] And when he returns again to the Socrates analogy in III.17.2, things seem to get worse. First, Thomas now explicitly admits that the hand/person analogy for the incarnation requires the rather bizarre idea of a Socrates taking on a hand as a 'new acquisition'. But there is another problem, too, more hidden: for it is in this section that Thomas reminds us (harking back to the discussion of the Trinity in I.29.4*corp*, see also I.3.3) that the *divine* nature in Christ is technically not distinct from the divine person (divinity being indivisible), which means that there is a kind of intrinsic asymmetry written into the idea of 'part/whole' as applied to Christ. So it must be that the whole/part analogy has an extra inappropriateness to it: it is not that two nature *esses* (parts) together *make up* one personal *esse*, but rather that one personal-*esse* (under another description, the divine nature-*esse*) assumes another nature-*esse*, this time a human one (in which, as a further complication, a soul does the work of animating the body). Climaxing on this complicated point in III.17.2, Thomas leaves his reader with a strong sense of the limited value of the part-whole analogue, *tout court*. Should we then be so surprised that in his text *De Unione Verbi Incarnati*, written about the same time as he was composing *ST* III, Thomas turns around and admits that the part/whole analogy finally fails in the face of the mystery of the incarnation? Negative theology is more appropriate to this 'ineffable assumption', he now avers; for the human nature is not '*properly* like a part in the whole'.[18] Whatever his final position on the pedagogical usefulness of the 'concrete part' analogy for the human nature of Christ, then, Thomas was in no doubt about its metaphysical inexactitude to a unique mystery.

---

[17] Hence the rather strained remark at III.2.4*ad*2 (my emphasis): 'This composition in the person from the natures is so described *not by reason of parts*, but rather by reason of number, even as a thing in which two realities concur can be said to be composed of them'. Thomas' earlier, rather whimsical, comparison in the *SCG* (IV.41.12) of a sixth finger for the human nature ('fitted' to the individual, but as a 'conjoined instrument') also shows a certain apophatic humour about such thought experiments: arguably one does well to remember the lessons of I.13, on metaphor and analogy, in this context.

[18] *De Unione Verbi Incarnati*, 2 (my emphasis), discussed by Cross in 'Aquinas on Nature', 198. Cross drives a strong wedge between this position and Thomas' view in *ST* III, one I find over-forced. A nuanced reading of the *ST* III account finds Thomas struggling with the part-whole analogy – still utilizing it but signalling its limitations.

The problem of the 'communicatio idiomatum'

By now we have charted some of the more demanding and difficult aspects of Thomas' account of the basic 'manner of the union' in Christ. However, when he goes on in *ST* III.16–26 to discuss what he had called in the *Prologus* 'consequent implications' of the incarnation, he turns first to a new cluster of philosophical complexities relating to the problem of the so-called 'communication of idioms' in Christ. This term in fact enshrines two sets of issues, closely related to one another. On the one hand, there is the problem of how one should rightly *speak* of the characteristics of Christ's human and divine natures and their relation. This, one might say, is a matter of semantic hygiene: it is easy to fall into misleading or doctrinally erroneous statements about Christ, especially vis-à-vis his earthly life (his suffering, apparent nescience on some matters, etc.), if one does not constantly remind oneself of the proper understanding of the metaphysics of incarnation, as already discussed. Secondly, however, there is the underlying ontological issue still to be probed: what exactly *happens to* the human nature when it is assumed by the Word? Chalcedon had ruled out any 'change' or 'confusion' of the natures, and yet clearly human nature had to be reconstituted in some way by the incarnation if the atonement was to be efficacious. These matters, it should be stressed, were not ones on which the patristic tradition had honed any consistent or systematic set of answers;[19] but the author who up to then had advanced the discussion most effectively, and whose work clearly lay open on Thomas' desk as he wrote this section of the III.16.1–12) was John of Damascus.[20]

In brief, Thomas answers the first question thus: if one is referring to the 'person' of Christ (the Son of God, the second person of Trinity), it is perfectly appropriate to *attribute* to him characteristics of both natures (which are of course hypostatically united, but not confused, in the suppposit). Thus, one may rightly say that 'The Son of God died on the cross' (understood as meaning the Son of God, in virtue of his humanity, or '*qua* human'). But what one may not say is that 'God' (*tout court*) or 'divine nature' suffered and died on the cross – one of which

---

[19] George Dion Dragas, 'Exchange or Communication of Properties and Deification: *Antidosis* or *Communicatio Idiomatum* and *Theosis*', *The Greek Orthodox Theological Revieiw* 43 (1988), 377–398, supplies an introductory survey of patristic accounts of the *communicatio* up to and including John Damascene. Wolfhart Pannenberg, *Jesus – God and Man* (London: SCM Press, 1968), 296–307, provides a clearer, albeit somewhat over-schematic, account of the *different* renditions of the *communicatio* in the patristic and scholastic era, and goes on to explain why the topic again became contentious in the Reformation and early modern periods.

[20] See John of Damascus, *De Fide Orthodoxa*, III, especially chapter 17.

claims would be blasphemous and the other absurd. By the same token, while it is correct to say that 'The Son of God is omnipotent, omniscient and impassible' (meaning, the Son of God, *qua* divine, has these characteristics), it is entirely incorrect to say that Christ's *human nature* is omnipotent, omniscient and impassible. Indeed, Thomas goes on to develop one of the most sophisticated and daring accounts in the scholastic tradition to allow for genuine human suffering and weakness in Christ, as well as for different types of developing knowledge during his incarnate life.[21] But everything depends here, for clarity's sake, on the correct application of what is called 'the reduplicative strategy' (Christ, *qua* God, being carefully distinguished from Christ, *qua* man, in any correctly-parsed christological statement). As Thomas puts it himself: 'While ... no distinction is to be made between the various Predicates attributed to Christ, it is necessary to distinguish the two aspects of the subject which justify the predication. For attributes of the divine nature are predicated of Christ *in virtue of* his divine nature, while attributes of the human nature are predicated of him *in virtue of* his human nature ...' (III.16.4corp [my emphasis]).

But is this just a linguistic conjuring trick? We can learn how to operate these semantic rules, but underlyingly an ontological query remains. Is Thomas implying that the 'concurrence' of the natures in the *hypostasis* occurs in such a way that they are still kept completely and hermetically sealed from one another, despite the 'union'? And how then can atoning transformation of humanity occur in Christ at all?

It is here that Thomas draws implicitly on the Damascene's solution to the problem, although it has to be said that – most unusually for Thomas – the detailed implications are left somewhat elusive in his *ST* III treatment. For John of Damascus, the crucial distinction to be made here is between an ontological 'confusion' or 'mingling' of the two natures (firmly ruled out, of course, by Chalcedon), and a participatory *deification* of the human nature in virtue of the union.[22] So too, Thomas: Christ's human nature was 'divinized' (III.16.3corp), he says, but not by any actual ontological leakage either directly between the

---

[21] See III.9–15, elements of which (relating to Christ's 'acquired knowledge' and 'disabilities' of body and soul) are strikingly daring within scholastic discussion.

[22] See again John of Damascus, *De Fide Orthodoxa*, III, chapter 17: the famous image of the 'heating of steel' is used for the 'mutual indwelling' of the natures – 'deifying' for the human nature, yet without actual 'mingling' with the divine nature. Richard Cross, 'Perichoresis, Deification, and Christological Predication in John of Damascus' *Mediaeval Studies* 62 (2000), 69–124, provides a sophisticated analysis of Damascene's complex position on this issue.

natures or even in virtue of their concurrence in the person. Rather, simply by their uniting 'in one subsisting subject' (III.16.3*corp*), 'the fact of being assumed *affects* the human nature' (III.16.5*ad*3 [my emphasis]) – though not, Thomas adds quickly, the divine one, which of course cannot be 'affected' by anything.

The problem of the two wills in Christ

Thomas' treatment of the two wills in Christ (a position defended at Constantinople III in 680–81 CE after the bitter 'Monothelite' controversy),[23] is consonant with his understanding of the *communicatio*, on which it follows, and it indicates a deep immersion in the heritage of Maximus Confessor and his scriptural exegesis of Gethsemane, as mediated again by John of Damascus. III.18–21 is one of the richest sections since it brings together all of Thomas' remarkable philosophical precision with his sensitive rendition of the gospel accounts of Jesus's life and passion. Here (III.18.3.1) Thomas first rehearses the view of the Damascene (following Maximus) in making a distinction between a 'natural' and a 'rational' will in Christ's human nature. However, as Thomas clarifies in the *corpus*, this distinction does not actually imply *two* human wills, since they merely denote different sorts of 'acts' within one 'faculty': one operating by 'natural instinct' (and connected to the sensuous realm), and the other by 'deliberation'.[24] Thus, it is 'natural' for a human to shrink from pain and death; and because Christ possessed all the authentic features of human nature, it is this struggle that is in evidence in Gethsemane. But this is at the same time a struggle which connotes the submission of Christ's complex human will to his divine will: in this sense, although admittedly paradoxically, we have to speak of Christ being hypostatically 'subject to himself' (III.20.2*corp*). Indeed, the whole phenomenon of Christ's prayer in his incarnate life witnesses to the same profound paradox: since Thomas will go so far as to say that there were aspects of the perfection of his human knowledge which Christ had to learn through his lifetime,[25] it is in his prayers that we see this yearning towards the full knowledge of beatitude being

---

[23] The whole of III.18 is taken up with the issue of the unity of Christ's will(s). See Thomas' historically-nuanced defence of Constantinople III in III.18.1*corp*.

[24] See III.18.5*corp*: 'There is the sensuous will, denominated will by participation; and the rational will, which may be considered as acting either by natural instinct or as modified by judgement'. For a more detailed analysis of Thomas' understanding of the various levels and types of will in Christ, see Corey Barnes, *Christ's Two Wills in Scholastic Thought: The Christology of Aquinas and Its Historical Contexts* (Toronto: Pontifical Institute of Mediaeval Studies, 2012), chapter 4.

[25] See again III.12.2.

worked out, and worked out on behalf of others. The result is a rich and dynamic account of struggling human desire as intrinsic to the act of prayer and as gradually conforming human selfhood to the will of the Father (see III.21corp, especially 21.4). The radicality of this dimension of Thomas' christology gives the lie to any suggestion of metaphysical rigidity or abstraction from the biblical narrative: it is in the sweat of Christ's prayerful agony and tortured desire that Thomas spells out the deepest existential implications of his account of the hypostatic union. For him, Christ suffers the *more* intensely for being (omniscient) God, not less (III.46.6).

CONCLUSIONS: CONTEMPORARY ASSESSMENTS DIVIDED

Thomas' sophisticated account of the doctrine of the person of Christ has attracted much new attention in recent years, perhaps primarily because of the fresh understanding of the importance of his scriptural and patristic insights for his doctrinal thinking (in the wake of the French *ressourcement* movement and the reforms of Vatican II), and then because of the more recent contrapuntal discussions between neo-conservative scholastics, *ressourcement* readers of Thomas, and analytic Thomists.[26] Suddenly Thomas' apparently arcane and dry doctrinal explications of the doctrines of Trinity and Christ look newly exciting and appealing (or at least worthy of the closest philosophical analysis and critique), against a backcloth of earlier neglect or prejudicial rejection.[27] In particular, many new studies have shown that Thomas cannot justly be accused of avoiding any of the messiness and human agony of Jesus's incarnate life: his doctrine of the 'hypostatic union' is precisely designed to be read in concert with his account of the passion and of the atonement wrought through it.[28] But apart from those who now explicate and defend Thomas'

---

[26] See Fergus Kerr, *After Aquinas: Versions of Thomism* (Oxford: Blackwell, 2002), especially chapter 10 on christology, for an accessible and attractive account of these divergences.

[27] The powerful influence of Jürgen Moltmann, *The Crucified God* (London: SCM Press, 1974), was just one manifestation of a strong trend in the latter part of the 20th century to set historical and metaphysical accounts of Christ into opposition and then embrace direct divine suffering in the light of the cross. For an unforgettably trenchant riposte to Moltmann's underlying presumptions (on Thomist lines), see Herbert McCabe, *God Matters* (London: Geoffrey Chapman, 1987), chapter 4.

[28] See especially Paul Gondreau, *The Passions of Christ's Soul in the Theology of Thomas Aquinas* (Münster: Aschendorff, 2002), whose excellent exegetical and philosophical work is representative of the many followers of Jean-Pierre Torrell OP.

christology on the *presumption* that he is likely to represent the acme of scholastic rigour and refined Catholic orthodoxy, there are at least two other forms of assessment manifest in contemporary discussion which deserve note. These are guided more by analytic philosophical goals and techniques than by prior commitment to ecclesial authority; and they agree that 'coherence' is a supreme philosophical good. What is perhaps bemusing is that they then diverge completely in their assessment of the success of Thomas' christological strategies.

We return here to the crucial divergence of opinion mentioned at the start of this chapter about the coherence of Thomas' *Summa in toto*. As we are now in a position to see more clearly, a great deal depends here, implicitly but strikingly, on a willingness or otherwise to accept the demanding features of paradox and mystery that are endemic to Thomas' account of the incarnation. If, with Richard Cross, one refuses at the outset the possibility of (logically incompatible) characteristics of humanity and divinity being coherently united in the 'person' of Christ through the assumption of human nature by the Word, then obviously the 'reduplicative strategy' is a mere scam, and the apparent changes of mind about one or two '*esses*' a sign of further uncertainty and confusion. Thomas' christological project is pronounced a failure.[29] If, on the other hand, with Eleonore Stump, one aims to tidy up after Thomas and provide a *better*, and more up to date, analogue for a 'parts/whole' model than he himself provided, then a different scenario unfolds, although it is one in which the still-insistent attempt to push back the edges of mystery and metaphysical uniqueness may ultimately also prove problematic. For it is revealing that Stump's heroic attempt to give new valency to the 'whole-parts' analogy (and thus to the 'reduplicative strategy') through a comparison with a molecule important to DNA transcription which is simultaneously 'coiled' and 'uncoiled', is fallible to the extent that it feeds off the 'parts' analogy which Thomas himself ultimately found so problematic.[30] As we have seen, Constantinople II's clarification of Chalcedon demands an *asymmetry* in any thinking about 'parts' and 'whole', since the Logos *is* the personal subject of the human life of Jesus of Nazareth; and that is ultimately what makes the idea of 'parts'

---

[29] See again Cross, 'Aquinas on Nature', and idem, *Metaphysics*, chapter 2. A probing critique of Cross's position is provided in Thomas Weinandy's review of the latter text: *The Thomist* 66 (2002), 637–643.

[30] See Eleanor Stump, 'Aquinas's Metaphysics of the Incarnation', in Stephen T. Davis, Daniel Kendall SJ, and Gerald O'Collins SJ (eds), *The Incarnation: An Interdisciplinary Symposium on the Incarnation of the Son of God* (Oxford: Oxford University Press, 2002), 197–218, especially 202–218.

so problematic, even given an ingenious new contemporary scientific analogue. If the 'reduplicative strategy' is to work, it must simply do so in the form of some such statement as this, echoing Thomas himself: 'The Son of God, in virtue of (or *qua*) his human nature, suffered and died'. And if that is too paradoxical to swallow, then Thomas' sophisticated christology (and indeed the whole post-Chalcedonian tradition he inherited) is unlikely to appeal at all.

I wrote at the beginning of this chapter that the metaphysical status of the account of incarnation in *ST* III is also crucial for the whole endeavour of Thomas' vision. If his philosophical strategies for unfolding the mystery of the person of Christ fail, then arguably his entire system of thought is under threat: as he himself admits at the start of *ST* III, the metaphysical paradoxes of the incarnation undergird everything that precedes and follows their enunciation. That is why the philosophical and theological decisions that have to be made in response to Thomas' account of the hypostatic union, as outlined in this chapter, are so crucial a matter in contemporary debates about the enduring theological importance of the *ST*.

Perhaps then the most important lessons for contemporary christology that emerge from our discussion of Thomas' are twofold, and both relate to intellectual developments of the modern period that seem to threaten the viability of Thomas' approach. First, one has to surmount the challenge of modern historical-critical approaches to the biblical Jesus, yet also acknowledge that metaphysical discussions of the person of Christ need not be accounted incompatible with these, but seen as two (non-competing) perspectives on the same reality. If one drives a wedge between them it is exceedingly difficult to recover any convincing christology in the Chalcedonian tradition at all, let alone in Thomas' form. Thomas of course knew nothing of these modern historiographical developments; but, as we have seen, his probing account of the human sufferings and mental development of Jesus eschews all docetism and invites a creative metaphysical response. Secondly, the essentially paradoxical idea of a divine Son who *takes on* a fully authentic and vulnerable human nature (with characteristics necessarily incompatible with those of divinity) has to be confronted and given some rigorously convincing philosophical explication: paradox is essential to the project, and this too has often seemed impossible (mere 'incoherence') from a modern philosophical perspective. If one falls at either or both of these two fences (historiographical, philosophical) the Thomistic christological game is certainly up, and certain profound negative soteriological implications inexorably accrue. It has however been the burden of this essay to re-examine Thomas' particular christological vision afresh and to commend it for its unique philosophical sophistication, biblical sensitivity and spiritual profundity.[31]

---

[31] In an earlier article ('Climax or Incoherence? The Place of Christology in Thomas' *Summa Theologiae*', *Providence: Studies in Western Civilization* 8 (2003), 60–69, here 67–8), I suggested that the most testing element in Thomas' christology is where his metaphysical account of the *communicatio idiomatum* intersects with his rendition of Christ's sufferings in the passion: for this theme, see Gondreau, 'Life of Christ', *infra*.

Life of Christ

PAUL GONDREAU

Amidst the Third Part of Aquinas' *Summa Theologiae* one finds a densely packed treatise, spanning questions 27–59, devoted to a theological reflection upon the principal events of the life of Christ. Long neglected in the history of theological commentary on the *Summa*, this treatise has only recently begun to receive the attention it deserves, chiefly by the renowned French Thomist scholar Jean-Pierre Torrell OP.[1] The aim of this essay is to give a general introductory overview of this treatise in the *Summa*.

THE MYSTERIES OF CHRIST'S LIFE IN AQUINAS' COMPREHENSIVE CHRISTOLOGY

The first thing to note is the significance of the placement of this treatise on the theological mysteries of Christ's life in the *Tertia Pars* of the *Summa*. Today's reader needs to be aware that Aquinas does not write as a modern author does, namely, in a somewhat loose knit, sequential fashion without a common thread combining all the arguments in a unified package, as if the *Summa* were composed of questions and articles that simply 'follow' each other.

Rather, consonant with the synthetic mindset of the High Middle Ages, Thomas writes architectonically in view of the larger organic unity of the work. Scholars of Aquinas, especially those of the French

---

[1] Jean-Pierre Torrell, *Le Christ en ses mystères: la vie et l'œuvre de Jésus selon saint Thomas d'Aquin* (2 vols.; Paris: Desclée, 1999), hereafter cited as *Le Christ*; the insights of this work were first imparted to me when Fr Torrell, still penning it, was my professor at the University of Fribourg, Switzerland, in the early 1990s. Other works that consider this treatise include: Ghislain Lafont OSB, *Structures et méthode dans la «Somme théologique» de saint Thomas d'Aquin* (Paris: Cerf, 1996), 401–34; and Leo Scheffczyk, 'Die Stellung des Thomas von Aquin in der Entwicklung der Lehre von den Mysteria Vitae Christi', in M. Gerwing and G. Ruppert (eds), *Renovatio et Reformatio. Wider das Bild vom 'finsteren' Mittelalter: Festschrift für Ludwig Hödl zum 60. Geburtstag* (Münster: Aschendorff, 1986), 44–70.

school, stress how the structural design (the *ordo disciplinae*) of the *Summa* plays as vital a didactic role in what Thomas wishes to communicate as the individual questions and articles themselves that compose it.[2] Aquinas weaves one article to the next, one question to the next, one treatise to the next, one part to the next, in a grand tapestry-like theological masterpiece, with the interspersing of prologues to introduce new parts or new treatises as tip-offs to the *Summa*'s overarching vision. Any reader who merely peers in from one of the windows of the *Summa* without taking in the edifice as a whole thus risks misconstruing what is glimpsed from the window.

So how does the 'window' known as the treatise on the theological mysteries of Christ's life (III.27–59) fit into the *Summa*'s edifice as a whole? The answer becomes clear when we keep in mind that the chief aim of the *Tertia Pars* is to offer a comprehensive christology as a way of completing the *Summa*'s 'golden circle of theology' – recall the *Summa* is constructed according to a theocentric circular plan of emanation from (*exitus*) and return to (*reditus*) God. As he expresses it in the *Summa*'s opening prologue, Thomas treats 'Christ, who as man is our way to God'.[3]

Put in other, more explicitly soteriological, terms, in fact, those of John of St Thomas (†1644), the *Tertia Pars* examines the Incarnate God who 'causes and acts as repairing the effects of sin which turned man from his ultimate end'.[4] There runs a pronounced soteriological undercurrent throughout Aquinas' entire christology, and the *Tertia Pars* wastes little time in confessing as much, as its prologue places the focus squarely on 'the Saviour of all'.

This soteriological concern explains in large measure why we find a treatise on the theological mysteries of Christ's life in Aquinas' comprehensive christology. Holding firm to the scholastic axiom that action follows being (*agere sequitur esse*), or that behaviour flows from a thing's

---

[2] Those stressing this include Jean-Pierre Torrell OP, Servais Pinckaers OP, Marie-Dominique Chenu OP (especially his *Toward Understanding Saint Thomas* [Chicago: Henry Regnery, 1964]), and Leonard Boyle OP, *The Setting of the 'Summa Theologiae' of Saint Thomas* (Toronto: PIMS, 1982).

[3] I.2*prol.* Christ as the way to God is a resounding theme in Aquinas' commentary on John's Gospel; for example: 'As man, Christ is the way: 'I am the way' (Jn 14:6); and as the Christ, he leads us to the Father as a way leads to its end' (ch6, lect5 [no 936]). See *Commentary on the Gospel of St John by St Thomas Aquinas*, vol. 1 (chs. 1–7), trans. James A. Weisheipl (Albany: Magi, 1980), and vol. 2 (chs. 8–21), trans. J. A. Weisheipl and Fabian Larcher (Petersham, MA: St Bede's, 1999).

[4] John of St Thomas (John Poinsot), *Introduction to the Summa Theologiae of Thomas Aquinas*, Bk. I, ch. 1, trans. Ralph McInerny (South Bend: St Augustine's, 2004), 11; here we find the phrase 'golden circle of theology'.

ontological constitution, Thomas views human salvation in a kind of two-step manner.[5] Human salvation begins with Christ's 'being' (ontology), or the fact that a human nature, for a soteriological purpose, subsists in the second Person of the Trinity. There follows the soteriological 'action' of the Incarnate God, since, as Thomas puts it in his commentary on John's Gospel, 'we obtain the fruit of the resurrection through those things which Christ did in his flesh (*in carne sua gessit*)'.[6] Aquinas accordingly opens the *Tertia Pars* with an extended reflection upon the doctrine of the Incarnation itself, that is, upon the doctrine of 'God made man for our salvation' (III.1–26); and this gives way to the treatise on the theological mysteries of Christ's life (III.27–59). This latter examines what the prologue to the *Tertia Pars* terms Christ's *acta et passa*, or that which Christ did and suffered or endured in the flesh, throughout his entire life, in view of our salvation.[7] In other words, this treatise considers the existential experiences of the Incarnate Word.

THE 'MYSTERIES' OF CHRIST'S LIFE

Aquinas often refers to these *acta et passa* as the 'mysteries of Christ's humanity' (*mysteria humanitatis Christi*), where *mysteria* captures what the Greek *mysterion* and the Latin *sacramentum* connote in relation to God's providential plan of salvation and to the role of Christ's saving actions (present in the sacraments) in that plan.[8] Hence the reason to dub this latter treatise, which rounds out the *Summa*'s comprehensive christology, the theological mysteries of Christ's life.

With the focus on Christ's saving actions in the divine plan of salvation, especially those mentioned in the Creed, Aquinas obviously does not pen this treatise to serve as a kind of 'biography' of Christ's life.[9] Still, the Gospel accounts provide the narrative backdrop to III.27–59; so much so that this treatise, after Jean-Pierre Torrell, can be termed a 'narrative christology'.[10] Thomas' endeavour is to comb the Gospels in order to extrapolate out of them the rich theological (soteriological) significance of the main events of Christ's life.

---

[5] See Torrell, *Le Christ*, 15–6.

[6] *In Ioannem*, ch 6, lect 5 (no 939).

[7] See prologue to question 27 for a reiteration of this. Insistence upon Christ's *acta et passa* emerges as a kind of mantra for Aquinas: for example, 'omnes actiones et passiones Christi' (III.48.6); or 'omnes eius actiones et passiones humanae' (*Compendium theologiae* I, chapter 212). See Torrell, *Le Christ*, 15, n. 6.

[8] See Torrell, *Le Christ*, 21–4.

[9] This is discussed at length in Torrell I, 261–6.

[10] Torrell, *Le Christ*, 15.

As signalled in the prologue to III.27, Aquinas organizes these main events around four principal poles: first, the Incarnate Word's entrance into the world (*ingressus*) (III.27–39); second, the Incarnate Word's course of life on earth and public ministry (*progressus*) (III.40–45); third, his leaving this world through his passion and death (*exitus*) (III.46–52); and, fourth, Christ's ascension to the Father and his subsequent crowning in glory and honour (*exaltatio*) (III.53–59).[11] This division should remind us of the overall *exitus-reditus* plan of the *Summa*; what III.27–59 may be said to offer us, in other words, is a microcosm of Thomas' entire enterprise of theology.[12]

A THEOLOGICAL METHOD OF THE FIRST ORDER

Historically, the first, and more speculative, treatise on the Incarnation (III.1–26) has garnered most, if not all, of the theological attention. With the Thomist commentarial tradition favouring the more speculative line of Aquinas' thought, and with III.1–26 examining the hypostatic union and its consequences, we can understand why short shrift has been given to III.27–59.[13]

Yet, given that Thomas' treatise on the theological mysteries of Christ's life is without parallel among the medieval schoolmen and constitutes what Jean-Pierre Torrell terms 'a profoundly original work', the neglect of III.27–59 is unfortunate.[14] This treatise stands second to none among all of Aquinas' writings as to the exemplary theological method it employs. In it he ramps up the primacy of the Bible and the Fathers in his theological ruminations and lets fly with an array of biblical and patristic references, some rather obscure, that should astound any reader, professional or lay, modern or medieval.[15] Here Aquinas brings to bear

---

[11] See John of St Thomas, *Introduction to the* Summa Theologiae, Bk. I, ch. 2 (trans. McInerny, 19).

[12] See Torrell, *Le Christ*, 17.

[13] Joseph Doré notes this in his introduction to Torrell's *Le Christ*, 3–4.

[14] 'To compare with the scholastic sources and parallel works that he could have used, Thomas appears as the first – and for a long time the only – to treat the mysteries of Christ as a packaged whole and for its own sake. It is in this manner that, all the while taking up a traditional theme, (Aquinas) offers a profoundly original work.' Torrell, *Le Christ*, 26–7.

[15] Torrell (*Le Christ*, 16–34) goes to great lengths to stress this. For the role of the Bible in theology, Thomas himself writes in I.36.2ad1: 'we should not say anything about God that is not found in sacred Scripture, either explicitly or implicitly'. On this point, Étienne Gilson (*Les tribulations de Sophie* [Paris: Vrin, 1967], 47) observes how 'the entire theology of Thomas is a commentary on the Bible; he advances no conclusion without basing it somehow on the word of sacred Scripture, which is the

the fruits of having previously commented extensively on the Gospels of Matthew and John and of having enjoyed singular thirteenth-century access to patristic writings and to the decrees of the early christological councils while serving at the papal court in Orvieto from 1261–65.[16]

CHRISTOLOGICAL GIVENS FOR THE THEOLOGICAL MYSTERIES OF CHRIST'S LIFE

As already indicated, with Thomas observing the axiom that action presupposes being, the treatise on Christ's soteriological 'action' (III.27–59) builds on and presupposes the earlier one on Christ's 'being' (the hypostatic union and its consequences [III.1–26]). Aquinas in fact assumes that the principles employed in the earlier treatise are retained firmly in mind all throughout the latter one. A doctrinal formulation of Christ's ontology, consequent upon the early christological councils, marks a necessary prelude to a narrative reflection upon the mystery of Christ's saving actions. The result is that the entire christological section of the *Tertia Pars* must be read as one organic whole.

For the reader who jumps right in at III.27, then, let us briefly enumerate (some of) the christological givens or principles that are operative in the earlier treatise on Christ's ontology, and which remain operative in the latter treatise on the mysteries of Christ's life.[17]

Most fundamentally, the professions of the early christological councils, especially Chalcedon's definition of the hypostatic union as the substantial joining of a divine Person (the Son or the Word) to an

Word of God'. As for the role of the patristic voice in Aquinas' theology, cf. C. G. Geenen, 'The Place of Tradition in the Theology of St Thomas', *Thomist* 15 (1952), 110–35; idem, 'Saint Thomas et les Pères', in 'Thomas d'Aquin (saint)', in A. Vacant and E. Mangenot (eds),*Dictionnaire de théologie catholique* (Paris: Letouzey et Ané, 1904-50), vol. 15,1, 738–62; Ignaz Backes, *Die Christologie des hl. Thomas von Aquin und die griechischen Kirchenväter* (Paderborn: Ferdinand Schöningh, 1931).

[16] The *Tertia Pars* and the *Catena aurea*, written after the stay at Orvieto, display a veritable burgeoning of patristic references not seen in Thomas' earlier works, including references to certain Greek Fathers for the first time in the Latin West, such as Victor of Antioch (5th cent.) and the Byzantine exegete Theophylact (†1108). This is chronicled by Louis Bataillon, 'Saint Thomas et les Pères: de la *Catena* à la *Tertia Pars*', in C.-J. Pinto de Oliveira (ed.), *Ordo sapientiae et amoris. Image et message de saint Thomas d'Aquin à travers les récentes études historiques, herméneutiques et doctrinales* (Fribourg: Éditions universitaires, 1993), 15–36, at 16. For more on the conciliar impact of the Orvieto years on Aquinas' theology, see C. G. Geenen, 'The Council of Chalcedon in the Theology of St. Thomas', in *From an Abundant Spring: The Walter Farrell Memorial Volume of 'The Thomist'* (New York: P. J. Kennedy, 1952), 172–217.

[17] These foundational christological principles are treated at greater length in my *The Passions of Christ's Soul in the Theology of St. Thomas Aquinas* (Münster: Aschendorff, 2002; reprinted by University of Scranton Press, 2008), 137–88.

assumed human nature, remain normative for any explication of the mystery of Christ. This means above all adhering to Christ's full divinity and full humanity: 'the good theologian *(bonus theologus),*' Aquinas asserts in his commentary on John's Gospel, 'professes the true faith *(veram fidem)* in both the humanity of Christ and the divinity of Christ'.[18]

As for Christ's divinity, Aquinas follows the Prologue to John's Gospel and the Hymn for the Philippians (Phil 2:6–11) and espouses what today we would call a high christology, or a christology from above: the divine Person of the Word who pre-exists from all eternity descends to the human condition in order to take on our common humanity.[19] Thomas rejects the claims: of Arianism, which denies the divinity and full humanity of the Word; of Nestorianism, which posits dual personhood in Christ (the divine Person of the Word joined to the human person Christ); and of monophysitism, which abbreviates Christ's full divinity and his full humanity by positing one fused, theandric nature in Christ that merely combines *elements* of the human and the divine. Following Nicaea, Ephesus and Chalcedon especially, Aquinas insists Christ is one acting subject, one Person, the divine Person of the Word, who is fully (substantially) joined to an assumed human nature. To be sure, Aquinas always looks upon Christ's human nature as subsisting in a divine Person, and one can never dissociate, even if we can distinguish, Christ's divinity from his human actions; it envelops his entire human life as saviour.[20] Though *verus homo,* Christ is not *purus homo,* to use Jacques Maritain's line.[21]

As for Aquinas' adherence to Christ's full humanity, there is little doubt, though little known, that there runs a pronounced anti-docetic undercurrent throughout all of his writings.[22] Thomas espouses the

---

[18] *In Ioan,* 20.6 (no 2562); similarly, III.52.2, holds: 'our faith is in both the divinity and the humanity of Christ, such that belief in one is not sufficient without belief in the other'. For more on Aquinas' theology of Christ's full humanity, cf. my 'The Humanity of Christ, the Incarnate Word', in J. Wawrykow and R. van Nieuwenhove (eds), *The Theology of Thomas Aquinas* (Notre Dame: University of Notre Dame, 2005), 252–76.

[19] See Torrell, *Le Christ,* 123.

[20] Ghislain Lafont (*Structures et méthode,* 355–9) insists this approach 'is truly unique to St. Thomas'. See III.2.6, for Thomas' views on Nestorianism and monophysitism.

[21] Jacques Maritain, *On the Grace and Humanity of Jesus* (New York: Herder, 1969), 70.

[22] Torrell makes this point repeatedly in *Le Christ;* see as well my own 'Anti-Docetism in Aquinas' *Super Ioannem:* St Thomas as Defender of the Full Humanity of Christ,' in M. Dauphinais and M. Levering (eds), *Reading John with St Thomas Aquinas. Theological Exegesis and Speculative Theology* (Washington, DC: Catholic University of America, 2005), 254–76.

view that the doctrine of the Incarnation means God has become man in the most fully human way possible. Thus his penchant for expressions like: 'the truth of [Christ's] human nature' (*veritas humanae naturae*); 'the truth of the Incarnation' (*veritas incarnationis*); 'the truth and integrity of [Christ's] human nature' (*veritatem et integritatem humanae naturae*); or the 'true man[hood]' (*verus homo*) of Christ. Aquinas' anti-docetism is on open display in particular in III.27–59, where a heavy emphasis is placed on the role of Christ's humanity in the work of our salvation.

Key to Aquinas' effort to underscore the soteriological significance of Christ's humanity is the christological given, drawn from John Damascene, that Christ's humanity acts as the 'instrument' (*organum*) of his divinity. Christ's divine Person acts through his humanity in the way a principal agent cause acts through a conjoined instrument, since the Word is the acting subject of this humanity.[23] Moved by the divine Person of the Word (like a brush moved by a painter), Christ's humanity produces human salvation.

Also at play is Aquinas' constant recourse to the soteriological principle, much celebrated for its patristic pedigree, namely, that what was not assumed by the Incarnate Word was not healed by him.[24] Aquinas invokes this principle when establishing the essential parts of Christ's human nature, such as his 'real body' (*verum corpus*) made of 'flesh and bones and blood,' his intellectual soul, his sensitive appetite subject to movements of emotion, and the like.

Another foundational principle operative in Aquinas' christology is that of credibility in the Incarnation. Faith in a God incarnate, necessary for human salvation, can be achieved only to the extent that we view Christ's humanity as fully *believable*. This need for credibility in the Incarnation, on Aquinas' account, shapes Christ's humanity in two divergent ways: on the one hand, Jesus takes on various weaknesses or defects that band him in solidarity with a human race suffering the consequences of sin (such as hunger, sickness, affliction, passibility, mortality), and which thereby allow him to atone for human sin; on the other,

---

[23] See III.19.1*corp* and *ad2* (the definition of instrumental causality comes in I.45.5); for Damascene's remarks, the source of this teaching, see *De fide orthodoxa*, bk3 chs15 and 19 (ed. Buytaert, 239 and 258). For more on this, see Thomas Joseph White, 'The Voluntary Action of the Earthly Christ and the Necessity of the Beatific Vision', *The Thomist* 69 (2005), 497–534, at 510–3.

[24] See, for example, III.5.4. Those Fathers who employ the soteriological principle include Origen, Irenaeus, Athanasius, Basil the Great, Cyril of Jerusalem, Gregory of Nazianzus, Gregory of Nyssa, Ambrose, Augustine, Cyril of Alexandria, Leo the Great, and John Damascene (Aquinas usually cites Damascene's formulation of the principle).

Christ assumes singular perfections that both verify his status as divine Saviour and assist him in his role as Saviour, such as absolute sinlessness, and with it consummate grace and virtue, as well as the fullness of knowledge and power.[25]

An additional christological given that Aquinas employs, more so in III.27–59, in fact, than anywhere else, is the 'fittingness' (*convenientia*) of the incarnate mystery; namely, that it was fitting for God to become incarnate, that it was fitting for the God-man to be born of a virgin, that it was fitting for Christ to live and die in the manner he did, and so forth.[26] The use of *convenientia* reveals Thomas' admiration for the coherence and ordered beauty of the divine wisdom manifest in the joining of our human nature to the Son of God. Aquinas knows, first, that God remains free in choosing the means by which to redeem the human race, but, second, that God desires that this end 'be attained better and more suitably'.[27] In view of God's economic plan of salvation, therefore, it was more 'fitting' or 'suitable', and thus beautifully wondrous and in harmony with human reason, for the Word to wed himself substantially to our humanity: 'Nothing more marvellous could be accomplished than that God should become man', Aquinas exclaims, revealing his Christ-centred spirituality.[28]

The last foundational principle operative in Aquinas' christology that we shall consider, and which is also omnipresent in III.27–59, is the notion of *imitatio Christi*, or Christ as exemplar to emulate. This principle surfaces, for instance, in Aquinas' penchant for the line 'Christ's action is our instruction'.[29] On Thomas' account, Christ alone provides an infallible model of human conduct, since he is the God-man who enjoys perfect moral rectitude.[30] Further, Christ acts as exemplar in two

---

[25] See III.7–13 for the perfections, and III.14–15 for the defects.

[26] Gilbert Narcisse OP ('Les enjeux épistémologiques de l'argument de convenance selon saint Thomas d'Aquin', in Olivera [ed.], *Ordo sapientiae et amoris*, 143–67, at 146–7) affirms that a 'torrent of suitabilities' runs throughout Aquinas' christology, with the *Tertia Pars* alone offering 108 uses of *conveniens* in reference to Christ; see as well Narcisse's larger work, *Les raisons de Dieu. Argument de convenance et esthétique théologique selon saint Thomas d'Aquin et Hans Urs von Balthasar* (Fribourg: Éditions universitaires, 1997). Torrell's *Le Christ*, 34–8, devotes considerable attention to the notion of *conveniens* in III.27–59.

[27] III.1.2.

[28] *In Ioan.*, ch2, lect3 (no 398); for nearly the same wording, see *SCG* IV.27.

[29] See III.40.1ad4: '*Christi actio fuit nostra instructio*'. For more on this expression, see Jean-Pierre Torrell, '«Imiter Dieu comme des enfants bien-aimés». La conformité à Dieu et au Christ dans l'oeuvre de saint Thomas', in Jean-Pierre Torrell, *Recherches thomasiennes. Études revues et augmentées* (Paris: Vrin, 2000), 325–35.

[30] '[T]he example of a mere human being would not be an adequate model for the entire human race to imitate…And so we were given the example of the Son of God, which

ways: first as moral or 'outward' exemplar, in that Christ's actions allow for outward imitation; and, second, as ontological or 'inward' exemplar, in as much as the Christo-conforming grace he confers upon all believers shapes our actions from within.

PERUSING THE THEOLOGICAL MYSTERIES OF CHRIST'S LIFE

We come, then, to III.27–59 proper. To recall, this treatise divides Christ's life into four principal events: *ingressus* (entrance into the world), *progressus* (course of life), *exitus* (passion and death), and *exaltatio* (ascension to the Father and crowning in glory).

Ingressus (III.27–39)

Thomas further subdivides this section into Christ's state *in utero* (qq27–34), his birth (qq35–36), his circumcision (q37), and his baptism (qq38–39). The first set of questions relating to Christ's conception contains a lengthy treatment of the Virgin Mary. Sometimes scholars identify this as the locus for Aquinas' 'Mariology'. While not entirely misleading, Jean-Pierre Torrell makes clear that this section remains 'resolutely christological', as it seeks to offer a theology of preparation for the Saviour's arrival – and thus a view of Mary not simply as 'a 'maternal transporter', a mere canal who serves to bring the Son of God into the world', but as an indispensable secondary agent in our salvation.[31] Indeed, because of her proximity to the source of grace (Christ), the Virgin Mary was sanctified to an unparalleled degree, though not so far as to be preserved from all stain of original sin (the doctrine of the immaculate conception).[32] (Other medieval theologians who agree with Aquinas on this include Bernard of Clairvaux, Alexander of Hales, Bonaventure, and Albert the Great.) The same line of reasoning extends to Mary's perpetual virginity: it was fitting (*conveniens*) because it points to the supreme dignity of her Son. Yet because she was at the same time married, Aquinas continues, 'in her person both virginity and marriage are honoured, contra those heretics who attack the one or the other' (III.29.1).

---

cannot err and which meets the needs of all human beings'. *In Ioan.*, ch13, lect3 (no 1781); for the same see *SCG* IV.54. See also III.40.2*ad*1: 'our Lord gave an example of perfection as to all those things which of themselves relate to salvation'.

31 Torrell, *Le Christ*, 47, 53 and 86.

32 'In every genus, the nearer a thing is to the principle [or cause], the greater the share it has in the effect of that principle.' III.27.5. For a fuller treatment of Mary's sanctification, see Torrell, *Le Christ*, 42–54.

The next set of questions (III.31–33) target Christ's belonging to our humanity and the unique quality of his humanity. Here Thomas' anti-docetism comes to the fore, as he presents a Christ fully subject to the laws of humanity. Yet given Christ's conception by the Holy Spirit – and Aquinas emphasizes the central role of the Holy Spirit throughout the whole of his christology[33] – the full humanity which Christ assumes gets donned with singular privileges. From the very instant of his conception, Thomas tells us, Christ's soul was full of grace and possessed the beatific vision: 'what belongs by nature to the Son of God belongs by grace to the Son of Man'.[34] Further, the truth of the hypostatic union allows us to attribute two generations/births to the Person of the Word: eternal generation from the Father and temporal generation from the Virgin Mary, by which the Word takes on our common humanity (Thomas utilizes the celebrated communication of idioms in order to predicate temporal birth of the pre-existent Son).[35]

On the circumcision (III.37), Aquinas, contra those who allege Christ's body was merely 'imaginary' (*phantasticum*) or 'heavenly' (*de caelo*), sees this as the supreme testament to the truth of his humanity and as providing an example of humility and obedience for us to follow (*imitatio Christi*). Insistent upon Christ's 'descent from Abraham' and 'submission to circumcision and the other stipulations of the Law', Thomas also shows here his detailed knowledge of and respect for all things Jewish and, in particular, the Jewishness of Jesus.[36]

Aquinas finds Jesus' baptism fitting (*conveniens*) since it bands him in solidarity with the sinful lot of humanity and because it provides us with an example of seeking baptism ourselves (qq38–39).

Progressus (III.40–45)
Thomas divides this section into Christ's manner of life (q40), his temptations (q41), his teaching (q42), and his miracles (qq43–45). On the Lord's manner of life, Aquinas identifies this with the ideal of his own religious order, namely, with a life of poverty and of itinerant 'preaching and

[33] See Torrell, I, chapter 7: 'To Speak of the Holy Spirit', 153–74.
[34] III.10.1arg3; here Thomas falsely attributes this wording to Augustine.
[35] III.35.1 and 2; see Torrell, *Le Christ*, 152–3. For more on the communication of idioms in Aquinas, see my 'St. Thomas Aquinas, the Communication of Idioms, and the Suffering of Christ in the Garden of Gethsemane', in J. F. Keating and T. J. White (eds), *Divine Impassibility and the Mystery of Human Suffering* (Grand Rapids: Eerdmans, 2009), 214–45.
[36] For more on this, see Matthew Levering, *Christ's Fulfillment of Torah and Temple: Salvation According to Thomas Aquinas* (Notre Dame: University of Notre Dame Press, 2002).

teaching[, whereby] one delivers to others the fruits of his contemplation' (III.40.1*ad*2). Undoubtedly standing behind this is Aquinas' defence of the mendicant way of life against the secular university masters who, equating spiritual perfection with the role of pastor, had called its very legitimacy into question.[37]

Recognizing the spiritual profit to be gained from Christ's temptations, Aquinas highlights the theme of Jesus' exemplarity in his treatment of this (Christ's example strengthens, warns and inspires us in our own temptations). Following John Damascene and Gregory the Great, Thomas insists Jesus could be tempted only by 'outward suggestion' from the enemy (*ab hoste*), as this can happen 'without sin', whereas interior temptation results from disordered impulses of the flesh (*a carne*), that is, from disordered affective movements (concupiscence), 'which cannot be without sin' (III.41.1*ad*3).[38] Seeking to explain how Jesus could be genuinely *drawn toward* a desirable though unlawful object, and thus be genuinely tempted, the French Thomist Jean-Hervé Nicolas offers the useful distinction that experiencing a good as *desirable* (such as stone being turned to bread [Luke 4:3]) is quite distinct from *desiring* that good; we can affirm the first in Jesus but not the second, which implies sin.[39]

On Christ's teaching (q42), Aquinas shows again his esteem for Jesus' Jewishness. It was 'fitting' (*conveniens*) that Christ's teaching 'should be directed at first to the Jews alone', since Christ's coming fulfils the promises made to the Jews and because 'by believing in and worshipping the one God, the Jews were nearer to God' (III.42.1).

If historical-critical exegetes, out of seeming embarrassment, tend to explain away Christ's miracles, Thomas follows a different path. Appealing to the doctrine that Christ's humanity acts as the 'instrument' (*organum*) of his divinity, Aquinas affirms that Christ, by virtue of his divinity, did indeed perform miracles, 'since only God can alter the order of nature' (III.43.2). This Thomas finds fitting, since his miracles 'confirm his teaching and show forth his divine power' and induce 'belief in the truth of his manhood' (III.43.3). Acknowledging that this proves

---

[37] For more on this controversy, see Torrell, I, chapter 5: 'Defender of Mendicant Religious Life', 75–95.

[38] I treat this at greater length in my *The Passions of Christ's Soul*, 350–64. For more on temptation of the flesh, see I-II.77.6; and for Christ III.15.2*ad*3. For Damascene, see *De fide orthodoxa*, III.20 (ed. Buytaert, 260); for Gregory the Great, see *Hom. in Evang.*, I.16.1 (*PL* 76:1135).

[39] Jean-Hervé Nicolas, *Synthèse dogmatique. De la Trinité à la Trinité* (Fribourg: Éditions universitaires, 1985), 407–8.

Christ to be 'the Saviour of all' (III.44.3), Thomas makes explicit the soteriological direction of this reasoning.

With the great miracle of the Transfiguration giving unparalleled witness to the clarity of Christ's divinity, Aquinas ends this section by devoting an entire *quaestio* to this event (q45). Here, too, the soteriological dimension emerges: the unveiling of Christ's glory in the Transfiguration arouses humans to desire the ultimate glory, that of eternal beatitude (III.45.3).

Exitus (III.46–52)

Thomas parcels this section into Christ's Passion (qq46–49), his death (q50), his burial (q51), and his descent into hell (q52). Not surprisingly, Aquinas' soteriology reaches a crescendo in this section, and the treatment of Christ's Passion, wherein Thomas examines the Passion in itself as well as its causes and effects, represents a priceless *chef d'œuvre* of spiritual theology. Of the many things that one could say of the treatment of the Passion (Torrell's *Le Christ* devotes one hundred and forty pages to it), we shall limit ourselves to the following.

Aquinas affirms that redemption by way of suffering does not ensue upon a kind of absolute necessity (not possible to be otherwise), but upon a 'conditional necessity'. Put in other terms, we need the Cross because by it we gain open display of God's exceeding love for us and an inestimable example of virtue (III.46.3). Further, in atoning for human sin, Christ in his Passion satisfies the demands of divine justice. While some modern scholars would have us believe Aquinas' theology of satisfaction, which otherwise gives scholastic expression to the rich biblical notion of atonement, introduces the 'monstrous' idea of 'propitiating an angry God',[40] Thomas' actual words on satisfaction, which stress God's mercy and Christ's love and obedience, tell a different story: that God himself should atone for human sin '*was in keeping with God's mercy*, since man of himself could not satisfy for the sin of all of human nature' (III.46.1*ad*3); and 'because of the exceeding love *(magnitudinem caritatis)* by which he suffered ... Christ's suffering constituted not simply a sufficient but a superabundant *(superabundans)* atonement' (III.48.2). This superabundance spills over into the Church, since 'the head and members are one mystic person'; in other words, by participating in his superabundant satisfaction, Christ's members can atone for their sins, too – our merits are Christ's merits, as it were.

---

[40] Gerald O'Collins, *Christology: A Biblical, Historical, and Systematic Study of Jesus* (Oxford: Oxford University Press, 1995), 206–7.

Aquinas evinces his personal devotion to the suffering Christ on the cross when confessing that Jesus 'endured every generic type of human suffering', namely, 'in his soul, as from sorrow, weariness and fear, and in his body, from wounds and scourgings' (III.46.5). This suffering in his soul, Thomas goes on to explain (III.46.6), comprised both spiritual and affective dimensions: 'The cause of [Christ's] interior pain was, first of all, the sins of the human race ... [and, secondly,] the loss of his bodily life, which is naturally horrible to human nature'.

And let there be no mistake: this is God himself who grieves and endures torturous bodily pain. Holding the communication of idioms and a symphony of patristic voices in mind, Aquinas affirms that God, in the Person of the Son, has suffered and died 'by reason of his assumed passible [human] nature' (III.46.12). Thus the integral role of Christ's humanity in the Passion, since, acting as the 'instrument' (*organum*) of his divinity, Christ's manhood 'causes' our salvation (III.48.6); Christ uses his body and soul to save us. Providing a remedy against any human sin or temptation (III.49.2), the instrumental efficacy of Christ's Passion, and the spiritual profit deriving therefrom, is truly inestimable.

When it comes to Christ's death itself, Thomas upholds its fittingness on the grounds that: it proves 'the veracity of his assumed flesh'; it helps us to brave our own death; it provides us with an example of dying to sin; and it 'instils in us the hope of rising from the dead' (III.50.1). The same reasoning extends to Christ's burial (III.51.1).

The treatment of Christ's descent into hell (q52) offers a fascinating reflection upon a mystery of the faith mentioned in the Creed. Noting that hell marks the ultimate penalty of sin, Aquinas argues it was fitting that Christ, who came to free us from the penalty of sin, descend into hell 'in order to deliver us also from going down into hell' (III.52.1). As for the actual descent, he observes that 'hell' (*infernus*) signifies three places: that of the damned, Purgatory, and that of the just awaiting the resurrection. Visiting 'in place' only the hell of the just, Christ descended into the other two 'not by passing through them locally with his soul, but by spreading the effects of his power in a measure to them all [namely, by shaming the damned and by giving hope to those in Purgatory] ... just as while suffering in one part of the earth he delivered the whole world by his Passion' (III.52.1*corp* and *ad*1).

Exaltatio (III.53–59)

This last section is parcelled into the resurrection (qq53–56), the ascension (q57), Christ's sitting at the right hand of the Father (q58), and

Christ's judicial power (q59). To those familiar only with modern biblical scholarship, which, manacled by the historical-critical approach, rarely ventures into such territory, this may seem like foreign terrain. But Thomas' concern, of course, is theological, that is, centred especially on what the Creed professes about Christ, and is thus wider ranging that what the historical-critical method can allow.

Following Paul (1 Cor 15:12), Aquinas appreciates that by overcoming death, Christ in his resurrection has proved he has power over evil in all its manifestations, including the grip sin holds on our hearts. Thus his resurrection 'completes the work of our salvation', as it allows us 'to walk in newness of life' (Rom 6:4) and gives us real hope for our resurrection (III.53.1). So if Christ's Passion, which works instrumentally in virtue of his divinity, is the 'cause' of our salvation (III.48.6), his resurrection, which also operates instrumentally in virtue of Christ's divinity, is the cause of our own resurrection (III.56.1 and 2).

In the age of modern scholarship it is not uncommon to find authors alleging Christ's body simply corrupted away. But on this score Thomas does not mince words: 'in order for it to be a true resurrection, it was necessary for the same body of Christ to be once more united with the same soul' (III.54.1). Nor does Aquinas fail to point out the docetic, and thus soteriological, stakes at play in the veracity of the resurrection, since if Christ had merely had 'an imaginary body (*corpus phantasticum*), then his resurrection would not have been true, but apparent' (ibid.).

Aquinas does not abandon the soteriological motif when considering Christ's ascension and crowning in glory. The ascension, too, 'causes' our salvation, inasmuch as it increases our faith (in things unseen), it uplifts our hope for eternal bliss, it orders the fervour of our love to heavenly realities, and it opens the way for 'our own ascent into heaven' (III.57.6). The salvific efficacy of Christ's humanity does not end there, since once seated at the Father's right hand Christ exercises supreme royal power. He does this by judging, 'even according to his human nature', whether to grant or deny each of us admission 'to the end of beatitude, which is everlasting salvation' (III.58.2 and III.59.2 and 4).

CONCLUSION

While we have certainly benefited from modern biblical scholarship, Aquinas' read on the principal Gospel events offers us a unique theological perspective that is rare to find today. It is a perspective that unites the Creed, in what it professes about Christ, with a narrative christology borne of the Gospel accounts. We have in the *Summa*'s treatise on the theological mysteries of Christ's life, then, something much more than a mere medieval relic: we have a theological treasure from which today's reader can learn and gain much.

Redemption

NICHOLAS M. HEALY

The third part of the *ST* brings 'the entire theological discourse to completion by considering the Saviour himself and his benefits to the human race' (III*prol*). Sent to 'manifest the truth' (III.40.1), everything Christ said and did was for the instruction of those around him (III.40.1*ad*3). He thus 'showed in his own person that path of truth which, in rising again, we can follow to the blessedness of eternal life' (III*prol*). Accordingly, *ST* III.1–59 consider the Saviour and his benefits from two perspectives. First, Thomas expounds his christology by discussing who Christ is as the Incarnate Word (qq1–26). Then (qq27–59) he considers the Gospel accounts of those things which he 'did and suffered' (Latin: *acta et passa*, III*prol*). The meaning of Latin '*passa*' is less specific than the English translation, 'things suffered', and denotes the simple passive 'things that were done' to him, in contrast to 'things that he did'. However, the contrast is significantly undermined by Thomas' contention that the Incarnate Word freely willed to suffer and die in order to redeem us and, moreover, maintained full control of events throughout (III.47.1). He was thus never simply passive, but was in a real sense 'the cause of his own passion [*passionem*] and death' (III.46.1).

ISSUES IN THE DOCTRINE OF REDEMPTION

As we would expect, Thomas follows the traditional reading of the scriptural story of salvation in Jesus Christ. The OT tells how humanity is no longer, as Adam and Eve once were, in a right relation to God. Our sinfulness is an offence that has distanced us from God, the consequences of which are described in the OT history of Israel, with its numerous depictions of God's wrath (and loving forgiveness!) in the face of human sin and depravity. The NT addresses this situation, telling how Christ came to redeem us, to reconcile us with God by making atonement for our sins ('at-one-ment', 'bringing together again'). In his treatment in

ST III, Thomas reserves the term 'redemption' and its cognates for a particular way of considering this part of Christ's work, following Paul's use of the metaphor (III.48.4–5, discussed later in this chapter). However, contemporary usage (including the title and much of the subject matter of this chapter)[1] extends the word's reference to cover all aspects of the atonement as well as the saving 'benefits' of Christ's work. So 'redemption' is now largely synonymous with what the scholastics called the *ordo salutis*, the entire 'plan of salvation' in Christ.

In this part of *ST* III, then, Thomas examines the various stages of this *ordo* – atonement/redemption, sanctification and salvation – in their relation to Christ. One of the most important issues has to do with agency: the 'who does what' question. The tradition has for the most part understood the NT to say that forgiveness of sins and reconciliation with God is 'objective' in that it is achieved by Christ without any contribution on our part at all. Christ acted 'for us and for our salvation', as the Creed puts it. In treating the issue, Thomas engages with Anselm's *Cur Deus Homo?* (written in 1098), already the classic position on objectivity. Anselm had argued that original sin is an offence against God that upsets the entire order (or 'rightness', 'justice') of creation. Drawing upon the metaphor of making satisfaction or giving compensation for an offence or a debt, Anselm argues that humanity owes God 'the debt of sin'. However, we are incapable of making adequate restitution because the offence affects all creation and, moreover, an adequate compensation must be greater than the original offence. So only the infinite God can make full satisfaction for our sins and restore the order of creation. God is loving and wills to do this, but God is also just, and 'divine justice', Anselm contends, can accept 'nothing but punishment as the recompense of sin'.[2] Furthermore, justice demands that the sinner make the satisfaction, since only the offender can justly be punished for an offence. Thus only God incarnate in humanity can make adequate satisfaction consistent with God's mercy and justice.

We will see later in this chapter how Thomas distances himself significantly from Anselm's argument, but he certainly agrees with its substance regarding objectivity. Forgiveness of our sins and reconciliation with God has been achieved by the Incarnate Word acting for us (III.46.1*ad*3). That said, however, we can and do contribute, as agents, to

---

[1] See Gerald O'Collins, 'Redemption: Some Crucial Issues' in S. T. Davis, D. Kendall SJ, G. O'Collins SJ (eds), *The Redemption: An Interdisciplinary Symposium on Christ as Redeemer* (Oxford: Oxford University Press, 2004), 1–22, here 5.

[2] Anselm, *Cur Deus Homo?*, I.24, in *St Anselm: Basic Writings*, trans. S. N. Deane, (2nd ed.; La Salle: Open Court, 1962), 249.

our salvation. Thomas spent much of the second part of the *ST* discussing our response to Jesus Christ, which is made possible – and made genuinely *our* action, too – by Christ's grace earned through his passion. The Dominicans and other religious orders were founded on the belief that our response to Christ's work is necessary for eternal life in him and that it requires both Christ's enabling grace and substantial effort on our part. According to Thomas, whatever we do by way of response will be limited, given who we are as finite creatures, and is not redemption (in the restricted sense). Yet it can be appropriate ('congruent') and, with the aid of the Holy Spirit, can even be truly worthy of our eternal reward ('condign'; I-II.114.3).

Earlier attempts to sort out the agency issue were not always so clear. Some monks had seemed to suggest we can respond adequately without grace, or that we can at least initiate a response by our own efforts alone, which is then rewarded by Christ's grace that, in turn, enables our further and more adequate progress – variations of the Pelagian heresy. A more recent controversy had been occasioned by the work of Peter Abelard (died 1142). He had defined redemption as 'that supreme love in us through the passion of Christ'.[3] The phrase suggested to critics like Bernard of Clairvaux (died 1153) that our redemption is achieved by our subjective response to the exemplary love of Christ displayed in his sufferings for us. Bernard worried that Abelard thereby undermined the objectivity of Christ's atoning work and so lapsed into another form of Pelegianism (later named 'exemplarism' or 'subjectivism'). Elsewhere, however, Abelard clearly maintains the objective aspect and, on the other hand, both Anselm and Bernard also write of our empathetic response to Christ's passion. The controversy thus seems to turn not on conflicting accounts so much as different emphases within what Caroline Walker Bynum has termed the one 'standard and multi-faceted medieval theory of the atonement'. Well aware of these issues, Thomas develops what Bynum correctly calls a 'complex theory where response and satisfaction interweave'.[4]

Thomas' treatment of the *ordo salutis* is not organized in the way we might expect in a contemporary systematics. His account is highly systematic in that it covers all aspects of the topic and shows their interrelations. But it is governed by somewhat different principles and concerns.

---

[3] Peter Abelard, *Expositio in epistolam Pauli ad Romanos*, book 2 (*CCCM* 11, 118), cited in Jaroslav Pelikan, *The Christian Tradition: 3 The Growth of Medieval Theology (600–1300)* (Chicago: University of Chicago Press, 1978), 128.

[4] Caroline Walker Bynum, 'The Power in the Blood', in Davis *et al.* (eds), *The Redemption*, 177–204, here 180, 181.

He breaks down complex issues into individual questions, whereas modern treatments of redemption tend to have a single organizing concept (rather like Anselm's focus on 'satisfaction'), or place Christ's redemptive work within a systematic treatment organized according to some theorized aspect of universal human experience, such as our sinfulness as exemplified by the horrific events of the twentieth century, or our tendency to violence in the face of goodness, or our need for a sacrificial victim. By contrast, Thomas keeps the focus not on us but on the triune God, in keeping with his understanding of theology's subject: God and things in their relation to God. Particularly evident, too, in this part of the ST is how Thomas' account is informed and guided by Scripture. For example, we find that what might seem to be a 'scholastic' question – in the negative sense of unnecessary and arcane – such as 'whether the passion is necessary', is actually occasioned by explicit statements to that effect in the NT (III.46.1). So, too, he devotes articles to each of the main metaphors used in Scripture to describe Christ's work, scripture's polyvalence itself arguably the main reason why Thomas chose not to base his treatment upon a single concept.

THE INCARNATION IS FOR OUR REDEMPTION AND SALVATION

We can now turn to examine some of the more significant passages of the ST in detail. The primary texts are those that focus on the Passion, but we should also look briefly at the initial articles of III.1, since there Thomas argues 'the work of the Incarnation was directed chiefly to the restoration of the human race through the removal of sin' (III.1.5). He notes in a later question that if circumstances were otherwise the Incarnation alone – without the Passion – would have saved us, because 'from the moment of his conception Christ merited eternal salvation for us.' However, there were 'certain obstacles which prevented us from enjoying the result of his previously acquired merits' (III.48.1ad2). These obstacles were, of course, our sinfulness and our need for reconciliation with God. Conspicuously absent from Thomas' account is any indication that God's displeasure with us is among the obstacles. Although Scripture tells of God's wrath, Thomas' doctrine of God indicates such passages must be read as metaphorical language. Our sinfulness cannot alter God, for God remains always loving and free both in God's self and in God's work in creation. God does not need anything other than God, for God is fully complete, good and loving, independently of anything created, including humanity. So the obstacles can only be on our part.

Christ's incarnation is therefore the beginning point of the process of changing *us* so that, after his resurrection and ascension, it will be possible for us, enabled by Christ's grace, to change ourselves to become like him.

Why did God choose this way to achieve our salvation? Was it the only way possible? Was it the best way, or could God's will have been achieved in a way more appropriate to what we know of God? These are recurring questions, posed in III.1 with regard to the Incarnation as such, later to the Passion and subsequent events. Thomas treats them by addressing what he terms the 'fittingness' of God's way of redeeming and saving humanity. Throughout the *ST* we come across the word 'fitting' (Latin *conveniens*), meaning 'reasonable' or 'appropriate'. Thomas' concern in addressing the fittingness of the Incarnation should be distinguished from a modern apologetics. A contemporary *apologia* for the incarnation would be couched in terms that all reasonable people could accept, and would try to counter secular disbelief or religious doubt by a logical and/or historical demonstration that Jesus Christ could have been, and very likely was, the incarnate Word of God. For Thomas and his medieval readers such an apologetics would be pointless. The incarnation is simply an article of faith and as such is logically unquestionable, as is our redemption and salvation in Christ. They were existentially unquestionable, too, in that few if any of his contemporary readers would have been likely ever to have had doubt about such matters. Instead, Thomas' concern is to bring out the fittingness and consistency of Scripture's claims and the Church's doctrines so that Christians may better understand and respond to the wisdom and glory in God's decision to bring about our redemption and salvation in just this particular way.

So in the first article (III.1.1), Thomas addresses possible worries that the incarnation seems inconsistent with what we know of God's perfection, immutability and freedom. On the contrary, he argues it is entirely consistent with God's *goodness*, and because goodness is 'God's very nature', it should govern our understanding of God's other attributes. In the second article, though, he agrees the incarnation is necessary for our restoration, a view that might seem to re-establish the inconsistency, since it would imply that God must follow a particular course of action if God wants to achieve our salvation, a suggestion that would undermine God's freedom and omnipotence. Thomas rules out any such implication by clarifying the usage of the word 'necessary' here, linking it directly to God's love for the world and 'the gift of his only Son' (John 3:16). God could have chosen any one of 'many other ways' to accomplish our salvation. God chose the incarnation as the means because it would result in the 'better and more expeditious attainment of the goal', our salvation. It was therefore 'necessary' in this relative sense, much as, Thomas remarks, it is necessary to ride a horse rather than walk if one must travel some distance expeditiously. Thomas then presents ten substantive reasons why it is the best way. Interestingly, the majority have to do with our subjective response to God's love displayed in the incarnation, supporting his suggestion that, absent the fall, we could have been brought to salvation by the grace of the incarnation without the passion.

A major controversy appears next (III.1.3), and one with direct implications for redemption: Whether God would have become incarnate if humanity had not sinned. Thomas notes 'there is a difference of opinion on this matter'. Some theologians, among them his teacher, Albert the Great, had argued the incarnation would have happened even if we had not sinned, a view with which Thomas himself concurred in his earlier *Commentary on the Sentences*. Others, including his colleague, Bonaventure, said it would not. Thomas – note how carefully! – says 'agreement with them [the latter] seems preferable'. His 'preference' follows from his understanding of Scripture and the limits of our knowledge of God: 'Those things that flow from the will of God alone beyond all that is due to creatures can come to be known by us only to the extent that they are handed down in sacred Scripture, which makes God's will known'. Logic, science or our experience gives us no independent knowledge of the 'will of God', to the reasons why God decides this happens rather than that. Certainly, God is free and omnipotent so, yes, abstractly we can agree that 'God *could* have been incarnate even if there had been no sin'. But since Scripture indicates 'the sin of the first man is given as the reason for the incarnation' (III.1.3), and offers no other reason that is not related to the forgiveness of sin, we cannot presume to declare that there *would* have been the incarnation had there been no sin. Such a declaration would be mere speculation and meaningless for faith. Thus the incarnation is for our redemption as well as our salvation.

THE PASSION

III.46 is devoted to the central redemptive action, Christ's passion as such, while the subsequent three questions (47–49) address its causes, efficacy and results. The first three articles of III.46 – which are parallel in some significant ways to the first three articles of I.1 – are a careful clarification of what it means to say that the passion is 'necessary' for our redemption and salvation. They should be taken together because the conclusions of one article are often nuanced further in the next, in part by engagement with Anselm. The first article addresses the question of necessity directly. Here Thomas must show the coherence between, on the one hand, the scriptural texts that say explicitly that Christ 'must' die for our sins (e.g., John 3:14) and on the other hand, the theological difficulties in saying that God 'must' do something. Thomas cannot admit to any necessity in God of that kind. If God were compelled to perform an action – or even merely *felt* compelled, morally or emotionally (God's love is not, of course, an emotion) – by something created it would mean that God is not truly God. Likewise Christ, as the incarnate Word, could not have been forced to suffer and die by those who killed him, nor could he have been compelled to suffer by God, since that would be inconsistent with the loving relations that constitute God's being. Rather, Christ suffered willingly, in loving obedience to the will of the Father (III.47.2*ad*2).

Yet there *is* a necessity here of another kind, because the goal that is sought – our redemption and salvation – requires Christ to suffer as the means to achieve it. The necessity in question is threefold. The passion must happen because, first, it is simply the way we are redeemed and, second, because the reward of Christ's suffering is his glorious resurrection and ascension into heaven. These reasons may suggest God's freedom is limited, or even that God is compelled to a certain course of action. But that is not the case. The kind of 'necessity' at play in the first two reasons is governed by the third, based upon Scripture: God freely and lovingly chose these very means to accomplish our salvation. Fundamentally, the passion is necessary solely because God wills it.

That does not make it arbitrary, however, as if it were merely an exercise of God's power to do anything in any way God chooses. In his response to one of the objections (III.46.1*ad*3), Thomas considers Anselm's contention that God's mercy and justice render the passion necessary because it is the only means by which the incarnate Word can make adequate satisfaction for our 'debt of sin'. Thomas agrees up to a point, but it is significant that Thomas uses the word 'consonant' here (Latin *conveniens*, 'fitting'), rather than 'necessary'. God willed the passion not because God had to satisfy a justice that is merely abstract and transactional, but because the passion displays the 'justice of Christ'. The passion is the concrete demonstration of God's goodness, the 'great love with which God loved us' (Eph. 2:4). It thus shows *greater* justice and mercy than if God simply forgave sins without the passion.

The point is sharpened further as Thomas answers the question of the second article (III.46.2), 'Whether humanity could have been freed from sin in any other way than by Christ's passion?' At issue here, once again, is the consistency of Scripture's witness and God's freedom. Thomas says that, 'absolutely' speaking, God could have chosen another way than the passion, but 'hypothetically' speaking, it can only be this way. Here Thomas uses 'hypothetical' in a way that sharply contrasts with our general and scientific usage. For us, a hypothesis is (roughly) a possibility to be explored further. For him, a hypothesis is the premise, here in the sense of what has actually happened. Given *these* events happened rather than others, it follows they are necessary and alternatives impossible. Thomas here is not, of course, stating the obvious fact that once events turn out one way rather than another it is impossible for them now to be different. Rather, his contention is that, since the events turned out this way, they *had* to have happened this way and not in another way. To be sure, such an inference would be invalid if made with regard to any normal events: you cannot infer from the mere fact that you had fried eggs for breakfast today that you necessarily had to breakfast in that particular way, or at all. Thomas' point here is theological, pertaining to events in their relation to God, all of which are 'foreknown and determined in advance by God'. Given that the passion happened (the 'hypothesis'), it follows that it must have been willed by God as part of 'the divine foreknowledge and plan'. Therefore it was a necessary event in the sense that it was impossible for it not to happen.

In the same article, a reply (III.46.2*ad*3) again takes up Anselm's contention that there could be no other way to address God's mercy *and* God's justice than with Christ making satisfaction by his suffering. Thomas is now in a position to deny this. First, it is evident that God could, 'absolutely' speaking, simply have willed to redeem us without the passion, for 'nothing is impossible with God'. Second, Anselm's concept of justice is drawn from the relation between an offender and the judge. The latter, who is not in any way injured or affected by the offence, must sentence the offender to a suitable punishment for the sake of social justice. Maintaining just societies and the rights of victims are not at issue here, however. Rather, as Thomas points out, the relation is more like that between a person who forgives another for an offence without demanding any recompense. That person 'acts mercifully, not unjustly'. Since the offence in question here is our sin against God, God could likewise justly have exercised mercy and simply forgiven us.

Thomas completes his treatment of the set of issues surrounding 'necessity' with the third article, 'Whether there was a better [i.e., more fitting] way to free us than by the passion of Christ?' (III.46.3) We now know the question makes little sense, since on the 'hypothesis' – the events recounted in Scripture – the possibility is inconceivable. Thomas' understanding of God and Scripture is such, as we have seen, that it *must* be the best way to get the job done. God could no doubt have brought about our redemption in some other way, but since God chose the passion as the means, it must on that account be the best means. So the article must address the hypothesis rather than reason abstractly (that is, independently of Scripture's account). We must ask instead: What makes the passion the best means of bringing about our salvation? Thomas notes that the best means to an end is the one that offers the most 'assets' that will help bring about the desired goal. So he sets out the chief assets, and in doing so makes the point that in the passion 'many things having to do with humanity's salvation over and above liberation from sin also converged' (III.46.3). The passion is the most expeditious means because it not only achieves our redemption (objectively), it also has a causal effect upon the subjective aspect of the *ordo salutis*, in regards to both enabling grace and our response. In the subsequent articles of q46, Thomas continues to discuss the various aspects of the passion to show how everything contributes to our redemption or our salvation, or both.

We move now to III.48, where Thomas discusses the proper usage of the primary metaphors used in Scripture and the tradition to describe the various aspects of Christ's work for us. The first two articles look respectively at 'merit' (or 'reward') and 'satisfaction' (Latin *satisfactio*, often translated as 'atonement'). Christ's passion is more than sufficient to make atonement for the sins of the whole world. But how, more precisely, is his achievement applied to us? Thomas answers this question in light of the doctrine of the Church as the Body of Christ, its Head, the Pauline analogy he had already examined in III.8. The Church here is very broadly conceived, for Christ is Head of all humanity, at least potentially, with the sole exception of those not predestined to salvation who have actually left 'this world' (III.8.3). Together, Christ and his Church 'form as it were a single mystical person' (III.48.2ad1), bound together by the grace of Christ's Headship which is passed on 'by Christ's own personal action on us'. Because we are one person, the merit Christ acquires for his suffering is poured out upon us so that we, too, receive the reward he has earned. And similarly, Christ's satisfaction pertains to 'to all the faithful as to his members' (III.8.5ad1).

Next Thomas addresses the 'figure' of sacrifice (III.48.3*ad*1). We have noted how, like Anselm, Thomas argues that our redemption was not something we could possibly achieve for ourselves. Christ redeemed us by offering himself as a sacrifice in our place and for our sakes, in free obedience to God's loving will. In the later Middle Ages there arose a tendency to conclude from scriptural references to God's anger that by his sacrifice Christ took upon himself the punishment desired by a wrathful God: the doctrine of penal substitution. Thomas does not make this move. (It is still often made, most evidently in some forms of Protestant evangelicalism and popular Catholicism.) *We* incur punishment, but it is largely self-inflicted. For we have placed ourselves 'in the devil's power by going along with him' (III.48.4*ad*2), thereby losing our freedom to serve God. It is from *this* punishment that Christ frees us, yet without his sacrifice being a punishment in our place (III.48.4). While normal social justice requires punishment of offences, the self-offering of the incarnate Word is an entirely different matter. The passion is the paradigmatic display of God's love for us, rather than punitive suffering to appease an angry God or to satisfy abstract justice.

Another way of explicating the meaning of Christ's work is to say that he 'ransoms' us in order to free us from our sin and our bondage to the devil. And so in III.48.4 and 5, we finally come to Thomas' treatment of the Pauline metaphor that gives the doctrine of redemption its name. To redeem or ransom someone is to buy their freedom from debt or servitude (figurative or literal) by paying what is owed or demanded. The significant questions here concern who is paid, what constitutes the price, and who the agent is. Some of the Fathers, influenced by Origen, had explained the passion as the price paid to the devil that freed us from his power. Later tradition found the notion that the devil is owed something by the incarnate Word entirely unfitting, and it was part of Anselm's great achievement to rule out any such implication by explaining redemption in terms of justice. Thomas argues the ransom was paid to God alone. Christ did not make restitution to the devil since that would be unfitting and, anyway, the devil is not owed anything (III.48.4*ad*3). The ransom itself is Christ's lifeblood. We should note that Thomas here stands at some distance from what Bynum calls the 'blood piety' of the later Middle Ages, with its focus upon the suffering of Christ, in which we may participate by means of our own pain.[5]

As for the agent of our redemption, it is, of course, not ourselves but Jesus Christ 'in his capacity as man'. His humanity is the 'immediate

---

[5]   Bynum, 'The Power in the Blood'.

cause', the one closest to the effect. The 'chief author' of our redemption, however, 'can be attributed to the entire Trinity', since Christ's life, given for us, 'belongs to the Trinity' and, moreover, 'it was the Trinity which inspired Christ the man to suffer for us' (III.48.5). Thomas explains this further in the concluding article of this question (III.48.6). The triune God is the principal cause of our redemption, while Christ's humanity is the 'instrumental cause'. When we use an instrument or tool, it contributes in its own way to the successful outcome of what we do and so can be said to 'cause' it. Thus the hook that catches the fish is the instrumental and immediate cause, whilst the angler is the primary cause; both can be said to catch the fish, but not in the same way. To be sure, Christ's humanity is not an instrumental cause in the same way as a fish-hook. He is animated by a rational soul and so acts in a fully human way (III.7.1ad3). His humanity is instrumental in that it is through the merits, the satisfaction and the redemption achieved in his humanity that Christ is the cause of grace in all of us. Thus the concept of an instrumental cause, drawn from John Damascene, enables Thomas to acknowledge the different kinds of contributions by the Trinity, Christ, and Christ's humanity, and to maintain an orthodox Chalcedonian christology.

The concluding question on the Passion (III.49) sums up its effects, both objective and subjective. So, for example, the first article explains how the passion frees us from sin: objectively by redeeming us, and subjectively by stimulating our love and faith, which also obtains pardon for our sins. In the second article Thomas addresses an issue that has troubled many Christians from the earliest times to the present day, especially those who have reflected on the dreadful events of the twentieth century: what difference did the redemption really make, given our obvious and ongoing sinfulness? Nothing seems to have changed. Are we not, then, still in bondage to the devil? Thomas argues that the many effects of the passion – the forgiveness of sins, our reconciliation with God, the curbing of the power of the devil, Christ's grace as Head of the Church, and the sacraments – now give us far stronger forms of 'self-defence against the wickedness of the devils' (III.49.2ad3). He points out, too, that 'the fact that some prefer not to use this remedy in no way detracts from the efficacy of Christ's passion' (III.49.2ad3).

The Christian life as Thomas conceives it requires all of us do all that we can to struggle against sin. For the 'plan for us was this, that we first conform ourselves to the model of Christ's passion and death in our own mortal lives, and only then [may we] attain a participation in the likeness of his resurrection' (III.56.1ad1). Thomas argues that, 'strictly speaking, the passion of Christ achieved its effect with regard to the removal of evil', and was indeed sufficient in that regard. Yet the events subsequent to Christ's passion – his death, resurrection and ascension – all contribute to our understanding of his redemptive activity and contribute in various ways to our salvation. The resurrection is the consequence of the passion, for 'Christ merited the glory of the resurrection by the humility of his passion' (III.54.2). As Head of the Church, his merits are applied to us so that we, too, may rise again in him. The resurrection, then, 'was both the first instance and the model of the good effects produced' by the passion (III.53.2*ad*3). The resurrection was 'necessary to increase our knowledge in faith' (III.53.2) and, more objectively, it initiated a new era, the time of the grace of Christ's headship and the movement towards the 'glory of eternity'. But our resurrection is not 'objectively' accomplished, as it were. It requires us to respond actively and appropriately to Christ's work throughout our lives, so as to make ourselves, by his grace, worthy of eternal life in him.

CONCLUSION

Thomas' treatment of redemption is at odds with many contemporary accounts. Modern theologians sometimes question the 'objectivity' of redemption and opt for various forms of exemplarism. They are less comfortable, too, with the notion that Christ remains fully in control. They focus on Jesus' humanity rather more than his divinity, and often argue that this is more in line with Scripture and our own experience. Some find the centrality of Christ's passion in Thomas' account oppressive rather than liberating, particularly because it is couched in terms of obedient self-denial and suffering. Contemporary theologians who discuss redemption tend to be more concerned with the sufferings of others or with theodicy issues.

Any engagement with Thomas on these and other matters would have to address his reading of Scripture, since it is evident that it guides so much of what he says about redemption. One might argue that Thomas' theological reflection on Scripture in this part of the *ST* is in some ways exemplary, at least in formal terms. Three aspects of Thomas' use of Scripture are particularly striking. First, we have already noted how – unlike Anselm, who relies heavily upon a single analogy to display the fittingness of the passion – Thomas seeks a broader and more flexible account by discussing the various metaphors that Scripture uses to describe Christ's work for us and its effects upon us. In this, Thomas avoids the sometimes reductive and overly theorized forms of systematic and moral theologies. He acknowledges the complexities and competing emphases found in Scripture, organizing them to accord with his view of the passion as the event that paradigmatically displays the fullness of the Trinity's love for us. Second, Thomas' focus is upon God, and he reads Scripture and does theology accordingly. Certainly he talks about us and about created realities, but only in our relation to God. For him, the triune God described by the Creed is the centre and organizing principle of theological inquiry and guides our reading of Scripture. We might argue that, as Christians, this is as it should be, for it is God revealed in Christ through the Holy Spirit who should govern how we should make use of what we know about other things, including our scientific and critical research. Finally, Thomas rules out the possibility of arguing back from creation to God's will by logical reasoning independent of what Scripture has revealed. We cannot explain God's decisions; we can only praise them, knowing they are good. So theology's task is to show their fittingness and correspondence with God's love. Thomas' refusal to engage in speculation contrasts significantly with a modern like Hans Urs von Balthasar, whose gendered metaphysics and reinterpretation of our redemption in dramatic terms reaches far into the being of the triune God. By comparison, Thomas' theology is indeed an obedient and humble reading of Scripture.

That said, Thomas was a thirteenth-century Dominican, and this, of course, influenced his understanding of Christianity. With his confrères, he believed that we should train ourselves by our efforts to follow our exemplar, Jesus Christ, so that we become like him – in our own way – as he is set forth paradigmatically on the Cross. Thomas seems to assume in his readers – quite reasonably, given they were monks and friars – an enthusiasm for such an effort, though he does acknowledge that many will fail in their efforts or not try at all. Some contemporary churchpeople have argued that Thomas is right, that every member of the church should respond to Christ's redemptive work by obedient and enthusiastic effort. Scholars (notably Stanley Hauerwas) have worked up theoretical versions of Thomas' discussion of virtues and sketched ecclesiologies that would support such a programme.

However, Thomas' account of the way of salvation, appropriate as it may have been for religious, may suggest to some contemporary lay people that he makes the Christian yoke too heavy, contrary to Jesus' words. His account may seem too sanguine about the possibility of truly conforming ourselves to Christ. Nor does it appear empirically as self-evident as Thomas seems to believe that those who are enthusiastic and obedient, and who make use of (or administer) the sacraments, are less sinful, all told, than others. Or if there is perhaps some difference, it does not seem sufficient. In addition, we are now far more aware of the psychological and sociological impediments to successfully living the Christian life as Thomas describes it. For these and other reasons, some might want to modify Thomas' understanding of our response to redemption to acknowledge a greater 'objectivity' in our sanctification and a greater dependence upon the sheer gift of salvation. We could do this in various ways, among which Thomas' understanding of the relation between Christ as the Head and his individual members might offer a point of entry. However, it is likely that any attempt to develop this or any other modification of Thomas would benefit from some appropriation of the model provided by this section of the *ST* for a contemporary form of scripturally based systematic theological reflection upon our redemption and sanctification in Christ.

Sacraments

OLIVIER-THOMAS VENARD OP

Aquinas had to choose where to place the sacraments in the pedagogical order of the *Summa*. By placing his questions on the sacraments in the third part of the *Summa*, he not only fulfilled his poetic and educational programme, he also made an important theological decision.[1] He assumed a more christological, than anthropological, view of sacraments. This is in accordance with his overall project of sacred doctrine, which treats of 'things', 'signs', 'the works of salvation,' only 'insofar as they have reference to God.'[2] More precisely, coming right after his study of the metaphysics and life of Christ, sacraments are placed in both a christological and an ontological light. Without any break of continuity, the reader moves from the mysteries of Christ to the sacraments of the Church 'which derive their efficacy from the Word incarnate himself.'[3]

Aquinas divides the matter in two: first the main features shared by all sacraments, then each separately. Questions 60–64 deal with several general issues raised by all the sacraments: what they are (q60); why they were instituted and are necessary (q61); what their effects are (qq62–63); how they come into being: who their author is and who may minister them (q64); finally, Aquinas ponders ways of conceiving the organization of the seven rituals (q65). Thereafter, questions 66–90 examine every sacrament in particular. This essay will focus on questions 60–65, and use the questions on baptism (qq66–71), confirmation (qq72), eucharist (qq73–83), and penance (qq84–90) to illustrate several points.

Aquinas' followers have sometimes reduced his theological analyses to rules aimed at defining the valid rituals, thus turning what were heuristic proposals into metaphysical statements, playing down their functioning as signs and overplaying the account of sacraments as causes. Thus, it might be helpful to synthesize Aquinas' main insights

[1] Many thanks to Gregory Tatum OP and Avital Wohlman for kind assistance.
[2] I.1.7*corp.*
[3] III.6o*prol.*

on sacraments in the *Summa* in three parts following the main three sources of light shed on them by their place in the structure of the *Summa*. Sacraments are (1) actions *of God* which flow (2) *from Christ* himself, for the benefit of (3) *human beings*, whom they empower to express their worship of God.

ACTS OF GOD FOR THE SANCTIFICATION OF HUMAN BEINGS

Even when he emphasizes the human need for sacraments, Aquinas cannot help adding a parenthesis admiring the wisdom of a benevolent God who devised sacraments as his main ploy to lead his bodily-spiritual creatures back to him: 'it is characteristic of divine providence that it provides for each being in a manner corresponding to its own particular way of functioning. Hence it is appropriate that in bestowing certain aids to salvation upon man the divine wisdom should make use of certain physical and sensible signs.'[4]

As we shall see, the category of sign, though necessary (since sacraments are for rational, interpreting animals), falls short of encapsulating what faith holds about the divine action in sacraments: it must be complemented with the category of cause, equally necessary and non-sufficient (since it could suggest automatic effects ignoring man's dispositions).

Sacraments as signs

The classification of sacraments as signs is a methodological choice made by Aquinas among other possibilities: causes, secrets or mysteries, oaths are other possible categories.[5] 'Sign' is a convenient analogical way to think about the seven sacraments. According to the Augustinian definition often quoted by Aquinas, 'a sign is that which, over and above the form which it impresses upon the senses, makes something else enter into our cognition.'[6] Classifying sacraments as signs enables one to think of two in one – the same with its other, the created and the Uncreated, humanity and God – without mixing categories, without diminishing the transcendence of God in any way whatsoever.

Moreover, talking of sacraments as signs allows Thomas to think of sacraments as a divine language. Minimally, sacraments imply the use

---

4   III.61.1*corp.*
5   Cf. III.60.1.1–3 and *corp.*
6   Augustine, *De Doctrina Christiana* XI.1 quoted, for example, in III.60.4*corp.*

of language. Words are required in the celebration of sacraments.[7] But sacraments may also be compared with words ontologically. Aquinas likes to quote Augustine: 'The word is conjoined to the material element, and the sacrament is constituted.'[8] 'What else are all these physical sacraments, except, so to say, so many visual words?' Aquinas wonders: 'The sensible elements of the sacraments are called words by way of a certain likeness, in so far as they partake of a certain power of signification, which resides principally in the very words' used in their celebration.[9]

Sacraments may also be compared to language in their functioning, analogous to a grammar: they are adapted to each stage of salvation history just as a verb is declined in tenses according to the time to be expressed.[10] Even deeper, the spiritual power of instrumental power is in the concrete sacrament as the meaning is in the pronounced word.[11]

Now, the end of the sacraments is to sanctify, that is to give grace, or divine life,[12] or the Holy Spirit – and only God can do this.[13] 'God alone enters into the soul in which the sacramental effect takes place; and no agent can operate immediately where it is not: [...] grace, which is the interior effect of the sacrament, is from God alone.'[14] For this reason, only God can determine how His life may be communicated, and decide what things may be used for the sanctification of humans.[15] The stress laid on the divine institution of the sacraments derives from an acute sense of the transcendence of God.

Thomas applies the same dynamic to the sacraments which he applies to scripture: only God knows God, and graciously pours His knowledge and grace on those he wishes. The fixity of sacraments is comparable to that of Scripture: they are signs chosen by God just as the words and symbols in Scripture are chosen by the Holy Spirit.[16] Therefore, whenever possible, Aquinas analyzes the sacramental words by means of the words pronounced by Christ in the Scriptures.[17] Moreover, the

---

[7] III.60.6*ad*1.

[8] Augustine, *Tract. in Joan.*, xxx, quoted in III.60.4*sed contra*; III.60.6*sed contra*; III.78.5*corp*; and *passim*.

[9] III.60.6, 1 and *ad*1.

[10] Cf. III.60.5*ad*3; III.61.4*corp*; III.68.1*ad*1.

[11] III.62.4*ad*1.

[12] I-II.110.3 and 4.

[13] III.64.2*corp*; III.62.1*corp*.

[14] III.64.1*corp*. Cf. I-II.112.1.

[15] III.60.5*corp*.

[16] III.60.5,1 and *ad*1; III.60.8, 1 and *ad*1.

[17] Cf. III.84.3*corp*, *ad*1, *ad*3, where Thomas uses Matt. 18:18f to defend the indicative, rather than begging, formula of absolution.

sacramental signs consist in sensible things just as in scripture spiritual
things are set before us under the guise of things sensible.[18] The theology
of sacraments turns out to rest on the same symbolic vision of reality as
the theory of the senses of the Holy Scripture devised by Aquinas.[19] Any
created thing can become a visible sign of the invisible, sanctifying reality. Both doctrines rest on the analogy of being.

But ultimately the category of sign is insufficiently precise to think
through Christian sacraments, for two reasons. The first one is cosmo-
logical: Aquinas' world is a semiotic one – a medieval universe in which
every creature is a sign of the creator God. In a universe made up of
signs of the sacred, the study of the seven sacraments requires further
precision.[20]

The second is historical-theological: in the *Summa*, Aquinas situates
the seven sacraments in the broad economy of salvation. Throughout
history God's salvation has been communicated in signs, and so Aquinas
talks of the Jewish sacred signs as sacraments. In talking of Christian
sacraments he needs more precision and thus talks of them as real, efficient causes of grace. Causality adds precision to signification.

Sacraments as efficient causes

The efficacy of sacraments is not a matter of proof or demonstration
but of the faith of the Church: 'we have it on the authority of many
saints that the sacraments of the New Law not merely signify, but actually cause grace.'[21] Indeed, sacraments are traditionally believed to com-
memorate and communicate the virtue of Christ's Passion, and their use
of exterior and material things does convey the notion of some efficacy.
Aquinas does not oppose sign to cause, but balances an Augustinian
view of sacraments as signs, and an Aristotelian conception of sacraments as causes, to assert that the sacraments of the New Law effect
what they signify.[22]

For Aquinas sacraments are made up of words and ritual elements:
words help to make the signification of rites more precise, but the rites
are not reducible to the signification of the words. The two interact: the
ritual elements, polysemic by nature, prevent the theologian from reducing sacramental signs to univocal signals.

[18] III.60.4*corp.*
[19] I.1.10*corp* and *ad1.*
[20] Cf. III.60.2.
[21] III.62.1*corp.*
[22] III.62.1*ad1.*

This is underlined by looking at the relations between the two pairs: words/elements and form/matter. The need to pin down the meaning of an overly polysemic sacramental sign with words is only the third argument (by fittingness) for using words in sacraments mentioned by Aquinas.[23] The pair form/matter appears only in passing, as an analogy.[24] The elements and the words form a united whole, that may be compared to that of matter and form. Aquinas does not suggest that elements and actions used in the sacraments would be mere passive matter which words would *a posteriori* inform as an active power. Both convey the meaning of the sacraments. The elements are integral parts of a sacrament inasmuch as it is a mystery (*mysterion*). Sometimes words themselves may even function as (part of) the matter of the sacrament. For example, in the sacrament of penance, the sins confessed are the 'remote matter,' the confession of sins is the 'proximate matter.'[25]

The reversal of form and matter prevents the theologian from reducing the sacrament to clear ideas derived from the sacramental words alone. Just as forms are not merely superimposed on matter, but result from its potentialities without exhausting them, so words are only the summit of a pyramid of signs built up by the meanings of all elements and actions comprised in the sacrament.

So much for any reduction of sacrament to sign: these are discrete notions. A mere sign can be a cause only by cognitively and morally influencing its recipient. At most, it would be a formal or final cause: no efficient causality is implied. The functioning of the sacrament as sign and the functioning of the sacrament as cause are not identifiable.

Aquinas links the efficacy of sacraments to the reality which they signify, rather than a particular understanding of signification. Sacraments are signs, but signs of God which cause remission of sins, granting grace, and bestowing holiness. As signs, sacraments perform a pedagogical role similar to any human teaching. Only God can 'touch' the spirit directly from inside: embodied creatures can only influence others from outside to produce the right concepts, by using material signs addressed to the senses, imagination and desire.[26] Thomas notices a possible delay between the performance of the rite and the actual welcoming of the gift of grace.[27] How is the sacrament as signification linked to the sacrament as efficient cause? These two aspects cannot be merely juxtaposed. For

---

[23] III.60.6*corp.*
[24] III.60.6*ad*2.
[25] III.84.2*corp*; III.84.3*corp.* Cf. also III.86.6*corp.*
[26] III.69.5*ad*2.
[27] Cf. III.69.4*ad* 2; III.69.10*sed contra.*

Aquinas this is not just concomitance. Sacraments are not only opportunities for God to grant grace, but they *cause* grace.

Good Aristotelian that he is, Aquinas locates the key to sacramental causality in the concept of instrumentality. For Aquinas, God is primary cause, but one which creates many secondary causes. The distinction between first, uncreated cause, and secondary causes proves crucial for understanding how the accidents of bread and wine remain after their Eucharistic transubstantiation.[28]

Among secondary causes, instrumental causes do not act by the power of their own forms, but their proper effect is taken over by the power of whatever main cause is making use of them, in order to produce an effect proportionate to its form. And for Aquinas sacraments take on this structure: instrumental mediations of God's power.[29] An instrument is an intermediary between cause and effect.[30] Whereas a main cause does not itself signify (rather it is signified by its effects, like fire by smoke), an instrumental cause may signify the main cause using it and the proper effect of that main cause, as any effect may do, without ceasing to be an actual cause causing its proper effects. For example, the pouring of water or the immersion of the baptism, while causing its proper effect of cleansing, signifies God's purifying action on the soul, and points to filial adoption as the proper effect of this purification from sin.

Were sacraments mere signs, one could think that they are conceptually graspable, understandable in every respect. Were they mere causes, one could assume that they are technically controllable, as if a human creature could produce grace. By defining them as both signs *and* causes without reducing one to the other,[31] Aquinas preserves the mysteries or sacraments from any epistemological or metaphysical reduction. As instrumental causes, sacraments appear as signs of a hidden, transcendent cause, sharing in the production of hidden effects.[32] The divine efficacy of the sacraments does not fit any ready-made category. Instrumental causality enables the theologian to firmly maintain God's transcendence while describing God's action in the sacraments: *both* the transcendence of the uncreated primary cause vis-à-vis its effects in creatures, *and* the immanence of its action in the creature God sanctifies, are maintained.

---

[28] Cf. III.77.1*corp in fine.*

[29] III.62.1*corp*; III.62.4*corp.*

[30] III.62.1*corp.*

[31] Cf. III.61.1*ad*1: The use of the sacrament 'is spiritual in virtue of the power inherent in the sacraments to convey meaning *and* produce effects.'

[32] III.62.1, 1 and *ad*1.

Sacramental characters

Baptism, Confirmation, and Holy Orders are believed to mark Christians once for all with spiritual, indelible seals or 'characters', deputing Christians 'to spiritual service pertaining to the worship of God.'[33] The existence of sacramental 'characters' is a traditional *datum* rooted in Scripture and in the ancient patristic metaphor of Christian life as military service and Christians as soldiers marked out for it.[34] The original literary and intra-ecclesial polemical circumstances surrounding the idea of sacramental characters led Reformers and anti-metaphysical theologians to suspect it to be mere speculation on a dispensable metaphysical chimera. Indeed, it is not very intuitive; but as we shall see, it comes as a necessary consequence of traditional beliefs in divine involvement in Christian sacraments,[35] if one grants metaphysical analysis of the human being.

The existence of the sacramental character is hardly obvious. It is uncovered through its causes and its effects. The definition of 'character' as a 'spiritual sign'[36] is a logical deduction from the fact that it is known as the effect of a sensible rite.[37] Being sensible is the main feature of the sign;[38] but a spiritual sign is counter-intuitive: is it more than an analogy? The classification of character as a kind of power (neither a passion nor a habit) is also the result of a logical reduction based upon an *a priori* definition by Aristotle,[39] not upon any experienced evidence.[40] Its 'localisation' in the powers (not the essence) of the soul,[41] namely the practical intellect,[42] is also a logical-metaphysical deduction.[43] In brief, the 'character does not belong to any given genus or species'; as divine,[44] it is an essentially analogical reality, in between rite and grace, like all other elements of the sacramental reality.

Sacraments' divine causality complicates any account of their structure as mere signs. They involve a level beyond any natural signification, granted by God's mercy, resulting in a threefold structure which does

---

[33] Ibid.
[34] III.63.1*corp.*
[35] III.62.2*corp.*
[36] Cf. III.60.4*ad1.*
[37] III.63.1*ad2.*
[38] III.60.4*ad1.*
[39] Aristotle, *Nicomachean Ethics*, II.5.
[40] III.63.2*sed contra.*
[41] III.63.4*corp.*
[42] III.63.4*ad3.*
[43] III.63.4*corp.*
[44] III.63.2*corp.* Cf. III.63.a3*corp.*

not coincide with the signifier/signified/referent pattern of linguistics. Patristic theologians distinguished: the sacramental ritual (*sacramentum tantum*); the grace given by God to those receiving the sacrament (*res tantum*), and, in between, the 'character' or marking of those receiving the sacrament (*res et sacramentum*). This character is both indelible and extrinsic – 'a certain kind of spiritual power introduced into [the soul] from without,'[45] superadded and activated by God.[46]

There are metaphysical reasons for sacramental character. Sacramental graces are supernatural gifts, which nothing natural can receive or transmit by itself. Reading Denys' teaching on the communication of divine life[47] in the light of Aristotelian metaphysical principles,[48] Thomas associates the need for a sacramental character as a potency, to the need for creatures to be able to become the subject (or the object) of acts of a kind superior to those of one's own nature. Only sacramental character provides the metaphysical possibility of an interaction without confusion of God and mankind, faith and reason, and grace and nature.

The main arguments are soteriological. God wants to save as many human beings as possible through sacraments communicating grace; sacraments must be conduits of God's will even if the humans who celebrate them are sinners. Aquinas illuminates this point with his theory of instrumentality. The 'minister has the same significance as an instrument, in the sense that the action of both is applied from without, yet achieves the interior effect from the power of the principal agent which is God.'[49] By being marked as an instrument of God's grace 'the ministers of the Church can confer the sacraments' – very good things indeed – 'even when they [themselves] are evil.'[50] The theory of sacramental character helps us understand how grace is infallibly offered by God though not infallibly received in the celebration of sacraments.

SACRAMENTS OF CHRIST

Aquinas' deployment of instrumental causality does not only result from metaphysical analysis of sacraments. Thomas was put on this track by the Greek Fathers, from whom he borrowed the idea of the human

---

[45] III.63.4*ad*2.
[46] III.63.5*ad*2.
[47] III.63.2*corp*.
[48] III.63.2*corp*.
[49] III.64.1*corp*.
[50] III.64.5*corp*.

nature being the instrument (*organon*) of the divine person in Christ.[51] Only God can achieve humanity's salvation, but this work was accomplished by His son through his human actions. Christ is the sanctifying holiness at work in and through the signs making up sacraments: it is he who makes of the sacraments – which are already (cognitive) signs – (efficient) causes. Thus, Christ is the source and model of sacramental instrumentality. He is the 'united instrument' and sacraments are the 'separated instruments' of God's causality.[52]

As early as in the prologue of the *Tertia Pars*, Aquinas presents the sacraments as benefits bestowed by Christ on the human race and means by which the latter attains the salvation that Christ achieved. The participation of sacraments in Christ's being and action is worked out throughout the questions on sacraments.

Sacraments, like Christ, derive from the mercy of God

'God did not cause his power to be restricted to the sacraments in such a way that he could not bestow the effect of the sacrament without the sacraments themselves',[53] so sacraments are needed just insofar as Christ is needed. Sensible signs of sanctification are needed for the same reason that the appearance of Christ is needed: a God-man to reorient embodied spirits, oriented towards material and sensible beings, quick to make idols and adore false divinities.[54] The Incarnation is an expression of the divine goodness communicating itself to humanity;[55] but considered from the side of fallen humanity, it appears first and foremost as a reparation ordained to glory, as the most fitting way of healing our misery.[56] Hence in the *Summa*, Thomas underlines the twofold nature of the sacraments, as both *elevans*, elevating humanity to the fullness of spiritual life, and *sanans*, healing sin and its consequences.

Aquinas fittingly attributes these to the two aspects of the Paschal mystery: Christ's Passion effected salvation, properly speaking, by removing evils; but the Resurrection did so as the beginning and exemplar of all good things.[57] Like other ancient authors, dealing with 'the Passion' Aquinas intends what we now call 'the paschal mystery' as

---

[51] See III.7.2*ad*3; III.8.1*ad*1 and the quotation of John Damascene, *De Fide Orthodoxa*, III.15, in III.2.6, 4 and *ad*4; III.7.1, 3.

[52] III.62.5*corp*.

[53] III.64.7*corp*.

[54] III.61.3–4.

[55] III.1.1*ad*2.

[56] III.1.2*sed contra*.

[57] III.53.1*ad*3; cf. also III.56.2*ad*4.

a whole. Both the Passion and the Resurrection together cause our justification.[58]

Sacraments share in the ontology of Christ

The ontology of sacraments is that of signs-instruments dispensing the causality of the first cause. They are isomorphic to Christ: the word is joined to the sensible sign, just as in the mystery of Incarnation the Word of God is united to sensible flesh.[59]

Moreover, as images and symbols of the reality of Christ's redemptive acts, sacraments participate in the realities they represent. This theme is particularly developed for the Eucharist.[60] Participation through representation (following common neoplatonist construals of the relation of images to their exemplar or archetype) is supernaturally accomplished by sacraments' institution by Christ himself, which is necessary for theological reasons, as mentioned earlier. Thomas does not define precisely what institution is.[61] But basically, he envisages the bestowing by Christ of a certain meaning and power to certain rituals, either by displaying it in his own actions during his life on earth (Eucharist), or by promising it for a later date (after his resurrection: Confirmation).[62]

His metaphysical understanding of sacraments enables Aquinas to endorse the literal meaning of the Scriptures dealing with sacraments.[63] It explains why they empower their receivers to share in Christ's mysteries: they are not mere 'technical tools' devised by God to spread the redeeming merits of the Passion to mankind; they are actual means to incorporate human beings into the body of Christ. The sacramental rituals insert believers into the historical saving action of Christ and unite them to Him severally: as the efficient causes of holiness (through His passion), as formal causes (He is *the* Icon of the Godhead), and as final causes (all returns to God through Him).[64]

Sacraments draw their efficacy from the power of Christ

Thomas links the efficacy of sacraments to the Incarnate Word from the very first question of his treatment of sacraments.[65] In patristic and poetic key, he uses the liquid metaphor of *effluence* – an image traditionally

---

[58] III.62.5*ad*3.
[59] III.60.6*corp*.
[60] Cf. III.73.4*ad*3; III.79.1*corp*; III.73.7*corp*; III.83.1*corp* and *ad*2.
[61] III.64.2.
[62] III.72.1*corp*.
[63] For example Gal 3:27 quoted in III.62.1*corp*; Rom. 6:3 quoted in III.61.1*ad*3.
[64] III.60.3*corp*.
[65] III.60*prol*.

used to speak about grace – to do this.[66] He also uses this imagery of the presence of a spiritual force within matter during baptism. Thomas says that water, refined by Christ's physical contact and blessing,[67] is able to reach even the most remote and subtle corners of soul.[68] The metaphorical continuity between material and spiritual strikingly suggested here by the liquid nature of water underlines the fact that only Christ can mediate between material and spiritual, natural and supernatural. The source of the effluence metaphor may be found in the piercing of Jesus' heart on the Cross, whence come blood (symbol of the Eucharist) and water (symbol of Baptism).[69]

The historical coming of the Word in flesh was necessary to transform the sacraments into causes. Before Christ, the sacred signs displayed in Judaism, rightly named sacraments,[70] were representative of the salvation to come, and acted in believers' lives through moral anticipation.[71] Christ's Passion had a certain final causality on them, but only through the spiritual acts of the faithful, expecting a Savior to come.[72] But an efficient cause cannot produce its effects in advance as a final cause can: Christ's Passion could only become an efficient cause in the signs commemorating it once it had happened. After the actual saving actions of Christ, sacraments representing them become efficacious providers of the redemption he achieved.

Sacraments participate in Christ's historical humanity. Grace is not a thing like a tangible gift: rather it is a share in the life of Christ, a participation in His death and resurrection. Christ did not deliver mankind from sin automatically, just by virtue of being God Incarnate, but voluntarily and intentionally, by choosing to atone for sins, by handing himself over to death.[73] Thus sacraments must be studied in connection with the mysteries lived by Jesus, the *acta et passa Christi* which Aquinas examines in the immediately preceding questions 27 to 59. Christ exerts his same unique priestly mediation in words and deeds before his glorification as in sacraments afterwards.

Indeed, the whole Christ is at work in the sacraments: past (memorial of the Passion), present (bestowing of sanctifying grace), future

---

[66] III.60.6*ad*3. Cf. already I-II.103.2*corp.*
[67] III.62.4*ad*3.
[68] III.62.4*ad*3.
[69] III.62.5*corp.*
[70] III.60.2*ad*2.
[71] I-II.107.2*corp.*
[72] III.60.6*corp.*
[73] III.62.5*corp.* citing Eph 5:2; cf. III.19.4*corp.*

(foretelling of future glory).[74] Aquinas insists that Christ's causality in sacraments is not just efficient (our sanctification through the voluntary offering in his Passion), but also formal (Christ himself is the plenitude of grace and virtues, the very form of our holiness) and final (the return of all things to God culminates in Him).

Christ's causality in the sacraments is both divine and human.[75] As man, He acts as the perfect instrument mediating the plenitude of grace which he suffuses in the sacraments as God. Interestingly enough, Aquinas teaches that Jesus could have shared this causality with other human beings (for example his apostles, who would then have had the power to devise new sacraments), but only to state that in fact He did not. The power and the authority of the Church over the sacraments is thus limited. Aquinas puts it in a way the Reformers could have agreed with: 'The Apostles and their successors are the vicars of God. [...] Hence just as it is not lawful for them to constitute any other Church so too it is not lawful to them either to hand down any other faith or to institute any other sacrament.'[76]

Sacraments imprint the character of Christ

As stated above, to confect and to receive sacraments, which are acts of God, humans need to be endowed with a special power, a character. Aquinas links sacramental characters with Christ first by means of Hebrews 1:3 which depicts Christ as 'the character of the Father's substance.'[77] He then explains that the sacramental characters are nothing but participations in Christ's priesthood, flowing from Christ Himself.[78] In the Eucharist, the minister marked by Christ's priestly character through ordination, is empowered to act in union with Him: *in persona Christi*, in the person of Christ.[79]

Christ uses sacramental characters to exert continually His priesthood by sacramentalising the worship of the believers in the Church. His power over them as *instruments* explains the paradox that they are both transitory (as any instrumental entity) and indelible (by virtue of its primary cause).[80]

---

[74] III.60.3*corp.*
[75] Cf. III.64.3 and 4
[76] III.64.2*ad*3.
[77] III.63.3*sed contra.*
[78] III.63.3*corp.*
[79] III.82.1*corp.*
[80] III.63.5*ad*1 and *ad*2.

Nevertheless, sacraments are also related to the full Trinity: by continuing the worship initiated by the incarnate Son, believers receive His character and make use of it, while they are granted grace by the Father, grace which is the gift of Holy Spirit.[81] Sensible sacraments (and sacramental characters) are more connected to Christ, the embodied Word, while their ultimate, eschatological effect is more closely attributed to the Holy Spirit.[82]

The order of the sacraments depends on their proximity to Christ

Although Thomas knows other ways of ordering sacraments (according to their necessity[83] or fittingness[84] for salvation), he prioritizes the criterion of 'greatness', which he understands following Denys the Areopagite as a degree in the ontological hierarchy.[85] The Eucharist is 'the greatest' insofar as Christ himself is present, and not just an action of Christ as in other sacraments. Whereas baptismal water or the oil of confirmation are transitory instruments of grace by participation, the Eucharistic bread and wine are miraculously deprived of their own substance, to become the signs of Christ's substantial presence. Thus the Eucharist is not one act of worship among others, but the fullness of adoration: Christ himself in the act of offering himself. The receiver of the Eucharist enters not only a *functional* relation to Christ like in the other sacraments, but an *essential* one. Christ is present substantially, as the very sacramental reality of the Eucharist.[86]

SACRAMENTS OF MANKIND: EMPOWERING AND EXPRESSING HUMAN WORSHIP OF GOD

God has no need of sacraments to save humanity: He could have saved humanity in many other ways than Incarnation.[87] But 'there was no more fitting way of healing our misery.'[88] Indeed, sacraments convey God's salvation to the human persons at all levels: ontologically (they fit as straddling the spiritual and material), biologically (they structure

---

[81] Cf. III.63.3, 1 and *ad*1 and III.8.1, 3 and *ad*3.
[82] Cf. III.63.3, 1 and *ad*1; 2Cor 1: 21 cited in III.63.1*sed contra*.
[83] III.65.3*corp*.
[84] III.65.4.
[85] III.65.3*corp* citing Dionysius, *De Eccl. Hier.* 3.
[86] III.73.1*ad*3.
[87] III.1.2.
[88] Augustine, *De Trinitate* XII.10, quoted in III.1.2*corp*.

human life from birth to death), and theologically (they are adapted to sinners called to grace and glory).

One of the most frequent images of human life Aquinas uses in the *Summa* is that of a journey from God to God. At the end of the exit-return structure of the whole work, he deals with the sacraments graciously given to mankind by its Redeemer. Since he has already treated them as ritual actions,[89] Aquinas here construes them as the divine means for perfecting the human life which he described in the anthropological questions of the *Prima Pars*; which he analyzed in the ethical, spiritual, and social teachings of the *Secunda Pars*; and which he depicted as redeemed by Jesus Christ in the *Tertia Pars*.

Sacraments as fitting the human condition

The first argument Thomas gives for the fittingness of sacraments for human salvation is ontological: they embrace both the material and immaterial sides of human life.[90] As signs, they are intended for humans.[91] The duality constituting signs mirrors the dualities of humanity (soul/body, interior/exterior, intellect/sense). Their hylomorphic structure mirrors that of human beings. For the Aristotelian Thomas, the senses provide the first, indispensable, step to human knowing, and for the Platonist Thomas, images received through the body mirror the spiritual reality accessed sacramentally. Rather than inviting a crude transactional view of sacramental grace, the form-matter language used by Aquinas provides a firm theoretical basis for any ritual, poetic, and artistic development of sacraments.

Sacraments convey salvation in all its dimensions, not only moral, but also epistemological. 'Signs are given to men, to whom it is proper to discover the unknown by means of the known.'[92] They fit the human need to attain intelligible or spiritual realities only through the mediation of sensible or material things.[93] The sacramental remedy is structured for its human recipient, 'for the visible materials in it touch the body, while the word in it is accepted in faith by the soul.'[94] Sacraments teach as signs, enabling humans to grow in knowledge of God. Aquinas certainly does not reduce their causality to efficient causality: sacraments empower the soul to reach God as its perfect *form*

---

[89] Cf. II-II.81.
[90] III.61.1*corp.*
[91] III.60.2*corp.*
[92] III.60.2*corp.*
[93] III.60.4*corp.*
[94] III.60.6*corp.*

or *end*.[95] Aquinas underlines the symbolic richness of the sacramental rites, whose pedagogical and mystagogical value he expounds.[96] Neither the post-Tridentine reduction of analogy to canonical regulation, nor the post-Vatican II impoverishment of symbols and ritual fit Aquinas' vision of sacraments.

In particular, sacraments are fitted to human biological condition. The structure of the seven sacraments is tailored to the ages and states of life. He conceives the fittingness of the seven sacraments in relation to human life in all its natural dimensions, both individual (birth: Baptism; growth: Confirmation, Penance, Eucharist; death: Anointing of the Sick) and social (marriage: Matrimony; priesthood: Ordination).

In typically medieval manner, Aquinas stresses the communal dimension of human life. For example, the sacraments of holy orders and matrimony achieve the perfection of man in relation to the community as a spiritual and physical whole.[97] More generally, by marking with a sign those who receive them, those sacraments conferring a character build up a community of persons bearing the mark of their designation for worship of God,[98] sometimes as agents (holy orders), sometimes as recipients (baptism). Although the mark must be spiritual, it is imprinted and known only through sensible means, such as the rituals themselves, or the parochial registers.[99] Characters have an ecclesiological dimension: they enable humans to build the pilgrim church. The Eucharist, which is the heart of the church, does not confer any character, but sacramental characters are required to celebrate it: the sacerdotal to give it, the baptismal to receive it.

Sacraments are adapted to the frailty of mankind

Although Aquinas stresses the instrumentality of ministers' actions, he is far from reducing them to machines. Ministers are a special kind of instrument since they are rational. They are not only moved by the primary cause; they also have to move themselves to produce the intended effect. Thus the truth and validity of sacramental rites depend not only on the authority Christ bestows on the elements or words, but also on the right intention and performance of their performers.[100]

[95] III.62.2*corp.*
[96] For example, III.66.10*corp.*
[97] III.65.1*corp.*
[98] III.63.1*corp.*
[99] III.63.1*ad*2.
[100] See the discussion about the form of baptism: III.66.5*ad*1.

Neither the words nor the elements signify or cause anything by themselves, but only when they are used by humans in the ways instituted by Christ.[101] For example, since a sacrament is like a sign, its truth depends on its signification, and on the right utterance of the instituted words: incorrect expression can invalidate the sacrament.[102] While signifiers are not efficacious by themselves, nevertheless appropriate use of words displaying the right meaning is required to perform a sacrament. Since that meaning is the one faith gives to words, some variations are possible, but the core meaning instituted by Christ must remain. This leads Aquinas to determine the elements and words which constitute the substance of the sacramental form for each sacrament.[103]

Even though the famous formula 'ex opere operato' captures the essentials of Aquinas' teaching on sacramental efficacy, it never occurs in the Summa. For a sacrament to exist, at least the intention 'to do what Christ and the Church do' is required.[104] In this respect, Aquinas proposes that pronouncing the words required by the Church suffices to do this.

This teaching gave rise to two different interpretations in theology and in canon law. Theologians would hold that the correct internal intention of the minister is necessary for the validity of the rite, as an obvious deduction from their status as animated instruments. Canon lawyers, on the other hand, wanting to define the validity of the rite, are satisfied with the 'external intention' manifested by the observance of the rites defined by the Church. They stress the fact that, by entailing the gift of characters, the dependence of sacramental grace on the minister's holiness is limited. Sacraments are designed for the benefit of all, so they must not be limited by the sinfulness of the ministers: their divine efficacy takes into account the fact that all ministers are not saints, and may even be sinners. It enables them to give even what they do not possess themselves.

This debate is interesting insofar as both parties face the objection of courting sacramental occasionalism. The theologians disconnect the causality of the primary cause from the instrumental cause, whereas the canon lawyers, in order to avoid a constant uncertainty as to the validity of sacraments (since the mental intention in the minister is unverifiable), must stress the freedom of a God unbound by His own institutions making good their defects.

[101]   Cf. III.66.1 (about baptism).
[102]   III.60.7, 3 and ad3.
[103]   III.60.8corp.
[104]   III.64.8ad1.

'He Who created you without you will not justify you without you.'[105] The efficacy of sacraments is partly dependent on the recipient's faith. For Aquinas, faith *and* the sacraments are two modes of uniting (*copulatio, continuatio*)[106] the self to the power (*virtus*) of the Passion of Christ: the former is invisible and interior, the latter visible, performed as exterior bodily acts.[107] Sacraments draw their efficacy from faith in Christ's passion.[108] Hence, instruction for those receiving the sacraments is required.[109] The faith and devotion of those receiving a sacrament can even make good a defect of intention in the minister, and obtain justification from sins.[110]

Sacraments meet the needs of fallen human beings

Sacraments sanctify as practical signs, starting from what we enjoy the most, namely bodily actions, thereby moderating humans' attraction to material things.[111] Aquinas combines a 'positive' conception of sacraments as perfecting humans,[112] with a 'negative' conception of sacraments as remedies against ignorance, weakness, and other consequences of sin. Sacramental grace entails both healing (the purification from sins) and exaltation (the perfecting of the soul with gifts pertaining to divine worship).[113]

Although Thomas aligns Baptism, Confirmation and the Eucharist with exaltation, and Penance and Extreme Unction with healing the consequences of sin,[114] nevertheless, in the same article Aquinas says all sacraments heal the defects caused by sin.[115] In any case, 'all sacraments are necessary for salvation in some manner,'[116] some for salvation only, and others for its perfection.

It might be argued that, by choosing to study sacraments firstly as signs, Aquinas was bound to consider them primarily as healing. Before sin humanity had no epistemological impairment, and senses and reason were harmoniously ordered, so signs were superfluous[117] for

---

[105] Augustine, *Sermo* 179, cited in III.68.4*sed contra*.
[106] III.62.5*ad2*.
[107] III.62.6*corp.*
[108] III.60.6*corp.*
[109] III.67.7*corp.*
[110] III.64.8*ad2*.
[111] III.61.1*corp.*
[112] Cf. III.65.2*corp.*
[113] III.62.5*corp.*
[114] III.65.1*corp.*
[115] III.65.1*corp.*
[116] III.72.1*ad3*
[117] Cf. *De Veritate* 18.2, *in fine*.

knowing and loving God, whose intelligible effects radiating throughout creation humans perceived intuitively.[118] No sacraments were needed.[119] Only after the Fall, once the sensitive and intelligible faculties were disordered, does the mediation of sensible signs such as the sacraments become necessary to cure ignorance and sin.[120] Thus, like signs, sacraments are not necessary to humanity *per se*, but they are indispensable to *fallen* human beings.

Sacraments fit the theological-historical condition of humanity. Having already studied at length the main features of life with grace in his treatise on the New Law,[121] in the *Tertia Pars*, Aquinas deals with the historical bestowing of such a gift through the Incarnation of the Word continued by the celebration of sacraments.

Aquinas' stress on the necessity of divine institution does not result from theological speculation ignoring the variations of the rites throughout history: it rather enhances the contingencies of history. Indeed, he agrees that the institution of the sacraments is known not only from Scriptures, but also 'from the family tradition of the Apostles.'[122] Hence his proposals leave room for further historical liturgical investigation exploring the preexisting Jewish rites transfigured in Christian sacraments in the beginnings of the Church, or their subsequent ritual and devotional developments.

Throughout time sacraments effect God's will to save all. The sacraments of the Old Law were different from those we know now: there is no abstract nature of sacraments, since they are mostly means of the divine mercy, pedagogically redeeming mankind step by step in history.[123] Since the sacraments of the New Law depend entirely on the historical incarnation of God, their forms and matters are more particular than those of the Old Law, and thus could be considered more exclusive.[124] Yet the most necessary ones, Baptism and the Eucharist, require elements (water and bread) 'such as people generally have in their possession or such as it costs little trouble to obtain.'[125]

Sacraments also prepare humans for eternal life with God. This eschatological aspect is much stressed at the end of these questions, when Aquinas identifies the Eucharist as the 'greatest' sacrament,

[118]   I.94.1corp.
[119]   III.61.2corp.
[120]   III.61.3ad2.
[121]   I-II.106.
[122]   III.64.2ad1.
[123]   III.61.3ad4.
[124]   III.60.5corp.
[125]   III.60.5ad3. Cf. III.67.3corp.

insofar as it 'contains' the substance of Christ himself, which is both the common spiritual good of the whole Church[126] and the foreshadowing of 'that enjoyment of God which will be ours in heaven.'[127]

CONCLUSION

Aquinas studies sacraments as mysteries of the faith: they escape any prior foundation. Scriptural proof is not available to justify them all.[128] In order to understand them, one must trust in the Church's tradition.[129]

Aquinas stopped writing the *Summa* while dealing with Penance.[130] While studying this sacrament whose 'confecting' (*facere*) entails 'acting' (*agere*), Aquinas could see the synergy of human effort and divine grace. This was a turning point for Thomas, who in his spiritual life was overwhelmed by God's empowering of humans to collaborate in his salvation out of pure friendship.[131]

From God to humanity, the sacraments continue the mediating mission of Christ as an endless overflowing of divine mercy. From mankind to God, by enabling human beings to minister and receive the grace of God, they build up a communal network of interactions welcoming God's grace. Ultimately, although God is not bound by the sacraments,[132] the elect are always saved by Christ in the Church, his mystical body.

---

[126] III.65.1*ad*1.
[127] III.73.4*corp.*
[128] III.72.4*ad*1.
[129] III.64.2, 1 and *ad*1, citing 1 Cor. 11:34.
[130] III.90.4.
[131] III.80.2*corp.* evokes a *reconciliatio amicitiae.*
[132] III.66.6*corp;* III.67.5*ad*2; III.68.2*corp;* III.72.6.

Part III

Catholic traditions

PAUL J. GRIFFITHS

Thomas Aquinas' *ST*, left unfinished in 1273, three months before his death, is now well into its eighth century of being read, taught, commented upon, admired, despised, copied, printed, analyzed, indexed, translated, glossed, dissected, supplemented, and epitomized. A large quantity of human effort has been focused upon it, certainly enough to make it reasonable to say that the *ST* holds a prominent place in the European literary archive. The *ST* was composed by a Christian thinker with the explicit intention of handing on 'what belongs to the Christian religion in a way suitable to the instruction of beginners' (I *prol*), and this means that on the surface of the text, at least, it belongs to the Christian part of that archive. And not only that, but since the fragmentation of Christendom in the sixteenth century, and most especially since the Council of Trent's (1545–1563) revisionist Catholic response to that fragmentation, it belongs to the specifically Catholic archive, sometimes even standing, *pars pro toto*, as a symbolic representation of the whole of that archive. This is not to say that it has prompted no response by non-Catholic Christians; they have sometimes read it and more often reviled it as symbolic of an unacceptable version of Christianity; neither is it to deny the significance of the increasingly frequent uses of it by non-Christians during the last half-century or so. But it is to say that a history of the *ST*'s reception and use will largely be an exercise in analysis of the Catholic archive.

There are, however, significant difficulties in the way of writing any such history. No one can read more than a tiny portion of the works responsive in one way or another to the *ST*. Even the bibliographies of such works are a crushing weight.[1] Also, while there are histories of

---

[1] Leonard Kennedy's *A Catalogue of Thomists: 1270–1900* (Houston: Center for Thomistic Studies, 1987), for example, lists 2,034 Thomists (though his criteria for determining who is a Thomist are relaxed), most of whom composed works in one way or another responsive to the *ST* – and that takes us up only to 1900. If this were supplemented by Bourke's two volumes of Thomistic bibliography, and by the online

Thomism, and while such histories always have something to say about the uses made by Thomists of the *ST*, they almost never disentangle such uses from the broader intellectual and institutional histories that they aim to tell, sometimes collapsing Thomism into the story of the *ST*'s interpretation, and sometimes relegating the *ST* to a walk-on role in that history.[2] There are, so far as I know, only two book-length studies that make some attempt synthetically to treat the history of the *ST*'s reception and use,[3] and even these make what they do in this respect ancillary to analysis of the literary form and thought of the *ST* as such. And while there are many specialist studies of particular Thomists, or of Thomism at particular times, these also rarely treat the use of the *ST* by itself. There is, then, no significant body of scholarly work on which to draw whose primary focus is the reception and use of the *ST*.

In this situation, modesty is essential. What I offer here is brief comment on three matters having to do with the *ST*'s place within the Catholic archive: its dissemination, its status, and its roles.

DISSEMINATION

The *ST* as Thomas left it in 1273, incomplete at III.90, contains something over 1.5 million words in Latin, and typically many more in the more prolix European vernaculars. It is a substantial portion of Thomas' corpus, comprising about 18 per cent of the whole. A work of this size is not easily disseminated as a whole, even in the days of print: almost all printed editions are in more than one volume, and some are in so many as to require a small bookcase to themselves – for example, the sixty-volume English/Latin 'Blackfriars' edition. The division of a large work into parts is even more necessary when manuscript is the only means of transmission, and since the *ST* clearly signals the places at

---

bibliography maintained by Enrique Alarcón (at http://www.corpusthomisticum .org/), the result would be a massive literature, growing by hundreds of works a year.

2 Useful histories or depictions of Thomism (of very different kinds) include: Géry Prouvost, *Thomas d'Aquin et les thomismes: essai sur l'histoire des thomismes* (Paris: Cerf, 1996); Romanus Cessario OP, *A Short History of Thomism* (Washington, DC: Catholic University of America Press, 2005); David Berger, *Thomismus* (Köln: Editiones Thomisticae, 2001), especially chapter 2; Fergus Kerr OP, *After Aquinas: Versions of Thomism* (Oxford: Blackwell, 2002); Mark D. Jordan, *Rewritten Theology: Aquinas After His Readers* (Oxford: Blackwell, 2006). None of these focuses exclusively upon the *ST*.

3 They are David Berger's *Thomas von Aquins "Summa theologiae"* (Darmstadt: Wissenschaftliche Buchgesellschaft, 2004), and Jean-Pierre Torrell OP's *Aquinas's Summa: Background, Structure, and Reception* (Washington, DC: Catholic University of America Press, 2005).

which it may most easily be divided (into four parts if the two sub-parts of *ST* II are counted separately), it is not surprising that the *ST* was rarely copied and transmitted *in toto*, but instead piecemeal.

Whether or not Thomas did intend the *ST*'s parts to circulate independently, or perhaps only acceded to the inevitability of this, it is certainly what happened. Among the surviving manuscripts of the *ST*, it is rare to find the entire quadripartite work copied and transmitted by a single hand and as a whole. Rather, the parts are copied and transmitted independently, with II-II being much the most popular, and III much the least.[4] II-II treats the particular virtues and vices in light of I-II's treatment of the virtues and vices in general, and the greater interest in disseminating this part of the *ST* suggests that the most common use of the work in the two centuries following its abandonment by Thomas was as a manual to train Dominican *novitii* in what we would call moral theology but what would likely have seemed to them preparation for the care of souls. The hearing of confessions is one of the foundational charisms and purposes of the Dominican order to which Thomas belonged and within which the *ST* was largely used during this period; and in order to do that well, training in the subject-matter of II-II is essential. This is no doubt among the more important explanations of the popularity of II-II, and of its separation from the rest of the work.

In the second half of the fifteenth century printing began to replace manuscript-copying, and the *ST* soon began, in whole or in part, to be disseminated in this way. The early (pre-1500) printed editions were mostly in part rather than in whole: the earliest appears to have been a 1463 edition of *ST* I. The most widely used printed edition of the entire *ST* between the sixteenth century and the nineteenth was almost certainly the 1570 Piana edition, named for Pius V. This edition appeared together with the commentary of Thomas de Vio (1469–1534), also called Cajetanus (after Gaeta, his Italian birthplace), based on his lectures on the whole *ST* delivered at Pavia during the first two decades of the sixteenth century. After the Piana edition, the *ST* was printed *in toto* in the nineteenth century editions of Thomas' complete *oeuvre*, among which the principal were the Parma (1852–1873), and the Vivès (1871–1880), supplanted by the Leonine (named for Leo XIII) edition

---

4   For statistics and discussion, see Leonard Boyle OP, 'The Setting of the "*Summa Theologiae*"' in idem, *Facing History: A Different Thomas Aquinas* (Louvain: Fédération Internationale d'Études Médiévales, 2000), 65–91, here 85–86; James A. Weisheipl OP, *Friar Thomas d'Aquino: His Life, Thought, and Works* (2nd ed.; Washington, DC: Catholic University of America Press, 2003), 360–361; Torrell, *Summa*, 92–93.

of the *ST* which appeared in eight volumes (1888–1896). This last edition was also printed with Cajetan's commentary, which had by then attained almost canonical status as an authoritative interpretation of Thomas. It is the Leonine version of the Latin text of the *ST* which has been reprinted in most of the manual editions of the twentieth and twenty-first century, sometimes with and sometimes without Cajetan's commentary. It is this version, too, which has most often been the basis of the nineteenth- and twentieth-century translations of the *ST* into European vernaculars.[5]

If the manuscript evidence suggests that the *ST* was rarely transmitted whole before 1500, and therefore also rarely studied or taught in that way, then the evidence of the printed editions suggests quite the contrary, that there was an increasing interest in disseminating the *ST* whole, and not only that but also transmitting it as part of two greater wholes. The first of these greater wholes was Thomas' entire corpus: those institutions and (rare) individuals who could afford the Parma or Vivès editions could thereby study not only the entire *ST*, but also its connections to and resonances with the rest of Thomas' work. These things would have been difficult or impossible before print. The second greater whole is that of Cajetan's commentary. The influence of this work as an interpretive frame for the *ST* was very great until recent times, and it came to assume such importance not only because of Cajetan's status as a systematic thinker in his own right, and as a Counter-Reformation intellectual warrior and therefore a Catholic hero, but also simply because his words were so often printed together with Thomas', as their frame and guide. If the *ST* had been disaggregated into its components by its manuscript-transmission, it was now subsumed into its commentarial context by its dissemination in print. In neither context was it often or easily treated in its own right as a conceptual or textual whole.

Electronic storage and display is now in a fair way to displace print as the principal means for the *ST*'s dissemination, whether in Latin or the vernaculars. A good deal of this remains parasitic upon print, displaying electronically only what was once displayed on the page, and preserving many of the visual conventions of printed media. But even when this is the case, the ease of access to the text given by the web, together with the easy use of various secondary tools (indices, concordances, and so on), is likely to mark a new and distinctively different

---

[5] More detailed information about the printed editions can be had from the bibliographical appendices to Weisheipl's *Thomas* and to Torrell I.

phase of the *ST*'s dissemination. It is too soon to offer detailed speculations about how the *ST* will be treated as a result of the move to electronic storage and display of the text; but it is perhaps worth noting that one effect, already evident, is to make it more likely that the *ST* will be mined (for data, for conclusions, for arguments, for tropes) than that it will be read.

Since the revival of Thomism signalled by Leo XIII's *Aeterni Patris* (1879), and the associated (but by no means identical) revival of particular concern with the text and content of the *ST* suggested by Pius X in his *Doctoris Angelici*, a document issued *motu proprio* in 1914, there has been renewed interest in the text of the *ST* of both a historical and a theological kind. The text has been disseminated in the Leonine edition, already mentioned; and there have been massive works of translation into the major European vernaculars, many of which have offered not only a vernacular version of the *ST*, but also the Latin text and considerable exegesis of both a historical-critical and textual sort. This work certainly signals an emergence of the *ST* from its carapace of commentary and epitome, and the work of translation has been paralleled with a renewed interest in the Catholic world in the structure and literary form of the *ST*. And, rather more remarkably, in English at least there is a significant number of *florilegia* of extracts from the *ST* in print in relatively inexpensive paperback editions. The number of these is increasing rather than decreasing, and this is principally driven by the needs of the American college and university market. It does, however, strongly suggest that at least parts of the *ST* are being taught quite widely in that setting, and, to the extent that students read what they are taught, also being read. But at this point, the *ST*'s dissemination is no longer a primarily Catholic matter: it is likely that the *ST* is now taught as much by Protestants and by secular historians and philosophers as by Catholics.[6]

The extent of the *ST*'s dissemination in both Latin and vernacular versions strongly supports the view that it is a classic of the Catholic archive. The same conclusion is supported by the number and kind of textual responses – commentaries, epitomes, reductions to system, expression in theses – to the *ST*. But it should also be noted that these textual responses have very often come to substitute for the *ST*, and that as a result the presence of the *ST* in the Catholic tradition has often,

---

6   On the twentieth-century translations of the *ST*, see Jean-Pierre Torrell OP, 'Situation actuelle des études thomistes', *Recherches de science religieuse* 91/3 (2003), 343–371, here 351–355. On the twentieth-century debate about how best to understand the structure of the *ST*, see Paul van Geest, Harm J. M. J. Goris, and Carlo Leget (eds), *Aquinas as Authority* (Leuven: Peeters, 2002), 187–200.

perhaps typically, been at one or more removes from the work itself, removes produced by absorption into commentaries or distillation into epitomes. This is typical for classics, and in this respect also the *ST* clearly is one.

STATUS

The importance of a work for a particular archive cannot be shown only by attending to its dissemination, essential though such attention is. It must also be shown by taking notice of the status explicitly granted to the work by the archive's guardians. Such status may be positive or negative. In the former case, the guardians say or do things that attribute to the work some particular favorable significance for the archive, or allot to it some special place therein. The limit-case of this, in Christian terms, is canonization. In the latter case, the guardians criticize the work, perhaps by saying why it ought not to be taken as representative of the archive, or why it is to be, in the extreme case, banned. The public guardians of the Catholic archive are, paradigmatically, the bishops with the Bishop of Rome at their head, but they are not the only ones: almost as important for the place of the *ST* in the Catholic tradition are those with authority in the religious orders. The *ST* has sometimes been the topic of pronouncements by these guardians of the archive, as, more frequently, have been Thomas himself and Thomism more generally. And the pronouncements have usually moved the *ST* closer to the canon than to the ban, though, especially in the early years, there were criticisms: the *ST* did not easily become a classic of the Catholic archive, and it has arguably never done so in the way its author might have hoped.

In 1277, three years after Thomas' death, two bishops, Étienne Tempier of Paris and Robert Kilwardby of Canterbury, condemned as untenable by the orthodox some theses taught by Thomas, among them some more or less directly derived from the *ST*. In 1279 there occurred the first of several critical responses to the *ST* by Franciscans, in this case by William de la Mare, an English Franciscan who published a list of 118 propositions to be corrected, most drawn almost verbatim from the *ST*; he also argued that the *ST* could not safely be used for teaching purposes unless these corrections were made. These early condemnations had mostly to do with inter-scholastic difficulties between Dominicans and Franciscans, the latter being more dubious than the former of the merits of using Aristotle and his Muslim interpreters as sources for the interpretation and elaboration of the deliverances of the faith. That these magisterial condemnations occurred at all – and so quickly, a bare few years after Thomas had written all he would write of the *ST* – suggests the importance that the work early assumed. It is important to recall, however, that Thomas' work was not identified in these condemnations solely with the *ST*, and so the condemnations, too, were not directed only at it.

So much, in brief, for the negative status given to the *ST* by the guardians of the Catholic archive. Interventions of that kind were quickly over, and following Thomas' canonization by John XXII in 1323, and the consequent lifting of the earlier Parisian condemnation, the *ST*, like Thomas' other works, became largely insulated from criticism and began its ascent toward iconic (if not quite canonical) status. At the Council of Trent (1545–1563), the *ST* was a definite presence: in the Council's Decree on Justification the textual presence of the *ST* is very clear, and sometimes approaches the verbatim.[7] This is not surprising given that a high proportion of the theologians active at the Council were avowedly Thomist, and would likely have had a close knowledge of the *ST*. In 1567, not long after the Council's conclusion, Pius V recognized Thomas as *doctor ecclesiae*, which is to say as one of the few whose thought and writing is of profound significance for the thought of the church. This recognition was not aimed explicitly at the *ST*, but it occurred as an important element in the Counter-Reformation's embrace of Thomas as a symbol of the Catholic Church's ability to renew itself intellectually and to counter Protestant criticisms. It was also at this time that commentatorial interest in the *ST* began to flourish in the schools of Paris and Salamanca; that the *ST* began finally to displace Peter Lombard's *Sentences* as the fundamental school-text in the houses of study of the religious orders; and that the well-established (since the fourteenth century) genre of painting Thomas as triumphant in victory over heretics and pagans, sometimes holding a text of the *ST*, began now to include representations of his triumph over the heresies of the Protestants.

In 1879, more than three centuries after Trent's use of the *ST* and the establishment of the *ST* as the emblematic counter-reformation text, the guardians of the archive returned to Thomas in Leo XIII's encyclical letter *Aeterni Patris*, issued in that year.[8] This letter was

---

7 Specifically: chapter VI of the Decree on Justification is close to III.85.5; the Decree's seventh chapter is intimate with I-II.112.4; and the fourth chapter of the Decree on the Eucharist is in part an almost verbatim reproduction of III.75.4. For some discussion, see Berger, *Summa*, 36–37.

8 On the importance of *Aeterni Patris* for the subsequent Thomist revival, and for the study of the *ST* in particular, see: Gerald A. McCool SJ, *From Unity to Pluralism: The*

concerned to place Catholic education – and especially clerical education – on a sound philosophical footing. For Leo, this meant founding
theological education upon what he called scholastic philosophy (§24),
a kind of philosophy which was, in his view, given its fullest and most
beautiful expression in Thomas' work. Not only, he thought, does theological education require scholastic philosophy: so also does the peace
and harmony of domestic and civil society (§28), and the appropriate
development of all arts and sciences (§29). Leo is careful to distinguish
the thought of Thomas himself from that of his interpreters and commentators (§31), a position entirely consistent with his advocacy of a
new critical edition of Thomas' works. What he wants is pure Thomas
('be watchful that the doctrine of Thomas be drawn from his own foun-
tains,' §31), and he wants it because he thinks it will serve as an effective counter to the errors of modernity, errors which, before the end
of Leo's papacy in 1903, were to become the subject of public controversy. For Leo, Thomas' philosophy – clearly distinguished from his
theology, against, according to the preponderance of modern interpreters, the meaning of the text – was the most effective bulwark against
error within and without the church; and because of this he speaks of
Thomas' wisdom and insight in very elevated language. The guardians
of the Catholic archive have often written fulsomely of the work and
character of the church's saints and doctors; but Leo's praise of Thomas
has never been equalled or even approached in intensity and range.
Thomas, as depicted in *Aeterni Patris*, is saint, philosopher, and teacher
to the world; without him, the church cannot fulfil its mandate to come
to a fuller understanding of what it teaches, and it is his work above all
else, that causes heretics to quail.

Thomas is lifted high in *Aeterni Patris*, but there the praise is given
to the man and his thought in general, not to the *ST* in particular.[9] The
praise of the man is repeated and intensified in a later letter, *Cum hoc
sit* (1880), which calls Thomas *sanctissimus inter doctos et doctissi-
mus inter sanctos*,[10] but still does not speak directly to the status of

Internal Evolution of Thomism (New York: Fordham University Press, 1989), and *The
Neo-Thomists* (Milwaukee: Marquette University Press, 1994); Jordan, *Rewritten
Theology*, 3–6; Kerr, *After Aquinas*, ch. 2; Torrell, *Summa*, ch. 6.

9 The *ST* is mentioned in *Aeterni Patris* only when Leo tells the story of its being laid
   on the altar 'together with sacred Scripture and the decrees of the supreme Pontiffs ...
   whence to seek counsel, reason, and inspiration' (§22). It is hard to find independent
   evidence that this was done.

10 *Cum hoc sit* is quoted to this effect by Paul VI in *Lumen ecclesiae*, a letter addressed
    to the Master of the Dominican Order on 21 November 1974, in celebration of the
    seven-hundredth anniversary of Thomas' death.

the *ST* among Thomas' other works. Such direct address is evident in magisterial texts from the early twentieth century. Pius X commends, in *Doctoris Angelici* (1914), attention to the *ST* as the best means of establishing the fundamental principles of Thomism in Catholic universities and colleges. And then, later that year, the Congregation of Studies in Rome proposed twenty-four theses as encapsulating just these fundamentals.[11] The theses reflect, in a highly abstract way, some positions argued for in the *ST*; and although their authority was disputed almost as soon as the Congregation had promulgated them, they were reaffirmed by Benedict XV after the death of Pius X, and this reaffirmation was then cited in the 1917 *Code of Canon Law* as the principal ground for requiring that teachers of philosophy and theology attend closely to Thomas' teaching – meaning, by implication if not explicitly, that teaching as found in the *ST*.[12]

The status given to the *ST* by the guardians of the archive in the first half of the twentieth century was, then, very high indeed. Thomas is the philosopher greater than whom none can be imagined; his work in general, and the *ST* in particular, is represented as the final, unsurpassable synthesis of philosophy and theology. No other text has anything approaching this degree of authority. But things soon changed. The texts of the Second Vatican Council, promulgated less than half a century after the 1917 *Code* and Benedict XV's reaffirmation of the twenty-four theses, give Thomas a place of honor, certainly, but a place among many others rather than one of unique authority;[13] and nothing was made of the *ST* in particular at that Council. Also the revision of the *Code of Canon Law* published in 1983, while it still gives Thomas' thought a special place when it comes to discuss the education of clerics (*s. Thoma praesertim magistro* – 'with St Thomas as their teacher in a special way'[14]), significantly tones down what had been said in the 1917 *Code*, which had come very close to requiring teachers of philosophy and theology to teach in accord with Thomas' doctrine. By the time we arrive at 1998's encyclical letter *Fides et Ratio*, by John Paul II, while Thomas is still given high praise for originality and profundity (§§43–44), that

---

[11] The theses were published in the *Acta Apostolicae Sedis* VI.11 (August 1914), 383–386. See Denzinger-Schönmetzer, §§3601–3624. For some discussion see Cessario, *History*, 25–26.

[12] *Codex Iuris Canonici* (1917), canon 1366, §2. See Torrell, *Summa*, 110–111, and Cessario, *History*, 27–28, for some discussion.

[13] Thomas' thought is still given an important place in clerical training in Vatican II's decree on that subject (*Optatam Totius*, §16).

[14] *Codex Iuris Canonici* (1983), canon 252, §3.

praise is muted by a clear and explicit denial that the church has any official philosophy (§76) – and therefore not Thomism – as well as by mention of many other philosophers and theologians, the praise of some of whom approaches, and perhaps exceeds, that given to Thomas.

ROLES

A work's dissemination is the extent to which it has found distribution; its status is the place explicitly given to it within some archive by that archive's guardians; its roles are the parts it plays within the tradition to which the archive belongs. These are distinct matters. A work can be widely disseminated and yet have low status; it can have high status and yet be narrowly disseminated; and even if widely disseminated and of high status – as, with some variation, the *ST* has been within the Catholic tradition – it may nevertheless not be widely read but rather used for other purposes. The *ST*'s principal roles have been two: as veiled pedagogue; and as site for intellectual controversy.

Thomas, it seems clear enough, had the education of his Dominican brothers in mind as among the proper uses of the *ST*, and perhaps as its principal use. And this was certainly among the earliest uses at least of the *Secunda Secundae*. The *ST* did not, however, soon gain a very prominent place as pedagogue, whether among Dominicans or at other sites for the training of clerics and religious. This was principally because of the dominance of Peter Lombard's *Sentences* as the standard textbook for theological training: even as late as the sixteenth century some Dominican houses of study – for example, Louvain – required its use and, thus, did not permit the *ST* to be used in this way. But by the sixteenth century, as religious orders other than the Dominican (especially the Jesuits and the Carmelites) began to make pedagogical use of the *ST*, and as the high status given to Thomas by the Council of Trent and further fuelled by the passions and energies of the Counter-Reformation began to be felt, the *ST*'s pedagogical prominence rose, and it began more often to be used as a whole rather than in part. By the late sixteenth century it was among the two or three works most widely used by the religious orders for clerical training: it had by then effectively displaced the *Sentences* as the standard theological text at Paris and Salamanca.

Once Thomas was declared *doctor ecclesiae* and the *ST* lay open on the lecterns of the lecture-halls of Paris and Salamanca, seemingly never to be closed again, it might have seemed that it would play its part as pedagogue without hindrance, and that generations of priests and religious would be formed by its words and arguments. Why would it not become the church's unrivalled pedagogue? And in one sense it did; but the very fact that it did almost at once cast commentatorial veils over its face.

Almost from the beginning, the *ST* had been epitomized and then offered to readers in short forms intended to make its quintessence easily and rapidly digestible. Probably the earliest of these epitomes, prompted by controversy among Dominicans, and between Dominicans and Franciscans, about the validity of some positions argued in the *ST* (and in other works by Thomas), was John of Quidort's *Correctorium*, composed at Paris around 1300. But this was only the first of many. Not long afterward, Giovanni Dominici epitomized the entire *ST* at the request of John XXII, as part of the proceedings that issued in Thomas' canonization in 1323. And the practice of epitomizing the *ST* continues to the present. Sometimes epitomes use principally or only Thomas' own words; and sometimes they provide none of them, but only a summary of the *ST*'s structure or content. In either case, the epitomes tend to veil the *ST* by effectively replacing it.[15]

There are also longer and thicker veils, so long that sometimes they make the *ST* itself seem short. These works are most often commentaries, sometimes line-by-line but more often article-by-article or question-by-question. The post-Tridentine elevation of the *ST* prompted the proliferation of these commentatorial veils, and they vary considerably in the degree of their intimacy with the *ST*'s words. Some are close to that text, paraphrasing and summarizing it; some are distant, taking shape as long discursive works occasioned by one topic or another raised in the *ST*, or by one or another lively local controversy, but not by a desire for close textual engagement. Cajetan's commentary has already been mentioned; because of its transmission with the printed text of the *ST*, it was among the most influential of the commentaries; but there were many others, most notably in the Spanish Dominican, Jesuit, and Carmelite schools from the sixteenth through the eighteenth centuries. Especially important among the Spanish commentators on the *ST*

---

[15] On John of Quidort, see Cessario, *History*, 49–50. On Giovanni Dominici see Torrell, *Summa*, 94–95. For a later example, see John Poinsot's (1589–1644) *Isagoge ad D. Thomae Theologiam*, an *explicatio* of the structure of the *ST*, available in English in Ralph McInerny (trans.), *John of St Thomas: An Introduction to the Summa Theologiae of Thomas Aquinas* (South Bend: St Augustine's Press, 2004). For modern epitomes see Peter Kreeft's, *Summa of the Summa* (San Francisco: Ignatius, 1990), the same author's *A Shorter Summa* (San Francisco: Ignatius: 1993), and Timothy McDermott (trans.), *Summa Theologiae: A Concise Translation* (Allen, TX: Christian Classics, 1989).

were Francisco de Vitoria (1492–1545), Luis de Molina (1535–1600), and Domingo Bañez (1528–1604). There are also important, though considerably less-studied, *ST*-commentaries from the eighteenth century, most strikingly (for sheer size), Charles René Billuart's (d. 1757) 19-volume commentary on the entire *ST*, printed at Brussels.[16]

A brief excursus on the form of Bañez's *ST*-commentary, the first part of which, on *ST* I.1–64, was published at Salamanca in 1564, and was based on Bañez's five-year course of lectures on the entire *ST*,[17] will illustrate how commentaries can veil what they expound. Bañez's ordinary procedure is to treat the *ST* article by article, without frequent reference to the topic of the question in which a particular article appears, or to the place the question has within the broader structure of the part or sub-part of the *ST* in which it occurs, and therefore largely without attention to the literary and conceptual structure of the *ST* as a whole. For each article, treated almost as a free-standing piece of work, Bañez provides a brief *summa articuli* in which the central thesis or theses of the articles is restated, usually in words close to Thomas'; this is then followed by a lengthy *commentarium*, sometimes ten times as long as the article it expounds, and rarely shorter than five times as long. This *commentarium* typically raises questions about Thomas' conclusions, often by adverting to what earlier commentators have said, and either defends Thomas against what might seem to be objections to his conclusions, or provides Thomistic nuance by reading those conclusions in a way that would not have occurred to Thomas but which is claimed to be *ad mentem D. Thomae* – in accord with the sainted Thomas' thought. These extended discussions are learned, subtle, and theologically interesting; but often distant from the text of the *ST*. Bañez's method casts a triple veil over the *ST*: first over its structure as a complete work, which almost completely vanishes; second by providing an epitome of the conclusions of each article, which it is hard to imagine students failing to use as a quick way of studying Thomas by avoiding his text altogether; and third, by extending the discussion of matters addressed in the *ST* into alien territory. These are not criticisms of Bañez; they are observations about a typical example of the *ST*'s veiling by commentary.

---

[16] On the *ST* commentary-tradition prior to the French revolution, see Torrell, *Summa*, 92–105; Cessario, *History*, 66–81; McInerny, *John of St. Thomas*, vii–x; Philippe Lécrivain, 'La Somme Théologique de Thomas d'Aquin aux XVIe-XVIIe siècles', *Recherches de science religieuse* 91/3 (2003), 397–427; Berger, *Summa*, 34–35.

[17] I have consulted an undated reprint, made in Dubuque, Iowa, of the 1934 edition of Bañez's *Scholastica Commentaria in Primam Partem ST s. Thomae Aquinatis* printed in Madrid as part of the Biblioteca de Tomistas Españoles.

It is at first sight paradoxical that the Leonine revival of interest in the text of the *ST* toward the end of the nineteenth century, together with the almost-canonical status of the *ST* as pedagogue from then until the 1960s, made the *ST*'s veils more impenetrable rather than less. Although teaching in religious houses of study and seminaries for the secular clergy was during this period usually in some sense *ad mentem D. Thomae*, it rarely involved study of the text of the *ST*, but rather of manuals still more distant in style, voice, and structure from that work than the sixteenth-century commentaries had been.[18] But perhaps this too is not really paradoxical: as a textual pedagogue increases in status, so it requires more and more textual handmaidens, so many that they eventually prevent the master from being seen.

The *ST* has, then, often played the role of veiled pedagogue, and to some degree continues to do so today. But this has been only one of its principal roles; the other is as a site for intellectual controversy. A work serves as such a site when it provides the terrain upon which disagreements of fundamental concern to the tradition get worked out. A preliminary distinction will be helpful in understanding how this works: on the one hand there are disagreements about what Thomas means by the *ST* (or, if you prefer a text-centered rather than an author-centered hermeneutic, what the *ST* should be taken to mean); and on the other there are disagreements about the truth of one controverted question or another – about the proper way to construe the relations between nature and grace, say; or between theology and philosophy; or about the significance that trinitarian doctrine should have in thinking about the doctrine of creation; or about the unity of the virtues; or about what ontotheology is and whether it is a bad thing. Once a work has become a high-status and widely-disseminated pedagogue, these two kinds of disagreement begin to merge. That is, it becomes difficult for the tradition to discriminate a question about the truth of some topic from a question about what the *ST* means. Disagreements about the one will be played out upon the field of the other. This is in part because it is difficult for participants in such debates to relinquish Thomas and the *ST* as allies and supporters; but it is also because it is difficult for any of the parties to such debates to accept that the *ST* may have no position or the wrong position on a debate of importance to the tradition. And so a good part of the history of Catholic theological controversy from the sixteenth

---

[18] Anthony Kenny, *A Path from Rome: An Autobiography* (Oxford: Oxford University Press, 1986), ch. 3, provides a richly detailed account of pedagogical method and texts at the Gregorian during the years 1949–1952, which abundantly illustrates this point.

century until now can be written by describing the ways in which the *ST* has been taken: as charter for a rigid two-tier nature-grace distinction or as defender of the opposite view; as a quarry for theses to be disputed, or as a work whose principal contribution to theology is structural and rhetorical; and so on.

The *ST*'s dissemination, status, and roles will no doubt change in the future. It is already the case that analysis of those matters requires attention to much that does not belong to the Catholic archive. The heroic synthesis of the truth of Catholicism that was lectured on in Paris and Salamanca and elevated to quasi-canonical status by Leo XIII and Pius X is now, perhaps, on the way to becoming a classic of the European archive whose appeal is less martial and more seductive. Of that Thomas would probably have approved.

Orthodox traditions

ANDREW LOUTH

The engagement of Eastern Orthodox theology with St Thomas Aquinas' *Summa Theologiae* is a complex and shadowy affair.[1] Within a century of Aquinas' death, some of the works of the theologian were available in Greek translation in the Byzantine world, and were greeted with both enthusiasm and dismay. Our understanding of this early Byzantine reaction to Thomism is complicated by a number of factors. First of all, the works of Aquinas became known in the full flush of the Palamite controversy, by which time positions had already hardened. Aquinas did not so much influence the controversy, as fit into largely predetermined positions, though often enough in a rather bewildering variety of ways. It is important to remember this, as our understanding of the engagement between Thomas and Byzantine theology in the fourteenth century is made the more difficult by the fact that in the twentieth century, the Palamite controversy came to be seen as definitive for understanding the nature of the schism between Eastern and Western Christendom – Palamism defining the heart of Eastern Orthodoxy in opposition to Western Christendom defined by Scholasticism (or sometimes by a more complex duality embracing Scholasticism and the emerging non-dogmatic mysticism of the Western later Middle Ages). Virtually all Orthodox scholarship on the fourteenth century – and most of the Western scholarship – has been affected by the sense that here we find the definitive nature of the schism (at a theological level), and this, in turn, has been affected by the more immediate encounter between Orthodox theologians (to begin with, mostly Russian Orthodox theologians) and the West that took place in the twentieth century. Put (too) bluntly, the controversy of the fourteenth century has been seen from the perspective

[1] For another account of the interactions of orthodox theologians with the *Summa* see Marcus Plested, *Orthodox Readings of Aquinas* (Oxford: Oxford University Press, 2012) which appeared several years after this essay was written. See my review in *First Things* 23/3 (1 May 2013), 63–4.

of the Russian Orthodox encounter with early twentieth-century Roman
Catholic theology, in which Aquinas appeared either as the inspiration
of a debased scholastic theology or as the hero of Neo-Thomism, and the
interpretative categories employed emerge from the twentieth-century
engagement rather than the fourteenth century, with the favoured view
being granted the palm of being 'existentialist'! Even to begin to disentangle this is more than can be attempted in a brief article, which must
therefore remain provisional.

The Eastern Orthodox encounter with the *Summa*, however, either
in the fourteenth century or the twentieth (or the centuries in between)
is not perhaps the place to begin. For Aquinas himself engaged with traditions that we would call Eastern Orthodox. Aquinas was indebted, in
his theology, to a long tradition of theological reflection that had been
shaped decisively by Eastern traditions. Indeed, although Aquinas is cast
in the Orthodox mind as the Scholastic, *par excellence*, this is to over-
simplify. Unlike many of the schoolmen, Aquinas' early education was
in a monastic school – at Monte Cassino, the monastery founded by St
Benedict himself – where *lectio divina* and a meditative approach to the
scriptures would have made prayer and study inseparable. This education was later supplemented by study at the University of Naples, an
imperial foundation independent of the Church, but the basis of Aquinas'
learning was monastic, and thus much closer to the tradition of what
the Byzantines called the 'inner wisdom'. Furthermore, it was argued
long ago that in his christology Aquinas was uniquely well informed,
in comparison with his contemporaries, by the Greek patristic tradition,[2] and more recently the once-popular idea that Aquinas departed
from an earlier Platonic tradition under the influence of the newly-dis-
covered Aristotle has been shaken, and a strong Neoplatonic influence
recognized.[3] Finally, it is worth mentioning that, when Aquinas died in
1274, he was on his way to the Council of Lyons in an attempt to heal the
schism between East and West. In general terms, then, Aquinas appears
more open to, and concerned for, 'Eastern' influences than the common
Orthodox preconception might suppose. In more strictly theological
terms, and especially in relation to the *Summa Theologiae*, Aquinas'
indebtedness to Eastern Orthodox tradition may be considered further

---

[2]   See Ignaz Backes, *Die Christologie des Hl. Thomas und die griechischen Kirchenväter*
      (Paderborn: Schöningh, 1931).
[3]   Argued *à outrance* in W. J. Hankey, *God in Himself: Aquinas' Doctrine of God as
      Expounded in the Summa Theologiae* (Oxford: Oxford University Press, 1987; see
      Fergus Kerr OP, *After Aquinas* (Oxford: Blackwell, 2002), 9–10.

with reference to two theologians determinative of the later Orthodox tradition: Dionysios the Areopagite and St John Damascene.

DIONYSIOS THE AREOPAGITE

The works ascribed to the disciple of the Apostle Paul, Dionysios the Areopagite, have had an unparalleled influence on Eastern Orthodox theology.[4] To put it briefly, these writings provided a unifying theological vision that picked up the characteristic emphases of Byzantine theology as they had developed by the beginning of the sixth century, when the *Corpus Areopagiticum* first appeared. It is a cosmic vision, focused on the Eucharistic celebration and associated sacramental rites, in which the heavenly and earthly realms are united; the whole created order is governed by a principle of hierarchy, by which everything is drawn more deeply into union with God, a principle of hierarchy manifest in its purity in the ranks of celestial beings; the creaturely orders are seen as engaged in praise of God, using the terms – the 'names' – by which God has revealed himself in the Scriptures, for the interpretation of which Dionysios introduces the terminology (borrowed from Neoplatonism) of apophatic and kataphatic theology (theology of denial and theology of affirmation); it is through this praise that creatures are united to God, and in this progress towards union there can be discerned a sequence of purification–illumination–union, the goal of which is an ecstatic union with God in love, experienced as darkness, since it is beyond any creaturely capacity. The writings of the Areopagite became known in the West, initially through the ninth-century Latin translations of Hilduin, abbot of St-Denys, and Eriugena; the version Aquinas knew was the still later revision by John the Saracen. In both East and West focus is initially directed towards the works on the hierarchies, which became the subject of repeated commentary; such an approach preserved a sense of the integrity of the Areopagite's vision. In the West, this approach seems gradually to fall away, so that with Aquinas it is the work, *The Divine Names*, to which he devotes a commentary. The extent of the influence of the *Divine Names* on Aquinas' theology, and especially on the *Summa*, is apparent from the index of citations of that work, given in Pera's edition of the commentary.[5] What lies behind this

---

4   See, most recently, the articles in *Modern Theology* 24/4 (2008), devoted to Dionysios and his reception.
5   Ceslas Pera OP (ed.), *In librum Beati Dionysii de Divinis Nominibus Expositio* (Turin and Rome: Marietti, 1950), 399–407.

new approach to Dionysios is not clear, but it may well have something to do with the fact that, while the liturgical rites on which Dionysios commented remained recognizably similar in the East, liturgical development in the West had led to a practice of liturgy significantly different from that presupposed by the *Ecclesiastical Hierarchy*. Although the *Celestial Hierarchy* remained important for Aquinas' angelology (for which he was justly famous), attention to the *Corpus Areopagiticum* in the West shifted to the *Divine Names* and the *Mystical Theology* – and there seems something emblematic in the fact that Thomas, and later schoolmen, comment on the *Divine Names*, while the *Mystical Theology* becomes the handbook of the emerging school of later medieval mysticism (compare, for example, the Middle English translation and commentary on the *Mystical Theology* by the author of the *Cloud of Unknowing*).[6]

This shift of attention heralds a change in interpretation, which may be brought out by noting an early comment on the *Divine Names*, preserved in the scholia. On *Divine Names* V. 8, the scholiast comments, 'As the cause of all, therefore, God is hymned; for he did not say, These things are *predicated* of the same, but properly speaking *hymned*'.[7] In other words, the *Divine Names* is about how we use language to praise God, not about the narrower logical issue of how we predicate qualities of God. This distinction seems to be lost to Aquinas; his commentary on the *Divine Names* is about divine predication, the connection with worship, explicit in Dionysios, has vanished.[8] This relates, as we shall see, to one of the principal bones of contention between Eastern Orthodox theology and Aquinas: the charge that for Aquinas and the Schoolmen generally, theology has become a matter of concepts, has been reduced to a rationalist enterprise. The *Summa Theologiae* itself can be cited in support of this contention – and also against it. The *Summa* is composed of *quaestiones*, questions, the genre that came to dominate Western theology in the newly founded universities. Although the *quaestio* is related to the older genre of questions-and-answers (*erotapokriseis*), that became important (and remained important) in the Byzantine world, in

---

[6] For an account of this development in the West, see the remarkable essay by Simon Tugwell OP, 'Albert and the Dionysian Tradition', in *Albert and Thomas: Selected Writings* (Mahwah, NY: Paulist, 1988), 39–95, 116–29 (notes).

[7] *PG* 4: 328A (my italics). The scholiast may be St Maximos the Confessor; this scholion does not seem to belong to the initial set prepared by John of Scythopolis.

[8] Of course, Thomas is eloquent in his praise of God in his hymns and prayers, most notably in the office he composed for the Feast of *Corpus Christi*. Nonetheless, he still takes the *Divine Names* to be a treatise on predication.

the world of the universities it developed its own role.[9] As Fergus Kerr has put it, the method behind the use of *quaestiones* in disputations, 'was not intended to reach a compromise or supposed consensus, by splitting the difference between conflicting interpretations. It allowed the disputants to discover the strengths and weaknesses of opposing views; but the aim was to work out the truth by considering and eliminating error, however common or plausible or seemingly supported by authority'.[10] The *Summa Theologiae* is a collection of *quaestiones*, in which Christian doctrine is interrogated, and set out as an array of propositions, supported and defended by reason. It could, in the circumstances, hardly be other than an exercise in conceptual theology. On the other hand, the structure of the *Summa* suggests something beyond this. The arrangement of the *quaestiones* is far from arbitrary; it can be interpreted as following a movement out from God into the created order, and then back through the human to God in a process of contemplation, the whole cycle being made possible by God's uniting himself with human kind and overcoming human sin in the Incarnation, death and resurrection of the Son of God. Underlying the conceptual distinctions there is a fundamental concern with the return of creation to God – reflected in the cycle, rest–procession–return, of Neoplatonic provenance – so that the core concern of the *Summa* is the deification, or *theosis*, of creation.[11] As Fergus Kerr puts it, in lapidary fashion, 'the *Summa Theologiae* is a study of the transcendental conditions of beatific vision; not foundationalist apologetics but a set of practices for receiving the gift of beatitude'.[12]

Another point of contrast between Dionysios and Thomas concerns their differing uses of the word analogy, *analogia*. This is perhaps less significant than it once was when Thomists reduced Thomism to the principle of *analogia entis* (analogy of being).[13] Nonetheless, *analogia*

[9] For the *Erotapokriseis*, see Yannis Papadoyannakis, 'Instruction by Question and Answer in Late Antiquity: the Case of Late Antique *Erotapokriseis*', in Scott Johnson (ed.), *Greek Literature in Late Antiquity: Dynamism, Didacticism, Classicism* (Farnham: Ashgate, 2006), 91–105.

[10] Kerr, *After Aquinas*, 8.

[11] See, fundamentally, M.-D. Chenu OP, *Introduction à l'étude de saint Thomas d'Aquin* (Paris: Vrin, 1954), 266–76. See also, A. N. Williams, *The Ground of Union: Deification in Aquinas and Palamas* (New York: Oxford University Press, 1999).

[12] Kerr, *After Aquinas*, 161.

[13] Classic account in Erich Przywara SJ, *Analogia Entis. Metaphysik* (Munich: Kösel & Pustet, 1932), recently translated, with additional material, by John Betz and David Bentley Hart, *Analogia Entis. Metaphysics: Original Structure and Universal Rhythm* (Grand Rapids: Eerdmans, 2014). The mid-twentieth century saw a rethinking of the place of analogy in Aquinas' thought. See Hampus Lyttkens, *The Analogy between God and the World: An Investigation of its Background and Interpretation*

is important to Aquinas, and is concerned with how we interpret our language about God: Aquinas seeks a middle way, the way of analogy, between the idea that our concepts apply to God in the same way as they apply in the created world (univocity), and the idea that our concepts as applied to God and to creaturely reality have nothing in common (equivocity). It is a conceptual puzzle. Analogy in Dionysios, however, means something completely different: it refers to the creaturely capacity to receive and understand; it is the *kata to dynaton* – 'as far as it is possible' – of Platonism, which qualifies anything we say about the creature's participation in the divine. Again, the contrast is between a conceptual issue and one concerned with our capacity to receive and understand.[14]

ST JOHN DAMASCENE

This perhaps provides a cue for consideration of the other 'Eastern Orthodox' influence on Aquinas: the work of St John Damascene. It is commonly asserted that the work known in the West as *De Fide Orthodoxa*, 'On the Orthodox Faith', by the Damascene, lies behind the dogmatic structures of Western Scholasticism.[15] It certainly seems to be true that this work provides the ground plan for the comprehensive surveys of Christian dogma put forward by the schoolmen, from the *Sentences* of Peter Lombard to the *Summa*s of High Scholasticism. But the step from the Damascene's *Century of Accurate Exposition of the Orthodox Faith* (as the Greek work might well be called)[16] to *De Fide Orthodoxa* is more than a matter of translation. St John Damascene's work belonged to the genre of the 'century', a collection of a hundred 'chapters' (anything from a sentence to a group of paragraphs), invented by the fourth-century monk of the Egyptian desert, Evagrios of Pontos, first used for collections of ascetic wisdom, and later incorporating

---

of its Use by Thomas of Aquino (Uppsala: Almquist & Wiksells Boktryckeri AB, 1952); and fundamentally George P. Klubertanz SJ, *St Thomas on Analogy: A Textual Analysis and Systematic Synthesis* (Chicago: Loyola University Press, 1960).

[14] See Vladimir Lossky, 'La notion des "analogies" chez le ps.-Denys l'Aréopagite', *Archives d'histoire doctrinale et littéraire du Moyen Age* 5 (1930), 279–309. The view I have presented as a matter of historical hermeneutics is discussed at greater length by Christos Yannaras in *To Prosopo kai o Eros* (4th ed.; Athens: Domos, 1987), 257–81 (translated by Norman Russell as *Person and Eros* [Brookline, MA: Holy Cross Orthodox Press, 2007], 201–20).

[15] For the view of the Damascene presented here, see Andrew Louth, *St John Damascene: Tradition and Originality in Byzantine Theology* (Oxford: Oxford University Press, 2002).

[16] Ed. by Bonifatius Kotter, *Die Schriften des Johannes von Damaskos II, Expositio Fidei* (Berlin: Walter de Gruyter, 1973).

succinct statements of Christian doctrine (e.g., by St Maximos the Confessor). But the century remained a monastic genre, and John would have been conscious of this. His *Century* covers Christian teaching in a roughly credal form – God–creation and human kind–christology and Redemption–Church, sacraments and worship – but though intended in some way to be comprehensive (aspiring to the fulness of the 'century'), it was certainly not intended to be exhaustive, nor is the structure particularly systematic. It is an account of Christian doctrine, intended certainly for monks living under Islam, who needed to be clear about what Orthodox Christianity stood for, but even more to help them to understand how to progress, through faithful prayer and worship, to union with God. The Latin version, *De Fide Orthodoxa*, translated by Burgundius of Pisa in the mid-twelfth century (probably 1153–4) is different in significant ways.[17] Apart from detailed points of translation, the most striking difference is that *De Fide Orthodoxa* is divided into four books: on God, on Creation, on the Incarnation and Redemption, on the Sacraments (though mostly about other matters). This division reflects the four books of Peter Lombard's *Sentences* – on the Mystery of the Trinity, on Creation, on the Incarnation of the Word, and on the Doctrine of Signs[18] – and underlies the sections of the medieval *Summa*, not least Aquinas' *Summa Theologiae*. But in such Latin dress, the Damascene's work now looks much more systematic, with pretensions to exhaustiveness, than the original Greek version.

How does this bear on Thomas' debt to Eastern Orthodox tradition as represented in the Damascene? First of all, *De Fide Orthodoxa* was, for Thomas, a treasury of Greek theology, which he draws on throughout the *Summa* and his other writings. The mystery of the Trinity, the doctrine of creation *ex nihilo*, the nature of the angels, the focal role of the human as God's image in the created order, the post-Chalcedonian developments of Byzantine christology, the profound sense of the importance of the bodily underlying both the Incarnation and the sacramental order of the Church: all this Aquinas draws on gratefully, even if some – even much – of it was firmly established in the Western

---

[17] For the text, see John Damascene, *De Fide Orthodoxa, Versions of Burgundio and Cerbanus*, ed. Eligius M. Buytaert OFM (St Bonaventure: Franciscan Institute, 1955).

[18] See Peter Lombard, *Sententiae in IV Libris Distinctae* (Grottaferrata: Editiones Collegii S. Bonaventurae Ad Claras Aquas, 1971–81). The closeness in date of Burgundio's translation and Lombard's *Sentences*, together with the fact that the division into sections of *De Fide Orthodoxa* is not found in the earliest manuscripts, makes one wonder whether the division of *De Fide Orthodoxa* is not a reflection of the books of the *Sentences*, and not vice versa, especially given the clearly Augustinian rationale of the Lombard's division.

tradition independently of the contribution of the Damascene's *De Fide Orthodoxa*. Secondly, however, the form of *De Fide Orthodoxa* may have suggested to Aquinas that Greek theology had a much more systematic form that was in fact the case. The form in which the Damascene's work was known in the Greek East was still as a century (or a variant on this); in fact, the commonest form in which it is found in medieval manuscripts is probably the original form intended by John Damascene – not as part three of *The Fountain-head of Knowledge*, as the existing preparatory letter to Cosmas of Maïuma suggests – but as the last two thirds of a work known as *One Hundred and Fifty Philosophical and Theological Chapters*, the first part being an introduction to logic known as the *Dialectica*, the model for Palamas' *One Hundred and Fifty Chapters*, his summary – and by no means exhaustive – statement of his position in the hesychast controversy.[19] The lack of system in Greek theology – both with the Damascene and Palamas – is part of a more profound sense of apophaticism before the mystery of God, which we know through participation and cannot express in any exhaustive way.

THE FOURTEENTH-CENTURY CONTROVERSY

We are now in a position to look at the other side of the engagement between Eastern Orthodox theology and Aquinas' *Summa Theologiae*: the reception of this work in the East from the fourteenth century onwards. This will fall into three parts: first, the engagement in the fourteenth (and fifteenth) century; secondly, the place of the *Summa* in Orthodox theology from the fall of Constantinople up to the twentieth century; and finally, engagement with the *Summa* in the twentieth century. We shall follow the chronological order, although, as already remarked at the beginning, the *ordo cognoscendi* is perhaps the reverse.[20]

---

[19] See my 'Τὸ σχῆμα τῆς Ὀρθοδοξίας στοὺς ἁγίους Γρηγόριο Παλαμᾶ καὶ Ἰωάννη Δαμασκηνό' [The Shape of Orthodoxy in Saints Gregory Palamas and John Damascene] in Georgios I. Mantzaridis (ed.), Ὁ Ἅγιος Γρηγόριος ὁ Παλαμᾶς στὴν Ἱστορία καὶ τὸ Παρόν [Saint Gregory Palamas in History and the Present] (Agion Oros: Iera Megisti Moni Vatopaidiou, 2000), 645–51.

[20] For a systematic attempt to present the history of (primarily Greek) Orthodox theology from the Middle Ages to the present, see Christos Yannaras, *Orthodoxia kai Dysi stin neoteriki Ellada* (Athens: Domos, 1992): somewhat abridged translation by Peter Chamberas and Norman Russell, *Orthodoxy and the West* (Brookline, MA: Holy Cross Orthodox Press, 2006).

Aquinas' works were by no means the first to be translated into Greek.[21] Already, at the end of the thirteenth century, Augustine's *De Trinitate* had been translated by Maximos Planoudes, and other works followed in the fourteenth century. Augustine's works were widely read, and not just among those in Byzantium who looked to the West with admiration. Even Gregory Palamas read Augustine's *De Trinitate*, though the use he made of it is sometimes surprising. As well as introducing into Byzantine theology Augustine's notion of the Spirit as the love between the Father and the Son, he also found in Augustine fuel for his attack on the double procession of the Holy Spirit![22]

The first work of Aquinas to be translated in Greek was his *Summa contra Gentiles*, the translation of which by Demetrios Kydones was published in 1354.[23] This seems to have been popular, with a wide circulation; at least forty manuscripts survive.[24] Demetrios later translated parts I and II of the *Summa Theologiae*, and his brother Prochoros translated some of the third part.[25] By this time the Palamite controversy was well under way. The tide had turned for St Gregory Palamas in 1347, with the accession to the imperial throne of John VI Kantakouzenos and Palamas' own elevation to the metropolitical throne of Thessaloniki, which was followed by Palamas' vindication at synods in Constantinople in 1347 and 1351. Palamas' defence of his position against Barlaam, the *Triads in Defence of the Holy Hesychasts*, had been published c.1338 and his *One Hundred and Fifty Chapters* between the two synods; the defence of Palamas by the monks of Mount Athos, the *Agioretic Tome*, had been issued in 1341. The principal issue of this controversy – whether through their prayer the hesychast monks could attain a deifying participation in God, and in particular whether the vision of the divine light was a vision of God himself, or a vision referring to God, or even simply an

---

[21] Fundamental for this period is Gerhard Podskalsky, *Theologie und Philosophie in Byzanz* (Munich: C.H. Beck, 1977). For the questions of translations from Greek into Latin, see esp. 173–80.

[22] See Reinhard Flogaus, 'Palamas and Barlaam Revisited: A Reassessment of East and West in the Hesychast Controversy of 14th-Century Byzantium', *St Vladimir's Theological Quarterly* 42 (1998), 1–32.

[23] On Demetrios Kydones, see Norman Russell, 'Palamism and the Circle of Demetrios Cydones', in Charalambos Dendrinos (ed.), *Porphyrogenita: Essays on the History and Literature of Byzantium and the Latin East in Honour of Julian Chrysostomides* (Aldershot: Ashgate, 2003), 153–4, and the literature cited there.

[24] L.G. Benakis, 'I parousia tou Thoma Akinati sto Vyzantio', in *Byzantini Philosophia: Keimena kai Meletes* (Athens: Parousia, 2002), 633–46, here 634.

[25] On Prochoros Kydones, see Norman Russell, 'Prochoros Cydones and the fourteenth-century understanding of Orthodoxy', in Andrew Louth & Augustine Casiday (eds), *Byzantine Orthodoxies* (Aldershot: Ashgate, 2006), 75–91.

hallucination – had been resolved by Palamas by utilizing the distinction between God's essence and energies, a distinction drawn from the Greek theological tradition going back to St Basil the Great, according to which God is unknowable in his essence, and yet truly known through his energies, which are not created effects of God's activity, but God himself in his activity. Those who opposed Palamas – initially Barlaam the Calabrian monk, then Gregory Akindynos (probably himself an Athonite monk) and the learned scholar, Nikephoros Gregoras – regarded the distinction between the essence of God and his uncreated energies as infringing the divine unity and simplicity, and effectively introducing into Christianity pagan polytheism. They made this point independently of any knowledge of Aquinas, but the availability of Aquinas' works in the Greek world provided further support for those who rejected the distinction between the divine οὐσία and ἐνεργεῖαι, such a rejection being implicit in the fundamental Thomist affirmation of the identity in God of *esse* and *essentia*, of existence and essence (see I.3.4).

There was a further issue on which Aquinas' voice was important, both for those who welcomed him and those who opposed him. This was the long-standing doctrinal issue between East and West that had frustrated the attempt at union at the Council of Lyons which death had prevented Aquinas from attending: the question of the *Filioque*, that is, whether the Holy Spirit proceeds from the Father, as the original version of the Niceno-Constantinopolitan Creed had asserted, or whether he proceeds from the Father and the Son (*Filioque*), as asserted in the Western addition to the ecumenical Creed. Aquinas' arguments in support of the *Filioque* in the *ST* (I.36.2) form a succinct version of the argument presented at greater length by Anselm in his *De Processione Spiritus Sancti* and like that argument proceed from purely logical considerations, without any direct reference to the witness of Scripture or the tradition of the Church.

Reactions to Aquinas varied. On the one hand, there were those who opposed his theological method, his use of Aristotelian logic ('syllogisms', though the Greek word συλλογισμός has a wider connotation than the English word); on the other hand, there were those who seemed to welcome his theological method, but lamented his theological position. Notable among the latter was Gennadios Scholarios, the first patriarch of Constantinople under the Ottomans, who apostrophizes Thomas thus: 'Come now, excellent Thomas, O that you had not been born in the West, so that you were bound to act as advocate for the deviations of that Church, both in the case of the procession of the Spirit and the difference between the divine essence and energies, for otherwise you would have been infallible in matters theological, as you are in matters ethical!'[26] (though Gennadios himself admired other aspects of Thomas' theology, e.g., his doctrine of transubstantiation). But such a reaction seems to have been rare. Those who attacked Aquinas on the matter of the Holy Spirit or the relationship between essence and energies also frequently attacked his theological method. Notable among those was Neilos Kavasilas, who succeeded Palamas on the throne of Thessaloniki, and whose attack on the Latin doctrine of the Procession of the Spirit includes an attack on the rationalism of Aquinas' argumentation (in modern language he opposed Eastern apophaticism to Aquinas' rationalism), but he also attacks the appeal made by the Latins to Scripture and the Fathers.[27]

The procession of the Holy Spirit was a defining issue between East and West. Those who were attracted by Thomas' theological method and embraced his theological opinion on this issue frequently ended up by making their peace with the Latin Church; these included Demetrios Kydones. In relation to the question of the relationship between the divine essence and energies, the situation was different. There were those, like Prochoros Kydones, the younger brother of Demetrios, who embraced Thomas' theological method and argued against the Palamite position, yet remained Orthodox. But there were others, like Theophanes III, Metropolitan of Nicaea, who were thoroughly Aristotelian, not just in their argumentation, but in their metaphysics, and from this position defended the Palamite understanding of the divine light of Tabor against the attacks of such as Prochoros Kydones. The tendency in scholarship over the last century to see the controversy in Byzantium in polarized terms – on the one side, Platonist, anti-Western monks, and, on the other, Aristotelian, Western-inclining lay scholars – is certainly simplistic and needs to be resisted. If so, the reception of Thomas and the Thomism of the *Summa* will be correspondingly complicated.

THE BABYLONIAN CAPTIVITY OF ORTHODOX THEOLOGY

The next stage in the reception of Thomas and the *Summa* is the period of what Florovsky called, borrowing from Luther, the 'Babylonian

---

[26] Quoted in Michael Rackl, 'Eine griechische Abbreviatio der Prima Secundae des hl. Thomas von Aquin', *Divus Thomas* 9 (1922), 50–9, here 52–3.

[27] See Nil Cabasilas, *Sur le Saint-Esprit*, ed. with introduction and translation by Hieromonk Théophile Kislas (Paris: Cerf, 2001).

Captivity of the Orthodox Church'.[28] In this period, the Orthodox Church, at first primarily the Church of the Ottoman Empire, increasingly found itself caught up in the aftermath of the Reformation in the Western Church. Protestants – and later Catholics – looked to the Eastern Orthodox Church for support in the ensuing controversy. In 1629, Cyril Loukaris, Patriarch of Constantinople several times in the 1620s and 1630s, published a *Confessio Fidei*, in which the Orthodox Faith was presented in thoroughly Calvinist terms. This produced a reaction within the Orthodox world, and led to Loukaris' condemnation at Constantinople (1638, 1642), Iaşi (1642) and Jerusalem (1672). The synod of Iaşi, as well as condemning Loukaris, ratified the *Orthodox Confession* of Peter Mogila, Metropolitan of Kiev, which, even in the revised form adopted by the synod, expressed the Orthodox faith, by contrast, in markedly Latin and Scholastic terms. In these confessions (and others: by Metrophanes Kritopoulos [1625] and Dositheos, Patriarch of Jerusalem [1672]), Orthodox theologians were attempting to express their faith in relation to the debates of the Reformation, and inevitably falling under the sway of issues and concepts quite foreign to traditional Orthodoxy. Those who inclined more to Roman Catholic ideas fell under the influence of the 'baroque' Scholasticism of the day. It was these Catholic-inclining confessions that became influential in the seventeenth and eighteenth centuries, and defined the approach to theology found in the theological academies, established first in Kiev and then later throughout Russia from the time of the Petrine reforms. Until the middle of the nineteenth century teaching in these academies was in Latin, using Western scholastic text-books, leading to an inevitable Latin influence.

How far one can think of this as any kind of engagement with Aquinas in general or the *Summa* in particular may be doubted. From the point of view of modern Thomist scholarship, the 'Thomism' of this period was debased (too indebted to Suárez, the sixteenth-/seventeenth-century Spanish Jesuit theologian and commentator on Aquinas), just as from the point of view of modern Orthodox theology, the Orthodox theologians of this period are generally dismissed as corrupted by their encounter with

---

[28] Florovsky actually says 'the "Babylonian Captivity" of the Russian Church', referring to the period from the Petrine reforms (see, *Ways of Russian Theology*, trans. Robert L. Nichols, [Belmont, MA: Nordland, 1971], 121), but others have extended it to include the period of the Greek Church under the Turkokratia: cf. the section entitled 'I vavylonios aichmalosia tis Orthoxias sta symbola' in Stelios Ramfos, *O Kaimos tou Enos* (Athens: Ekdoseis Harmos, 2000), 188.

Western theology. The Orthodox theologians may have drunk deep, but the source was thoroughly muddy.

Modern Orthodox theology

The revival of Eastern Orthodox theology over the last two centuries was mostly in fairly conscious opposition to the West. The influence, at first in the Slav countries and then in Greece, of the *Philokalia*, a collection of Byzantine ascetical texts compiled and published by St Makarios of Corinth and St Nikodemos of the Holy Mountain in 1782, has ensured that an important strand in Orthodox theology has laid emphasis on prayer and spiritual experience, and looked back to St Gregory Palamas. The initial intellectual reception of the *Philokalia* was among Slavophils, such as Kireevsky and Khomiakov, who were anxiously seeking to define what it was that distinguished the Orthodox experience of the Slavs from the newly encountered West. Russian personalism as opposed to the perceived individualism of the West, the Russian sense of *sobornost'*, 'togetherness': it was with a sense of identity defined in such terms that the Russian intellectuals, expelled by Lenin in 1922, found themselves in a welcoming, but unfamiliar West. It is not surprising that, out of the encounters with Western thinkers through groups such as the 'Berdyaev Colloquy' in Paris *entre deux guerres*, a sense of Orthodox identity emerged that rejected the narrow 'scholasticism' of seminary theology and – for some at least – fashioned itself as a kind of mirror image of the Neo-Thomism of Maritain and Gilson. It called itself the 'Neo-Patristic synthesis' (perhaps in conscious opposition to – and imitation of – 'Neo-Thomism'), and it is hardly surprising that it saw the hesychast controversy as a kind of archetypal clash of West and East, of 'Thomist scholasticism' and 'Palamite spiritual experience', of Western essentialism and Eastern existentialism (despite the fact that the Thomas of Neo-Thomism was also cast as an existentialist). This sense of the meaning of Orthodoxy has been immensely fruitful, and has been received and developed throughout the Orthodox world: by Stăniloae in Romania, Popovich in Serbia, and with great *élan* by theologians and philosophers of the stature of Zizioulas, Yannaras and Ramfos in Greece. Such a sense of where Orthodoxy stands is not very propitious for any authentic encounter with Aquinas, or with his *Summa Theologiae*. There is some positive appreciation of Aquinas in Ramfos, but it seems to be based on secondary sources, rather than any engagement with Aquinas, still less with his *Summa*.[29] There has been some

---

[29] See Ramfos, *O Kaimos tou Enos*, 135–41 (I owe this reference to Norman Russell).

attention paid to Aquinas by the remarkable Russian scholar and poly-
math, Sergei Averintsev († 2004), who also translated some passages
from his works; his interest seems to have been inspired by the theories
of art expounded by Neo-Thomists such as Maritain and Gilson.[30]

A genuine Orthodox engagement with the *Summa Theologiae* of St
Thomas Aquinas has yet to begin. It will demand of the Orthodox a willingness to abandon (or at least put on hold) a tendency to see the 'West'
as the cause of the problems of modern civilization, and trace these back
to the Middle Ages and the Schism. Whether this is possible remains to
be seen.

---

[30] See, for instance, his 'Jacques Maritain, Neotomism, Katolicheskaya theologiya
iskusstva' [Jacques Maritain, Neo-Thomism, the Catholic Theology of Art], *Voprosy
Literatury* 10 (1968), 126–43.

Reformed traditions

CHRISTOPH SCHWÖBEL

LUTHER AND THOMAS AQUINAS: A CONFLICT OVER AUTHORITY?

The early Protestant Reformers have mixed attitudes to the *ST* and its author. In Martin Luther's writings we find relatively frequent references to Thomas, although not exact quotations.[1] Luther gleefully reports on Thomas' girth.[2] Luther repeatedly relates in his table talks how the dying Thomas experienced such grave spiritual temptations that he could not hold out against the devil until he confounded him by embracing his Bible, saying: 'I believe what is written in this book.'[3] At least on some occasions Luther seems to speak approvingly of Thomas' taking refuge in faith grounded in the Bible in the face of spiritual crisis (*Anfechtung*), one of the central topics of Luther's own existential understanding of faith. But he could refer to Thomas as a 'Sophist',[4] 'not worth a louse',[5] he could also at different stages in his life speak of Thomas as '*Divus Thomas*', 'this holy man'[6] or as a man of 'great genius'[7] who had tragically been misunderstood.

What Luther actually knew of Thomas Aquinas' theology is a matter of debate.[8] While anti-Protestant polemic at the turn of the nineteenth to the twentieth century had been eager to describe Luther as an 'ignoramus' with regard to his knowledge of scholastic theology and especially of Thomas Aquinas, later research by Catholic scholars, most notably

---

[1] Luther's references to Thomas have been carefully analysed by Denis R. Janz, *Luther on Thomas Aquinas. The Angelic Doctor in the Thought of the Reformer* (Wiesbaden: Franz Steiner, 1989).
[2] WATR 2, 192, 14–193, 2 (12 July 1532).
[3] Cf. WA 38, 148, 13ff (1533).
[4] WA 10 I, 115, 7ff (1522).
[5] WATR 2, 193, 3 (1532).
[6] WA 1, 658ff.
[7] WA 40 III, 112, 35ff.
[8] Janz, *Luther on Thomas Aquinas*, 96–98.

Joseph Lortz, lamented the fact that he had known so little of Aquinas because otherwise he would not have felt obliged to reject Thomas and the whole of scholastic theology as an aberration from orthodox doctrine.[9] Had Luther not been trained at Erfurt and Wittenberg in the *via moderna* but at Cologne, the German capital of the *via antiqua* in the Thomist tradition, so the argument goes, the outcome of what became the 'Reformation' might have been quite different.

However, is it true that Luther knew so little of Thomas and the scholastic tradition? A careful study suggests otherwise. Denis R. Janz has shown that his knowledge was by contemporary standards impressive. Janz can ascertain that Luther had extensive knowledge of Thomas' theological writings, though perhaps not of his commentaries on Aristotle. He concludes: 'Comparatively speaking, his acquaintance with these writings fell far below the level of a contemporary such as Cajetan. And yet it may have been equal or better than that of some Thomists such as Prierias.'[10] Luther probably knew Aquinas through his reading of Pierre d'Ailly and especially Gabriel Biel who, as Thomas Farthing has shown, reliably reports on the *Sentences Commentary* and the *ST* – apart from the teaching on sin, grace, and justification where Biel presents an Occamist version as that also endorsed by Thomas.[11] However, this alone cannot account for the fact of Luther's sometimes rather pointed criticism of Thomas' views on these matters. Rather, it seems not unlikely, as Janz shows, that Luther had first-hand knowledge of Aquinas through his writings, very probably also of the *ST*. This is not only suggested by circumstantial evidence – there were 40 copies of the *ST* alone in the four libraries at Erfurt when Luther studied there – but also by a careful analysis of the points which Luther challenges when he refers explicitly to Thomas Aquinas. This seems to suggest that he knew all parts of the *Summa*. Janz summarizes his findings: 'It is important to underscore the fact that Luther did not utterly despise the *ST* or regard it as worthless. One senses here a grudging recognition of greatness even in a book which contained, from his point of view, great error.'[12]

Another observation is relevant here. Luther's discussion of doctrinal points where he refers to Thomas is usually, even when critical,

[9] Joseph Lortz, *Die Reformation in Deutschland* (Freiburg: Herder, 1939).
[10] Janz, *Luther on Thomas Aquinas*, 111.
[11] John Farthing, *Thomas Aquinas and Gabriel Biel: Interpretations of German Nominalism on the Eve of the Reformation* (Durham, NC: Duke University Press, 1988).
[12] Janz, *Luther on Thomas Aquinas*, 110.

quite measured. As doctrinal opinions, Thomas' views have to be taken seriously, even where Luther disagrees with Thomas. How then are such strong statements to be understood as where Luther condemns Thomas as 'the source and stock of all heresy, all error and of the obliteration of the Gospel (as his books demonstrate)'? Janz argues that, whatever Luther might criticize in Thomas' opinions, the main target of his attack and polemic is the *status* which was ascribed to Thomas not only by Thomists but also, at least in Luther's view, by the authorities of the Roman church. It is thus certainly no accident that Luther's main opponents in the controversy triggered by his critique of indulgences in the ninety-five theses were Dominican Thomists: Konrad Wimpina, Johannes Tetzel, Silvester Prierias and Cardinal Cajetan. Luther's main protest against the authority ascribed to Thomas becomes already clear in his response to Prierias' attack on Luther's views in the ninety-five theses in *De Potentia Papae Dialogus* (1518). In his response, *Ad dialogum Silvestri Prierias de potestate papae responsio*,[13] Luther sharply attacks Prierias' habit of only referring to the authority of Thomas to refute his views and he responds by adducing arguments from Scripture, from the Fathers, from canon law and from reason against Prierias' 'Thomist' authority – a truly catholic response:

> 'You Thomists are to be gravely reprehended that you dare put the opinions and often false meditations of this holy man before us in place of articles of faith, and you only care for that, just as you consider nothing beyond Thomas as worthy of your reading, so you do not want to see anything false in him ...'[14]

Consequently, Luther argues, the Thomists regard anyone who seems to contradict Thomas as a heretic. Thus in 1518 Luther saw the unique status accorded to Thomas by some of his followers as a case of *misplaced authority*, conflating the authority of one important theologian with that of other teachers of the church, of Scripture and, ultimately, with that of Christ. In this connection Luther's critiques of Thomas acquire a fundamental theological significance. If the appeal to the authority of Thomas has these consequences, it is no longer just a case of misplaced authority but of *displaced foundations*. The appeal to a human word has displaced the Word of God, God's self-presentation in Christ and through the Spirit, and reliance on human work has displaced the sole trust in God's work.

[13] WA I, 647–689.
[14] WA I, 658, 1ff.

Luther's engagements with Thomas on questions of method and doctrine fall into this pattern. Where he engages with Thomas and the *ST* on specific theological issues, which do not seem to touch on this fundamental question, he treats him like another important theologian whose opinions are to be taken seriously, indeed so seriously that they have to be criticized. Where Luther suspects that appeal to Thomas in dealing with doctrinal matters is a symptom of misplaced authority leading to displaced foundations, his criticism can be savage, as in the case of the accusation of doing theology on the basis of Aristotle and not on the basis of God's self-disclosure as testified in Scripture. The most trenchant criticism in this fundamental respect assumes that Thomas, in following Aristotle, has displaced faith with human virtue. This is a fundamental distortion of the understanding of justification because it replaces trust in God's work in Christ with the exercise of human virtue as described by Aristotle.

> 'Paul says: Nobody fulfils the commandments but by faith alone. Love is nothing but faith. There Thomas is in error with his followers, that is with the Aristotelians, who say that somebody becomes virtuous through practice. Just as a harp player becomes a good harpist by long practice, so these fools think they achieve the virtues, love, chastity and humility though practice. It is not true. They become deceivers and the devil's martyrs ...'[15]

Luther's criticism reflects a situation where the traditional contest of the plurality of *viae* of doing theology – the University of Wittenberg, founded only in 1502, offered the *via Thomae* and the *via Scoti*, and, in 1508, added the *via moderna* in the statutes of the university[16] – was gradually being replaced by the dominance of the Thomist way. The Thomist way, however, was no longer one way among others but it had became *the* way, based on its own paradigmatic textbook, the *Summa Theologiae*.

VARIETIES OF REFORM AND DIVERSITIES OF RECEPTION

During the time of the Reformation the *Summa Theologiae* replaced Peter Lombard's *Book of Sentences* as a textbook in the catholic institutions

---

[15] WA 10 III, 92, 17ff:
[16] Janz, *Luther and Thomism*, 112.

of theological learning and training. In 1526 the *Summa* was introduced as the authoritative doctrinal textbook at Salamanca, followed by Leuven at the end of the century. Cajetan's commentaries on the *Summa*, the first on the entire work, published between 1507 and 1522, became the commentary which served as the template for the whole 'period of the commentaries', the second phase in the reception of Thomas' thought.

The period of the commentaries coincided with the Tridentine reforms in the Roman Catholic church, and the *Summa*, interpreted in the style of Cajetan's commentary, became one of its most important instruments. It is not surprising that legend tells us that a copy of the *Summa Theologiae* lay next to the Bible on the altar at the Council of Trent. Tridentine Catholicism must be regarded both as a reform movement within the Roman Catholic church and as a doctrinal response to the challenges of the Reformation. The attempt at securing the foundations for the Roman Catholic church is combined with the critical reaction to the formation of the Protestant churches. In this context the *ST* was used both as a foundational text and as a critical instrument, the bulwark against Protestant aberrations. In this sense the *Summa* became both a Catholic and a Roman work, the Roman Catholic classic. This, in turn, shaped the way theologians in the churches of the Reformation referred to the *ST*: it was only rarely seen as representing a common tradition of the Catholic church and of the churches of the Reformation, but most often as the theological authority on which Roman Catholics based their arguments for not following Protestant reforms.

The concrete ways of referring to the *ST*, however, depended on the ecclesial context and on the character of the reformation in that context. John Calvin is a second generation Reformer who could presuppose the work of the first generation and was concerned with determining the further course of the Reformed movement, primarily in the context of its spreading and increasing pluralisation. In addition, Calvin, like Melanchthon, belonged among those theologians trained in the tradition of humanism whose knowledge of scholastic theology, in which they were never trained, was limited. So the references to Thomas in Calvin are few.[17] This seems surprising, to say the least, because systematically one can point to many structural similarities and common problems, treated by both Thomas' *ST* and by Calvin's *Institutes*, often overlooked and misconstrued by Catholic and Protestant interpreters

[17] Janz, *Luther on Thomas Aquinas*, 111f.

alike.[18] Calvinist theology on the continent before the rise of Reformed Scholasticism, so it would seem, developed in its major strands without an extensive critical engagement with Thomas' *Summa*. This, however, implies that the early Calvinists had no qualms about any agreement of their doctrines with the teaching of the *ST*. The need for critical engagement, it seems, did not arise.

England provides a different picture. As early as 1522 Henry VIII had attacked Luther's critique of sacramental theology in *De captivitate Babylonica* in his *Assertio Septem Sacramentorum*, probably with the underlying intention of gaining Roman support for his marriage plans. A long, drawn out, and particularly acerbic exchange followed in which Luther robustly polemicised against Henry as the 'king of lies' and the 'king by God's disfavour'.[19] The peculiar character of the English Reformation, as primarily a political process, only finding its theological foundations after the event in a measured approach to reform, determined the mixture of continuities and discontinuities in its relationship to the magisterial theologians of the Roman church, most notably Thomas Aquinas. It may also be that the lasting influence of some of the refugees from the Continent was a factor in establishing a positive attitude towards Aquinas. In 1547 Peter Martyr Vermigli (1499–1562) fled to Oxford. His teaching, though not Thomist in any strict sense of the word, showed remarkable parallels to Aquinas and he frequently refers to Aquinas to support his own doctrinal position.[20] Perhaps the enduring influence of Martin Bucer (1491–1551) who migrated to Cambridge in 1549 laid some of the foundations for a positive attitude towards Thomas and his *Summa*, since as a Dominican friar Bucer had received his first philosophical and theological training through the writings of Thomas.[21]

Furthermore it seems that Thomas and his *ST* were natural allies for Richard Hooker (c. 1554–1600) in creating an Anglican theology of worship and church order, in the English context, in which the disparities between different strands of the Reformation with regard to questions

[18] Arvin Vos, *Aquinas, Calvin and Contemporary Protestant Thought: A Critique of Protestant Views on the Thought of Thomas Aquinas* (Washington, DC: Christian University Press, 1985).

[19] Dorothea Wendebourg, 'The German Reformers and England', in eadem (ed.), *Sister Reformations – Schwesterreformationen. The Reformation in Germany and England – Die Reformation in Deutschland und England* (Tübingen: Mohr Siebeck, 2009), 94–132, especially 96–112.

[20] John Patrick Donnelly, 'Calvinist Thomism', *Viator* 7 (1976), 441–55.

[21] Marin Greschat, *Martin Bucer: A Reformer and His Times*, (Louisville: Westminster John Knox, 2004), 24.

of church order were far more dominant than the contrast to the Roman Church, Thomas could be referred to without immediately engaging with Thomist theology as a key element of Tridentine Roman Catholic identity definition. The dominant feature of the *Summa*, construing a dialectical continuity between nature and grace from a theological stance that could be supported by philosophical arguments, made the *Summa* an important resource for theologians with a non-sectarian outlook like Hooker, without in any way compromising their views on the *theological* foundations of authority in the church. Earlier research has tended to see Hooker's *Of the Lawes of Ecclesiastical Polity*, the first four books of which were published in 1594 (the fifth in 1597; the last three after his death), simply as an application of the teaching of the *Summa* to the situation of English church and society at the end of the 16th century. More recent research has emphasized with particular reference to the question of natural law, so central in the *Summa* and the *Lawes*, that, while the influence of Thomas is not be denied, it is a mistake to set it against the influence of the magisterial Reformation.[22] The true contrast appears between Thomas and the Reformers and the radicalism of Walter Travers and Thomas Cartwright and others in the context of the debates surrounding the Admonition to Parliament in 1592. With regard to the influence of the *Summa*, H. R. McAdoo could roundly state:

> 'Hooker's writings on law and reason stem from the *Summa Theologica*, which together with the emphasis on practical divinity also found in the *Ecclesiastical Polity*, play a recurring role in the development of theological method as the century progresses.'[23]

The structural analogies to the treatise on law in the *Summa* (I-II.90–108) and the direct references to both Thomas and Aristotle in the first book of the *Lawes* provide ample evidence for this statement. And yet, this does not constitute a contrast to the teaching of the Reformers if we bear in mind that for Hooker the term law unites what Luther distinguished as law and gospel, so that the 'divine law' as found in Thomas Aquinas also embraces what Luther distinguished as Gospel from the law in the one will of God the creator. However, if one accepts the substantive continuity of views on the law between Hooker and the Reformers on the

---

[22] W. J. Torrance Kirby, 'Richard Hooker's Discourse on Natural Law in the Context of the Magisterial Reformation', *Animus* 3 (1998), 30–49.

[23] H. R. McAdoo, *The Spirit of Anglicanism: A Survey of Anglican Theological Method in the Seventeenth Century* (London: A&C Black, 1965), 8f.

Continent, which neither called the sufficiency of scripture for salvation into question nor collided with the principles of *solus Christus, sola gratia* and *sola fide*, there is no basis for accusing Hooker of promoting 'Romishe doctrine' as was done in the Admonition controversy, any more than there is for construing his theology and ideas on the polity of the church as an anticipation of what the nineteenth century then construed as the *via media* of Anglicanism. The enduring influence of the *Summa* as a formative factor in what became Anglican theological method is, perhaps with some degree of exaggeration, celebrated by McAdoo:

> 'No picture of the development of theological method in the seventeenth century which hopes to achieve a degree of verisimilitude can fail to take account of the influence of the *Summa Theologica*. Nor can it fail to note that the point of entry of its influence is mainly though not entirely in connection with the function of reason and in connection with matters involving certain clearly defined aspects of practical divinity, such as law, acts and happiness considered as the ultimate good. The influence of the *Summa Theologica* preceded and reinforced the quest for a reasonable theology as this went in other directions, impelled by other influences and evoked by varying situations. It strengthened the search, in circumstances different from its own origins, for that which it was itself designed to be, a theology of synthesis in which the claims of faith and reason were not mutually exclusive.'[24]

This judgment, which McAdoo can support with his findings from the writings of Archbishop John Bramhall (1594–1663) and Bishops Lancelot Andrewes (1555–1626), Robert Sanderson (1587–1663) and John Wilkins (1614–1672), also indicates that the influence of the *Summa* is primarily to be found in matters of theological method, and questions of theological cosmology and anthropology, sometimes, as in the case of Bramhall, as a means of criticising the 'new philosophy' of a Thomas Hobbes and its underlying views of human nature and society. It does not so much extend to matters of christology or soteriology where, as in the case of Hooker, the continuity with the questions and answers of the Reformation is essentially maintained. The interesting question, however, remains, whether a kind of pragmatic Thomism is at least one ingredient of the 'spirit of Anglicanism'.

---

[24] McAdoo, *Spirit of Anglicanism*, 383f.

THE AGE OF CONFESSIONAL DIVISION AND THE RETURN OF METAPHYSICS: REJECTIONS AND RETRIEVALS

The time of the Reformation was an age of rhetoric. When contentious issues arise that cannot simply be solved by appeal to authority, the hour of rhetoric has come. Of the seven liberal arts it is rhetoric which became the paradigmatic discipline in the Reformation. This is particularly true in Reformation countries where rhetoric was undergoing an exceptional flourishing in academic education and in all areas of society where the right course of action had to be negotiated between parties relying on different authorities. Philipp Melanchthon is the key figure here. His reordering of doctrinal arguments, relying exclusively on rhetoric and dialectics, summarized in the structuring of the doctrinal content by the *loci* of rhetoric, became standard for the Lutheran Reformation. Calvin's training as a lawyer brought with it a rhetorical influence, and in the Calvinist circles the anti-Aristotelian polemics of Peter Ramus (1515–1572), together with his emphasis on the distinction between rhetoric and dialectics (logic), gained widespread support. Confessional differentiation and the, often unsuccessful, negotiation of the possibilities of inter-confessional political cooperation, go hand in hand with the rise and fall of rhetoric.

The age of rhetoric is followed by the age of metaphysics. Was it frustration with the dominance of rhetoric, which remained on the surface of meaning, rather than plumbing the depths of the connection between meaning and being, which prompted the metaphysical revival at the beginning of the 17th century? In philosophy, it is clearly a frustration with a methodical virtuosity that seemed disengaged from the questions of the nature of reality which found its clearest expression in the rejection of a Ramist understanding of rhetoric and logic. In theology, it was the feeling that the very content of faith, the *res fidei*, was in danger of being lost in mere words. The rediscovery of Aristotelian metaphysics in Protestant philosophy in Germany occurred before Francesco Suárez (1548–1617) and his *Metaphysicae disputationes* became known, but it received an important second impulse through the new turn to metaphysics in the Catholic territories. Thomas Aquinas became the 'new classic' in the Catholic revival of metaphysics and the Protestant philosophers, especially from a Lutheran background, had no difficulty in regarding Thomas as the greatest teacher of medieval times, in spite of all the theological differences.[25] The revival of a 'scholastic' philosophy in Protestant territories and the establishment of a 'scholastic' theology occurred almost simultaneously, and the two developments could support and reinforce one another. Thomas and the Protestant philosophers and theologians were united in their return to Aristotelian metaphysics and a scholastic mode of intellectual inquiry. In Thomas' case the scholastic approach is elaborated in the disputational style of the *Summa*, in the case of the Protestant philosophers and theologians in their use of a systematic mode form of exposition and their employment of numerous distinctions, normally proceeding from the 'onomatology', the analysis of the concepts in their relation to the phenomena, to the pragmatology, the analysis of the signified phenomena according to the principles of Aristotelian metaphysics, normally employing the scheme of four causes. Although the boundaries between philosophy and theology were still a matter of debate and philosophers included theological questions as a matter of course in their metaphysics, theologians not only employed the methods of philosophy in theology but also themselves wrote philosophical textbooks. The philosophy which was cultivated especially in the Lutheran theologians interpreted itself as a 'received philosophy' (*philosophia recepta*) which attempted to summarize and systematize the core of the metaphysical tradition against philosophical innovations which they regarded as both philosophically and theologically destructive. A good example is the *Vade Mecum sive Manuale philosophicum* (1654) of the Hebrew scholar, Lutheran polemicist against Bellarmine and the Semi-Ramism of the Calvinist Schools, and philosopher Johann Adam Scherzer (1628–1683), one of the teachers of Leibniz. The philosophical ecumenism of the Aristotelian schools is documented in the fact that Scherzer bases his philosophical definitions on the collection of the Catholic theologian John Thierry *Definitiones philosophicae in*

---

[25] Max Wundt, *Die deutsche Schulmetaphysik des 17. Jahrhunderts* (Tübingen: Mohr, 1939), 12, writes that especially the Lutherans regarded Thomas as the greatest teacher of the Middle Ages and emphasizes that the Protestant theology of the seventeenth century was not infected by the modern prejudice that the philosophy of the middle ages is essentially Catholic and has nothing to say to Protestants. This is connected to the rejection of nominalism by Reformed and Lutheran theologians alike which is aptly summarized by Donnelly: '... when Protestants came to recast their theology in to a scholastic form, they rather consistently avoided nominalism as a base. Insofar as the roots of Protestant scholasticism go back to the Middle Ages, they tend to go back to the *via antiqua* and Thomists. Protestant fruit grows well on the Thomist tree, even better than on the bad nominalist tree.' Donnelly, 'Calvinist Thomism', 454.

scholis celebriores (Cologne, 1644), supplemented from similar collections by Dominican and Jesuit theologians.[26] It is hardly surprising that the *Summa* is frequently directly and indirectly referred to.

The continuing presence of the *Summa* as an important part of the received philosophy of the Lutheran metaphysicians should not detract from the differences that have to be noted in more strictly theological matters. While Thomas regards theology as a *scientia speculativa* ('speculative science') the Lutheran theologians understood theology as a *scientia eminens practica* ('an eminently practical science': M. Chemnitz and many others) or even as *sapientia eminens practica* ('an eminently practical wisdom': D. Hollaz) insofar as it leads sinful humans through faith and sanctification to eternal life, and reconstructs analytically the steps necessary for reaching this goal. But the interest of the Lutheran theologians in the renewal of metaphysics is still more specifically motivated. As Walter Sparn has shown, the Lutheran theologians have a special interest in their reception of Aristotelian metaphysics.[27] Their question is how the distinctive claims of a Lutheran christology that the union of the person of Christ exists as the co-existence of essentially disparate substances which nevertheless communicate their attributes to one another – a christology of radical personal union which is normally summarized in the catch-phrase *finitum capax infiniti* – can be metaphysically grasped in its own significance and developed in a metaphysical view of reality. How can the 'new language' which Luther had seen as necessary for christology be metaphysically related to the 'received language' of Aristotelian metaphysics. In this way a tension is introduced into the relationship of a christologically based theological metaphysics and the universal claims of metaphysics which one cannot find in the same way in Catholic or Calvinist metaphysics of that time. This means that Lutheran theologians refer to the theology and philosophy of the tradition, including the *Summa*, not only selectively, as theologians in the tradition of the Reformation, but also critically with regard to their specific christological criteria.

If one surveys the whole field of Protestant school theology in the seventeenth century one finds that the *Summa* could be referred to constructively as part of the received tradition in all philosophical

---

26 A list of the works referred on which the manual is based provided by the introduction by Stephan Meier-Oeser in the reprint of the *Vade Mecum* in the edition of 1675: Stephan Meier-Oeser (ed.), *Vade Mecum sive Manuale philosophicum* (Stuttgart-Bad Cannstatt: Frommann-Holzboog, 1996), VII–XVII.

27 Walter Sparn, *Die Wiederkehr der Metaphysik: Die ontologische Frage in der lutherischen Theologie des frühen 17. Jahrhunderts* (Stuttgart: Calwer, 1976).

matters and critically in those theological questions where the teaching of the Reformation differed from the theology of the *Summa*. A good example for this is the theology of the Reformed scholastic John Owen (1616–1683), sometimes referred to as 'Cromwell's Archbishop', in whose works we find both frequent references to the *Summa* and many structural analogies to Thomas' thought.[28] Owen can refer constructively to the *Summa* in his doctrine of God and in his christology. He can even adopt the notion of infused habits in order to describe the operation of grace in regeneration and sanctification.[29] With regard to the doctrine of justification he remains, however, as his *Doctrine of Justification by Faith* (1677) amply demonstrates, adamant that the notion of infused habits has no place in a doctrine of justification in the tradition of the Reformation.

There is, however, one theologian in the Lutheran tradition, who claimed Thomas' support exactly for those questions where the teaching of the churches of the Reformation and the teaching of the Roman Catholic church had the most decisive differences. Johann Georg Dorsche (sometimes called Dorsch, 1597–1659) was Professor at the universities of Strasbourg (since 1627) and Rostock (since 1653). During his time in Strasbourg he was the teacher of Philipp Jacob Spener, the founder of pietism. Dorsche must have made the discovery that Thomas Aquinas is closer to the teachings of the Reformation than contemporary Thomist teaching would suggest relatively early on. Already in Strasbourg he started to make excerpts from Thomas' writings, not only of the *Summa* but also of his exegetical writings and the commentary on Dionysius. He discussed his findings with the former Dominican Johann Gerhard Schobenius. In 1656 he published at last the fruit of his researches, the voluminous work with the title *Thomas Aquinas, Confessor veritatis evangelicae Augustana Confessione repetitae*.[30] The work is by no means a simple attempt to reclaim Aquinas for the Protestant cause. It is a highly differentiated and sophisticated conversation with Thomas which results in three observations: (a) Thomas argues for hypotheses with which the Lutheran doctrine could be defended; (b) those elements of Catholic doctrine which are now claimed as infallible because they contradict Lutheran teaching are of lesser importance for Thomas; and (c) Thomas would regard the

---

[28] Christopher Cleveland, *Thomism in John Owen* (Burlington, VT: Ashgate, 2013).

[29] See Cleveland's interpretation of sanctification in Owen's *Discourse on the Holy Spirit*, ibid., 99–116.

[30] A digital version of Dorsche's work can befound: http://digital.slub-dresden.de/id367808935.

Lutherans where they diverge from his own teaching not as heretics. Formally the work follows the four volumes of Cardinal Bellarmine's *Disputationes* against the heretics, but it is not an exercise in confessional controversy. Dorsche seeks to establish that Thomas' teaching is much closer to the evangelical truth which had been 'repeated' by the Augsburg Confession than anti-Lutheran polemics from the Thomists would suggest. The Augsburg Confession itself is rarely referred to but always treated as a statement of the catholic truth of Christian faith and not as a particular document of Lutheran teaching. Much more emphasis is placed on those medieval and contemporary catholic authors who would support Dorsche's reading of Thomas. Although the eight sections of Dorsche's work cover the whole of Christian teaching (Scripture, Christ, the Office of the Pope, the church, the sacraments, the original state of humanity, sin and regeneration) one can distil from it Dorsche's reading of Thomas' understanding of what the Lutherans regarded as the core of their teaching in the so-called exclusive, or '*sola*', articles. The principle *sola scriptura*, Scripture alone, is supported with statements from the *Summa* that we may not assert anything about God which cannot be found, literally or substantively, in Scripture.[31] This applies especially to everything that can be said about salvation.[32] Because Christ is in both natures the mediator, his suffering can be the ground of our salvation so that Christ alone (*solus Christus*) is perfect mediator between God and humanity.[33] The most extensive treatment is devoted to the principle that we are saved by God's grace alone (*sola gratia*). Justifying grace, even according to Thomas,[34] is not necessarily an infused habit of grace. God can accept humans into his grace. And although Thomas regards predestination as an act of the divine intellect, it is nevertheless an act of God's considered will. Dorsche here tries to show that divine intellect and divine will are not to be regarded as in any sense mutually exclusive. With regard to justification he can applaud Thomas' statement that Christ's resurrection is the cause of our justification.[35] And on the crucial Lutheran doctrine that we are justified by faith alone (*sola fide*) Dorsche quotes those passages from Thomas where he speaks, following Paul, about faith alone and adduces multiple references from the church fathers to justify this statement.

---

[31] I.36.2*ad1*. In this and the subsequent footnotes I follow Dorsche's references to Aquinas' writings.

[32] *In Dionysii Librum De divinis nominibus*, c.1.

[33] III.48.5.

[34] I-II.110.1; III.2.10.

[35] *Ad Rom.* 5, lect 1.

This presupposes a view of faith where according to Aquinas faith and charity may not be separated as two different habits.[36] If justifying faith is perfect faith then it includes charity in the fullest sense. There are, however, also numerous points where Dorsche notes differences. They are interesting differences because they raise the question whether Thomas occasionally contradicts his own teaching. Can one say with Thomas that the believer can be certain of his faith while denying that the certainty of faith includes certainty of grace?

Dorsche's recommendation of Thomas Aquinas as the confessor of evangelical truth, which presents many more convergences between Thomas and the teaching of the Augsburg Confession than we can enumerate here, is so interesting in the context of the seventeenth century because it does not claim continuity between Lutheran and Thomist Aristotelian metaphysics (the whole work never refers to strictly philosophical issues) but because it discovers the agreements between the two in relation to the truth of the gospel. There is relative agreement, relative to the evangelical truth, which allows for differences of doctrinal interpretation. This is the highest possible compliment a Lutheran theologian can pay to the *Summa* and its author.

'SCHOLASTICISM' – THE SHADOW CAST BY THE ENLIGHTENMENT AND THE RISE OF HISTORICAL CONSCIOUSNESS

The Enlightenment interpreted itself as the age of illumination. The light of reason cast a shadow which created the view of the Middle Ages as the dark ages and turned scholasticism with Thomas Aquinas as its chief representative into a by-word for philosophical obscurantism, lost in conceptual sophistry and bound to the alien authority of the church. This is especially true of the view of scholasticism which became prevalent among Protestants after the Enlightenment. The appeal to use one's own reason as opposed to the authority of others, or to start from experience rather than received traditions, produced a mirror image which seemed so evident in its negative connotations that it did not require any rational justification. The new approaches in philosophy and theology tried to establish self-evident foundations beyond the acquired knowledge of a received tradition. 'Scholasticism' became a pejorative term, denoting everything that was opposed to one's own orientations and was rejected as 'a grave disease of the human spirit' (Diderot), 'false

[36] II-II.4.4 and II-II.5.3.

philosophy' (Hume), or 'learned gibberish' (Locke). Much of Luther's polemics against 'scholasticism', which after the Council of Trent had become synonymous with Catholic thought, could be repeated in an entirely new sense, especially when Luther was celebrated as a precursor of the autonomy of the individual subject confronting the authorities of state and church head-on.

The more Protestantism aligned itself with modernity, supposedly inaugurated by the Reformation, the less interest it could develop for scholastic philosophy and theology, except as a negative mirror image of its own programmatic orientations. The loss of Protestantism's own 'scholastic' philosophy and theology in the seventeenth century was a side-effect of such a view. The philosophical critique of the Enlightenment by the Romantics did not lead to a recovery of Thomas Aquinas and the *Summa* as a conversation-partner for Protestant thought.

The rise of historical consciousness and the self-interpretation of Protestant theology as a primarily historical discipline leads to a new engagement with the sources of medieval thought and a thorough reassessment of Thomas' *Summa*. Adolf von Harnack's judgement in his magisterial *Lehrbuch der Dogmengeschichte* is characteristic of this view of Aquinas. After a meticulously researched and concisely documented exposition of Thomas' thought and its transformations in later medieval times, he comes to the conclusion that Thomas' account of grace remains consistently ambivalent. On the one hand it looks back to Augustine, on the other hand, it points forward to the dissolution which Augustinianism would undergo in the fourteenth century. From a religious view-point, Harnack contends, Thomas intends to insist on the sole efficacy of divine grace; but the way in which he develops this theme already points in the opposite direction.[37]

It is not surprising that the elevation of Thomas Aquinas as the authoritative teacher of the church in Pope Leo XIII's encyclical *Aeterni Patris* in 1879, his inauguration of the Leonine edition of Thomas, and the declaration of the normative status of twenty-four philosophical Thomist theses by the Congregation for Studies (1914) did not help a constructive engagement with the *Summa* by Protestant theologians. The prescription of the *Code of Canon Law* in 1917 that philosophy and theology should be taught according to the doctrine, method and principles of St Thomas seemed to support all Protestant

---

[37] Adolf von Harnack, *Lehrbuch der Dogmengeschichte, 3. Bd: Die Entwicklung des kirchlichen Dogmas II/III* (4th ed.; Tübingen: J.C.B. Mohr, 1910). On the doctrine of grace cf. especially 624–644, and Harnack's conclusion on 642f.

prejudices about the character of Roman Catholic theology. The coalition between Neo-Thomism and Anti-Modernism contradicted the self-understanding of modern Protestant theology of the time. The more Catholic philosophy and theology distanced itself from the heritage of modernity and positioned Thomas as the antidote against all modern aberrations, the more Protestant philosophers and theologians aligned themselves to the Kantian heritage and to the legacy of German idealism. In response to Catholic views of Kant as the low point of the history of philosophy, Kant was celebrated as the 'philosopher of Protestantism'.

THE ANALOGY OF GRACE

The decisive turning-point in Protestant theology, which was inaugurated with the second edition of Karl Barth's *Epistle to the Romans* (1922) and which found its magisterial expression in the *Church Dogmatics*, is often connected with Barth's strictures against the *analogia entis* (analogy of being) as an 'invention of the Antichrist',[38] occasionally read as a wholesale rejection of the Catholic tradition, and so implicitly of Thomas Aquinas and the *Summa*. Barth himself, however, distanced himself from this remark at the end of his life as being nothing more than a literary flourish which slipped from his pen while viewing St Peter's in Rome from the Monte Pincio.[39] The context of this remark is important. Barth critises his own earlier *Christian Dogmatics* (1927) in the preface to *Church Dogmatics*, five years later, seeing his earlier work as a continuation of the tradition 'Schleiermacher-Ritschl-Herrmann' which he now considers to be the certain downfall of Christian theology. Theology is confronted with a choice of between 'the play with the *analogia entis*, legitimate only on Roman Catholic ground, between the greatness and misery of an allegedly natural knowledge of God in the sense of Vatican I, or a Protestant theology which nurtures itself from its own sources and stands on its own feet, finally liberated from such secular misery'.[40] From this context, it is clear that Barth here regards the *analogia entis* as the Roman Catholic version of doing theology on 'secular' foundations instead of starting with the founding event of God's revelation in Christ. The analogy of being is here regarded as virtually the same as modern

---

[38] K. Barth, *Die Kirchliche Dogmatik* (Zürich: TVZ 1932), I/1, viii.
[39] Conversation with students in Wuppertal, 1.7.1968, in: Karl Barth, *Gespräche 1964–1968* (Zürich: TVZ, 1996), 484f.
[40] Barth, *Kirchliche Dogmatik*, I/1, viii.

theology of the 'line Schleiermacher-Ritschl-Herrmann', as the Roman-Catholic attempt as 'natural theology', basing theology on 'natural', non-theological foundations. In this way, it can be regarded as an invention of the Antichrist, the counter-figure of Christ. In the next paragraph Barth, confronts the accusation, already levelled against his earlier *Christian Dogmatics* that he walks on the well-trodden paths of 'scholasticism' so that his theology displays 'catholicizing tendencies'. Barth deals with that ironically by admitting that the history of the church does not start for him in 1517, that he is able to quote Anselm and Thomas without signs of revulsion. The most interesting and the most beautiful problems of dogmatics start, he contends, where one would have to end if one believed the 'fairy tale' of the 'barren scholasticism' and the 'Hellenic thought forms of the church fathers'.

This twofold perspective mirrors the treatment of Thomas and the *Summa* in the *Church Dogmatics*. Where Barth sees in Thomas a representative of 'natural theology', he is sharply critical, oblivious to the fact that in Aquinas one cannot find a concept of pure nature that could be interpreted in a secular way, as does 'natural' in Barth's understanding of 'natural theology'.[41] Where he deals with the *Summa* apart from this specific context, his reading is highly appreciative and engages Thomas in constructive argument. Where Barth leaves the modern paradigm of Protestant theology behind (and in this sense does theology in a post-modern fashion) he is the Protestant theologian of the twentieth century whose work contains by far the most frequent references to Thomas Aquinas and the *Summa*.

It was Hans Urs von Balthasar, the translator of Henri de Lubac's *Catholicisme* (1938) and *Surnaturel* (1947) into German, who spotted Barth's misunderstanding of 'nature' in Aquinas and who sensed the proximity of Barth's theological endeavour to the interpretations of Aquinas in *nouvelle théologie*. As the *Church Dogmatics* unfold, Barth's understanding of grace developed in a way which shows many parallels with the distancing of the *nouvelle théologie* from Neo-Thomist formulae. If God's revelation in Christ is to be understood not only in an epistemological but in an ontological sense, then the incarnation cannot remain external to God's being. One must then assume a real communication of divine being and act in Jesus Christ if the full divinity of Christ is not to be compromised. Since Christ is the incarnate creative logos, the 'being together of God and man' in Christ, the fulfilment of all

---

[41] Eugene Rogers Jr, *Thomas Aquinas and Karl Barth: Sacred Doctrine and Natural Knowledge of God* (Notre Dame: University of Notre Dame, 1995).

history in this particular historical story, the Christ event illumines the way in which the being of the whole created order is from the beginning directed towards grace. Barth can therefore say that salvation is more than being. Created being strives for and is lacking grace which it cannot possess itself but which can only come towards it from God, because grace is, in its very nature, participation in the being of God by something other than God.[42] The analogy in this way proceeds from grace to being, from the Incarnation and God's saving grace in Christ to God's grace in his creative, conserving and governing action. From this christological focus, Barth seems to share de Lubac's main thesis that nature and grace cannot be understood as two separate realms, and that nature must be understood as being directed towards grace as its fulfilment. He would, however, have resisted the way in which this view is generalized in some forms of transcendental Thomism. The analogy rests on its christological foundation and can only be extended towards all humans on this particular basis; it is only anthropologically inclusive because it is christologically exclusive. If one reads Barth's conversations with the *Summa* in the 'small print' of the *Church Dogmatics* one can follow the different stages of this *rapprochement*.[43]

NEW BEGINNINGS: FROM PROTESTANT THOMAS STUDIES TO ECUMENICAL CONVERSATIONS WITH THOMAS THE THEOLOGIAN

A new era of engagement by Protestant theologians of Thomas and the *ST* began in the years before Vatican II, gathered momentum during the Council and has continued ever since. Protestant studies on Thomas have their correlate in studies by Roman-Catholic theologians on Luther, or comparative studies of Thomas and Luther on issues which had been regarded as confessionally deeply divisive.[44] In all these studies there is a conscious attempt to avoid the confessional stereotypes that have characterised the respective other. This, however, necessitates

---

[42] This is a summary of part of the argument of *Kirchliche Dogmatik*, IV/1, 7. Hans Urs von Balthasar quotes this passage in the second edition of his *Karl Barth* (Cologne: Jakob Hegner, 1962), iii, as evidence for the fact that Barth had buried the hatchet in his war against the *analogia entis*.

[43] Bruce L. McCormack and Thomas Joseph White OP (eds), *Thomas Aquinas and Karl Barth: An Unofficial Catholic-Protestant Dialogue* (Grand Rapids: Eerdmans, 2013).

[44] Cf. Stephan H. Pfürther, *Luther und Thomas im Gespräch. Unser Heil zwischen Gewissheit und Gefährdung* (Heidelberg: Kerle, 1961); Otto Hermann Pesch, *Theologie der Rechtfertigung bei Martin Luther und Thomas von Aquin: Versuch eines systematisch-theologischen Dialogs* (Ostfildern: Grünewald 1985).

avoiding some of the long-established strategies of making Thomas and his theology the standard of Roman-Catholic identity definition after the Reformation and against the different varieties of modernist thought after the Enlightenment. In this respect, historical research, attempting to see Thomas in the context of his times has an important critical function for theological interpretation.

The beginning of a new era of Protestant Luther studies is marked by a study from Sweden, Per Eric Persson's *Sacra Doctrina: Reason and Revelation in Thomas Aquinas* (1957). Here we find what becomes characteristic for the new era of Protestant Thomas research, a conscious turn to Thomas the theologian, disregarding Neo-Thomist use of Thomas as the primary resource for the refutation of modernist errors. Consequently, the *Summa* cannot simply be interpreted as a collection of propositions. The theses that Thomas defends can only be understood in the context of the overall argument. The key concepts of 'reason' and 'revelation' appear in this way as embedded concepts which cannot be properly understood without their references to Scripture, to the tradition of the teachings of the church and without the use they make of philosophical distinctions and theories. Attention to the whole of the *Summa* demonstrates that it is organized on the basis of the different, but connected, ways in which God is present to the world as its transcendent cause. Some of the most important results appear as by-products of this strategy of interpretation, namely that for Thomas 'tradition' is not a second independent source of doctrinal judgement complementing Scripture (as the Council of Trent posited against the Protestant *sola scriptura* principle) but is treated by Thomas as the interpretive effect of the understanding of Scripture and so becomes an interpretative tool for understanding Scripture.[45]

In German-speaking contexts the first monograph on Thomas is Thomas Bonhoeffer's study on Thomas' doctrine of God as a problem of language, which, in the heyday of the Word-of-God theologies, appeals to Thomas in order to solve the problems surrounding this understanding of theology. The author surprises the Protestant reader when he announces on the first page that Thomas' *Summa* is the 'most accomplished Christian dogmatics we have', and talks about '*the* classic Christian dogmatics' on the next page.[46] This presupposes a hermeneutic

---

[45] Cf. Per Erik Persson, *Sacra Doctrina: Reason and Revelation* (Oxford: Blackwell, 1970), 69f.

[46] Cf. Thomas Bonhoeffer, *Die Gotteslehre des Thomas von Aquin als Sprachproblem* (Tübingen: J. C. B. Mohr, 1961), 1.

strategy which reads Thomas as a pre-Reformation theologian (not as 'a voice in the choir of post-Tridentine theologians') who invites Protestant theologians to read him as Protestant theologians.[47]

While Bonhoeffer does not refer to Roman-Catholic Thomas research but tries to elucidate Thomas' doctrine of God by means of post-Heideggerian hermeneutics, Ulrich Kühn's study *Via Caritatis. Theologie des Gesetzes bei Thomas von Aquin*[48] investigates Thomas' theology of law from the perspective of the Lutheran distinction between law and gospel. Carefully tracing the interpretation of law from the *Commentary on the Sentences* in the context of salvation history, through the *SCG*, where it is developed in the context of a metaphysics of creation, Kühn interprets the treatise on the law of the *ST* as the integration of these aspects in a view of the law which leads humans on the way of charity. The free devotion to God in love, developed from the perspective of the calling of the human creature to be its own law and so to correspond to the will of God, is interpreted as the end which God intends from the beginning through the law of nature, which he preaches in the old law and fulfils through the interior power of the Holy Spirit in the new law.[49] The achievement of *ST* is therefore the systematic integration of the emphases of the *Commentary* and *SCG* in the unifying perspective of the way of love. Thomas can, for Kühn, be seen as a theologian of the Gospel, as an evangelical theologian, since the way of love is rooted in the love in which God bestows both being and the direction towards communion with God on the human creature.[50] And so Kühn can claim Thomas from the Protestant side as one 'our own fathers in faith'[51].

The questions surrounding the treatise on law in the *ST*, its anthropological presuppositions and implications for the theology of grace, have played a major role in the Protestant interpretation of the *ST*. Hans Vorster analysed the understanding of the freedom of the will in the *Summa* and in Luther's *On the Bondage of the Will*.[52] He shows that Luther argues against an understanding of the freedom of the will, exemplified by Erasmus, where human freedom can independently compete or cooperate with divine freedom and can in this way contribute to the

---

[47] Op. cit., 3

[48] Ulrich Kühn, *Via Caritatis. Theologie des Gesetzes bei Thomas von Aquin* (Göttingen: Vandenhoeck & Ruprecht, 1965).

[49] Cf. ibid., 220

[50] Cf. ibid., 272.

[51] Ibid., 13.

[52] Hans Vorster, *Das Freiheitsverständnis bei Thomas von Aquin und Martin Luther*, (Göttingen: Vandenhoeck & Ruprecht, 1965).

constitution of salvation; when it comes to Thomas' *ST*, Vorster shows that human freedom is embedded in the principal and comprehensive causality of divine action. Could Thomas' and Luther's conceptions of freedom be compatible? The question returns in Rochus Leonhardt's inquiry into the doctrine of beatitude in Thomas writings.[53] If achieving beatitude is dependent on human activity, although God's beatitude is the source and measure of all beatitude (*ST* I.26), free will as an implication of human rationality (*ST* I.93.6) must be considered as a prerequisite for realizing the human destiny. Is this compatible with the crucial Protestant conviction that God is the sole author of salvation? To demonstrate this is the aim of Stephan Gradl's study *Deus beatitudo hominis*.[54] Gradl offers a careful analysis not only of the theology of beatitude in I-II.1–5, but also of the presuppositions and implications of Thomas' view of beatitude in *ST* I and *ST* III. The result is truly provocative:

> Thomas' doctrine of beatitude, conceived in this way is [his] doctrine of justification. It is an explication of that which, according to Luther, is the only legitimate subject-matter of theology – the relationship between sinful and lost man and the saving and justifying God.[55]

If this can be substantiated, then the relationship between Thomas and Protestant theology cannot be restricted to the question of the compatibility of their respective teaching. The question must be raised whether Thomas' teaching offers constructive inspirations for a Protestant theology of happiness.[56]

THE *ST* IN REFORMED TRADITIONS: FROM FOE TO FRIEND?

A comprehensive history of the reception of the *Summa* in the Protestant tradition in its various strands has not yet been written. We could only offer a few examples from a complex and multi-layered process. The most recent developments however show that there is a certain progression in the way in which the *ST* is treated in Protestant theology: from conflict and contradiction to the possibility of compatibility, and finally to considerations of whether the *ST* can be claimed as a pre-Reformation

[53] Rochus Leonhardt, *Glück als Vollendung des Menschseins* (Berlin: de Gruyter, 1998).
[54] Stefan Gradl, *Deus Beatitudo Hominis. Eine evangelische Annäherung an die Glückslehre der Thomas von Aquin* (Leuven: Peeters, 2004).
[55] Op. cit., 154.
[56] Op. cit., 364–383.

resource for the Protestant way of doing theology. If Protestantism is interpreted as an entirely new beginning in the history of Christianity, as Protestants have sometimes been tempted to do, the preceding centuries of Christian history are left to the Roman-Catholic church, something neither Luther nor any other Reformer ever thought possible. In fact, the specific points that make Protestant theology Protestant will be lost if they can no longer be understood in the context of the prevenient debates in the history of Christian thought and life.

It has also become clear that the concerns of the contemporary context in which theology is done shape the way in which theologians relate to the past and construe the narratives connecting the past and the present. Thomas studies in particular, and not only from a Protestant perspective, create the impression that the past – including Thomas and his *ST* – is constantly changing, inflected by the interests and concerns of the present. It is here that collaboration between historians and systematic theologians and philosophers is necessary. Historians are not exempt from their own inflections of the past, and the histories of their discipline create a heightened awareness of this issue. But systematicians and philosophers are also able to contribute by reminding historians that important thinkers in history did not write their works as sources for future historical research, but to defend truth claims that need to be taken seriously across the centuries. In fact, it is their truth claims and the convictions which motivated their actions which turned the work of theologians (and, of course, other agents in history) into 'sources' for later generations.

If we consider whether there is a specific set of criteria which has shaped the Protestant reception of Aquinas and his *Summa* it seems best to refer to one distinction which Luther made in *De servo arbitrio* which seems to lie at the roots of typically Protestant concerns in relating to the history of Christian doctrine and thus to Thomas Aquinas and the *Summa*. Luther states: 'It is necessary to have an absolutely certain distinction between the power of God and our power, between God's work and ours, if we want to lead a pious life.'[57] This distinction stands behind the exclusive *sola* particles of the Reformation, insisting that salvation and faith can be constituted by God alone in Christ through the Holy Spirit and can in no way be regarded as a human work. It is this distinction which lies at the critique Luther levelled at the practice of the late medieval Roman church and the theologies which legitimized such practices. It is this distinction which shapes the relation between divine and human work and determines the logic of

---

[57] WA 18, 614, 15–16.

divine-human cooperation in the Protestant tradition. There is no cooperation between God and humans in the constitution of salvation and faith, this is the work of God alone; but the constitution of faith aims at enabling humans to cooperate with God on the basis of this categorical distinction and relationship. Protestant theology would be ill-advised to leave the notion of divine-human cooperation to the Roman-Catholic and the Orthodox traditions. The life of faith is a life that is enabled to do the will of God on the basis of what God has done and does and which is given to us in faith in the clear awareness that our 'natural' capacity for acting in obedience to the will of God is utterly perverted by sin.

Thomas' teaching on these matters seems to be clear. Fergus Kerr points out that Thomas was fond of quoting Isaiah 26:12 'Lord, thou hast wrought all works in us' (*ST* I.105.5) and states:

> Indeed, when Thomas speaks of 'co-operation' between creatures and God, he almost always rules out the picture of two rival agents on a level playing field. On the contrary, he sees it as the mark of God's freedom, and ours, that God causes everything in such a way that the creature 'causes' it too.[58]

The Protestant engagement with Thomas always revolves around the question whether the distinction between God's action and human action as the basis for their relationship has been consistently maintained in the whole of Thomas' theology, and whether it is consistent with his employment of philosophical theories like those of Aristotle. If it were to be shown, as many, especially Catholic, studies of Thomas Aquinas and the Reformers suggest, that 'the unresolved and perhaps unresolvable difference over the question of grace between Lutheran and pre-Reformation theologies'[59] can be resolved in the case of Thomas, and that the real difference exists between Lutheran and Catholic *post*-Reformation theologies, then, what Fergus Kerr calls 'the most intractable division in the history of Western Christianity', would become more tractable and, if such a comment may be permitted to a Lutheran, Thomas Aquinas would appear as a not easily underestimated resource for Roman-Catholic church reform.

Does this also apply to the thorny questions surrounding the problem of 'natural theology' and the relationship of reason and revelation? For Luther Christian faith implies certainty because it is constituted in the threefold self-giving of the triune God. Because of its constitution in

---

[58] Kerr, *After Aquinas*, 143.
[59] Kerr, *After Aquinas*, 148.

God's revelation the certainty of faith cannot be deceived.[60] Ultimately, the certainty of faith, which implies certainty of salvation, rests on the fact that God is truth and can neither lie nor be deceived. The passive constitution of faith is therefore the foundation for any form of active knowing in matters theological. The role of reason in theology is thereby defined by its relationship to faith. Reason does not have a constitutive role for faith, its function rests in explicating and elucidating what can be known in faith, as it is disclosed by the respective and internally related lights of nature, grace and glory. It seems difficult to see here an 'intractable division', since Thomas states in the *Summa* on the relationship between theology and other sciences: '... other sciences derive their certitude from the natural light of human reason, which can err; whereas this derives its certitude from the light of divine knowledge, which cannot be misled.' (I.5*resp*) If, as Thomists today insist in unison, there is no concept of pure nature in Thomas, so that nature appears as an embedded concept, which receives its meaning and end in the framework of God's creative action, and if there is no pure reason, so that reason is equally directed towards illumination by the light of the *scientia divina*, if the Aristotelian concepts of nature and reason have already undergone a conceptual re-formation by being systematically embedded in the architecture of the *Summa*, it would appear to be time that some of the 'anxieties' of Reformed theologians be laid to rest.[61]

Surveying the examples of the interpretation of the *Summa Theologiae* in the Protestant tradition one wonders whether the time has come not to focus primarily on contrasting and comparing the *Summa* with the various conceptions of Protestant theology, but to take their common self-understanding seriously in assessing them as theological explications of the *fundamentum fidei*, given in God's revelation and witnessed in Scripture and its interpretive traditions. This would mean viewing the *Summa* and the various Protestant expositions of Christian doctrine not primarily as if they were self-sufficient systems of thought in relation to one another, but to view them (and their mutual relations) in relation to what they all see as their respective common ground and subject-matter. Could it be that such a way of seeing the *Summa* in the Protestant tradition would find increasingly that Thomas Aquinas, the *doctor angelicus* could legitimately be regarded as a *doctor evangelicus*?

---

[60] WA 18, 651, 7
[61] Cf. The section 'Barthian Anxieties' in Kerr, *After Aquinas*, 139–144.

Non-Abrahamic traditions

FRANCIS X. CLOONEY SJ

There are numerous vantage points from which to think about the *ST* and world religions. The most obvious and fundamental approach is to seek out interreligious diversity in the text by sorting out the disputes inscribed within the *Summa Theologiae*, for example, by tracing Aquinas' reliance on Jewish and Muslim thinkers. But since fundamental work in this regard has been done very well by Burrell and others (for instance, see Fodor and Bauerschmidt), I will not repeat it here.[1] Rather, I consider other points: points of doctrine that are recognizable and arguable across religious boundaries, and that the *ST* enables us to handle with both clarity and flexibility (1); stylistic features of the *ST* conducive to thinking about world religions and engaging their religious intellectuals in real conversations (2); light the *ST* might shed on Christian ways of thinking about world religions (3); reflection on the *ST* in relation to Hinduism (chosen here as an important but neglected parallel), both in terms of how we can see the *ST* anew in light of Hindu scholastic literature, and how the *ST* was used in reflection on Hinduism by Catholic theologians in India (4); a brief concluding reflection on whether the *ST* and other theological systems remain useful in today's religiously diverse world (5). While any of these points might well be discussed in greater detail, it is worthwhile in this brief essay at least to propose them for further reflection.

THEMES

The *ST* treats topics that are of broad interest among religious intellectuals; even when discussing Catholic doctrine, it is never narrowly sectarian. We can easily list key themes in the *ST* that are of interest

---

[1] See Jim Fodor and Frederick C. Bauerschmidt (eds), *Aquinas in Dialogue: Thomas for the Twenty-First Century* (Oxford: Blackwell, 2004).

in the interreligious context: God's nature and existence; God as creator and in relation to created reality; God as One and as Trinity; God
as complex in divine simplicity; God as knowable in revelation and
in nature; the differences among God, angels, humans, and animals as
conscious beings, and their respective relationships to material reality;
the meaning of divine embodiment, and God's incarnation in Jesus;
distinctive human actions, virtues and sins, and the objective and subjective features of the ethical life; the meaning and efficacy of rites
and sacraments; death, resurrection, and the ultimate human destiny.
Inevitable and expected differences aside, all of these topics have interreligious pertinence; thinkers in other religious traditions have discussed many of the same points, with concrete reference to particular
beliefs in their own scriptures and traditions. Likewise, in multiple
religions God is recognized to have by definition certain perfections;
the world, whether or not created *ex nihilo*, is recognized to be entirely
dependent on God; if divine embodiment is recognized as possible and
salutary, it is also understood as free of necessity or imperfection.

The *ST* is also important as an authoritative text. Whichever topic
is taken up, the *ST* is thought to provide a reliable Christian contribution to the interreligious conversation. For instance, from a base in
the *ST* one might discuss with Muslims or Hindus the possibility of a
demonstration for God's existence, the possibility and nature of divine
embodiment, or the manner of human knowledge of God. Or, Aquinas'
views on the necessity that God is one only (I.11.3) and that God is
incorporeal (I.3.1–2) might well be debated interreligiously – with various thinkers, Christian and other, taking up various nuanced positions.
Since Aquinas does not neatly distinguish philosophy and theology,
such thematic conversations can begin without indicating faith or
confessional loyalty as a non-negotiable starting point. Themes such
as nature and grace, right practice and sin, might be argued in accord
with reason and usefully so, without any immediate concession to the
authority of revelation; there is room for multiple starting points and
avenues of approach that more or less require faith, and one always benefits from discussion, even when issues of substance are at stake. The
fluidity of philosophy and theology promotes subtler and not entirely
fixed distinctions, and facilitates better interreligious conversation
on a range of issues where both reason and faith play a role. The *ST*
thus provides a rich site for reflection on religious and theological concerns even beginning simply with the possibility of natural knowledge
of God.

STYLE: THE *ST* AS TEXT

Were our emphasis merely on doctrinal conclusions, the settled conclusions of the *ST* might serve to foreclose rather than foster discussion; some readings of the *ST* give this impression that its positions are final and there is nothing to discuss. But the *ST* also models a kind of theological learning that can flourish across religious boundaries, and so we must distinguish the *ST* that came to be respected as *the* authoritative systematization of Catholic doctrine from the teaching text that shows us how to think about issues of religious importance. When its manner of presenting doctrines is taken into account, we find considerable room for discussion among the proponents of the *ST* and religious experts in other religions. While clearly asserting Christian doctrinal positions – because they were the topic of discussion, because they were true – the *ST* takes seriously both counter-position and position for the sake of productive debate, and in this way repeatedly shows the complexity and seriousness even of positions that are in the end rejected. Even when the questions seem doctrinally closed, theological method and form may still open productive ground for discussion, as the *ST* exemplifies modes of thinking fruitful for interreligious exchange. I suggest four starting points for our consideration.

First, it is important to recall the evident wholeness of Aquinas' system, in the context of which his insights, from the strongest to the weakest, have their full meaning. This wholeness provides an integral map for Christian doctrine in its various parts, so that no particular issue stands on its own, and no particular contrast with another tradition's belief is allowed to become decisive on its own. This wholeness distinguishes Catholicism's openness to its others but, upon reflection, should also be taken to encourage the expectation that other traditions too likewise possess this kind of wholeness.

Second, the *ST* offers a model for disputation, demonstrating how to foster honest and fruitful argument among traditions. Its generously conceived argumentative patterns exemplify how to pose disputes, what to do when they arise, and even how to accentuate differences for the sake of clarification. It takes seriously the view that multiple positions need to be considered, before judgments are made final. Hearing attentively adversarial positions and responding to them with care is necessary to any conclusion that takes objections into account and subsumes their partial wisdom. (The same dynamic, it can be noted, is operative in the great Hindu treatises, where 'adversarial' views are *purva-paksas*, 'prior positions,' to be integrated into the *siddhanta*, 'the achieved conclusion.')

The *ST* aids us in better understanding that interreligious argument is worthwhile if we proceed, even in the interreligious context, with this same determination to listen and understand before making judgments. Merely stating conclusions is not good or useful theology.

Third, each question and its articles also model a necessary multidimensional argument, wherein sharply posed questions, appeals to scripture, tradition, and 'secular' sources, the positing of distinctions, and constructive thinking about doctrine, are all intertwined, found inseparable and on the same page. Readers are instructed by arguments that draw on reason and scripture, and commentaries that are both exegetical and philosophical, with no single perspective adequate. Rather, a space is created in which a reader can choose her or his approach to the matter at hand, giving top priority to arguments, or scriptural warrants, or patterns of reasoning. This complexity and non-homogeneity provide a better way of setting up probable disagreements even in an interreligious context, since participants, coming from traditions with equally complex resources, can find many places to make a beginning to the conversation. Conversation is key.

Fourth, it makes sense to read the *ST* as oriented to the exposition of moral science, practical knowledge, and the nature and goals of human action. According to Jordan,[2] its lessons are accordingly distinguished: conclusions hold only for the most part, judgments are applicable in particular circumstances, dependent on the *exemplum* as illuminating instance; however firm one's reasoning, conclusions are always limited, while actually living the virtuous life is a matter of grace rather than merely a rational conclusion exclusive of all others. The theological instruction offered in *ST* I sets up the practical consideration to follow in I-II and II-II; the instructions on virtue and vice offers patterns for practical choice and action, and prudence, wisdom in application, and therefore judgments are at stake. All of this makes the *ST* akin to the great philosophical and theological systems of many religions, which likewise see reasoning and analysis as oriented to practical goals which cannot be encompassed by discursive logic.

THE *ST* AND OTHER RELIGIONS

On the particular issue of religions – if for the moment we accept 'other religions' as marking issues important in the world of the *ST* – Aquinas

---

[2]   Mark Jordan, 'What the *Summa of Theology* Teaches', in Idem, *Rewritten Theology: Aquinas after His Readers* (Oxford: Blackwell, 2006), 136–53, here 150–3.

may appear inflexible regarding doctrine, clearly relegating the infidel to inferior status; this is so, even if his actual use of Greek, Jewish, and Islamic sources is sophisticated. As a matter of course he used a language of 'heathens,' 'pagans,' and 'idolatry,' and theorized the natural and revealed in a way that has authorized the Christian relegation of pagan religions to the merely natural realm; views that still influence much Christian thinking on religions today. Yet here too his heritage has more positive results, since his distinction of nature and grace – distinct but never separable realities – may be taken to ground a generous, distinctively Catholic perspective on religions. Modern Catholic writing in the theology of religions is indebted to the *ST*, of course, and scholars from Louis Massignon, Karl Rahner, and Bernard Lonergan, to Raimon Panikkar, Jacques Dupuis, and Gavin D'Costa, are all indebted to Aquinas in their efforts to construct a non-reductive, constructive and open yet still *Catholic* view of other religions.

In II-II.2, for instance, the discussion of faith opens some interesting avenues for thinking about God's work among people who have no explicit faith in Christ. Under II-II.2.7, in addressing the question, 'Whether it is necessary for the salvation of all, that they should believe explicitly in the mystery of Christ?', Aquinas first sets up stringent standards, affirming the claim that 'There is no other name under heaven given to men, whereby we must be saved.' (Acts 4.12), but he also prizes implicit faith and its efficacy among those who are open to divine providence: 'They did, nevertheless, have implicit faith through believing in Divine providence, since they believed that God would deliver mankind in whatever way was pleasing to Him, and according to the revelation of the Spirit to those who knew the truth, as stated in Job 35.11: "Who teacheth us more than the beasts of the earth."' The basic idea of relations with heathens is treated in II-II.10, where Aquinas assesses the value of communicating, arguing, and having regular contact with unbelievers. 'Unbelief' is discussed in terms of sin and culpability (articles 1–3), the life of the unbeliever (article 4), kinds of unbelief (articles 5–6) and then, most interestingly, a series of cases by which the Christian-unbeliever relationship is worked out: whether argument with them is appropriate (yes: article 7), whether compulsion is appropriate, to make believers (no: article 8), whether Christians can be in communication with them (yes: article 9), whether unbelievers can rule over Christians (yes: article 10), whether their rites should be tolerated (yes, in part: article 11) and their children forcibly baptized (no: article 12). Even if his arguments may affront today's Hindu or Muslim reader by their content and phrasing, patient readers will find that the complexity and nuance of his positions open the door to more complex and interesting discussions with people of other traditions even today. There are things to argue about; in conversations that should be encouraged.

Or, to take one other example: at II-II.94 Aquinas insists on the gravity of the sin of idolatry; he dismisses proffered justifications for the worship of images, such as universal human custom, respect for higher beings that are not God, and civic necessity. His analysis considers how idols might be understood to stand in crudely for spiritual beings, or actually be more grossly worshipped in their materiality. He also suggests (in article 4) that idolatry began in human veneration of images of deceased loved ones, though he still sees this process of deification as a grave evil. Of course, Aquinas had no firsthand knowledge of pagan worship as actually practised, nor had he access to the pertinent texts of living religions, but even in this necessarily inadequate situation, his analyses are complex and multidimensional. Even if idolatry is the gravest of sins, in article 3 Aquinas distinguished the objective gravity from the subjective factors that moderate the culpability of the idolater. The *ST* thus fuels the intellectual hostility of missionaries to Hindu image worship, leaving little ground for a serene discussion of the matter, but allows for a consideration of subjective factors that affect how people act. While strict adherence to his stance on idolatry would bode ill for conversation with traditions such as Hinduism, where images are worshipped, careful reading suggests that his nuances still leave room for some conversation, while ruling out simplistic attitudes toward 'the pagan' and 'the idolater.'

THE *ST* AND HINDUISM

It is instructive also to consider the *ST* and particular religions, since at a certain point generalizations cease to be interesting. Here I limit myself to Hinduism, the major religion *least* noticed in Christian theological discussions. Of course, Aquinas had no access to Hindu religious systems, and it is necessarily a matter of conjecture to think generally about the *ST* and Hinduism. We can presume that Hinduism would be allocated to the realm of the natural, deficient due to its lack of revealed truths, and due to the Hindu commitment to what Aquinas would have counted as idolatry. Yet too, Hinduism is comprised of numerous integral systematic traditions, with significant scholastic systems richly parallel to Catholicism; almost any of the points made thus far in this essay might be explored comparatively with respect to Hinduism; in fact, the *ST* has often come to mind among those Christian theologians venturing to understand Hinduism. Here I proceed in two ways. First, I reflect on some of the analogous structures found in Hindu scholasticism, with an eye to how knowledge of such parallels can enliven our consideration of the *ST*. Second, I offer just a few examples of how the *ST* has actually been used by Christian thinkers in India in their reflection on Hinduism.

The *ST* in light of Hinduism: some theoretical reflections

The *ST* is clearly of great use in interreligious inquiries that are genuinely theological, since it offers a full version of Christianity as a coherent system of thought, as a starting point for Christians studying other religions, but also for religious intellectuals in other religions who wish to understand Christianity. It is a scholastic text, arguably an example of *scholasticism* such as may exist in multiple cultural and religious contexts.[3] If so, not only does the *ST* open ways of thinking about other religious traditions, it is also profitably read in light of other scholasticisms.

I have already mentioned that many of the themes prominent in the *ST* make sense in other religious contexts; its theses about God, humans, and the world, along with underlying problems, have recognizable parallels in Hindu theological contexts.[4] Here we can focus on how the *ST*, as Christian teaching and as system, might appear in light of Hindu scholastic systems. In lieu of much needed work by Hindu thinkers who study the *ST* carefully – work that to my knowledge has not been done – I offer just a few initial remarks on reading the *ST* in light of Hindu scholastic writing. The wholeness of the *ST* would make sense to a Brahminical thinker trained in the traditional modes of Hindu theology and philosophy, and at this point, the most useful comparisons may lie in the formidable project of comparing the *ST* to whole Hindu scholastic texts. In Hinduism too we find distinctive theological themes that will be in part at least recognizable to students of the *ST*: the theorization of and gradation of forms of right knowledge (*pramana*), the nature and force of the practical knowledge revealed in ritually-oriented scriptures and enacted in ritual practice, problems arising due to the diversity of expressions evident in very different scriptural texts, the role of corporeal existence in the development of the self, the problem of action

3 See the comparative essays in José Ignacio Cabezón (ed.), *Scholasticism: Cross-Cultural and Comparative Perspectives* (New York: SUNY Press, 1998).

4 See Francis X. Clooney SJ, *Theology after Vedanta: An Experiment in Comparative Theology* (New York: SUNY Press, 1993); 'Imago Dei, Paramam Samyam: Hindu Light on a Traditional Christian Theme', *International Journal of Hindu Studies* 12/3 (2008), 227–55.

and its results with respect to divine sovereignty, the nature of God as person and as ultimate reality (Brahman), and the tension between the all-inclusive divine apprehension of reality and the hierarchical caste distinctions that mark traditional Hindu society. We have seen that the *ST* is best read as oriented to ethics and issues related to virtue, and this practical turn is all the more clear in Indian systems which read the sacred texts and commentaries on them for the sake of the liberative knowledge situated in its proper, efficacious contexts. Even if some classic Hindu texts are relentlessly rational, dedicated strictly to the clarification of ideas, the preponderance of systematic Hindu discourse emphasizes the direct connection of proper exegesis and the consequent proper knowledge to transformation and liberation.

If we wish to explore specific parallels to the *ST*, we can first consider Indian logic (Nyaya), and Udayana's *Nyayakusumanjali* (tenth century),[5] which in its five books takes up arguments for and against the idea that God, a world-maker possessed of maximal positive attributes, exists: (1) the nature of causality; (2) the nature of right knowledge and the possibility of knowing objects beyond the senses, just as it is only through the scriptures that we can know surely the efficacy of religious actions; (3) the consideration and rejection of arguments against the existence of God posed on the grounds that God cannot be known by the several means of knowledge; (4) further arguments defending epistemological realism and the knowability of the divine, in experience, by observation, and in Vedic revelation; (5) finally, an actual positive demonstration of the existence of God. While the *Nyayakusumanjali* and the *ST* converge content-wise at a number of points, they stand closer still in their shared respect for clarity of thought, proper use of language, and insistence on learning through argumentation. Both the classic scholastic texts testify that clear thinking and proper distinctions remove key obstacles to an affirmation of God's existence and nature properly understood.

But given the rather narrowly focused logical argumentation of the Nyaya, it does not offer the most interesting analogue to the *ST*. A closer example lies in the various Vedanta systems and, in particular, Vedanta's key systematic text, the *Uttara Mimamsa Sutras* (early centuries CE).[6] In 450 brief verses, Badarayana, the author, organizes the key texts and

---

[5]   Udayanacarya, *Nyayakusumanjali*, trans. N. S. Dravid (New Delhi: Indian Council of Philosophical Research, 1996).

[6]   See Francis X. Clooney, 'Samkara's Theological Realism: the meaning and usefulness of gods (*devata*) in the Uttara Mimamsa Sutras Bhasya', in Bradley J. Malkovsky (ed.), *New Perspectives on Advaita Vedanta: Essays in Commemoration of Professor Richard De Smet SJ* (Leiden: Brill, 2000), 30–50.

teachings of the Upanisads with an eye to right practice and the right overall theological context for that practice. There are many topics and theological strategies in the UMS that Aquinas would recognize: the nature of ultimate reality, and our means for knowing it; proper explanations of human-being in its similitude and difference from God; the destiny of the self after death; the defectiveness of adversarial views that make God too material, or inadequately explain the relation of God and the world. There are four main sections to the UMS: *samanvaya* (on the coherence among the basic teachings of the Upanisads regarding Brahman, ultimate reality), *virodha* (rejoinders, argued rationally, to competing and opposing religious and philosophical views), *sadhana* (the harmonization of texts and means for the sake of theology and practice of meditation), and *phala* (the end result of the path of meditative knowledge, the post-mortem journey of the soul). These sections, with their several subdivisions, are richly complex, as reason, exegesis, argument, and meditative practice remain intertwined – much as in the *ST*, even if the UMS commentaries largely follow the UMS in considering problematic scriptural texts rather than theological questions.[7] Each smaller unit (*adhikarana*), more or less equivalent to an article in the *ST*, presents a text considered in terms of important doubts regarding its meaning. Once the problem is stated, adversarial interpretations are considered and, finally, a correct position is defended by a best reading of the contested texts, and by supporting reasons intended to undercut alternate readings. As in the *ST*, the student who works his way through each of the units is educated not only in right meaning, but also in regard to how to read and think properly, consonant with right exegeses and right ethical and spiritual behavior. An additional promising ground for comparison lies in the insight, noted above, that the *ST* is ordered to practical, ethical reflection; if so, with that focus we also find various qualifications regarding applied, practiced truth, approaching but never absolutely articulating truth. This ethical turn is in a sense also appropriate to the Vedanta, in keeping with its concern for a right way of living that is conducive to liberation meditation.

But when we step back and review the *ST* in light of the main topics of the UMS and the exegetical and contemplative orientation of the Vedanta commentators, we also notice differences; here I can only suggest several. First, the *ST* does not appear to be structured around

---

7 See George Thibaut (trans.), *The Vedanta Sutras with the Commentary by Sankara* (2 vols.; Oxford: Clarendon, 1890), Idem (trans.), *The Vedanta Sutras with the Commentary by Ramanuja* (Oxford: Clarendon, 1904).

contemplative knowledge or around the exegesis of texts essential to contemplation, whereas these concerns are clearly central to Vedanta. In the *ST* right exegesis seems less often to be at the center of the inquiry, even if texts are cited decisively, whereas in the UMS, the right reading of texts is *the* main point. Such differences may at first make the *ST* seem more accessible – one can read it without attention to meditation practice or the technicalities of exegesis – but one is also left without the entrée the UMS offers to those willing actually to read the sacred texts it is exegeting, and consider the implications of various readings for right contemplative practice. So too, the Vedanta commentators on the UMS distance themselves from the ideal of logical truth put forward in the Nyaya, and would be willing to see their knowledge as 'scientific' only in the sense that right knowledge confirms the higher truths known only through scripture; whether or not either the *ST* or UMS viably claim the title of true knowledge, as science, requires further exploration. In any case, the dynamics of learning may differ: the Vedanta schools are accessible primarily to those willing to enter into their worlds, and to engage in right practice as well as right thinking, in a communal setting; while it may be that the *ST* presumes such commitment too, it may not be as explicit in this regard.

Finally, sectarian traditions too – dedicated to the worship of deities such as Narayana or Siva – offer us important 'summa-like' works. For example, we have the *Nyaya Parisuddhi* (The Purification of Logic), *Nyaya Siddhanjana* (The Healing of Logic), and *Srimad Rahasyatrayasara* (The Essence of the Three Auspicious Mysteries) of Vedanta Desika, the fourteenth-century theistic Vedanta theologian. Together, these works offer a comprehensive view of Hindu faith in its rational, scriptural and experiential dimensions; for comparative purposes, only a Christian work as large and complete as the *ST* can stand next to them. Similarly, we can find formidable parallels in Tamil Saivism (in works such as the *Siva Jnana Bodham* of Meykandar [thirteenth century or earlier] and its commentaries), in Bengali (Gaudiya) Vaisnavism (in works such as the six related treatises [*samdarbha*] of Jiva Goswami [sixteenth–seventeenth centuries], or in Kashmir Saivism (in works such as the *Tantraloka* of Abhinavagupta [tenth–eleventh centuries]). But here we can conclude with a simpler point: the *ST* holds its own when read alongside these great systems, and finds in them 'peer texts' that provide bases for the fuller comparative reflection that the *ST* itself facilitates and expects.

The *ST* and the interpretation of Hinduism in Christian India

We can also profit from observing the use to which the *ST* was put in the Catholic interpretation of Hinduism in the seventeenth to twentieth centuries, when the *ST* served as *the* standard for Catholic theology and for an integral philosophical and theological apprehension of reality. In the early seventeenth century Roberto de Nobili SJ (1579–1656) was already applying principles gleaned from the *ST* to Hinduism. In *The Report on the Customs of the Indian Nation*, he refers explicitly to the *ST* three times in the course of his defense of Catholicism's adaptation to local customs.[8] The *ST* (I-II.3; II-II.180) describes the state of human happiness as a state reached only in contemplation of God; according to de Nobili, this notion of a basic human longing for God allows us to appreciate the ideals of happiness stated in Indian texts, and thus the Hindu ideals regarding liberated persons who have reached that happiness.[9] Christians are at liberty to use pagan insignia if these help bridge the gap between Christianity and a particular culture; for this he refers us to II-II.3 (and probably II-II.3.2) to show that Christians need not be entirely forthright and ostentatious in their faith if this serves no good purpose, but only causes disturbance or scandal.[10] The *ST* rules that purely religious symbols cannot be used by Christians, and that there is no problem in using things simply possessed of natural value. But regarding a third, more ambiguous category – things and actions that are natural but nevertheless overlaid with superstition in some particular setting – these can be used (II-II.3).[11]

Aquinas and the *ST* appears elsewhere in de Nobili's writing as well. Anchukudam notes de Nobili's appeal, in his 1610 *Responsio*, to the *ST* in his analysis of Hindu religion as superstition and idolatry, and likewise in his appeal to it in defending his adaptation of Christianity to the Indian context.[12] In *Dialogues on Eternal Life*, though without quoting the *ST* (or any other source), de Nobili evidently relies on Aquinas' views on reason and revelation to argue for the need to accept a divine

---

[8] Anand Amaladass and Francis X. Clooney SJ (trans. and eds), *Preaching Wisdom to the Wise: Three Treatises of Roberto de Nobili* (St Louis: Institute of Jesuit Sources, 2000), 53–229.

[9] Ibid., 65.

[10] Ibid., 155.

[11] Ibid., 201.

[12] Thomas Anchukandam SDB, *Roberto de Nobili's Responsio (1610): A Vindication of Inculturation and Adaptation* (Bangalore: Kristu Jyoti Publications, 1996), 55.

Word that goes beyond what Indians could learn on their own even while still being in harmony with reason; here too, he draws on the *ST* on the aetiology of idolatry.[13] In his *Refutation of Rebirth*, a criticism of Hindu views of reincarnation, de Nobili draws on the *ST*'s article on the resurrection of the body (III.79.1), and his argument regarding the unity of body and soul as matter and form, and the impossibility of the human soul taking on bodies of other species, and for this refers to the *ST*. This model recurs in the generations after de Nobili, as later Jesuits in India too, though never spelling out a theory of the relevance of the *ST* to India, in many specific instances either explicitly or implicitly turned to the *ST* to clarify issues, justify their own judgments, and in general make a bridge between orthodox Christianity and religious India.[14]

At the end of the 19th century, Brahmabandhab Upadhyay (1861–1907), a Hindu convert to Christianity and then to Catholicism, counted Thomism, represented particularly by the *ST*, as setting the standard for what counted as Catholic theology and therefore authoritative – and convincing, in his efforts at interreligious accommodation – Christian teaching. Upadhyay (as quoted in Lipner) says that Thomas is 'the most accredited representative of the philosophy of the Western world, as well as the greatest master of Catholic theology.'[15] His detailed argument on the existence of God, recounted by Lipner,[16] clearly uses the five 'proofs' in the *ST* as the standard for understanding and defending Hindu equivalents. Similarly, Upadhyay's explanation of evil as a deficiency of the good draws on Aquinas,[17] as does his refutation of reincarnation.[18] In arguing for a new, indigenous seminary education appropriate to the Indian context, Upadhyay takes this to mean that students would have to learn Vedanta, the great Indian theological system – along with the philosophy of Aquinas.[19]

The most systematic and extensive effort to bring Aquinas as quintessential Catholic thinker into a constructive dialogue with Hindu thought was that of Pierre Johanns SJ (1882–1955). In the series known as 'To Christ through the Vedanta' published in the *Light from the East* in Calcutta in the 1920s and 1930s, Johanns analyzed in detail the

---

[13] Amaladass and Clooney, *Preaching*, 279-303.
[14] Ibid., 13-18.
[15] Julius Lipner, *Brahmabandhab Upadhyay: The Life and Thought of a Revolutionary* (Oxford: Oxford University Press, 1999), 194.
[16] Ibid., 111-5.
[17] Ibid., 137-8.
[18] Ibid., 139-41.
[19] Ibid., 210.

various Vedanta traditions of India; inspired by the seminal work of de Nobili and Upadhyay, he undertook this study as it were with the eyes of Aquinas.[20] While unsurprisingly critical of the 'natural' systems of the great Vedanta thinkers Sankara, Ramanuja and others, Johanns' more important point was that they did indeed contain correct insights, even if in fragmentary form that lacked the order and full integration of doctrines found in the *ST*. Johanns applied to the religions of India the claim that in Aquinas we find a synthesis of truths known only in parts, without full integration, by earlier Christian theologians and even by the fathers of the Church: 'We have said that in the Catholic philosophy of Saint Thomas, we find all the important doctrines met with in the Vedanta. But in the Thomistic system we have an organic whole. It is one harmony in which the different Vedantic systems find their proper setting. Their discordance disappears. The loose members combine into one organism, one harmonious body of truth.'[21] By appeals to the integrative system of the *ST*, he thus ventured to criticize the Vedanta theologians without entirely dismissing their important insights, and to integrate them in accord with the *ST*, without denying their particular truths. Thus, for example, after his detailed presentation and critique of Sankara's and Ramanuja's Vedanta systems, he points out weaknesses in their understanding of creation – due to their ignorance of creation *ex nihilo* – but also how, in light of the Catholic Thomistic synthesis, the best insights of both, often seen as contrary to one another, could be saved and reconciled. In Johanns' view, the *ST* thus provides the key even to a proper understanding of India's own great theological systems.

With comparable acumen but a slightly different intent, in the mid-20th century Richard De Smet SJ (1916–1997) relied on a capacious Thomistic understanding of theological reasoning in order to portray the Vedanta thinker Sankara as a theologian; the *ST* after all provides a rich and nuanced understanding of 'theology,' that does not diminish or straightjacket even a great Indian thinker.[22] At the end of his doctoral thesis, De Smet highlights the role of the Church in preserving human wisdom – now in India, as it did in the ancient Mediterranean. He cites with hope the treatise on grace (I-II.109.1*ad*1): *quidquid verum, a quocumque dicatur, est a Spiritu Sancto,* (in his translation): 'All truth, no matter who speaks it, is from the Holy Spirit.' De Smet grounds his

---

[20] Pierre Johanns, *To Christ through the Vedanta*, ed. Theo de Greef (Bangalore: The United Theological College, 1996).

[21] Ibid., vol. I, 5–6.

[22] Richard De Smet, *The Theological Method of Sankara* (Rome: Pontifical Gregorian University, 1953).

own generous openness to Sankara in Aquinas' defense of the human capacity to know the truth, to live morally, and thus to prepare for grace – even 'before' grace. Here, too, the *ST* is assumed to open the way for a more constructive relationship between the religious thought of India and Christian theology. With a missionary's hope that places full understanding in the future, De Smet concludes, 'And there will come a time, we hope, when the question that worries many of the responsible Indians, namely, how to save the doctrinal treasures of their past, will find an answer in the new synthesis of the Indian traditions with the teaching of Christ.'[23] We can add, though, that despite his continuity with Johanns, De Smet is reluctant to identify inadequacies in Vedanta; he has moved into a new realm, where a correction of Vedanta in accord with the *ST* becomes virtually impossible. And yet, the *ST* is still relied on to shed light on Indian thought.

In her *Sankaracarya's Concept of Relation*, Sarah Grant, RSCJ (1922–2002) also uses the *ST* for the sake of clarification rather than critique.[24] She offers a detailed and subtle analysis of the problem of the divine-human, infinite-finite relationship. To explain it, she draws constructively on both Sankara and Aquinas (relying primarily on the *ST*, even if also a wide range of Aquinas' other works). *Sankaracarya's Concept of Relation* is a dense and difficult study – inevitably so – of the concept of relation between the infinite and finite in Sankara, read in light of Aquinas' teaching on relation. The major portion of the work examines Sankara's teaching in detail, with attention to his Sanskrit terminology. The Indological inquiry is in turn followed by a twofold comparison of Sankara's views with Aquinas' – with respect to the theological/philosophical teaching on relation, where their positions are compared and contrasted – surprisingly close on many points, considering common expectations about 'nondualism' and 'theism,' and then with respect to the place of relation in their overall intellectual and spiritual apprehensions of reality. Grant argues that both Sankara and Aquinas struggle with the notion of a non-reciprocal relation between the finite and the infinite; they come up with similar solutions, despite their quite different metaphysical systems. Even Aquinas' terminology of creator and created, properly interpreted, can be accommodated in Sankara's system which, expected differences aside, is surprisingly sympathetic to Aquinas' understanding of creation. Grant's presupposition

---

[23] Ibid., 345.

[24] Sara Grant, *Sankaracarya's Concept of Relation* (Delhi: Motilal Banarsidass Publishers, 1999).

is, in any case, familiar: to take the measure of a thinker like Sankara, it is to Aquinas and his *ST* that we must turn.

Two other examples may be added more briefly. The three lectures by Ignatius Puthiadam SJ, that comprise his *God in the Thought of St. Thomas Aquinas and Sri Madhvacarya* is an exhaustive comparison of the doctrine of God in the writings of Madhva, a theistic Vedanta theologian, compared with the philosophy of Aquinas set forth in the *ST*.[25] The first lecture offers an overview of the two systems, while the second focuses on the nature of God, and the third on God and the world. Interestingly, Puthiadam indicates that he is comparing Madhva's full philosophical and theological system with Aquinas introduced only on a philosophical level.[26] Puthiadam insists that Aquinas, as philosopher, is interestingly illuminative of Madhva as religious thinker, but the implication is that when Aquinas' reflection on revelation comes to the fore, the room for comparison will become more limited.

And, finally, Gaspar Koelmann, SJ offers yet another nuance that pertains more to style and general disposition. His *Patanjala Yoga Sutras* is almost entirely an analysis of the Sutras and not a comparative study, but he admits to approaching yoga with a scholastic, Thomistic perspective.[27] His evident training in Aquinas does not make him reject or minimize yoga as an integral religious and philosophical system. Rather, it seems that his scholastic sensitivities have enabled him to appreciate the nuances of the Yoga commentarial tradition; by his own scholastic training, he has become able to read properly another scholastic work. Koelmann cites the *ST* a number of times, in very specific detail: he clarifies and distinguishes the Yogic understanding of consciousness by pointing to the Thomistic understanding of consciousness in potency and the role of the agent intellect (I.45.1*ad*1), and explaining agent intellect as a distinctive but not conscious illuminative power (I.79.4*ad*3). Koelmann also draws on I.79.4*ad*1 and I-II.10.1 to explain how God illumines the mind and how matter figures in this process. Throughout, Koelmann is interested in clarifying yogic theory – and for this instinctively turns to the *ST*. He likewise explains the yogic teaching on matter and spirit by a lengthy footnote making a comparison with the scholastic (and largely Thomistic) view of act

---

[25] Ignatius Puthiadam SJ, *God in the Thought of St.Thomas Aquinas and Sri Madhvacarya* (Madurai: Dialogue Series, 1981).

[26] Ibid., 82.

[27] Gaspar M. Koelman SJ, *Pantanjala Yoga: From Related Ego to Absolute Self* (Poona: Papal Athenaeum, 1970).

and potency,[28] and, finally, by reference to Aquinas' distinction of the *objectum formale quo* and the *objectum formale quod*, he explains the nature of Yoga's 'determination'/judgment as a material and intellectual act.[29] The overall effect is to show how the Yoga theorists, in a quite different context, had a rather different yet still systematic sense of knowledge that needs to be understood in its totality and nuance. And again: for Koelmann too, it is almost taken for granted that the *ST* is the premier Christian systematic text, the one able to rise to the task of illumining the great Indian systems.

THE *ST* IN TODAY'S INTERRELIGIOUS CONTEXT

In closing, I can only concede that much more needs to be said with respect to still other fields of comparison. The historical relationship of the *ST* to Jewish and Islamic sources is of fundamental importance; the suggested thematic, stylistic, and historical links to Hindu tradition offer distinct possibilities and new insights into the *ST*. Other possibilities and problems will of course arise in relation to Buddhism, for instance, or by a greater challenge still, in reference to the oral traditions of Africa, the Caribbean, and Native Americans.

Yet we can also wonder what the future holds. Historical connections and intellectual homologies such as we have explored have a classicist tone to them; they may be only of limited value, given today's much wider religious diversity. Religious pluralism confronts us with a world that seems to exceed the great scholastic systems of any culture, and raises questions about their limits, including what they miss and what they exclude. But even so, we can hope that re-reading the *ST* and its counterparts in other religions in light of one another will provide us with solid and flexible grounds for a grasp of the new realities that today's diversity is bringing upon us. And as long as we are aiming at fruitful and intelligent interreligious dialogue, the themes, styles, and subtleties of the *ST* provide us with grounds and models for the conversations that still need to happen.

---

[28] Ibid., 78–9.
[29] Ibid., 97.

Index